Joe Moakley's Journey

★ ★ ★ ★ ★

MARK ROBERT SCHNEIDER

★ ★ ★ ★ ★

Joe Moakley's Journey

From
South Boston
to
El Salvador

★ ★ ★

NORTHEASTERN
UNIVERSITY PRESS
BOSTON

★

Northeastern University Press
An imprint of University Press of New England
www.upne.com
© 2013 Mark Robert Schneider
All rights reserved
Manufactured in the United States of America
Designed by Eric M. Brooks
Typeset in Whitman by Passumpsic Publishing

University Press of New England is a member of the
Green Press Initiative. The paper used in this book meets
their minimum requirement for recycled paper.

Library of Congress Cataloging-in-Publication Data
Schneider, Mark R. (Mark Robert), 1948–
Joe Moakley's journey: from South Boston to El Salvador / Mark
Robert Schneider.
    p.   cm.
Includes bibliographical references and index.
ISBN 978–1–55553–807–1 (cloth : alk. paper) —
    ISBN 978–1–55553–808–8 (ebook)
1. Moakley, John Joseph, 1927–2001 2. United States. Congress.
House — Biography. 3. Legislators — United States — Biography.
4. United States — Politics and government — 1945–1989. 5. United
States — Politics and government — 1989– 6. Legislators —
Massachusetts — Biography. 7. Massachusetts — Politics and
government — 1951– 8. South Boston (Boston, Mass.) —
Biography. 9. Boston (Mass.) — Biography. I. Title.
    E840.8.M63S36   2013
    328.73'092 — dc23   [B]   2012038709

5 4 3 2 1

For Judith

CONTENTS

Illustrations follow page 142.

A Regular Joe

Congressman John Joseph Moakley styled himself as a regular Joe. He studied sheet metal in high school, but dropped out to join the Navy. He went to college in Miami only for a semester; mostly he boxed during that brief sojourn. "Joe" Moakley hesitated to enter law school when he considered the size of the law books. (His father advised: "But you only gotta read 'em one page at a time.") No one ever accused him of being an intellectual.

Like most congressmen on his side of the aisle, he was shaped by the New Deal, the Fair Deal, the New Frontier, and the Great Society. Moakley and his teachers—his predecessor John W. McCormack, Rules Committee chairman Claude Pepper, and colleague and mentor Speaker Tip O'Neill—were liberal pragmatists: blue collar, not Blue Dog, Democrats. They were untutored Keynesians who believed that government was supposed to help people. "Help" meant putting people to work on projects that met human needs when the private sector didn't do that. Moakley entered politics at a time when the United States was the world's greatest industrial power, and when Boston, if in decline relative to other cities, could fairly be described as a diverse manufacturing center. Young men like Moakley earned a good living working on the docks, building homes, or making precision parts on milling machines and lathes. They all belonged to unions, and the AFL-CIO mobilized its ranks to turn out a Democratic labor vote on Election Day. The face of George Meany, the cigar chomping AFL-CIO president, was recognizable to millions.

In Massachusetts the industrial working class was predominantly Catholic, and it was socially conservative. There was no divorce, no abortion, and red-baiting Wisconsin senator Joe McCarthy was not a villain. Martin Luther King was not a hero. Construction unions and tradition passed good jobs on from father to son, and African Americans were kept out, from the iron workers to the police departments. During the early years of the war in Vietnam, State Senator Moakley focused on cleaning up Boston Harbor. At first he instinctively supported the president and the fighting men. During Boston's busing crisis of the 1970s, Congressman Moakley kept a low profile. He was a familiar type: an economic progressive and a social conservative.

By 1983, he had served in the U.S. Congress for ten years. Thanks to Tip O'Neill, he sat on the powerful Rules Committee, the House's traffic cop. Moakley had his finger in every pie. As a generalist with no particular specialty and a fair-minded temperament, he was the perfect man for the job. He was respected by all as a diplomatic back-room negotiator, not as an orator or flashy self-promoter. He held a safe seat based in his own South Boston neighborhood in which he'd lived his entire life. His district extended through African American Roxbury, into the diverse Jamaica Plain neighborhood, and out into working-class suburbs inhabited by many Irish Catholics who had prospered and improved their circumstances — just like Moakley himself.

That year he was approached by Jamaica Plain constituents who asked him to vote against Ronald Reagan's support for the military regime in El Salvador, and against aid to the "contra" rebels in Nicaragua. Moakley already was with them on those issues. They also wanted Moakley to promote legislation that would temporarily protect undocumented Salvadoran refugees — "illegal aliens" to most of Moakley's constituents — from deportation. These Salvadorans might be killed in the civil war from which they had fled if they went back. After consulting his young aide Jim McGovern, Moakley decided to help the Salvadorans secure temporary legal status.

Many Americans knew that in 1980 Archbishop Oscar Romero had been gunned down in his church, and that four American churchwomen had been brutally murdered in El Salvador. But the Reagan administration continued to bankroll the military regime (it had a powerless civilian president) responsible for those crimes and thousands like them. Yet Moakley had every reason to hand this issue off to someone else. While polls showed that the American people opposed Reagan's policy in Central America, the polls also showed that nobody much cared, ranking the issue's importance well down on a list headed by an economy in recession. Moreover, the voters who were concerned constituted only a tiny minority of the public, and they clustered in academic communities far removed from Moakley's district. He could easily have told the visiting activists to take their case to Tip O'Neill, whose district included Harvard, or Barney Frank, whose district included towns like Newton and Brookline, where the Harvard professors lived.

He didn't. The situation angered him. Moakley sometimes related a story about himself as a boy. He and his father once encountered a big kid beating up a smaller boy. "What are you supposed to do?" his father challenged. Joe replied that he didn't know the boys and it wasn't his problem. His father disagreed. Joe stepped in and ended the fight. He never forgot the lesson, and siding with the underdog became part of his constitution. In later years, when speaking about El Salvador, Moakley would often say, "I always hated bullies." Like all good stories it might be apocryphal, but the impulse was characteristic of the man.

Moakley knew little about El Salvador when he started on this journey. By agreeing to champion the cause of these technically "illegal aliens," he thus brought to the surface a deeper problem in American life: the tension between cosmopolitans (people who feel at ease in international settings, are curious about other cultures, who learn from books) and provincials (people who suspect such behavior as being inherently un-American). During the 1980s, he never spoke much in his district about the issue. He presented himself as a "meat and potatoes," regular Joe concerned with the same lunch-bucket issues with which he was generally identified. Other liberal congressmen — such as Gerry Studds from the Massachusetts Cape Cod/South Shore district, Stephen Solarz of New York, or Michael Barnes of Maryland — were known as the leading opponents of Reagan's Central America war policy, not Joe Moakley.

In November 1989, six Jesuit priests in El Salvador were rousted from their beds and shot as they lay face down on the ground; their housekeeper and her daughter, witnesses, were also murdered. At first, the George H. W. Bush administration echoed the Salvadoran military's line that the rebels might have done it, a claim that was preposterous on its face. House Speaker Thomas Foley asked Moakley to lead a House delegation to report on the Salvadoran investigation into the murders. From that moment until the time of his death, issues of Central American justice, peace, and economic development became Moakley's cause. This was an unusual transformation in American politics and the main subject of this biography.

It is this part of his life that distinguishes Moakley from many similar figures whose biographies generally reveal a lifetime of meritorious, if undramatic, compromise in closed committee rooms—the place where the sausage gets made in Congress. Yet, on behalf of those figures, it should be said that neither historians nor political scientists pay them enough attention. Historians have lately pursued social history to the detriment of political history, now too often dismissed as the domain of elite white men. Political scientists have written many excellent volumes on the institution of the Congress, but few biographies—a genre that does not fall under the heading of "science." In addition, the imperial presidency and growth of the national security state have focused money, public attention, and academic discourse upon an overly powerful executive branch. Hence, we have few congressional biographies but many presidential ones, often written by journalists.

★ ★ ★

Joe Moakley was influenced by various political traditions. Everyone who worked for him said that the part of his job that he liked most was helping individual constituents. To them, he was the man to whom you turned when some branch of the bureaucracy refused to provide the proper service because you filled out the forms too late. In this sense, he descended from ward bosses like Martin Lomasney, or Mayor James Michael Curley, who provided services directly to their constituents. Moakley remembered that breed—the politician as provider—from his own childhood. Ward boss politics had its limitations, especially when practiced by people like Curley, whose corrupt practices had left Boston a stagnant city when Moakley first ran for office in 1950.

Moakley similarly learned from Democratic leaders during the great midcentury era of reform, from the New Deal to the Great Society. Moakley idolized Congressman John W. McCormack, who worked with President Franklin Roosevelt to get the money for the housing project he lived in. Moakley went to law school on the GI Bill, one of the most effective and popular government programs that raised the standard of living for millions during the Truman administration. Moakley had been a state representative during the 1950s and was out of office during the Kennedy administration, but he admired Jack Kennedy; he first announced for Congress while posed under Kennedy's portrait.

Moakley was shaped by the immigrant backgrounds of his parents. His father's parents were Irish immigrants; Moakley's paternal grandfather died when Joseph A. Moakley, the congressman's father, was an infant. His mother's parents came from northern Italy. The union of these two South Boston residents was an unusual marriage across ethnic lines during the 1920s. While their relationship did not last long, the poverty of their circumstances reminded their three sons that immigrants faced a tough time in their adopted country, and contributed mightily to its development. It is very possible that, confronted by the plight of the Salvadoran immigrants, Joe Moakley thought back to his immigrant, Italian-speaking grandmother who lived in the house with them.

Finally, Joe Moakley was a true son of South Boston. He never lived anywhere else. He wanted the approval, love, and votes of his neighbors. During the busing crisis of the 1970s he opposed busing to desegregate the schools, but he refused to join the race-haters who accounted for the hard core of the antibusing movement, many of whom spewed their vitriol on him. Old friends spat at him. This period was the hardest part of his life. He had days when he didn't feel like getting out of bed. Moakley survived that crisis, and among his proudest honors was to be voted South Boston's "Man of the Century" shortly before he died.

Joe Moakley's five journeys to El Salvador and three trips to Cuba changed his life. They serve as a paradigm for the way in which face-to-face, lived experience is the best teacher about our world. Moakley did not initiate this part of his life by himself, but his instinctive compassion caused him to follow the best impulse of his heart. He showed his constituents how good they themselves might be.

Most of Moakley's life story was overshadowed by the towering figures of his era, Speaker Tip O' Neill and Senator Ted Kennedy, who wielded great power during their long careers. Moreover, in the course of Moakley's half-century in politics, starting in 1950, four fellow Bay Staters made credible runs for the presidency: Jack Kennedy was elected; Michael Dukakis won the nomination; senators Ted Kennedy and Paul Tsongas sought but did not get their party's nomination. As most congressmen from major metropolitan areas discover, governors, mayors, and senators typically capture the local headlines. However, from the vantage point of a decade after his death, I believe we can see how unusual Moakley's political career was, and how it highlights the possibility that other "Regular Joes" might do something truly noble during the course of their careers.

Of course, we are living in ever more cynical times. Voters stay home more. The institutions that shaped Moakley—labor unions, the Catholic Church, and the Democratic Party—have diminished. Industries closed up shop, their workers retired or dispersed. Labor unions shrank, playing less of a role in public life, so that today virtually no one can identify the head of the AFL-CIO. Just after Moakley died, the Catholic Church was racked by a scandal in which it was revealed that a small number of priests had sexually abused a larger number of victims. Church membership declined and churches closed. Gradually, people dropped out of both political parties and candidates stopped identifying themselves by political party. In the words of an insightful sociologist, people were still going bowling, but not in leagues. They were bowling alone.

And yet, in part because of Joe Moakley, his city and state blossomed. His name adorns a courthouse, a park, a law library, a technology center on a state college; the name of his wife, Evelyn Moakley, identifies a new bridge. The down-at-heels 1950s city—James Michael Curley's Boston—has become a magnificent, attractive downtown due in part to his efforts.

El Salvador became Moakley's "adopted" other country. It still has enormous problems: powerful drug cartels and criminal gangs; an economy buffeted by downward global trends; hurricanes and earthquakes wreaking terrible destruction. Yet El Salvador is a much better place to live today than it was in January 1983, when Moakley first began to pay it attention. The death squads no longer do their evil business; airplanes no longer bomb rural villages. Moakley's political equivalents won the last presidential election. An established Salvadoran-American community contributes to its homeland's economy and culture. There is hope. When I visited El Salvador in 2012, the minister of public works told me that he was planning to build—using private, rather than public money—a bust of their nation's best American friend, Joe Moakley, in front of the Foreign Affairs Ministry.

This book tells the story of Joe Moakley's journey, from South Boston to El Salvador.

ACKNOWLEDGMENTS

Writing this book led me to unfamiliar places, and I was fortunate to have guides along the way. I decided to write about Joe Moakley in part because I teach at Suffolk University, which holds his papers. Luckily for me, my chairman in the History Department, Bob Allison, is also the president of the South Boston Historical Association, as well as being a close student of the history of the city. I am grateful for his help in arranging interviews and explaining the labyrinth of the city's politics. At the Moakley Archive, Director Julia Collins Howington, Associate Archivist Nicole M. Feeney, and their colleagues Michael Dello Iacono and Sonali Munshi were extraordinarily helpful and unfailingly cheerful. Undergraduate Eric Kebschull volunteered to be a research assistant, and got his first look at the contents of archival boxes. In Miami, Valerie Samet reviewed the student newspaper for signs of Moakley.

I owe a debt of gratitude to all the informants for this volume. Of the places that figured prominently in Moakley's life, the place that I understood the least was Washington, DC. Thanks first of all to my Washington hosts, human rights activists and dear friends Kate Titus and Judith Armatta. Special thanks to Patrick McCarthy for granting an extensive interview and critiquing two chapters insightfully. Congressman Jim McGovern took time out from a busy schedule to do a long interview and review an early draft of one chapter. Fred Clark sat for two interviews that inform three chapters. No informant necessarily agrees with my interpretation of events in this book. Thanks as well to all the others who shared their memories.

In El Salvador, I had a great deal of help. Barbara Goldoftus put me in touch with Jack Spence, who led me to Dr. Charlie Clements, now director of the Carr Center at Harvard University, and Jeff Thale of the Washington Office on Latin America. I am also grateful to Stephen LaRose, Moakley's El Salvador issues director from 1996 until 2001. Jack, Jeff, Charlie and Stephen connected me to my El Salvador guides. Loly de Zuniga arranged my interviews in El Salvador, and long-time Americans-in-residence Sister Peggy O'Neill, Eugene Palumbo, and Cristina Starr translated and shared their wisdom about the country with me. Special thanks to translator Gene Palumbo, who had to put up with me for two and a half long days as we navigated various San Salvador appointments.

My old friend Professor Mark Brodin of Boston College Law School read the busing chapter and advised me on the federal lawsuit. At University Press of New England, Stephen Hull carefully read the penultimate draft, asked the right questions, and helped me to stay on point. Copy editor Martin Hanft improved the manuscript further; the errors that appear are all mine.

Finally, my wife, Judith Beth Cohen, a writer and teacher, read much of the manuscript and kept reminding me to tell a story about a man's life, one that had a beginning, middle, and end — a tale with a narrative arc. I hope I have succeeded.

Joe Moakley's Journey

★ ★ ★ ★ ★

1

* * * * *

Chronicle of a Death Foretold

On February 2, 2001, Congressman John Joseph Moakley stepped to the podium in the jury room of the courthouse that everyone in the audience knew would soon be named for him. Just two months shy of his seventy-fourth birthday, Moakley remained a vigorous, sturdy man, with a round, friendly face marked by bushy eyebrows, a close-cropped white beard, and a slightly rearranged nose. More than fifty years earlier, as a young boxer in Miami, he had been billed as the "Boston Bull," and if he now appeared portly and avuncular, the congressman still looked like a man who could not easily be moved from the ground upon which he stood.

Almost two hundred people packed the room—the stars of the Boston press corps, fellow politicians, labor and civic leaders—most somber, some tearful, greeting each other with the camaraderie and affection of highly visible people who have known each other for years. Together they constituted the elite through whom a city, metropolitan area, and state make themselves a community. Joe Moakley was the most beloved member of this tribe. First elected to the state legislature in 1952 and the U.S. Congress twenty years later, Moakley didn't have an enemy among them.

They knew what he was going to say. The night before he had told the *Boston Globe*, "I went in for a checkup and the guy said, 'Don't buy any green bananas.'" Moakley had a rare, untreatable form of leukemia—high-grade myelodysplastic syndrome—and he had only a few months to live.

"First I think it important to put to rest a rumor floating around town the last couple of days. No, I am not a candidate for ambassador to Canada," he cracked, referring to recently inaugurated President George W. Bush's nomination of Massachusetts governor Argeo Paul Celucci for that post. The crowd chuckled. "Despite today's headlines, I consider myself a very lucky guy," he continued. Echoing baseball star Lou Gehrig, whose Yankee Stadium farewell speech he might have heard as a boy, Moakley was at peace with himself, confident that his life had been well lived. "I started in this business as a bread and butter Democrat and I stand before you today as a bread and butter Democrat." Never given to self-promotion, he mentioned some of the urban projects to which he had contributed—among them the cleanup of Boston harbor, the "Big Dig," and Third Harbor Tunnel. "In fact, you're standing in one of my accomplishments right now—so please don't spill anything. . . . My favorite bird is a crane—and we have lots of them in Boston."

Still, he had to tell the truth in his own words, face to face with his colleagues and friends, in front of the cameras and tape recorders, to the Boston public. He choked up and struggled for a moment: "Today I am announcing . . . that I'm serving my last term in the Congress." The disease was "neither curable nor treatable," and while "the man upstairs hasn't told me anything yet," the doctor had spoken frankly.

Then Moakley turned to what he regarded as his central achievement. "But of all the things I've done, perhaps what remains closest to my heart is my work in El Salvador. I may not have been a foreign policy expert . . . in fact, my idea of a foreign affair used to be driving from South Boston to East Boston for an Italian sub."[1] This was a self-deprecating line he had used for years. Joe Moakley, a regular guy, a blue-collar politician with little formal education, a lifelong South Boston resident whose early training was for a career as a sheet metal operative, had confronted the generals of a brutal regime backed by presidents Ronald Reagan and George H. W. Bush. In November 1989 Salvadoran soldiers had murdered six Jesuit priests, two of whom Moakley had known personally, along with their housekeeper and her daughter, at the end of a reign of terror that had killed almost seventy-five thousand people. Despite the Salvadoran military's cover-up of the crime, Moakley condemned the real culprits in a stinging report to the Congress, hastened the legal indictment and imprisonment of some of the guilty, and cut in half U.S. military aid to El Salvador. He influenced the warring parties in the civil war to make peace. In small Salvadoran villages, poor people remembered his visits to their huts built of cane stalks and thatch. In Boston, Joe Moakley was proud to be an accessible "Southie" politician, never too busy to help a constituent; to the poorest Salvadorans, he was a powerful friend who wouldn't forget them.

Now he was going to die. He probably had only a few months to live. What would he do?

For Moakley, this was not a tough question. A widower who had been married for thirty-nine years, he now enjoyed a quiet private life. His wife, the former Evelyn Duffy, had been his close companion and best friend. They had been childless, but Moakley was not alone at the end. After Evelyn died, in 1996, Moakley reunited with a childhood romance, Barbara Cheney, who kept a very low profile in public but was now his "significant other," and the first person he told about the preliminary diagnosis he had received ten days before the press conference. After Barbara he notified his two closest colleagues, district director Fred Clark, and his former aide, now Congressman Jim McGovern of Worcester. Both of them referred to Moakley as a "second father," as did others with whom he worked.

Moakley had, in fact, faced this question before. Around the same time that Evelyn contracted the brain tumor that would take her life in 1996, Moakley was afflicted with a liver cancer that required a transplant. When, confronted by these twin catastrophes, he prepared to announce his retirement, the plucky Evelyn restrained him.[2] There was only one thing he really loved to do, and that was his job. He would continue to do the meticulous congressional work until the very end, but in the midst of it, there was to be a recessional—no pomp and circumstance, but a sentimental, mostly wise-cracking Boston Irish Catholic farewell.

* * *

Two weeks later, on February 27, President George W. Bush delivered his first State of the Union address. The country had just been through the searing electoral contest between Bush and Vice President Al Gore, a see-saw election night battle that deadlocked, with the Florida vote in dispute until the Supreme Court shut the process down in Bush's favor. This was the president's first speech since the inauguration. Bush wanted to present himself as a "compassionate conservative," but he was also determined to drive home his chief objective, a $1.6 trillion tax cut for the wealthiest Americans, an idea that Moakley rejected. Shortly before Moakley entered the hall, Bush's chief of staff, Andy Card, of Holbrook,

Massachusetts, told him that the president would commend his service during the talk. Bush's motive was certainly sincere, but the show of appreciation for a dying rival would have the added benefit of helping to sell the generally unpalatable package to skeptical Democrats and independents. After announcing that he would triple the budget for reading programs, the president extended his gratitude to Moakley, "a fine representative, and a good man. I can think of no more fitting tribute to Joe than doubling the budget for the National Institute of Health," the president declared. Moakley, visibly moved, seated next to Congressman Charley Rangel of Harlem, rose to a standing ovation that lasted for a full twenty seconds. He had become, for that brief moment, a symbol of national unity.[3]

In the middle of March, the president honored Moakley again at his first signing ceremony in the White House Rose Garden, a bill naming the federal courthouse in Boston for him. This was House Resolution 559, passed just after the news conference, motivated by Moakley's Massachusetts colleagues and backed by such ideological rivals as Texas Republican Dick Armey. His two brothers, Tom and Robert, the twelve-person state congressional delegation, and his staff members accompanied him. Bush hailed Moakley's "sharp sense of humor in the face of adversity" and reflected, "If Speaker [John] McCormack and Speaker [Thomas 'Tip'] O'Neill were here they'd say 'Well done John Joseph Moakley. You served your constituents and your Congress and your country with honor and distinction.'" As the president signed the bill, clouds overhead parted and the sun shone through. "You know, it's nice to be on the same side of the grass that the monument that honors you is on," the congressman quipped. This was, in fact, a rare honor, as federal buildings were usually named only for the deceased. He reassured his colleagues that he felt fine. And in a gently partisan assertion of the positive role of the federal government in improving American life, he noted how the construction project had spurred the local economy and revitalized the neighborhood in which the courthouse stood, in the area between downtown and South Boston. Moakley could remember collecting fruit that fell off the freight cars there as a little boy.[4]

A few days later Saint Patrick's Day arrived. On the eve of Boston's great Irish celebration, the John F. Kennedy Library honored Moakley at its building on the University of Massachusetts campus in Dorchester. Moakley's old friend William Bulger took the podium. The crowd was seated at green-covered tables in the library's capacious auditorium, whose glass wall opened onto Boston Harbor, symbolizing the Kennedy family's love of the sea. Bulger was the once powerful president of the state Senate; now, appointed by former Republican governor William Weld, he chaired the state university system. Seven years younger than Moakley, Bulger had been Moakley's neighbor in the Old Harbor housing project from the time it opened in 1938. Moakley lived at #51 Logan Way, the Bulgers at #41; young Bob Moakley, Joe's brother, had informed Bulger's mother about the attack on Pearl Harbor. Steeped in Jesuitical erudition, Bulger had also been touched by the blarney stone. He could quote classical philosophers extemporaneously, or, with equal eloquence, tell an amusing story about a South Boston inebriant. He began his speech with Moakley's loyalty to his neighborhood, "a place where roots ran deep, tradition cherished," and where citizens held "a fierce sense of fidelity to friends and neighbors. No one absorbed those values more thoroughly than Joe Moakley." The crowd fell silent, sensing that indeed one political era was coming to an end—the days of torchlight parades and active citizen involvement, of Mayor James Michael Curley, John McCormack, Tip O'Neill, Bulger himself, and Moakley—supplanted by the age of television advertisements and email. This was the theme of *The Last Hurrah*, the Edwin O'Connor novel about Curley that mourned the death of oratory and personal politics.

A screen was lowered and a retrospective video played: Moakley visiting a senior citizens' home; gabbing at the Galley Diner, a working class hole-in-the-wall up on P Street where the congressman consumed huge breakfasts; being praised by Tom Lyons of the New England Shelter for Homeless Veterans and Tommy McIntyre of the Bricklayers' Union; Moakley in Cuba accompanied by Cardinal Bernard Law to attend the papal Mass in Havana; clips of numerous medical clinics and schools his legislation had benefited; Moakley in El Salvador. The lights came on, and Senator Ted Kennedy, roughly quoting Yeats—"how lucky I was to have such friends"—invited Moakley up to the dais to speak: "Come up Joe, we love you."

Moakley was not a great orator; in fact, he rarely gave a public speech unless he had to. This one he had worked on diligently with speechwriter Joe Moynihan. Moynihan was a typical Moakley guy who had worked his way up the staff ladder from intern and driver, another version of Moakley himself as a young man. Moynihan came out of North Quincy High School, Bridgewater State College, and the army; there was nothing fancy about him, and he didn't have Ivy League credentials. But he talked the way Moakley talked, and naturally put the right words on paper for him.

Moakley hit all the right notes that night. After thanking the Kennedy family and expressing his discomfort at being memorialized, he declared that "I feel like Huck Finn and Tom Sawyer overhearing the eulogies of their death." It was funny, a little morbid, but rang true. Then he told an amusing story about an incident that had occurred when he was a state representative in 1960. Dressed in a golf shirt and Bermuda shorts, Moakley had arrived at Hyannis Airport to pick up a friend when he accidentally ran into Senator Jack Kennedy, returning home after a primary victory in the presidential campaign. They shook hands, a photographer snapped the picture, and the headline the next day announced that Joe Moakley was the only member of the state legislature to welcome Kennedy home after his victory—a lucky break for an aspiring young politician. Moakley recounted how the New Deal and GI Bill had changed his life by opening new opportunities for him in housing and education; how his own first 1952 election as state representative took place in the year that Jack Kennedy became a senator and Tip O'Neill a congressman; how he hoped he had lived up to the promises enunciated in president-elect Kennedy's "City on a Hill" speech to the Massachusetts legislature on January 9, 1961, which he had heard as a member. He celebrated his neighborhood and his hometown, where he had learned the values that would guide him. In this room full of local politicians, he might have stopped there.

Instead he launched into a seventeen-minute peroration on El Salvador (in a thirty-seven-minute speech), visibly coming alive with the fighting passion of a younger man. He confessed his ignorance about the subject until he had been introduced by constituents to the problems faced by Salvadoran refugees living in his district, fearing for their lives if they were deported. He had his aide, Jim McGovern, look into the situation, and the Salvadorans' plight became his battle for the rest of his life. Then in 1989, he was asked by Speaker Tom Foley to investigate the assassination of the Jesuit priests. "What I saw was a bully, and I hated bullies all my life . . . We poured six billion dollars into their military . . . Reagan and Bush were firmly committed to them. [But] at the end, we cut off all their aid in a monumental vote."[5]

The next day Moakley was exhausted. He had marched in every South Boston Saint Patrick's Day parade since his first campaign in 1950, except for the one in 1996, just after Evelyn's death. This time he rode in a car as honorary chief marshal, waving to the crowd with his tam-o'-shanter cap. But he was too worn out to attend Southie's traditional corned beef and cabbage political breakfast. A banner hung inside Iron Workers' Local Seven Hall declaring "We Love You, Joe," but a bittersweet atmosphere pervaded the room. This year, the forty-fifth anniversary of the event, neither senators Kennedy nor John Forbes Kerry appeared, there was no phone call from the president, and the oratory fell a little flat. The morning's highlight was a satirical song performed by a local official that cleverly imagined naming everything in the city for the congressman. Moakley participated by speakerphone. He had spent the day before in his office, reading the letters of support that poured in. "All these years in politics I could never get in the paper," he cracked. "All you have to do is announce you're going to die."[6] The implication was that he should have thought of it before!

Fred Clark had been busy behind the scenes on Moakley's behalf since joining his staff as a young man in 1982. Born in working-class Brockton, a former shoe manufacturing center, Clark was an unassuming, low-key fellow, blessed with the same dogged determination and attention to detail that characterized his patron. Tall, dark, and handsome, Clark had attended Oliver Ames High School in North Easton and then Bridgewater State College before running a state representative's campaign. In the 1982 redistricting, Moakley's 9th District picked up five new south-central Massachusetts towns, including Easton, and Clark came on board, running Moakley's next election campaign, rising to district director, and later earning a degree from Suffolk University Law School. He would become Moakley's right-hand man in Massachusetts, speaking to the congressman daily, always out of sight, until the end. This was true for many Moakley staffers, an unusual pattern among congressional employees, who often harbor their own ambitions and leave for higher positions as soon as they can. Moakley's people stayed. They were like family.[7]

Along with Moakley's former law partner, William Shaevel, Clark persuaded the modest congressman to permit the establishment of a charitable foundation in his name. They held fundraisers in Washington and in Boston, and raised $2.2 million to start. After the Washington benefit, Clark scheduled two events for Moakley on April 18. In the afternoon, Senator John Kerry addressed the formal courthouse dedication: "The truth is that he has been writing his name in our history and our hearts for about half a century," Kerry announced. And to Tip O'Neill's dictum that "all politics is local," Kerry added a "Moakley Corollary that certain values and commitments are global as well." In a special touch, tugboats pulled the USS *Constitution* up behind the building, and the crew fired a nineteen-gun salute, honoring Moakley's World War II naval service. A fire department boat spewed a plume of water skyward. At this local tribute, Moakley, looking wan and tired, spoke briefly on a favorite theme. "I learned very early as a child that it is very important to never forget where I came from." Tommy McIntyre, president of the Bricklayers' Union, observed that his members had laid 1,752,000 bricks in the building. Later that night two thousand people packed the Hynes Auditorium at the fundraiser for the charitable foundation. A formal portrait, for which Moakley had posed with some difficulty as his disease progressed, was unveiled. The video rolled again. And when Moakley spoke, he emphasized El Salvador here as well. "I enjoyed constituent service, but in all honesty, one of the highlights of my career was helping bring to justice the murderers of six Jesuit priests, their housekeeper and her daughter, in El Salvador." In a newspaper photograph the next day, Moakley was shown facing the camera, waving to the crowd, his features brimming with emotion.[8]

There was to be one last hurrah. It was anticlimactic. Some journalists were already observing that that, while the plaudits were not at Moakley's instigation, it was all getting to be too much. *Boston Globe* columnist Joan Vennochi opined, not without justice, that the effect was "over-kill," and that there was nothing left to say. Yet everyone was caught in an unavoidable human drama about how to die with dignity, and how to show love for the dying, and there is never a right answer. Moakley had served in both branches of the state legislature, the U.S. Congress, and briefly on the city council, and the city of Boston had yet to arrange its tribute. Moakley appeared dutifully on April 29 at a ceremony renaming the former Columbus Park, where he had played as a boy, for him. The park was to have a series of paired obelisks marking entryways at nine locations, with historical markers and a low curving stone wall at two ends, and the project was tastefully completed as a fitting tribute to the man and his neighborhood. Moakley gave a last short speech. He said a few words about El Salvador here too, but at home, in his old neighborhood, these words probably meant the most:

> Of the many lessons that I've learned in the course of my life, the four I value the most are those that I learned as a child: never forget where you came from; people form their day to day opinions of life through their kitchen window; loyalty is the holiest good in the human heart; and, do unto others as you would have them do unto you. . . . If St. Peter came down here and said, "Hey Joe, you done a great job. As a reward, you can have anything on earth that you want," I'd say, "Saint Peter, thanks for the thought, but actually, I'm doing exactly what I want to do. I wouldn't change a thing. Just let me keep doing my job."[9]

Mercifully, there would be no more public appearances. Moakley still had to get ready for the posthumous one, though. Loyal to the end, he had been going to the same barber, a young man of thirty-five named Ed Del Tufo, for years. His shop was in Dorchester's Neponset Circle, just a regular joint with low rates for a neighborhood clientele. Moakley loved the place and came two or three times a week to have his hair trimmed. Over time, the two men had become close; another father-son type relationship. Del Tufo had a gentle manner and adoring kids; they called the congressman "Mr. Mobley," confusing him with a character from a children's book.

When he knew he was dying, Moakley asked Eddie to cut his hair one last time, and Eddie went to the house on Columbia Road. Characteristically, Joe asked him if there was anything he needed. Eddie said, "I'm fine. You're thinking about me now? You ought to be taking care of yourself."[10]

Moakley held one last private dinner in Washington at Legal Sea Foods, a Boston-based chain, with his congressional staff, Massachusetts colleagues Marty Meehan of Lowell, Richard E. Neal of Springfield, and Peter King of New York, a Republican. "It was a night I'll never forget because we all knew the significance," Meehan said. "He was at the top of his game, telling stories." Neal, who had dined weekly with Moakley for the last thirteen years in Washington, remembered him as "the last link" in a chain going back to Speaker John W. McCormack.[11]

Moakley had enough to do just reading and responding to the influx of mail. The letters came from colleagues, former colleagues, friends and family, people whose lives he had touched without meeting, constituents, people from outside the district who admired him: the mother of a son he had nominated for West Point; a Cape Cod minister who visited El Salvador in 1987; a doctor who had treated him earlier; the parents of an autistic boy for whom his staff had intervened to ensure that he got the appropriate school placement. "On the one hand you don't know me, but on the other, I'm sure you do," wrote Kevin Maguire. "My parents were from the projects," and he recalled how torn he felt during the mid-1970s Boston busing crisis. Like Moakley, Maguire felt loyal to his neighborhood, but "the people on those buses were human beings too—more like us than not," and he told Moakley how proud he was of his conduct in those days and for his work in El Salvador. Or another one from a Salvadoran refugee in Hartford, Connecticut, whose husband, a labor leader, had been tortured by the regime and who had testified to it in Washington, showing his acid burns. The man died the following year. She wanted help for her daughters.[12]

Late in April, Moakley got a letter, in Spanish with English translation, signed by President Fidel Castro Ruiz, and addressed to "Honorable Congresista Joe Moakley," remembering their conversations and disagreements, expressing his gratitude for Moakley's efforts to end the U.S. trade embargo, normalize relations between Cuba and the United States, and offering "my friendliness and my deepest solidarity." Fidel Castro recognized that Moakley was an opponent of communism, but the two men understood each other. "With your fighting spirit . . . you will be able to endure, with the dignity and strength that have always characterized you, your present difficulties."[13]

Moakley did not miss this deathbed opportunity to appeal to the Cuban leader's sense of the possible. A week before his death, he composed a letter that he entrusted to Jim McGovern to deliver in person. He suggested that Castro break the deadlock between Cuba and the United States. Castro should invite President Bush to Cuba for talks, and to address the Cuban people directly, as Pope John Paul II had done in 1998.

Moreover, he should acknowledge that he held political prisoners and release them. Finally, he confided, "I now face an adversary that I cannot hope to beat. As you said in your letter to me, we have always had open and frank discussions. And it is because of this history between us that I take this opportunity and appeal to you to try—one more time—to take a bold step on the path to restore relations between our two nations."[14]

Finally he had to stop. "He did it to the end, with the intravenous tubes sticking out of his arms, until he couldn't do it anymore," Fred Clark remembered. In the week before he was hospitalized he worked every day, calling Clark and aide Kevin Ryan regarding the details of these last services to his constituents. "He never complained," Clark said. On May 21 he entered Bethesda Naval Hospital. After a few days the doctors decided that the end was near, and Barbara Cheney, brothers Tom and Robert, and close members of the staff came down to say good-bye just as he entered a drug-induced coma. The hospital was eerily quiet over the Memorial Day weekend, with much of the staff on vacation. Each person spent some time alone with him and said a final farewell, until the congressman's journey ended, fittingly, on Memorial Day. His friends and family stood together in a circle, holding hands. Then Jim McGovern and the staff went outside to give the reporters the news. "He was like a second father to me. He was my best friend," McGovern said. Much of the staff felt the same way, and some of them cried.[15]

* * *

Moakley had died a childless widower. Brothers Tom and Robert were relieved to find that he had already worked out the funeral arrangements. Fred Clark was the second person Moakley told about his impending demise. Clark had had no idea what was coming when Moakley called him to his office. In February the congressman was in full stride; he had traveled in January for a face-to-face meeting with Pope John Paul II at the Vatican, and to visit Massachusetts troops in war-torn Kosovo. Clark was stunned. He probed the possibility of alternative courses of treatment, but Moakley gently confirmed that the doctors had been unanimous in their verdict. They both choked up; they both shed a tear; Clark told him that he loved him. Then they got down to work. They planned the press conference, began the discussion of the funeral, and by mid-April Clark had completed a legal document that outlined the appropriate ceremonies for "a man of simplistic taste" whose funeral would "reach out to every person." Moakley wanted the final service to be at Saint Brigid's, his own church in South Boston, a modest venue that invited the idea of moving it to Holy Cross, the mammoth South End Cathedral, but Moakley wouldn't have it. So Clark suggested that the wider public, especially his devoted trade union supporters, would line the streets outside the church, holding signs, a last "stand-out" as Boston political professionals call the practice. Moakley shed a tear at that image. But he did give in on another detail. His best friend, colleague, and mentor, Tip O'Neill, a national figure, had lain in state at the State House. Moakley, who was unknown outside Massachusetts, and humble to the end, thought that he wasn't worthy of a similar honor, and worried that it would look pretentious and that no one would come if his casket lay there. Clark assured him that the line would never stop.[16]

★ ★ ★

The local and national media covered McGovern's announcement live or shortly thereafter. That night, there was a moment of silence at Fenway Park before the Red Sox played the Yankees. From Mesa, Arizona, President Bush called for a national moment of silence. "Joe loved America, and he will be sorely missed," the president said. Boston Mayor Thomas Menino ordered the flags to be flown at half-staff; Acting Governor Jane Swift and Cardinal Bernard Law uttered words of appreciation.

The next day a naval honor guard accompanied the casket home to South Boston. Moakley's brothers, Barbara Cheney, and staff members were waiting at the airport. A political cartoon showed Saint Peter calling his name in heaven, and the newspapers filled with stories—a constituent who had called Moakley's office with a minor request who was startled when Moakley himself answered the phone; a news report about Alice Faye Hart, an African American woman on kidney dialysis whom he had helped to keep her home; a letter from a professor whose son had served in the Gulf War recalling a visit to Congress. There was a fond remembrance by Irish human rights activist Padraig O'Malley, now an old friend and Boston resident. O'Malley had visited Moakley in his office just before he returned to Washington for the last time. They watched a Public Broadcasting Service video on El Salvador in which Moakley appeared. Moakley recalled telling a Salvadoran general that he was "full of bullshit," to which the man, his hands figuratively dripping with blood, replied, "You can't use that type of language with me." Moakley chuckled. "He laughed all the way to the grave," O'Malley wrote, and cried in the elevator.[17]

On Wednesday, May 30, the open casket lay in state at St. Brigid's while family, friends, and neighbors paid their respects. Ed Del Tufo had cut Moakley's hair one last time again, the first time he had ever cut a dead man's hair. When he passed through the receiving line, Barbara Cheney threw her arms around him and cried, telling him how much Joe loved him. To his astonishment, all the top aides, including Congressman Jim McGovern, whom he had never met, knew exactly who he was.[18]

Moakley had lived among his neighbors for his entire life, acquiring his modest home at 1812 Columbia Road as a young married man and never moving. After Evelyn died, Bulger had talked Moakley into opening up the home on Christmas Day as part of a house tour to benefit the LaBoure Center, a neighborhood institution. Moakley reluctantly agreed, but enjoyed the experience. The next year, Bulger called again, this time in August. "Sure," Moakley replied. "The Christmas decorations are still up." "What?" Bulger exclaimed. "Hey, I live by myself," Moakley replied. "If a goddamn hippopotamus died in my house tomorrow, who'd know the difference but me!" That was the regular Joe his neighbors knew well.[19]

The morning of the funeral dawned bright and sunny. Just as Clark had predicted, thousands of neighbors thronged the streets outside to pay their respects. Meanwhile Air Force One touched down at Logan Airport. For the first time since Inauguration Day, Al Gore, Bill Clinton, and George Bush were in the same place together, seated in the front pew, along with Ted and Vicki Kennedy, Governor Jane Swift, House Majority Leader Richard Gephardt, and Michigan congressman David Bonior, a leading spokesperson for peace in Central America. Bush waved to Gore as they took their seats, and chatted with Clinton. The casket, draped in white, lay in the aisle to Bush's right. Louise Day Hicks, Moakley's neighbor and opponent in two congressional races, quietly took a seat in a back pew. In death, Joe Moakley had brought them all together.[20]

Congressman Jim McGovern felt a torrent of mixed emotions. When Moakley told him he was going to die, he'd asked McGovern to give the second part of the eulogy, on his congressional career. Like Clark, McGovern started asking about second opinions.

"No more doctors," Moakley had said. "I'm having Chinese food. What do you want?"

McGovern agreed to deliver his part of the eulogy, but Cardinal Bernard Law blocked it. McGovern was a social liberal; the cardinal was hostile to the liberation theology Jesuits, and he didn't want a long eulogy about the El Salvador priests. Moakley agreed to a compromise: McGovern would offer a prayer. Just before the funeral, one of the cardinal's acolytes "instructed me like I was a school child" about what to say. McGovern was furious. The night before the funeral, he stayed at the Seaport Hotel instead of going home to Worcester, went down to the bar, and wrote out an outline on a cocktail napkin. The prayer was for the souls of the martyred Jesuits. McGovern sensed the cardinal steaming as he spoke. When he returned to his pew, Senator John Kerry leaned over to compliment him. So did President Bush.[21]

Bulger therefore delivered the entire eulogy; he had warmed up for this moment at the Kennedy Library, and he repeated some of the same lines. They were pitch perfect, mixing humor, tenderness, and civil and religious values. In the solemn church interior with its dark wood and spare white walls, massed with grieving mourners and robed choristers, the podium lined with green flowers, Bulger loosened up the crowd, just as Moakley would have wanted, with a funny story.

"Joe told me a lot of things to say today, so I'll just read them," he began, and the crowd laughed. Bulger launched into a tale about himself and former governor Bill Weld, whose nomination as ambassador to Mexico was being blocked by the ultraconservative Jesse Helms. Weld asked Bulger to put in a word for him with Helms. Bulger, now state university president thanks to Weld, replied, "Why really! We in the academy are above mere politics!" The anecdote perfectly inverted the traditional roles of upright Yankee and conniving Irish politician, to the crowd's delight.

"He lived his entire life on this peninsula, and it was here in this place that his character was shaped." South Boston's residents loved it as a clearly defined community, in a way that few urban places were anymore, a place in which people lived, worked, and died, knew their neighbors, raised their children, drank and prayed together, a village in the midst of a city. Bulger related how Moakley had upheld an "ideal of brotherhood" throughout his career, demonstrated a proper blend of humility and pride, and, at the end, had not been afraid of death. Finally, a last word to

Moakley's spirit: "You were never pompous, seeking the applause of the grandstand. . . . Fare forward, good friend."

Moakley had been a sincere Catholic, a regular at Mass at Saint Brigid's. Cardinal Law, dressed in his white surplice and red cardinal's hat, backed by a host of church dignitaries, spoke a final prayer of commendation; a parishioner raised the crucifix aloft; the cardinal swung his smoking censer around the casket in ritual purification; the choristers launched into song—"Jesus remember me when you come into your kingdom"; the procession filed toward the door. Slowly, moving as if floating on air, the military guard revolved the casket on its caisson. Observers could see presidents Bush and Clinton shake hands. The chorus intoned the words of Handel's *Messiah*: "Hallelujah! Hallelujah! And He Shall Reign Forever and Ever!"

Outside, all was brightness. An eight-man military guard slid the casket gracefully into the hearse. Bagpipes and drums sounded a spirited "Anchors Aweigh!" for the former sailor. The family gathered around, brothers Tom and Robert, their wives, adult children, and grandchildren. The cortege started off, and now it was the common person's turn. Thousands lined the route, many bearing the jaunty blue and teal campaign signs that splayed Moakley's name angled upward. This was campaign director Clark's "last stand out." People stood with their hands over their hearts as the hearse motored slowly past, circling east to Castle Island and turning west past Moakley's house on Columbia Road. Construction workers, teamsters, bus drivers, electrical linemen, firemen, teachers. and nurses waved American flags or placed hard hats over their hearts.

Air Force One flew home overhead. The country was at peace, and with the Cold War over, had no enemies. The economy was sound, the national budget balanced. The future seemed bright and promised more of the same. Political life would go on, as usual. The election for Moakley's open seat was scheduled for September 11, 2001.

Clark remembered that as the procession headed south on the expressway toward Braintree, where Evelyn was buried, cars in the northbound lane stopped, drivers got out, and saluted. On television, Moakley's old pal Tommy McIntyre, president of the Bricklayers' Union, observed of Moakley that "he had the body of a boxer but the heart of an angel."[22]

He did, once, have the body of a boxer, and the big heart was a constant in the man's life. But where did they come from?

2

★ ★ ★ ★ ★

Southie Was His Hometown

I n October 1903, Elario and Antonia Scappini boarded the passenger vessel *Cambroman* at Genoa and sailed for faraway Boston. Originally from Parma, they joined hundreds of other northern Italians on that crowded ship, seeking economic opportunity. Boston was not an unknown land, for the couple almost certainly would have had letters from Antonia's brother Giuseppe Lamoretti, who already lived there. They were both thirty-three years old and in good health. With them was their six-month-old daughter, Leonara. After a journey of several weeks, they arrived at the Port of Boston on October 31, carrying the equivalent of fifteen dollars in cash. These were Joe Moakley's maternal grandparents.[1]

Boston had a bustling Italian community located in the North End, but its inhabitants came from southern Italy—Sicily or Naples. Elario and Antonia Scappini were northern Italians. Boston's small northern Italian contingent, mostly of Genoese origin, settled mainly in the South End, with a few in South Boston, a peninsula protruding from Dorchester, just south of downtown Boston. That was where Giuseppe Lamoretti lived, at 283 Dorchester Street. By the time of the 1910 census the Scappinis had established themselves a few doors down at #289, and later they would own the building at #291. Daughter Leonara, seven years old in 1910, had a year-old baby brother Luigi (Louis), and a four-year-old sister Mary. Seventeen years later, Mary would give birth to the future chairman of the Rules Committee of the House of Representatives.[2]

On the 1910 census form, Elario declared that he spoke English at home, but that was probably only to his children, because Antonia spoke only a few words of the language.[3] Elario was a grocer—a fruit dealer who perhaps began with a pushcart and later ran his own store below the apartment. About 1913, his brother Roberto arrived from Italy.[4] A family studio photograph, likely taken in that year, shows the proud Scappini family: a sturdy, mustachioed Elario surrounded by wife Antonia, the three children, and brother Roberto, gaze soberly into the camera, recording their domestic contentment for future generations.[5] Years later, Elario's grandson Joe Moakley would bear a physical resemblance to his maternal grandfather: both men were round-faced and possessed a certain stout grounded solidity about their frames.

As northern Italians, Elario and Antonia Scappini did not naturally fit in anywhere. Yankee and Irish Bostonians both typically regarded Italians as undesirable aliens. Most Italian immigrants to Boston enjoyed community life in the North End, but northern Italians and southerners didn't mix. The Scappinis signaled their isolation from the wider Italian community by choosing to live in a mostly Irish neighborhood. They were, therefore, twice marginalized. This unusual social situation may have encouraged Elario to assimilate into American life: on May 24, 1915, he became a citizen of the United States.[6]

Disaster struck the family in 1919. The influenza pandemic that had begun in the wake of World War I, traveling around the world with returning soldiers, killed between 20 and 40 million people. The flu struck Boston late in August 1918 as returning soldiers at Fort Devens succumbed, usually within three days of showing signs of infection. In September scores died daily, and on October 1, more than two hundred died. All public places closed—schools, theaters, and public events came to a halt. Corpses piled up for lack of gravediggers.[7] Elario died on February 17, just after his forty-eighth birthday.[8] Mary Scappini, his thirteen-year-old daughter, dropped out of school to help the family.

★   ★   ★

Moakley's paternal ancestors arrived earlier than the Scappinis. Born in Galway in 1863, Bridget A. Connolly immigrated to America when she was only sixteen years old; it's not clear whether she came alone or with relatives. Six years later she married Thomas Mochler, also an Irish immigrant, who was a year older and who later changed his name to Moakley. They lived at 28 Leonard Street in Dorchester in 1898, and could be found at 78 Granger Street, then at 54 Granger, and finally on Clayton Street. All three streets abut each other in a hardscrabble district between Dorchester's Fields Corner and Savin Hill neighborhoods. Thomas worked as a porter, hauling freight. A son, Thomas F., was born in 1887, followed by Mary, then Rose, Peter, John, a baby James who did not survive, then Agnes Rita, and finally Joseph A. Moakley, born July 27, 1904. Five months later, on New Year's Eve, Thomas, the father of the family, died at age forty-two.[9]

Joseph A. Moakley, then, grew up as a fatherless boy, raised by his mother, brothers, and sisters. Bridget was now a widow with seven children. Fortunately, Thomas F., the eldest son, was by then seventeen and able to work; by 1910 he had a good job as a brakeman for the railroad; Rose worked as a bookbinder; and fourteen-year-old Peter as a messenger.[10] Joseph A. Moakley went to school through sixth grade and learned to read and write.[11] By age twelve or thirteen he was working on his own. On July 30, 1922, when Joe was a few days past his eighteenth birthday, his mother, then living at 50 Charles Street in Dorchester, died in Sandwich, on Cape Cod, of a cerebral hemorrhage.[12]

Probably around the time of his mother's death, Joe signed up for a hitch in the Coast Guard. Two days before his twenty-second birthday in 1926, Joseph A. Moakley, a seaman living with his brothers at 819 5th Street in South Boston, married Mary R. Scappini, twenty, a blade wrapper (she probably worked at the Gillette razor factory) living at 291 Dorchester Street.[13] This was an unusual marriage made across lines of ethnicity and temperament. As historian Thomas H. O'Connor observed, "The prospect of a marriage between an Irish boy and an Italian girl in those days . . . was apt to create as violent an explosion among members of both families as a 'mixed marriage' between a Catholic and a Protestant."[14] But in this case, both the groom's parents were deceased, and the bride had only her mother, who did not speak English. It is not clear how the couple met. They lived at opposite ends of the South Boston peninsula, Mary not far from Andrew Square in the Lower End, and Joe near City Point at the peninsula's tip: if he looked right coming out of his door he would have an excellent view of the Marine Park green that crested out toward Castle Island. It was not a shotgun marriage. Their first child, John Joseph, was born almost exactly nine months later, on April 27, 1927, followed by brothers Tom and Robert at year-and-a-half intervals.

The marriage flew in the face of societal norms. South Boston, it is true, was not simply an Irish enclave. It was the most Irish of Boston's neighborhoods, but it included pockets of Lithuanians, Italians, Poles,

Anglophone Canadians, and even Albanians and Russians. As historian O'Connor explains, the community prided itself on common civic participation across ethnic lines. Yet each group lived in its own neighborhood—Poles near Andrew Square, Lithuanians nearby just west of Dorchester Street, and a small Italian enclave on Third Street between H and L streets. Each ethnic group attended separate churches, and people generally did not intermarry.[15]

Joseph A. Moakley and Mary Scappini were divided not only by ethnicity but also by temperament. Joe senior was an irrepressible fountain of energy. Years later, his sons remembered him, with good humor, as a big, tough man. He worked out in the basement, doing pushups with all three boys sitting on his back. He punched a speed bag and a heavy bag. He had attitude. Joseph A. Moakley, then a laundry truck driver, listed his nationality on the 1930 census as "Yugoslav." One can imagine this wise guy thinking, "My name's Moakley, what the f . . . do you think I am?" as he mocks the census official's questions. He could be tough, but protective, with his boys too. Tom Moakley remembers the first time his father caught him with a pack of cigarettes, and gave him a whack that sent him sprawling across the room. "He cursed every sentence," Robert Moakley remembered with a chuckle.[16]

In the late 1930s, Joseph A. Moakley opened the first in a string of taverns. The initial venture was a partnership, with restaurateur Tommy Dorgan, located downtown, across from the old Hotel Bradford on Tremont Street. A second was on Dorchester Avenue near South Station; the last graced the Savin Hill neighborhood of Dorchester. A teenaged Tom Moakley is photographed at one of them, standing next to a beaming father who is pouring a drink, flanked by two uniformed waiters. This rare photograph shows Joe Sr. as a vibrant man whose charismatic life energy leaps out at the viewer. His bright black eyes and erect posture project the look of a man who lived life to the full.

On one occasion, Joe was driving in the rain with his two younger boys, and he stopped to pick up a priest who was trudging through the downpour. This good deed did not go unpunished. The priest started in on Moakley, complaining that he served women at his saloon. No, I don't, Joe replied. That did not satisfy the padre, who offered his general objection to alcohol, but Moakley had heard enough. "You know, if you weren't wearing your shirt inside out, I'd take you outside and punch the shit out of you," he rebuked the man of God, and unceremoniously kicked him out into the storm. The younger brothers remember two separate occasions when their father took them along to watch him collect money from a deadbeat. When the man refused to pay up, Moakley punched him in the face.[17] The father was showing his sons how to survive in an urban jungle.

Joe Moakley was also active in politics. He and his young boys campaigned for the obscure Charles F. Hurley of Cambridge when he ran for governor in 1936. Hurley rewarded Joe with a job as a bodyguard. One day the governor passed Joe his coat. "I'm not your valet, I'm your bodyguard," he snapped as he tossed it back.[18]

Joseph also worked for John E. Kerrigan, South Boston city counselor and, briefly, acting mayor. Kerrigan, while occupying the latter office in 1945, disappeared for a few months, only to turn up in New Orleans, where he claimed to be studying tourism. Reporters started asking questions, and it soon came out that he had followed a showgirl there. Years later, Congressman Joe Moakley would remember his father offering him the sage advice to live every day of his political life as though it would appear on the front page. Kerrigan's misadventures probably contributed to this bit of paternal wisdom.[19]

The elder Joe Moakley left his wife sometime after his third son was born. They were Catholics in Boston, and divorce was out of the question. He took up with his girlfriend, Maida Comeau, of Nova Scotia. She already had two girls, Lorraine and Barbara. Joe Sr. spent the rest of his life with her, marrying her after his wife, Mary, died in 1959. In the depths of the Depression, Mary had to raise three boys alone, although her husband remained financially and emotionally responsible toward his sons. He checked up on them regularly and remained an active presence in their lives. Congressman Joe Moakley never publicly acknowledged that his father had lived with another woman when he was growing up.[20]

Mary Scappini was different from her husband in every imaginable way. Her sons remember her as sweet, gentle, self-sacrificing, a doer of quiet good deeds for the neighbors as they all struggled through the Depression. She was a devout Catholic and took the boys to communion every day when they were little. Her death certificate did not show a social security number, so she may not have worked after marrying, or worked "off the books," relying upon her husband and brother, and later, her sons, for support. Until the early 1930s they lived at 291 Dorchester on the second floor, over a hardware store. Grandmother Antonia Scappini made wine in the basement and constructed scooters for the boys out of two-by-fours salvaged from the barrel factory behind the house. The barrels also stored chocolate, and the boys would lick the staves. "Our first taste of chocolate had splinters in it," Tom Moakley recalled.

At some point after Joe Sr. moved out the family migrated to different apartments in South Boston, often because Mary couldn't pay the rent. The longest stay was at 5A Bateman Place, now called Bantry Way, the second floor of a triple-decker on a quiet L-shaped street. Their nearest neighbor was Jimmy Kelly, who grew up to be a city councilor and a leader of the antibusing movement in the 1970s; the building is today marked in Kelly's memory. Until they moved into the Old Harbor housing project in 1938, Mary and her boys never had a heated apartment, warming themselves at the oven in winter. "Everybody was poor, but we just didn't know it at the time," Joe remembered, just before he died.

The boys attended the John Boyle O'Reilly School, the Nazareth School, the Thomas N. Hart School (they transfigured its abbreviation, T.N.H., into "Tony's Nut House"), and finally South Boston High School. At the Nazareth School the nuns condescended to the boys as mere public school children, but when Robert won the spelling and history prizes the ribbing stopped.

Mary took her boys to church. Joe was not an altar boy, but he remained a practicing Catholic throughout his life. All three boys were baptized at Saint Augustine's just up the hill on Dorchester Avenue, an imposing red brick edifice marked by a towering steeple and crested with a gold painted cross. Its three majestic pink stone entrances were framed by carved yellow geometric designs—an impressive sight for small boys. Mother took them later to Saint Brigid's, then Saint Monica's, and finally back to Saint Augustine's when they returned to the original neighborhood, first at Old Harbor project and at last back at 291 Dorchester Street.

The Moakley brothers were imbued with their father's mischievous spirit as well as their mother's compassion. Each brother had his own crowd. They rarely played together, but did similar things at different ages. Water is nearby everywhere on a small peninsula, and the boys would go crabbing from a bridge, with a burlap bag draped over a barrel hoop and sunk with a brick to serve as an improvised net. Fish were so plentiful before Boston Harbor became polluted that you could kick them out of the shallow water or trap them in a towel using minnows for bait. In summer they had cookouts at Columbus Park, even if there was just a potato for lunch, and go swimming at Carson Beach. In the evening, Joe hung out on his corner at East Fifth and H Street, in front of a variety store that anchored a three-story brick building extending along both sides of the northwest corner. There the boys would choose up sides for football on Saturday morning. The family had a radio, probably purchased during better times. Tom Moakley remembers listening to "The Shadow," a popular detective broadcast whose signature introduction— "The Shadow Knows!"—was followed by a menacing cackle. Sometimes grandmother Scappini would take the boys to the movies, even though she herself couldn't understand the words.

And of course, the Moakley boys went to work as soon as they could, even during the Depression. Joe worked for a while at the South Boston Market on Broadway. He loved potato salad, and apparently it made up part of his wages. One day he saw an employee sneeze into it, and Joe never ate it again; the image must have stuck. Bob worked at a livery stable, and Tom sold papers and shined shoes. When they were older, sometimes Tom and Bob would salvage scrap metal and peddle it from a rented horse and wagon as young entrepreneurs. In 1938, when Joe was eleven, the Moakley family was among the first to be admitted to the new Old Harbor housing project. They moved into #51 Logan Way, and nearby was the Bulger family at #41. Billy, the younger brother, was just five when eleven-year-old Joe moved in, so they didn't play together. William Bulger remembers Joe's father visiting and throwing a football around with his boys.[21]

Joe Moakley was influenced by all these aspects of his childhood. All four of his grandparents were immigrants, the grandfathers both dying at an early age. His Italian-born grandmother did not learn English. His parents came from different ethnic groups that had both faced discrimination. This connection to the life experience of immigrants would resonate later in his career.

The breakup of his parents' marriage made Joe the man of the house when he was still a child. He had to learn responsibility early. Yet he always had a roof over his head, and learned values of compassion and courage from parents who no longer loved each other but who loved them. The housing project, and later the GI Bill, taught him that government could help people too.

The Moakley brothers had good childhoods. They loved their neighborhood. They experienced "Southie" as a special place, which it is. Clearly defined geographically by its peninsula, it had a definite boundary with its only neighbor, Dorchester. An urban village in a big city, it had enough population density so that children of the same age could interact free of adult supervision and develop their character in sports, games, school, and church. If there were few trees in South Boston, there were, on the other hand, several parks and water all around. There were lots of places to go: parks, a beach enlivened by a spectacular edifice called "the headhouse"; the L Street bathhouse; a pleasant causeway leading out to Fort Independence on Castle Island; two movie theaters; and playing fields for baseball and football. Few children ever left the neighborhood. Beacon Hill or Harvard Square were far-off, distant places to children, even to high school students. A breezy Tin Pan Alley–type song, "Southie Is My Home Town" expressed neighborhood pride. Few other neighborhoods in the country had a local anthem that people sang with emotion.

Fathers typically worked nearby, in those factories still operating in Southie's Lower End along Dorchester Avenue, at bustling South Station: on the docks, as teamsters, cops, mailmen, or firemen, in the construction trades, or in the more distant shipyards in East Boston and on the Quincy Fore River. There was no need to leave the safe boundaries of this close-knit community in which people knew each other and looked out for one another. South Boston had its criminal underworld, but in the 1930s its violence was mostly intramural.[22]

★　★　★

On September 11, 1941, fourteen-year-old John Joseph, now called "Joe" like his dad, entered South Boston High School, an impressive building perched atop the district's Telegraph Hill. Opened in 1901, the three-story yellow brick structure boasted a classical triangular crest graced by toga-clad figures guarding a shield of the city. The entranceway was anchored by four graceful columns decorated with small classical martial busts. Most spectacularly, the entrance commanded a sweeping view down East Sixth Street to the harbor, while the view to the south looked down the steep G Street hill to Carson Beach and across Dorchester Bay.

Abutting the school was the historic tower marking the location from which George Washington's cannon forced the British fleet in Boston Harbor to evacuate the city on Saint Patrick's Day, 1776.

Joe would have trudged up the hill to school, first from the apartment on Logan Way, and later from another on Frederick Street, a little connecting alley near an industrial building. He earned grades of B and C, took a shop class where he learned to work a sheet metal press, and studied mechanical drawing. Boston was still an industrial city, and John Joseph worked in a factory after school, earning thirty cents an hour while apprenticing at a trade that required measurements to a thousandth of an inch. A skilled worker earned a good, steady living, and the likelihood is that young Joe, the son of two parents with grammar school educations, imagined sheet metal work to be his future. He also joined the football team.[23]

Three months after Joe entered high school the Japanese attacked Pearl Harbor. William Bulger remembers Bob Moakley running over to tell his mother the news.[24] South Boston rallied as one man to the colors. Its sons had served in the Spanish American War, as the memorial plaque in the entranceway of the high school announced, and in the Great War. Now, a greater war had begun.

Toward the end of his second year in high school, fifteen-year-old John Joseph Moakley dropped out to join the Navy. He was "running with an older crowd," he remembered just before he died. They were all enlisting, and he mentioned to his father that he was thinking about it as well—but he was underage. Joseph A. Moakley took his son's considerations as intentions to join the Navy. One day he drove up to a corner where Joe was hanging out. "Well . . . you said you were going to join the Navy," he announced. "We got the papers here for you. Come on, let's go."[25]

Young Moakley's history teacher, a Mr. O'Leary, remembered John Joseph as a shy young man, and he tried to discourage him; his teachers knew that he was too young. Moakley senior doctored his son's birth certificate, changing the "7" in 1927 to a "5"—a transparent forgery that probably did not fool the Navy recruiting officer at the Fargo Building. There were other boys who did the same thing, but there weren't many. Enlistment worked out well for young Joe, although his father was probably motivated by a desire to boast to his pals that his son was wearing a uniform. There was no shame in waiting until the legal age for military duty; those ages were picked for a reason. The more objective Mr. O'Leary probably had it right. Joe Moakley's mother did not seem to have a vote in this decision, the way Joe remembered it.[26]

Joe's physical exam revealed a young man in good health with one surprising defect: it said he was color blind. The officials wrote "C.B." on his orders; young Moakley believed it meant "Color Blind." Actually, he had been assigned to a Construction Battalion, whose initials caused the units to be called "Seabees." The unit's sporting insignia showed a buzzing bumblebee adorned with a sailor's cap, brandishing a machine gun in its front hands and construction tools in the rear ones. Moakley was inducted in March and reported to Camp Allen in Norfolk, Virginia.

These "Fighting Seabees" were a creation of Rear Admiral Ben Moreell, commander of the Navy's Department of Yards and Docks. In peacetime, experienced civilian engineers directed complex construction projects for a small navy. Moreell had those who enlisted commissioned as military officers and placed them in charge of new units that would play a crucial role in winning the war. In the Atlantic and Pacific theaters, Seabees expended $11 billion to build four hundred military bases. More than 8,000 officers commanded 325,000 men, all trained to defend what they built.

Moakley had taken military drill instruction in high school, so the officers at first put the green young man in charge of marching the older men around the parade ground previous to starting formal boot camp. The older guys let him hear about it after they broke ranks; it would have been difficult for a sixteen-year-old to bark out orders to grown men with jobs, wives, and children, but he did it. After boot camp the men got a week of jungle training. Next they were formed into the Special Tenth Naval Construction Battalion. One section was assigned to the Atlantic Theater, stationed at Exeter, England, and Moakley's section was shipped out, probably by troop train, to the West Coast Seabee staging area at Port Hueneme, California. From there they boarded ships for Hawaii.

The "Special" Seabee units were stevedores—port workers who off-loaded construction supplies and goods for the troops. In all there were 151 regular Seabee Battalions and 39 specials. They did a good job, besting civilian longshoremen. The Pacific Theater was organized into three "roads to victory"—North, Mid Pacific, and South Pacific—along which the Seabees built 441 piers, 2,558 ammunition magazines, 700 square blocks of warehouses, hospitals, gasoline storage tanks, and housing for 1.5 million men. American industry and construction skills won the war just as much as military valor.

Compared with the lives of combat soldiers, Seabees had "good wars." They typically lived in Quonset huts, slept on cots, ate three meals a day, and enjoyed recreational activities. Moakley, like most Seabees, was never under fire. The weather on Hawaii was better than the weather in Boston. Pictures of the young sailor show a smiling young man, relaxing with his buddies. He had courageously volunteered to go into harm's way to defend his country and found himself, in effect, with a day job in Hawaii for a year.

On March 8, 1945, the unit shipped out to a forward area on Samar in the liberated Philippines. After the Japanese surrender, Moakley was reassigned to the 28th Special Battalion, which sailed for Yokosuko, Japan, as other men were demobilized. Moakley remained on duty until February 1946, when he returned home and was discharged after almost three years, having earned the rank of Seaman First Class and the appropriate service ribbons. He had been one of the youngest Navy sailors and was discharged two months before his nineteenth birthday. Still chronologically a teenager, he was now a young man with the life experience of a mature veteran.[27]

World War II changed its veterans profoundly. The war pitted an alliance of the great Anglophone democracies and dictatorial Soviet Russia against the most evil totalitarian regimes in human history. American veterans returned with a great sense of shared sacrifice and pride in their country. Young men who had never ventured beyond the confines of their neighborhood had served alongside men from all over the country and seen the world. While they served in a Jim Crow military, they had fought against ideologically racist enemies whose atrocities staggered the imagination and reinforced American patriotism. They all become less parochial, less ethnically identified, more "American" in their self-conception. Their service would be a lifelong source of pride when they returned to civilian life.

Seaman Moakley came home to the house he had left in South Boston three years earlier. His mother now lived at 172 Dorchester Street with brothers Tom and Bob. His father listed his address as the same place, but he continued to cohabit with Maida Comeau, operating "Joe's Café" at 280 Tremont Street downtown. While Joe was away in the Navy, the school committee in 1944 had awarded the young sailor a high school diploma.[28] Now a high school graduate who had served his country in wartime, young Joe Moakley prepared to attend college.

The GI Bill passed during the Harry Truman administration after the war allowed veterans to attend college at very low cost, and the colleges began to swell with returning soldiers and sailors. Joe, who had only a year and a half of high school, enrolled at Newman Preparatory Academy in Boston's fashionable Back Bay. In the fall of 1946 he earned B grades in French, English, civics, and ancient history, and the next semester he earned Cs in algebra, economics, modern history, and French. On weekends he played football on a team sponsored by his father's tavern. Newman was important to him. Young Joe forged a lifelong friendship with one of his teachers, Mr. Coen, who taught French and English there for decades. Moakley addressed a Newman graduation years later, speaking warmly of the school's influence on him.[29]

Joe's direction still wasn't clear. After he finished school, his father and Maida Comeau left for Miami to open a tavern. The reasons for the move remain obscure, but after the war many Americans did set off for some other part of the country, just to see it. Joseph A. Moakley's sons were grown, and nothing necessarily tied him to Boston anymore. It is also possible that as a man accustomed to using his fists to collect bad debts, he had his own reasons for leaving town for a while. Joe Moakley went with his father, but remembered the Miami part of his life only hazily. One picture from 1947 shows young Joe, fishing rod in hand, posed happily with a big marlin.[30]

In 1948 Joe entered the University of Miami in the education program, where he stayed for only one semester. When not in class Joe boxed in the school's intramural tournament, billed as the "Boston Bull," an exotic character from faraway New England. He fought in the light heavyweight intramural tournament and was favored to win, losing in an upset in the final bout. He must have trained hard to do so well. Another picture from that time shows Moakley in the ring, landing a blow against a taller opponent before an enthusiastic outdoor crowd.[31]

In 1948 or 1949 Moakley returned with his father to a stagnant city still dominated by Mayor James Michael Curley, who was completing his fourth term in office and preparing for a fifth run in 1949 at age seventy-five. Joe moved back in with his mother while his father and Maida settled in Dorchester. He still had no definite plans, but sheet metal work was clearly in his past. He was back in his familiar neighborhood, encountering old friends and considering his future.

William Bulger remembers strolling with Joe Moakley on Carson Beach, and the two of them, one a young man and the other a teenager, discovered that they already shared mutual political ambitions.[32] Moakley's hopes were probably shaped by seeing how politics affected people's life possibilities. In office he would excel at delivering constituent services; virtually everyone who knew him said that he was "always helping people out." His political career would be a life of service to neighbors he knew and a neighborhood that he loved. "Southie" was his hometown, and he never left it again.

3

★ ★ ★ ★ ★

From Curley's Boston to Kennedy's America

Sometime in 1949, a chance encounter set Joe Moakley on his life's course. Fifty years later, just before he died, he remembered it "like it was yesterday."

Joe boarded the Bayview bus at Knowlton Street and ran into two football buddies, Henry "Looper" Doherty and Martin Carter. Joe was just back from Miami University, and his pals were impressed. Not many people they knew had been to college.

"Why don't you run for city council?" Carter asked.

"What?"

Carter insisted: "You're young, you're a veteran, someone our age—you know, we got to have somebody represent us."

Doherty added, "Those old guys, they don't know."[1]

The story reveals much about the narrow horizons of these young men. No particular issue bothers them. They aren't thinking about the different perspectives of Mayor Curley or his challenger, City Clerk John B. Hynes, in the upcoming mayoral race. They have not been inspired by national events, such as Minneapolis mayor Hubert Humphrey's stirring speech at the 1948 Democratic convention, attacking segregation and causing the "Dixiecrats" to bolt the party. They aren't considering the Progressive Henry Wallace campaign that year, or the rise of Joe McCarthy. Their focus is totally local, and there's nothing special that they want to change, except the generation that holds power.

Moakley would have been just twenty-two, and he had probably cast his first vote for Harry Truman the year before. Moakley considered the offer, but Boston city politics was a snake pit. The upcoming election promised to elevate incumbent mayor James Michael Curley to a fifth term, and Moakley might not have wanted to be part of that atmosphere.

Discretion seemed the better part of valor, so he demurred. That fall Moakley enrolled instead at Bentley College in the Back Bay, which he attended for a year, long enough to earn him a job in 1950 as an insurance examiner at a state office. Nevertheless, a seed had been planted.

Then-congressman Curley had won his fourth term in 1945, defeating Joseph A. Moakley's friend, the acting mayor, John Kerrigan. That year Congressman Curley had the aid of one of his old nemeses, Joseph P. Kennedy, whose son Jack was just back from the Navy with political ambitions of his own. Joe Kennedy wanted Curley's 9th District congressional seat for his son Jack so he secretly offered to underwrite Curley's mayoral campaign to vacate the congressional seat, thus putting the strangest of fellows in bed.[2]

Back on his throne, King Curley extracted the royal fifth out of every municipal transaction, having the bribes delivered to a bagman ensconced across from City Hall on School Street. One sign of Boston's municipal corruption under Curley was that the city paid sixty-four dollars to install each parking meter, while Cambridge paid only twelve. As mayor, he was sent off to federal prison in Connecticut on a charge of mail fraud, pardoned by President Truman, and gratuitously insulted Acting Major John B. Hynes upon his return from prison. It made good newspaper copy. Hynes soon declared his candidacy for mayor. Surveying the state of the city, Curley's biographer Jack Beatty saw a "corrupt mayor, a corrupt City Council, a corrupt press, a swollen city payroll, a dying city economy, and the highest city taxes beneath the wandering moon: such was the Boston scene as the 1949 election began." Hynes won the election. It was Curley's "Last Hurrah," chronicled in fiction by writer Edwin O'Connor in a memorable book of the same name. Curley would run on to the end, almost to his death in 1958, but the era was over, a half-century of some accomplishment, massive grafting, economic stasis, and coarsened political discourse.[3]

Hynes inaugurated a new, scandal-free political atmosphere. Doherty and Carter approached Moakley again in 1950, this time suggesting a run for the state representative's race. Now they had some more guys with them, in effect having formed a political club in search of a candidate. They included John "Sleepy" Lynch, Pat Loftus, Dave Keefe, Joe Murphy, Herbie Arrigal, and Paul O'Donnell. This time Moakley said yes.[4]

In 1950, the Massachusetts House had 240 representatives. Densely populated South Boston was divided into two wards—Ward 6, which lay entirely in the northern part of the neighborhood and included the wealthier precincts of City Point and "Pill Hill"; and Ward 7, which included the Lower End and a southern strip of South Boston, as well as several precincts in the Savin Hill section of neighboring Dorchester. Moakley's gang lived in the poorer Ward 7, which had the advantage of being represented by two delegates. Republicans didn't stand a chance in a working-class district, so the real election came in the September primary.

Campaigns for state representative were merely popularity contests, devoid of issues. State representatives rarely appeared even in the neighborhood newspapers, except on ceremonial occasions or when they were promoting some bill of local concern. The incumbents in Ward 7 were decent men with minor achievements to their credit. James F. "Jimmie" Condon, then fifty-one, a World War I veteran active in the South Boston Citizens Association, was much beloved for inviting children down to his farm in rural North Easton for annual outings. William F. Carr was the other incumbent. Six newcomers challenged them.[5]

Moakley possessed only mediocre oratorical skills. In those days before television, politics was street theater. Candidates commandeered busy corners, surrounded by their noisy entourage, and hyped their abilities to passersby before decamping for the next intersection. Herbie Arrigal or John "Sleepy" Lynch would introduce Moakley, who typically garbled his lines, and his supporters would proceed to the next fiasco. Moakley was so uninspiring that Arrigal began extending his introductions, leaving less for the candidate to say at each stop, until finally, after a lengthy introduction he just got up and said, "And I'm Joe Moakley!"[6]

What Moakley lacked in oratorical skills he made up for in energy, organization, and a winning personality. His real skill was that he knew how to listen and take voters seriously. Moakley established a headquarters at Dorchester and 8th streets, from which Pat Loftus dispatched campaign teams. He personally knocked on as many doors as he could. He remembered people's names and what they wanted government to do on their block. His campaign slogan, "Make the Right Change," and youthful wartime service appealed to the rising generation. His first advertisement noted his membership in the Veterans of Foreign Wars, the American Legion, the Massachusetts State Employees Association, and the South

Boston Irish Club. He almost won. Condon registered 4,854 votes, Carr 3,568, and Moakley came in third with 3,369, only 199 votes short. The next in the pack finished with 1,558. Moakley must have shown some personally attractive characteristic to distinguish him from his rivals. For a young man in his first race, it was an impressive showing, and he came out of it determined to try again. In the general election, Democrats did well in 1950, with Governor Paul Dever winning re-election. No Republicans contested for office in South Boston.[7]

★ ★ ★

The year marked a turning point for Moakley in another part of his life. During the campaign he went to a Cambridge social event where he met Evelyn Duffy, a lively and attractive young woman born a month before him. One of Moakley's companions asked her to dance but was turned down. Moakley tried next and she said yes. The first guy was too short.

They got to know each other better and a relationship developed. It wasn't easy at first, because Evelyn wasn't interested in politics. Evelyn lived with her parents on Eustis Street near Porter Square in North Cambridge; she worked at a bank. Her father had been born in Ireland and her mother in Canada. She was vivacious, playful, a woman who smoked and drank, and, while the word would be invented only a few years later, she was hip, a fan of Frank Sinatra. An early class picture shows her at age eleven at the Agassiz School near Harvard Square. All the girls are wearing frumpy dresses—except one, who is already clad in sophisticated black and looking into the camera like a fashion model surrounded by old ladies.[8]

There was more. Evelyn was a widow. She had married the boy next door, Ernest Forster Buckley, in August 1942, claiming on her marriage certificate that she was eighteen years old when she was really not yet fifteen and a half, a stunning parallel to Moakley's lie about his own age. In that sense they were two of a kind, precocious kids affected by the winds of war. Ernie joined the army in November. Two years later, on December 26, 1944, he was wounded in action by shrapnel in the knee and taken prisoner. A letter on German stationery reached his mother the following month, assuring her that he was OK. Ernie remained in German hands until April 14, 1945, just before the German surrender. In November the army redressed his wound and mustered him out of Company B,

422nd Infantry, on November 23, 1945, at Fort Dix, New Jersey. Evelyn wrote her husband a Christmas card in 1946, but there is no record of him after that date. The likelihood is that he died of his wounds. Evelyn kept the cards, the pictures, and his medals to the end of her life.[9]

★ ★ ★

Joe Moakley ran again for state representative in 1952. The year would mark another turning point in American politics. General Dwight D. Eisenhower easily defeated Illinois governor Adlai Stevenson, whose bald dome and intellectual demeanor led a journalistic wag to coin the descriptive term "egghead," which became part of the American vocabulary. Eight Massachusetts Republicans and six Democrats won U.S. House seats. Among the Democratic House victors was Thomas P. "Tip" O'Neill, who won a tough primary campaign in the safely Democratic 11th District vacated by Jack Kennedy.

The major campaign of that year was for the U.S. Senate seat held by incumbent Henry Cabot Lodge, Jr., who had first entered the U.S. Senate in 1936 when he bested perennial candidate James Michael Curley. Governor Paul Dever considered challenging Lodge but figured he was unbeatable. That decision opened the field for ambitious young Congressman John Fitzgerald Kennedy, who, backed by his father's millions, visited almost every town in the state and won by seventy-five thousand votes. In a battle of dynasties, Kennedy triumphed as Lodge faded. A new star, and a major force in state politics, had risen.[10]

Moakley's 1952 campaign, like 240 other down-ticket races, took place in the shadow of this major showdown. In Ward 7 one incumbent, Carr, had moved up to the school committee, and that opening attracted a total of ten candidates for the two seats. The new rivals were experienced and formidable. They included Thomas A. Sullivan, a member of the powerful Electrical Workers Union Local 103, backed by an array of labor officials; and City Councilor John J. McColgan, whose fourteen siblings alone could be a significant vote-getting force. Moakley's reorganized campaign committee now included reinforcements George Logue, longshoreman Basil Quirk, and Jess Hurney. This campaign too was apparently issue-free. Moakley not only won, but he topped the ticket with 4,838 votes to Condon's 4,236; Condon barely squeaked past McColgan, who received 4,008. Moakley did it with shoe leather, paying more attention to the Dorchester precincts this time. In the general election, a Republican received a paltry 2,431 votes, to Condon's and Moakley's totals of more than 11,000 each.[11]

The Republicans, however, regained control of the Massachusetts State House that year. The House had been solidly Republican from 1867 until 1948. In 1948 the triumphant Democrats swore in as Speaker another rising star in the party, Cambridge's Thomas P. "Tip" O'Neill, who was first elected in 1936 at the age of twenty-three. The Democrats maintained their majority in the following election, but the popular Eisenhower helped the Republicans to regain a state house majority of 123–117 in 1952. Moakley entered the legislature the same year that Tip O'Neill went to the U.S. House of Representatives and Jack Kennedy became a senator.[12]

As a freshman representative in the minority party, Moakley wielded almost no power. Like most state representatives, Moakley kept his day job (he was an insurance examiner for the state), since his legislative salary was only forty-five hundred dollars, too little to live on. Legislators typically showed up in the afternoon to cast their votes. Early arrivals huddled in the corridors, bent over card games. The party leadership herded the members like sheep. State reps had no office, no phone, and no staff. Many of them wanted the job only to boost their law practices and paid little attention to state business. The ambitious stayed a few years, and if they could not move up, dropped out of politics altogether.[13]

Moakley pushed a few bills that showed his own concerns. One would require out-of-state automobile renters to purchase liability insurance. Moakley pointed to six automobile accident fatalities in his district alone. The insurance lobby naturally opposed the bill, but Moakley got it passed even in a Republican House, probably because it penalized out-of-state residents. Another, which would end automatic higher rates for younger drivers, didn't pass.[14]

Moakley's next idea was more revealing of the tone of national politics. He proposed that any candidate for office who had been a member of the Communist Party within the last ten years be required to disclose his membership on his nominating papers. During that session other representatives put forward similar restrictions on suspected communist activity. Moakley was hopping on the bandwagon and singing his own patriotic tunes. The country was in the depths of the 1950s witch-hunt, and as is the nature of witch-hunts, everyone had to stand up and be counted in the struggle against the witches.

Moakley thus came into political life representing a community that was prolabor on economic matters and conservative on civil liberties and social issues. Boston's ethnic and religious complexion made it more conservative than other industrial, big-city states that had more diverse populations. The splintered Massachusetts Democratic Party was not necessarily more "liberal" than the Republican Party. Yet from 1952 to 1960, Moakley inhabited a Boston political world that was gradually shaking off the legacy of its first half-century.

Several years later, political scientist Murray Levin argued that the overlapping Irish and Catholic (55 percent) influences in Boston helped produce Boston's conservative and corrupt political climate because its homogeneity eliminated bargaining between ethnic groups. In New York and Philadelphia, he posited, the Irish were just one faction among native-born Protestants, Italians, Germans, Dutch, Jews, African Americans, Slavs, and others, all of whom had a place at the table.[15]

There were additional factors as well. The Irish nationalist experience, usually viewed as part of the global anti-imperialist struggle, also carried within it a conservative component. All anti-imperialist movements had to decide whether they would emulate the modernity of the colonial power and become democratic, secular, intellectual, and commercial. In India, for example, Mohandas Gandhi, with his homespun clothing, represented the traditionalist response, while his colleague Jawaharlal Nehru favored modernization, and the two men worked a synthesis. In Ireland, by contrast, the traditionalist, Catholic, antimodern wing led by Eamon de Valera triumphed over the modernist wing led by Michael Collins. De Valera was a frequent and popular visitor to Boston, and his Catholic conservatism influenced Boston's Irish-American community.

Further, the decline of industry in Massachusetts in the 1920s, as textile mills and shoe factories moved south, led to a series of losing, defensive strikes in the nearby manufacturing cities of Lawrence and Fall River. By the 1930s the state's labor movement was retreating, while the movement in the Midwestern industrial states organized the vibrant Congress of Industrial Organizations, which included African American workers in its ranks. Boston therefore was largely bypassed by the migration of African Americans out of the South in the 1920s. Boston's small African

American community remained largely invisible to white Bostonians. South Boston concentrated all these factors. It was the most Irish and most Catholic neighborhood. By the 1950s neither Jews nor blacks lived there; Protestants were scarce, and communists probably nonexistent.

Moakley ran for re-election in 1954. In addition to the insurance and communist bills, he had also sponsored legislation to raise jury duty compensation, maintain state aid to education, allow pay increases for civilian employees of police departments, and he opposed antilabor laws. This time Ward 7 had been reorganized into ten precincts. Although Moakley was an incumbent, he ran just as hard as he had in 1952. The *South Boston Gazette* covered his kick-off speech at campaign headquarters in September. His advertisements announced that he had new labor support from the American Federation of State, County, and Municipal Employees and the Brotherhood of Railroad Trainmen. Moakley topped the ticket again, showing that his previous high tallies were no fluke. He garnered 3,425 votes in a field of seven in the primary, and 8,533 in the general election, besting his colleague Condon, who was also elected, by a few votes.[16]

After this victory, Moakley held a safe seat and felt secure enough to embark upon the next step of his professional career. He was accepted to the Suffolk Law School for the graduating class of 1956, along with several other working-class legislators. His one semester of college at Miami and one year of finance training at Bentley were sufficient to gain him admittance. Suffolk was then located in a single building, named for its founder, Gleason Archer, and conveniently located across Derne Street from the back entrance to the State House. Legislators could attend either day or evening sessions, and on occasion, a messenger would be sent scurrying from the legislative chamber to summon a student out of class to cast a vote. If the fellow hurried, he could hustle over in four minutes.[17]

Sixty-two students entered Suffolk that year. Eight of them were state legislators, and some of the others went on to successful careers in the Boston bar or bench. Suffolk then occupied the lowest rung on the totem pole of Boston legal education. Moakley flunked Professor David Sargent's course on trusts, but later he made the dean's list.

Moakley's academic struggles in Sargent's class could be ascribed to his busy life. He lived with his mother back at 291 Dorchester Street, the home in which he had lived as a child, and by this point was probably her main financial support. He held a day job as an insurance examiner, and another one as a state representative. He had a girl friend, and he had classes to take.

Moakley got through law school with the help of a friend, Jeanne M. Hession, one of two women in the class and a legal secretary by day. One night he offered Jeanne a ride home; she was a constituent of his. Joe encouraged her to run for class president, and she won. Since Joe and the other legislators couldn't attend every class, Jeanne agreed to type up her notes, making carbon copies, and share them with the young legislators. With Jeanne's help, Moakley graduated from Suffolk Law in June 1956 and was admitted to the bar on April 23, 1957.[18]

Joe's long courtship of Evelyn Duffy is probably best explained by Evelyn's ambivalence toward Joe's political career. He wanted to postpone marriage until he got his law degree. A picture from May 1955 shows Evelyn at the swinging Latin Quarter nightclub at a merry table of ten, as her male companion, looking somewhat inebriated, nuzzles Evelyn's shoulder. The male companion is not Joe. Joe probably realized that he had better propose before he lost her. His brother Tom had married his high school sweetheart, Doris, in 1952, and Robert married a girl also named Evelyn three years later. Joe and Evelyn married on February 10, 1957, at Saint Peter's Church in Cambridge. Bob served as best man. Evelyn came to live with Joe in an apartment in South Boston.[19]

* * *

Meanwhile, the city was changing around them. Mayor Hynes ended the old ethnic polarization and forged a new alliance with Yankee investors previously scorned by Curley as "the State Street wrecking crew." He reached out to previously marginal ethnic groups like the Italians and Jews, and appealed to middle-class Irish-Americans in the West Roxbury neighborhood. At the same time, the Catholic Church replaced the militant Cardinal William O'Connell with Archbishop Richard Cushing, whose views were ecumenical and inclusive. Hynes set out to revitalize the city by building a "New Boston" that would be cleared of crowded, substandard housing and replaced by modern, city-financed housing projects in the Brighton, South End, Jamaica Plain, Roxbury, and Dorchester districts. Hynes won re-election in 1955, defeating South Boston's leading political figure, Senate president John E. Powers.

During the Hynes administration, the wrecking ball and new construction projects produced jobs for union labor but destroyed Boston's West End and the "New York streets" section of the South End. These were both vibrant and diverse neighborhoods to the people who lived in them.[20] The state legislature largely stayed out of the process, and Moakley cast no votes. It's not clear what he thought about it. As a backbencher, even when his party recaptured the majority in 1954, never to lose it again, Moakley's opinion wouldn't have mattered much anyway. His subsequent record indicates that Moakley was a sensitive supporter of urban renewal who would have favored doing whatever was possible to maintain the existing communities. His generation wanted change, and the construction unions always wanted the work.[21]

On another front, state politics was changing in the same direction as Jack Kennedy's ambitions gathered steam. In 1956, Kennedy, who generally remained aloof from the state political machinery, tried to put his own man in control of the state apparatus. The head of the state party was an old-timer from western Massachusetts, William "Onions" Burke, whose soubriquet derived from the chief product of his farm. Burke was closely allied both with South Boston congressman John McCormack and with Curley, both of whom opposed another Adlai Stevenson run for the presidency in 1956. Kennedy wanted to replace Burke with former Somerville mayor John M. "Pat" Lynch, a continuation of the generational battle unfolding within the party. A showdown played out at Boston's Bradford Hotel, coincidentally located across the street from Joseph A. Moakley's tavern. A drunken, screaming Burke lost the battle as JFK waited outside in a car.[22]

Again, it is not clear what Moakley made of this change in the political landscape, an analogue to the modernization of Boston's physical landscape. Two powerful figures in his political firmament were aligned on different sides of this struggle. South Boston state senator John E. Powers had been a strong Kennedy supporter in the 1952 campaign, organizing the effort in Boston. Congressman John McCormack was in the Burke camp. Moakley made a lifelong career of staying out of intraparty battles, and he may have decided to avoid them as a result of this experience. "He stayed away from state conventions," staffer William Shaevel later recalled. "You only made enemies there."[23]

Two years later Kennedy faced a sacrificial Republican lamb, William

Celeste, who lost by more than 800,000 votes, the worst beating at the Massachusetts polls a Republican had ever received. A week later Kennedy was attending a family function in Los Angeles when he learned that Curley had died.[24] In that same election, Moakley easily retained his seat, running unopposed in the general election. Democrats widened their majority in the State House, winning 145 seats to the Republican's 95. In the Senate, Democrats won a majority for the first time, choosing John E. Powers of South Boston as their president.

Moakley, now a young veteran in the House, rose to a leadership position as majority whip. The Speaker was John Forbes Thompson from Ludlow in central Massachusetts, first elected to the House ten years earlier and to the top leadership in the 1957 session. Thompson was a large, imposing man, weighing about 275 pounds, with a big jaw, brushed back-blond hair, and, when he needed it, a menacing scowl. He ruled the House with strict discipline, earning him the nickname the "Iron Duke." Thompson was also a nasty drunk. He was famous for suspending House deliberations so that he and his claque could retire to a North End restaurant from which he would return inebriated and in a foul mood. Former state representative Beryl Cohen grimly recalled one late-night session in which Thompson wanted to ram through a transit bill that would raise fares on the Massachusetts Transit Authority.

"You're for it," Thompson instructed the freshman representative.

"No, I'm not," said Cohen, whose Brookline constituents relied on public transportation.

"Then get the fuck out of here," Thompson snarled.[25]

This was the man for whom Joe Moakley had to round up votes in 1958. He couldn't stand it and began to look for a way out.

The following year, John Hynes would complete his second term as mayor. The office would be open, and Senate president John E. Powers of South Boston looked certain to succeed him. Powers had the backing of labor and much of the press, the friendship of Cardinal Cushing, and a long career in state politics dating back to 1938. Born in 1910 to a streetcar motorman, he'd had to leave school in the eighth grade when his father was killed in an accident. These tragic circumstances no doubt shaped a fierce determination to succeed and honed his ambition. Powers faced the additional challenge of being short in stature, growing up in a world in which charisma was equated with size. Powers had won every election he entered except one, when he lost the 1955 mayoral race to Hynes.

Powers announced on March 31, 1959, at a $100-a-plate dinner at the Statler Hilton. Cardinal Cushing attended. Powers's headquarters bustled with busy staffers, fanning out around the city with posters and billboards, sending out press releases, stuffing envelopes. It was a sure thing, but Powers had lost once and wasn't taking any chances. He beat four rivals, taking 34 percent of the vote, not enough to prevent a run-off. His nearest challenger was John Collins.

Collins was shaped in the same non-confrontational mode as Hynes. He had been a state legislator from Roxbury and now served as the city's registrar of probate, a low-visibility position. In 1955 he had been stricken with polio, and as a mayoral candidate that probably won him a certain amount of sympathy; it equated him, of course, with FDR. Nobody gave him a chance. His kick-off dinner charged $15 a plate. Senator John F. Kennedy publicly endorsed Powers, as did Republican senator Leverett Saltonstall. So did everyone from South Boston and Dorchester, including Congressman John W. McCormack, his nephew Edward McCormack, and Representative John Joseph Moakley, who had his eye on Powers's Senate seat.

Powers vowed to lower the city property tax to attract new business, and to make up any revenue shortfalls by restricting tax abatements; Collins favored a sales tax. Voters don't choose candidates on these fiscal schemes upon which reasonable people might reasonably disagree. As political scientist Murray Levin pointed out in an analysis of the campaign, voters choose images that relate to their ideas of proper governance. The candidates held a television debate. Historian O'Connor concluded that Powers "came across . . . as a tough, arrogant, old time machine politician." Collins's slogan read "Stop Power Politics." Then, a few days before the election, the IRS raided a bookie joint, whose office bore a Powers campaign poster that appeared in newspaper photos. Powers lost by twenty-five thousand votes in a low-turnout election, a huge margin.[26]

Probably the second-most unhappy man in the city after the votes were counted was Joe Moakley. He couldn't run against incumbent Powers for his Senate seat. He was stuck.

Two months later, on January 2, 1960, Jack Kennedy announced his

candidacy for the presidency. John E. Powers, smarting from his mayoral defeat, hopped on the bandwagon. At some point in 1960, Powers
put out the word that he wasn't going to run for the Senate again; he
was going to Washington with Jack Kennedy. The 4th Suffolk District
included four wards beside Moakley's: the 6th, which covered the northern section of South Boston; and three others, in Dorchester, the South
End, and Roxbury. All the state representatives in Powers's district met to
assess each other's ambitions. They agreed to stay out of Moakley's way.
Moakley announced for the seat in mid-July. Later, Powers, disappointed
in his quest for a Washington job, jumped back in. He expected Moakley
to back out.[27]

Moakley didn't. He had probably always viewed Powers warily. Moakley didn't like bullies, and he perceived Powers to be one. Powers had a
Napoleonic short man's imperiousness that brooked no dissent; Moakley
would have seen in Powers a cannier, sober version of the Iron Duke.
Meanwhile, William Bulger announced for Moakley's open state rep's
seat. While recognizing Powers's abilities, Bulger, with his typical dry
wit, remembered Powers as "a close accountant of the slightest criti-
cisms, and it was said he never held grudges longer than three or four
decades."[28]

Sure enough, the campaign turned ugly. Moakley had never run *against*
anyone before. In a two-seat district, he never attacked opponents; he
respectfully motivated himself. Powers ran big ads in the South Boston
newspaper charging that Moakley supported a sales tax, and reminding
voters that it was silly to replace the Senate president with a freshman.
He accused Moakley of failing to make a lot of roll calls, dubbing him,
"Take a Walk" Moakley.

Moakley fought back at a three hundred–strong campaign rally in
Dorchester. His slogans were "It's Time for That Change" and "The Old
Ways Will Not Do," echoed JFK's generational appeal, but indicated no
substantive differences from Powers. He asserted that he had voted
against the sales tax nine times, admitted that he had missed some roll
calls, but no important ones (like most young state representatives, he
had a day job). He charged that Powers was inaccessible, and that if he
were elected he would not be. In the only meaningful part of the discussion, Moakley backed urban renewal projects such as Mayor Collins's
new Government Center in seedy Scollay Square, and the Prudential

complex in the Back Bay. All the state representatives sided with Moakley and encouraged their supporters to do so as well. Some observers predicted an upset, but it was not to be. Moakley lost by a big margin, 15,108 to 9,565, and the outcome made the front pages. A class act in defeat, Moakley showed up in person at the Ward 7 Democratic Club to concede graciously. Powers, just as Bulger characterized him, treated Moakley as a permanent enemy. It was the way he operated.[29]

In the general election six weeks later, William Bulger won his race for Moakley's seat and went over to the Ward 7 Democratic Club, standing on a table with Powers, their hands clasped above their heads in victory.[30] But the biggest winner that night, in a very close election, was now president-elect John F. Kennedy. The New Frontier was about to begin, and thirty-three-year-old Joe Moakley would be on the outside looking in. The ride that had begun on the Bayview bus was over.

4

★ ★ ★ ★ ★

The Invisible, the Blind, and the Visionary

Mary Scappini Moakley, Joe's mother, died of heart disease on Mother's Day in 1959, at age fifty-three.[1] She had been a quiet doer of good deeds, a member of the church faithful, and a good mother. She lived her whole life in South Boston, and at the end she lived in the house into which she had been born, at 291 Dorchester Street, back at St. Augustine's parish. All three of her sons had turned out well, and for a woman of her generation, that probably mattered more to her than the fact that her husband had abandoned her for another woman. Her children were happily married and she had grandchildren. It had been a good life, if touched with sadness.

Joe and Evelyn bought a modest house looking out at the sea at 1812 Columbia Road on the south shore of the peninsula, a short walk to Castle Island. They would live there until their deaths. Brothers Tom and Robert worked as Boston police officers. Tom had served in the Coast Guard, married his high school sweetheart, Doris, and was starting a family. Of the three brothers, Tom most resembled his father physically; he was tall and handsome, with a long face and ruddy Irish complexion. Robert had worked as a longshoreman and served twice in the army, including a stint in Japan after the war and later in Korea. He was built more like Joe, and had inherited the family political gene; by the mid-1950s Robert was among Joe's most trusted advisors.

Joseph A. Moakley was living with Maida Comeau in Dorchester when his wife died. John Joseph reported Mary's personal information to the authorities when his mother died; he was the head of the family now. The relationship between father and sons was shifting as the boys started successful careers and happy marriages. None of Joe Senior's saloons ever proved financially successful. The one at 280 Tremont, across from the

Bradford Hotel and Shubert Theater, had a perfect location but for some reason never quite worked out. He finally had to take a job at the Massachusetts Turnpike Authority.[2] Evelyn Duffy Moakley now had her husband all to herself after Joe lost the Senate race to Johnny Powers. While she shared in her husband's triumphs and defeats, this loss might not have been so bitter for her. She was and would remain a private person, partisan on her husband's behalf but not especially interested in politics and jealous of her husband's time. She had been widowed once and didn't want to become a widow to her husband's career. She and Joe never had children, and that fact probably made Joe's time spent with her all the more precious.

Joe established a law office just up Dorchester Street from his mother's house, past Saint Augustine's and across from the O'Brien Funeral Parlor, where he could attend wakes and meet prospective clients. Everyone at a wake remembers his own mortality—and there would be Joe Moakley, the attorney, offering his condolences. Maybe it was time to draw up a will or add a codicil? Moakley had street-smart business sense. He entered a partnership with Daniel Healy, a former longshoreman, who, like Joe, had come to the law late and was a Suffolk graduate. Where Joe was gregarious and good at sizing up people and cases, Healy was meticulous and detail-oriented. Bill Shaevel, who joined their firm later, remembered that the two men had a "wonderful partnership."[3]

The office at 149 Dorchester was also located just down from the South Boston District Court, to which they brought many of their cases when they had some discretion. The squat District Court sat on Broadway, just past its intersection with Dorchester Street atop Mount Washington. The simple three-story red brick structure was designed with functionality, not the majesty of the law, in mind; like most local courts it is a place where deals are struck to resolve the rival claims of petty thieves and policemen. The main courtroom was white walled, square shaped, furnished with plain wooden benches for clients who will not be there long, and lit by sunlight from three oval widows on the western wall. An elevated judge's rostrum, from which the judge might balefully survey the human dramas appearing before him, overlooked a clerk's desk and attorney's table.

The Honorable Thomas E. Linehan, a fair-minded jurist who dispensed no favors, presided over the court in the years that Moakley worked there. Bill Shaevel remembered one such case that would have been typical of a criminal trial before the court. A longshoreman was apprehended on suspicion of stealing a cargo of stereos that had disappeared from the docks. The federal authorities, who had charge of the docks, informed the state police of their suspicions about the man, whose premises were searched, revealing the missing merchandise. The man was thereupon arrested, but something was lacking in the paperwork between the law enforcement agencies. Judge Linehan found that the search had been improper. The longshoreman went free. On the courthouse steps, he asked Moakley, "So you mean I can go get those stereos now?"[4]

Moakley had no illusions about arguing before the Supreme Court, but even in the early 1960s he wanted more than to spend his time defending petty thieves or drawing up wills. So he kept his eye on the political scene. The earthquake of 1960, when Jack Kennedy won the presidency, was about to receive an aftershock.

★ ★ ★

Edward J. McCormack, Jr., thirty-nine years old, was the nephew of Congressman John W. McCormack, and in 1962 he announced his candidacy for the U.S. Senate seat that Jack Kennedy had vacated just before assuming the presidency. At the president's request, Governor Foster Furcolo then appointed Benjamin A. Smith, the mayor of Gloucester, to hold the seat until an election could be scheduled. From Joe Moakley's perspective, his neighbor Eddie McCormack deserved the seat next. Son of South Boston's "Knocko" McCormack, a clownish figure frequently photographed in his World War I doughboy's uniform, Eddie took after his sober uncle rather than his oddball father. He had served in the Navy, was elected to two terms on the city council, and won the state's attorney general post in 1960 by 450,000 votes. In that office, he established a civil rights division. He had climbed the ladder of office and paid his dues.[5]

Eddie McCormack was not particularly surprised when Ted Kennedy, a mere thirty years old, jumped into the race on March 14, claiming that "He Can Do More for Massachusetts," a frank reference to his presumed pipeline to the White House should he win. Ted Kennedy had never run for anything, had dropped out of Harvard when it was found that another student had taken an exam in his place, and had worked only as an assistant district attorney in Suffolk County. Kennedy biographer Adam

Clymer concluded that no sitting senator had come to the office with so thin a resume. Kennedy's bid angered not just local politicians of Moakley's ilk but also distinguished Harvard professors and *New York Times* Washington bureau chief James B. Reston. "One Kennedy is a triumph, two Kennedys at the same time are a miracle, but three could easily be regarded as an invasion," Reston declared. Moreover, McCormack was probably the more liberal candidate. He favored the elimination of nuclear weapons, and as a former longshoreman had New Deal instincts that Kennedy did not yet have. But Kennedy out-organized McCormack at the state convention, out-campaigned him in the primary, captured the nomination, and destroyed his Republican opponent in the 1962 election. A new Kennedy star rose in the Bay State firmament.[6]

Joe Moakley loyally supported Eddie McCormack in this election but maintained his regard for the Kennedy family. He was out of office and could afford to say little if he wanted to get back in. Taking sides in intraparty fights was always a risky gamble. Some in South Boston, sensing who the victor would be, backed Kennedy. One of them was Roger Kineavy, a longshoreman and Navy veteran, soon to be a Moakley supporter. He remembered how personal that campaign was. "Eddie McCormack's father, 'Knocko.' He used to see me on the street, and he says, 'You son of a bitch. You're for Kennedy.'"

By barging in, out of turn, by bringing his vast financial resources to bear against a local favorite son, Kennedy had broken an unspoken rule of proper ethnic solidarity. The right thing for young Ted Kennedy to have done was to run for Eddie's vacant seat, which still would have been an act of unprecedented brashness, but would at least have been understandable. Ambition had to be balanced against propriety and respect for one's colleagues. For Moakley, and others like him, the core issue was that a man stayed loyal to his friends.[7]

This principle had some merits, but its limitations would soon be revealed when Boston entered the deepest crisis in its history, one that would last for two decades.

★ ★ ★

On June 11, 1963, members of the Boston National Association for the Advancement of Colored People confronted the Boston School Committee at a stormy meeting. Led by Ruth Batson and Paul Parks, 125 black and white activists insisted that the city's schools were segregated in fact and that the school committee should acknowledge and address the problem. Batson had been working on the issue since 1951, when she learned that her own children were using inferior textbooks in an overcrowded classroom. Over the next decade the NAACP, Freedom House, and Citizens for Boston Public Schools documented the situation in a variety of reports that clearly demonstrated racial disparities. Thirteen schools were 90 percent black. Average annual spending on white elementary schools was $350 per pupil, while in black schools it was $229. The school department functioned like an Irish job trust. People in authority loyally helped their friends and neighbors. The school committee had been overwhelmingly Irish and Catholic since the turn of the century, as were the superintendants and teachers. J. Anthony Lukas, in *Common Ground*, the Pulitzer Prize–winning book on the desegregation battle, found that "[in] the mid 1960s one investigator counted 68 Sullivans, 61 Murphys, [and] 40 McCarthys . . . in the system."[8]

Boston's black civil rights activists had a proud history of struggle going back to Crispus Attucks and the Boston Massacre, and continuing through the abolitionist period, the Civil War, and beyond; black Bostonians such as William Monroe Trotter challenged Booker T. Washington's acquiescence to the Gilded Age's Jim Crow laws; black and white Bostonians helped launch the fledgling NAACP in 1909. Most Irish-Americans were indifferent to the black struggle. The two great exceptions were John Boyle O'Reilly, a late-nineteenth-century romantic nationalist who saw the brotherhood of oppressed Irishman and Negro; and in the twentieth century, Cardinal Richard Cushing. However, African American Bostonians in 1963 were still a smaller percentage of the city's population (sixty thousand people, or 9 percent in 1960) than were their equivalents in New York or Chicago, which already had black congressmen.

Boston's racially liberal past, coupled with the small size of the community, made black Bostonians more integrationist than nationalist. The Marcus Garvey "Back to Africa" movement of the 1920s attracted relatively few followers in Boston, compared with the mass movement it generated in Harlem. Ruth Batson and Paul Parks, therefore, crystallized the major trend of Boston black community activism when they stood before the school committee. They were visionary leaders of an imagined, integrated Boston.

Boston's African American activists and their white allies had some hope that the five-person school committee might act in their favor. Louise Day Hicks of South Boston had been elected to the school committee in 1961 and become its chairperson in January 1963. A burly woman with an oddly ill-fitting prim voice, she was the dutiful daughter of the prominent, now deceased Judge William J. Day. He had been a respected denizen of the City Point district who looked down on politics as a sordid business and revered the law as an elevated one. If Louise had gone into politics, she nonetheless honored her father's principled respect for the law. She was not consciously a racist. In fact, she had been one of nine women in a class of 232 students at Boston University Law School, where she formed a small study group that included three black students. In 1963 Paul Parks had driven her home to South Boston after a meeting, an unusual act of racial intimacy in and of itself, during which she indicated that she was sympathetic to the problems of the black community.

Ruth Batson made the major address at the June 11 meeting. Years later a documentary film, made for the *Eyes on the Prize* civil rights documentary series, shows her appealing for "some goodwill and common sense" to resolve a difficult but not insoluble problem. Batson did not charge the school committee with deliberately segregating the schools, but she did argue that the committee had to acknowledge that de facto segregation existed and that it was inherently unjust. The obvious solution was to build new schools along the racial borders and make appropriate pupil assignments to gradually balance the ratios.

It was not to be. Hicks made no comment that night but turned the microphone over to School Superintendent Frederick J. Gillis, who denied that there was a problem because he did not deliberately segregate the schools. A few days later the school committee met with four black representatives, but after seven hours nothing was resolved. Hicks, no intransigent, then met privately with Parks and Muriel and Otto Snowden, directors of Roxbury's Freedom House. They produced a compromise statement from all four participants, which, although it did not accept that "de facto segregation" existed, seemed sufficient to head off a threatened school boycott by Negro parents. The black leaders released the statement, and then Hicks charged that the statement had been altered. Another meeting at the home of Governor Endicott Peabody also failed to resolve the deadlock, and black parents organized a one-day boycott in which more than eight thousand students attended Freedom Schools or stayed home. From that point on, all serious negotiations were off. Hicks dug in her heels, refused to compromise, and defended herself before adoring white crowds that echoed her views. Cardinal Cushing and even President Kennedy implored Hicks to negotiate further with black leaders, but at the August 15 school committee meeting she ruled the black leaders out of order when they pressed the issue.

The black activists walked out. Later, Alabama segregationist George Wallace approached Hicks, seeking an alliance that she rejected with disgust. Louise Day Hicks was not consciously a racist and she was not a segregationist. Wallace was both those things. The tragedy was that Hicks could not walk a mile in the Negroes' shoes, as president Kennedy asked white Americans to do in his June 11, 1963, speech, made coincidentally on the day of the Boston School Committee confrontation. She could not see them. They were invisible to her. A long struggle that would peak eleven years later had begun.[9]

Two months later Martin Luther King gave the famous "I Have a Dream" speech at the March on Washington, called to promote Kennedy's civil rights bill. A few months later President Kennedy was assassinated in Dallas and Vice President Lyndon Baines Johnson became president. A liberal New Dealer from the Texas Hill Country near Austin, he had voted cautiously against most civil rights measures. He now promised to fulfill King's and Kennedy's dream and push the civil rights bill through Congress. The bill was signed in June 1964, beginning the end of an era that would conclude the following year with the passage of the Voting Rights Act.

As the Civil Rights Act made its way through Congress in 1964, South Boston held its annual Evacuation Day Parade. This patriotic celebration honored the flight of British troops from Boston on St. Patrick's Day 1776. A proud tower rising from Telegraph Hill commemorated the victory; it echoed the Bunker Hill Monument in Charlestown. The event was traditionally patriotic and military in character, not Irish, and would remain so until the NAACP joined the 1964 parade hoping to rekindle the spirit of John Boyle O'Reilly among the South Boston Irish. The NAACP unfurled a banner depicting the martyred John F. Kennedy, bearing a green lettered slogan: "From the Fight for Irish Freedom to the Fight for U.S. Equality." The activists were greeted with a barrage of rocks and bottles and a homemade sign that said "Go home, nigger. Long live the spirit of independence in segregated Boston."[10]

★ ★ ★

Soon after, Johnny Powers resigned his Senate seat to become clerk of the State Supreme Judicial Court. Joe Moakley responded by gaining control of the Ward 7 Democratic Party Committee. His slate won the election with Moakley topping the ticket, while a rival slate of Hicks, Bulger, and Condon placed second. The battle for Powers's seat now opened up. Moakley entered the primary race immediately.[11] The question of civil rights for Negroes, in a district that now included black voters in North Dorchester, Roxbury, and the South End, never came up. Black people remained invisible.

Moakley ran on his record as a state representative, but once again the campaign was not about issues. Brother Robert, Patrick Loftus, and Roger Kineavy organized a vigorous effort for Joe. They opened four campaign headquarters in the district, knocked on doors in the housing projects, and visited merchants in Roxbury and Dorchester, not just South Boston. The campaign even sponsored a basketball team, "The Moakley Senators," in a park league. He took out a large ad in the South Boston newspaper in which a dozen citizens testified that Moakley's "honest and friendly" character, prolabor views, and eagerness to get shade trees planted made him a "regular all around fellow."

Any of his five rivals might have said the same, but the leading contestants looked like old-timers out of Boston's past, one of them running a picture of himself shaking hands with Curley. Moakley looked like the future. He never attacked his opponents, and he didn't advance a central theme. He won an incredibly absolute majority with 12,144 votes. His nearest rival got 4,224. Evelyn appeared in the newspaper, beaming alongside her husband, sporting fake handlebar mustaches as they thanked the voters on election night. In November, Lyndon Johnson defeated Barry Goldwater and Moakley carried the 4th Suffolk District by nine to one with 27,104 votes, to 2,845 for his obscure Republican rival. Joe Moakley would be back doing what he most loved to do.[12]

Moakley took office in January 1965 just as the climactic events of the decade-long national civil rights struggle came to a head. In March and April of 1965, Martin Luther King joined civil rights activists in Selma,

Alabama, as they demanded the right to vote. Their struggle contributed to the passage of the 1965 Voting Rights Act that guaranteed all citizens the right to vote. In signing the act, President Johnson privately observed that white Southerners would begin to leave the party. He was right. The Voting Rights Act transformed the face of American politics. Southern and Northern whites would begin to vote for a Republican Party that pandered to their racial resentments. This was the beginning of the end of the New Deal coalition that had improbably joined Northern blacks and Southern racists in the same Democratic Party.[13]

Shortly after the Selma demonstrations, with national emotions running high, Martin Luther King came to Boston to campaign for civil rights in the North, his first effort in that regard. He arrived just after the commissioner of the Massachusetts Board of Education, Owen Kiernan, released a blue ribbon panel report on racial imbalance—a polite word for segregation—in the state's schools. The report identified fifty-five racially imbalanced schools in the state, forty-five of them in Boston.[14]

Predictably, Louise Day Hicks was "appalled" by the report, which, she charged, was written by "a small band of racial agitators, non-native to Boston, and a few college radicals who have joined in a conspiracy to tell the people of Boston how to run their schools, their city, and their lives." This opinion was shared by three other board members. Hicks had denied all along that segregation existed, and suggested that the issue be settled by a referendum. Her colleague William O'Connor denied "that racial imbalance is harmful." Only the Back Bay's Arthur Gartland on the committee supported the report, and he would not be re-elected. (The Boston School Committee was elected by citywide, rather than district, voting.) The NAACP demanded new hearings before the school committee to revisit the question that Hicks had closed.[15]

The 1954 *Brown vs. Board of Education* Supreme Court decision had made segregation illegal precisely because it *was* harmful. The idea of settling the question by means of referendum denied the minority a basic human right; this was the very "tyranny of the majority" that the Founding Fathers had designed a system of checks and balances to prevent. The commission had included Hicks's neighbor Edward McCormack, and South Boston's Richard Cardinal Cushing. Hicks was wrong on every point.

King toured Roxbury in the company of black leaders. He was warmly received by Republican governor John Volpe at the State House, where

Lieutenant Governor Elliot Richardson reminded King that they had met in Selma. Democratic mayor John Collins met King and a delegation of black leaders, bearing a set of proposals to improve race relations, at City Hall. Brookline state senator Beryl Cohen worked with black state representatives Royal Bolling, Franklin W. Holgate, and Michael Haynes to have King address a joint session of the legislature, which concluded with the stirring call of the "I Have a Dream" speech to "Let Freedom Ring." The only place King was not welcome was at the Boston School Committee, to which he was invited on the condition that local Negro leaders would not speak, an insulting demand designed to preclude a visit. On Friday, April 23, King led a march of more than twenty thousand from the South End to the historic Boston Common, where he called on citizens to "march in Boston until the walls of segregation come tumbling down." The religious community participated enthusiastically, including a contingent of Catholics, spearheaded by the Catholic Interracial Council, whose numbers formed a solid block in the march. King left Boston feeling upbeat and inspired.[16]

Within months, the Voting Rights Act passed, and by August, African Americans began to register to vote by the millions as racists stood by gnashing their teeth. Yet August 1965 was also the month of the Watts, Los Angeles, race riot, in which dozens were killed and millions of dollars in property were destroyed, beginning an era of racial polarization in American life. In Boston, the school committee, rather than gradually desegregating the schools, decided instead to hold double sessions in the black schools while seats in nearby white schools remained vacant. Governor Volpe angrily protested, pointing out that 400,000 students in the state rode buses to school without any objections.[17]

At this historic juncture the Massachusetts State Senate took a third and final reading on a Racial Imbalance Law, first proposed by Roxbury state representative Royal Bolling and promoted in the Senate by Beryl Cohen. Bolling had failed to pass the bill two years previously, but the national attitude toward civil rights had shifted dramatically from 1963 to 1965. The bill mandated that school districts report to state authorities their racially imbalanced schools, along with plans to redress the problem. Failure to comply would result in a cut-off of state aid. Democratic and Republican leaders together drafted funding language so that jurisdictions with imbalanced schools could obtain state money to comply, and an appeal mechanism was established. In the House, white Boston members voted against the measure. In the forty-member Senate, the "ayes" carried a voice vote, and no one had to be recorded by name for or against. This was a historic vote—no other state passed similar legislation; it was very much in keeping with Boston's antislavery tradition. At the signing ceremony in the State House Hall of Flags, executive and legislative leaders were joined by civil rights activists, fair housing proponents, business leaders, and liberal Catholics such as David Nelson, African American leader of the Catholic Interracial Council, and Father Robert Drinan, dean of Boston College's Law School.[18]

Freshman senator John Joseph Moakley largely avoided this controversy. He was only one of forty senators, and only one of seven from Suffolk County, but he also represented substantial numbers of African Americans. He did make two recorded votes on the Racial Imbalance Act on the second reading: a "Yes" vote on an amendment to have the Commonwealth fund 40 to 65 percent of school district costs necessary to comply with the law; and a "No" vote on an amendment to use 50 percent as the benchmark figure for an imbalanced school.[19] Those votes suggested how difficult his position was. On the final voice vote he was opposed.[20] Had Moakley voted "Aye" he would have been spurned by all his South Boston colleagues and turned out of office in the next election. In fact, no one challenged him in the next two elections, either in the primary or general election.[21]

Boston's stormiest election in the 1960s would pit the descendants of two prominent fathers, Louise Day Hicks and Secretary of State Kevin White, against each other, again testing Moakley's loyalties. Hicks had become the symbol of intransigence against desegregation; White had the support of the black community, and attracted young reformers like Barney Frank. Moakley had friends in both camps and stayed out. "He was nowhere, no place," Kineavy remembered.[22]

A few weeks after the election, Moakley's father died, at age sixty-three. He had enjoyed the satisfaction of seeing his sons grown and prosperous; he was grandfather to a growing brood of Tom's and Robert's children. They called his wife, Maida, "Nanna" in recognition of her integration into the family. Four of Joe's colleagues from the Senate, several state representatives, and an assortment of officials attended the funeral, despite a freak November snowstorm that blanketed the city.[23]

Moakley kept quiet on other issues that were important to the black community. By 1970 Boston's black community would reach 16 percent of the
city's total, with 104,000 counted in the census. Yet the black vote was
divided among four Boston senatorial districts, and no African American had won election to the state Senate. The three black state representatives, Royal Bolling, Michael Haynes, and Franklin W. Holgate, urged
that the legislature redraw the districts to produce a majority black district. This would be done shortly after Moakley left the Senate in 1970,
with the cooperation of three Jewish state senators who agreed to "lose"
one of "their" seats, but Moakley didn't take a stand either way. In addition, perhaps with his eye on a future congressional race, he opposed
legislation requiring that Boston policemen meet a residency requirement, a move that would help increase black representation in the overwhelmingly white police force. Finally, he supported the death penalty,
a position usually opposed by African Americans because racist police
departments sometimes sought convictions regardless of the facts, especially when the alleged perpetrator was black.[24]

Over the next few years, Moakley opposed busing to achieve desegregation, but he also warned that state and federal laws must be obeyed and
violence abjured. As the mood in South Boston turned increasingly ugly
regarding African American aspirations, Moakley did not champion civil
rights claims. Mel King, a prominent civil rights activist in this period,
didn't remember Moakley at all from the 1960s. Moakley did not ignore
black voters, and he visited Roxbury with black state legislator Michael
Haynes.[25] But he was sitting on a barbed wire fence on the busing issue,
and he hastened to address other matters closer to his heart, issues that
he felt united, rather than divided, his black and white constituents.

★ ★ ★

One of those issues was housing. In January 1968, Moakley was well into
his second term and he acceded to the chairmanship of a committee later
known as Urban Affairs. He assigned to the housing issue a new young
staff member, Bill Shaevel of Newton. Shaevel originally came to Moakley fresh out of New England School of Law through a Ford Foundation
grant to state legislatures, most of which did not have the money for staff

members. Having lived in public housing, and representing a district of renters, Moakley proposed and passed a bill that would make it more difficult to evict tenants without cause. Henceforth landlords could be challenged at a hearing if they evicted an unoffending tenant.[26]

Much more controversial was a bill to expand public housing statewide. Boston faced a severe housing crisis. Like most major cities in the late 1960s, white residents moved to the suburbs as the economy boomed and the GI Bill facilitated low-interest mortgages on mass-produced housing. In most cities, new black migrants moved into what became extensive black neighborhoods, forming either a "ghetto" or "black community," depending upon point of view. This problem was exaggerated in Boston because bankers anticipated white riots if black migrants purchased homes—or even attempted to rent—in most white neighborhoods. The banks and real estate agencies cooperated clandestinely to "redline" Boston, funneling black people only into the mostly Jewish neighborhoods of Roxbury and Mattapan.[27]

An additional problem was that Boston had a relatively lower total tax base than most cities because it had so many universities, churches, and hospitals. Half the city's property was tax exempt. In addition, the urban renewal projects of the 1960s had removed vast swaths of housing in the South and West Ends occupied by "slum" housing and replaced it with Route 93 running through the heart of the city, the new City Hall and Government Center, and luxury housing. Although the city's population would decline from 698,901 in 1960 to 580,000 twenty years later, changing demographics reduced the number of inhabitants per unit by one person. The net result, despite the population decline in Boston, was that one in five residents of the total metropolitan area lived in substandard housing. Moakley concluded that 123,000 Bostonians needed low-rent housing, and that only 335 such units had been built in the past six years. In Boston, there was nowhere left to build, and in the suburbs, nobody wanted low-rent housing. The poor, many of them black, were stuck.[28]

Moakley proposed a series of measures to combat the housing crisis, most importantly a "snob zoning bill" that would override suburban town edicts prohibiting low-income housing by zoning only for large lots. Nobody in the suburbs wanted Boston's poor, especially if they were black, but nobody would say so in those terms. Builders want to build for the rich, owners fear a decline in their property values if low-income people move in, and town managers worry about increased costs generated by people who contribute less in taxes and may require additional services. Moakley's bill, written by a joint committee, told the suburban towns that they would have to surrender these privileges for the common good.

The "snob zoning bill," predictably, was defended by a coalition of suburban liberals based in the churches and temples, and vigorously opposed by "not in my backyard" property owners. As chairman of the Joint Legislative Committee, Moakley received a high volume of mail from outraged home owners, none of them his constituents, some of them frankly stating that they didn't want urban "riffraff" in their town. Their state senators and representatives more diplomatically alleged that the bill violated home rule.[29] They might have added that this was precisely South Boston's objection to the Racial Imbalance Law, but none made the connection.

In addition, Moakley wanted, and got, new revenues for building public housing. For this he had to overcome the objections even of Democratic colleagues like James "Blackie" Burke, chairman of the Ways and Means Committee, who frankly told Moakley he didn't like public housing. Moakley might have stood up in the Senate and made a speech, but that was never his style. He went to Burke, reminded him that he himself had lived in public housing, and asked Burke to back the funding as a personal favor to him. Burke did. That was Moakley, the behind the scenes legislator, working successfully for the public good as he saw it.[30]

A second issue that drew Moakley's attention was environmental degradation. Moakley opposed an idea to locate the 1976 Bicentennial celebration on Boston's Harbor Islands. Boston would be a logical place to host the event as one of the two leading centers of the Revolution, Philadelphia being the other. Builders, hotel and restaurant owners, charter bus operators, and even taxi drivers would benefit enormously should their city be chosen as the host. A report by the Arthur D. Little consulting company anticipated a $2.2 billion bonanza from millions of visitors, figures derived from recent experience at the 1967 Montreal World's Fair.[31]

Not so fast, Moakley cautioned. From his post in the Senate, Moakley worked to influence city officials who would also have a say in the decision. In April 1969 he appeared before a city council committee and spelled out his objections. They were based largely on environmental impact concerns, a concept just beginning to emerge in the late 1960s. To place the Fair on the islands, landfill would have to be dumped into the harbor, and no one had calculated its effect on the polluted water. In 1969, eight 100-year-old conduits were dumping raw sewage directly into the harbor. Tides removed the outflow, and the likelihood was that the landfill would interrupt that flow. Moreover, despite profits for developers, the city of Montreal, Moakley argued, was a net loser and was still paying $1.5 million a month to meet its obligations.[32]

Moakley had the support of a united South Boston on this matter; he had just been honored by the community newspaper as "Man of the Year," largely for this stance, and Louise Day Hicks campaigned on this issue too.[33] Whether the costs really outran the benefits is difficult to determine. Philadelphia didn't think so, and it got the Fair. But Moakley's environmental concerns were genuine. The discussion of the Fair turned Moakley's attention to what the Harbor Islands should be used for.

Moakley's opposition to the Fair was based on a detailed preliminary study by urban planners and economists at the Massachusetts Institute of Technology. As chairman of a special legislative committee established in 1966, composed of five Boston and South Shore senators, nine state representatives, and eight governors' appointees from government, business, and labor, Moakley commissioned the report in June 1968. "The Harbor Islands" was released in April 1969 and discussed at a conference convened by Moakley in late June. The report, with which Moakley concurred, argued that the Commonwealth should begin a process of acquiring the thirty islands and nearby peninsulas for the purpose of planned development. At the time, the islands were held by a Byzantine hodgepodge of competing governmental entities and private owners, many with rival agendas. Some islands were partially owned by combinations of these entities: towns, counties, the Metropolitan District Commission, Massachusetts, and various federal agencies.

This jurisdictional anarchy led to the pollution of the harbor. Meanwhile, as the coastal population expanded, developers obtained more housing and commercial permits from Boston to Cape Cod. The MIT report observed: "Vast amounts of raw and treated sewage, along with some industrial wastes, are discharged into Boston Harbor." It concluded that the Commonwealth legally had a controlling interest in making final determinations. Moakley thus led the first coordinated long-range planning effort that took seriously environmental issues in the harbor and islands.[34]

While Moakley was in the Senate, he advanced other environmental issues as well. He opposed the expansion of Logan Airport and recommended that carriers be required to adjust flight patterns and employ quieter engines to conciliate residential abutters—his constituents. He went after the Boston Edison Company, whose sprawling South Boston plant employed his constituents but pumped noxious smoke into the atmosphere. For this offense, the utility had been cited sixty-nine times—and paid a measly fifty-dollar fine each time. Moakley proposed fines of twenty five thousand dollars and two-and-half-year prison terms for company executives. He wanted mandatory antipollution devices installed on automobiles and charged the auto industry with "utter disregard for human life." At the first national Earth Day ceremonies, Harvard University invited only one state legislator—Joe Moakley.[35] Moakley would work on this issue throughout his career; if he was among the cautious on race relations, on the clean-up of Boston Harbor he was a visionary.

While Moakley was an early environmentalist, it would be wrong to conclude that he was also a social liberal. Dispensing information on birth control was illegal in Massachusetts until the late 1960s. Moakley was among only eleven senators to oppose a change in the law. It is not clear whether Moakley was voting his conscience or making a political calculation in opposing the bill. It would, and did, pass without his vote. He probably figured that a vote in favor would hurt him in conservative South Boston, and that he was doing no harm by voting against it. However, he had plenty of cover to vote in favor if he felt that that was the right thing to do. Cardinal Cushing issued a statement during debate on a legalization bill that Catholics were not obligated to vote against non-Catholics practicing birth control. Moakley opposed abortion too.[36]

Moakley also supported the death penalty. Massachusetts had a death penalty, but the state had not carried out an execution since 1947. Various legislative campaigns to abolish the death penalty stalled in the face of popular opposition. By 1967, eight men waited at Walpole State prison's death row to be electrocuted. In February that year, Moakley voted against abolition of the death penalty and against a moratorium on executions pending a study. The state was in the grip of a crime wave, and not one involving black perpetrators but white ones. In recent years, forty-three men had been killed in gangland-style slayings related to loan sharking alone. Moakley's two brothers were policemen, many of his constituents were policemen, and Moakley would have been way out on a limb had he voted against the virtually unanimous opinion of law enforcement officers on this score; the likelihood is that he was voting his conscience on the death penalty. The death penalty in Massachusetts would be overturned by a 1975 decision in the Supreme Judicial Court.[37]

On economic and social issues such as health care, however, Moakley was a strong partisan for government action to help the middle class and poor. He served on the special commission to implement Medicaid in the state. Along with Senator Beryl Cohen, he advocated an expansion of medical facilities through the establishment of new municipal authorities empowered to issue bonds. This bill failed in the Senate because hospital employees' unions feared they would lose job security under the measure. Moakley and Cohen amended the bill accordingly, but senators concluded that the new provisions would discourage potential bond purchasers. Health care limped along. Moakley himself, like Ted Kennedy, who was proving to be a diligent senator, favored some form of universal health-care coverage and was looking for a formula to increase the availability of medical care.[38]

Moakley began the 1960s out of office, looking like a man with a limited political future. He closed the decade as a leader in the state Senate on issues such as housing and the environment. He had his eye on a congressional seat too. When Speaker John McCormack announced his retirement, Joe Moakley was ready to run.

5

★ ★ ★ ★ ★

Moakley versus Hicks

S peaker of the U.S. House John William McCormack was a formidable poker player, known for holding his cards close to his vest and maintaining an inscrutable demeanor. Although he was seventy-eight years old and completing his twenty-first term, only his wife, Harriet, and his closest aides knew that he would announce his retirement on May 20, 1970. His colleagues in the Massachusetts delegation were informed of the fact two hours before the news conference.

McCormack had been Speaker of the U.S. House since the death of Sam Rayburn, taking over in January 1962. When he rose to the top leadership, *Time* magazine described him, accurately, as a "tall, gaunt man, with a shock of white hair, rimless glasses and a thin lipped smile." In truth, he looked like a figure from the distant past even in 1962—a man born in 1891, a World War I veteran in a landscape shaped by World War II, the space race, and rock and roll. The first time the Speaker flew on an airplane was in late 1961 to attend Rayburn's funeral. By 1970, to a generation that was protesting the war in Vietnam, smoking marijuana, and dancing to the Rolling Stones, McCormack looked like a figure from nineteenth-century literature—Ichabod Crane or Mr. Micawber.

There was some truth to that image. The cultural revolt of the 1960s and 1970s located the sources of militarism and imperialism in an uptight culture of emotional repression that frustrated humanity's inner longing for pleasure and joy. McCormack didn't drink, dance, or even socialize much with his colleagues—a seemingly humorless Puritan in a den of congressional bourbon-swillers. He dined quietly with his wife every evening in their apartment at the Hotel Washington. "Old John" exemplified routine. He arrived at the House at the same time every morning, and ordered the same cheese sandwich and chocolate ice cream for lunch every day. John McCormack rarely appeared in the headlines, and probably few Americans in the 1960s could identify him.

In Congress, Majority Leader John W. McCormack rounded up the votes to pass Franklin Roosevelt's New Deal program. Its fruits included the Old Harbor housing project, today named for McCormack's mother, in which Joe Moakley had lived as a boy. McCormack helped push through parts of Truman's Fair Deal, such as the GI Bill, from which Moakley had also benefited. McCormack's rise to the office of Speaker continued a tradition of House leadership based in Texas and Massachusetts that went back to John Nance Garner and would end with Tip O'Neill, the "Austin/ Boston Connection," as political scientists dubbed it. McCormack fashioned the majorities, which included substantial numbers of Republicans and no Southern Democrats, that passed the Civil Rights Bill of 1964 and the Voting Rights Act of 1965. The story of the legislative "Second Reconstruction" has gone down in American history as the work of John F. Kennedy and Lyndon Johnson, but few remember that "Old John," Speaker McCormack, had led those bills through the House. And when McCormack announced his retirement, the one unfinished item of business that he regretted had not been completed was a constitutional amendment that would guarantee the right of eighteen-year-olds to vote.[1] Then why did he look like an out-of-touch old man?

The reason was that McCormack supported the war in Vietnam.

The House took its first vote on Vietnam in August 1964 after a murky incident in the Gulf of Tonkin off the North Vietnamese coast. The resolution cited the centrality of Southeast Asia to American interests and empowered the president "to take all necessary steps, including the use of armed forces" to defend the region. In his masterful biography of the future House Speaker, *Tip O'Neill and the American Century*, John A. Farrell describes an exchange between the representatives of the 8th and 9th districts of Massachusetts. The two men, mentor and protege, were seated at a table among others in the House dining room before the vote, and O'Neill remarked that "there was something screwy about the whole thing." Later, O'Neill remembered that "everybody kind of looked at me aghast," and McCormack summoned him to his office, warning him not to vote against the resolution. "Tom, it will be determining that you're a traitor if you were to do a thing like that," McCormack admonished, and O'Neill joined the 416–0 majority in favor. It would become the one vote that O'Neill most wanted to take back at the end of his career.[2]

In 1965, President Johnson would use the Gulf of Tonkin Resolution to escalate the war. President Kennedy had sent sixteen thousand "advisors" who were inevitably drawn into the fighting. But the central problem for the Americans was that Vietnam had no liberal middle class to lead the nation toward democracy; its middle class was either too closely tied to the old French colonialists or had fought against the French and become communists. Johnson sent combat troops, ultimately half a million on the ground at one time, to defeat the enemy. Presidents Truman, Eisenhower, Kennedy, Johnson, and Nixon saw the war as an effort to end global communist aggression in which neighboring countries would fall like "dominoes" should communist dictatorship win in Vietnam. They believed that there was an international communist conspiracy to take over the world, and that the communists responded only to force. This Cold War consensus was accepted by the vast majority of Americans, from academia to the man in the street. To John McCormack, Vietnam was a battleground in the war of freedom against dictatorship.[3]

After Johnson escalated the war and resumed the draft, a small minority launched a radical critique against the war. Student antiwar activists argued that the Vietnamese were waging a war of national liberation against an unyielding imperialist power—first the French and then the Americans—and they happened to have communists, along with others, in their leadership. They saw the Vietnamese struggle as part of a global anticolonial revolt, like the postwar independence movements of Gandhi in India or the Algerians against the French. The activists pointed out that the war was killing hundreds of thousands of innocent civilians, and therefore should be ceased immediately and all troops withdrawn. To the "peaceniks," the South Vietnamese regime was an illegitimate dictatorship that repressed its noncommunist opposition of students and Buddhists. As the body count on both sides skyrocketed, the antiwar movement became steadily more determined, and larger.[4]

Somewhere between those camps, the broad American public adopted a middle position, expressed in infinite variation but whose common theme was: the war can't be won and isn't worth it anyway. Tip O'Neill had expressed his doubts in private to McCormack in 1964, but he defended the war in public over the subsequent three years. In February

1967 his eldest son Thomas, Jr., invited him to speak to the Boston College Democrats. O'Neill told the students that he had been briefed by the president, by Secretary of State Dean Rusk and Defense Secretary Robert McNamara, and that the war should and could be won. In the discussion period, student leader Patrick McCarthy, who would have been regarded as a moderate on many other Boston area campuses, stood up and asked, "Have you been briefed by the other side?"

McCarthy was his class president, the son of a San Francisco labor lawyer and grandson of a former mayor. But he was a Democrat, no revolutionary firebrand, and he would drop out of BC a few months later to join the army and serve in Vietnam himself. McCarthy's challenge made O'Neill think. Over the next few months, he began asking probing questions, and was in turn sought out for a clandestine rendezvous with dissident intelligence officers who had concluded that the war was unwinnable unless the United States was willing to risk a confrontation with Russia or China. O'Neill was a product of patriotic, working-class North Cambridge, and those people made up his committed base. He hesitated. But as the war continued, a letter from the antiwar mother of a son in the army finally persuaded Tip O'Neill that his working-class constituents had had enough. So had he. In August of 1967 he sent out a newsletter urging an end to the war. President Johnson summoned O'Neill to his office and called him a "son of a bitch." In October, as protestors marched on the Pentagon, McCormack gave an emotional speech on the House floor in favor of the war. Tip O'Neill's change of opinion represented a seismic shift in the national debate on the war. He had chosen principle over loyalty to his chiefs, Johnson and McCormack.[5]

In the following year, the most turbulent in American history, the United States suffered a nervous breakdown as the country lurched spasmodically toward O'Neill's position. In January the National Liberation Front launched an offensive, attacking scores of cities and briefly occupying the American embassy in Saigon. Minnesota senator Eugene McCarthy challenged LBJ in the New Hampshire primary and jolted the establishment by capturing 43 percent of the conservative Granite State vote. Bobby Kennedy jumped into the race behind him, and when Senator Joe Moakley hosted the annual St. Patrick's Day political gathering at Dorgan's Restaurant, all the nervous participants of a divided state Democratic Party were walking on eggshells. "Hawks or Doves?" one reporter queried new Mayor Kevin White, and he blurted out, "Chickens." At the end of the month, President Johnson, realizing that support for the war within his party had crumbled but not willing to admit it, announced dramatically on television that he would not seek re-election. Four days later, Martin Luther King was assassinated, and two months after that Bobby Kennedy was gunned down after claiming victory in the California primary. At the August Democratic national convention, prowar and antiwar factions tore themselves apart as Chicago mayor William Daley's police clubbed antiwar protestors in the street. Hubert Humphrey won the nomination but lost the general election to Richard Nixon, who claimed to have a secret plan to end the war.

With Nixon in office, the Democrats felt unconstrained in their opposition to the war, and the Johnson-Humphrey Cold Warriors steadily lost ground to a rising generation of antiwar activists within the party. Both sides radicalized, consensus disappeared, and emotional polarization became normal discourse. McCormack came under attack from a variety of liberal House leaders, most prominently Richard Bolling of Missouri, Phil Burton of California, and Morris K. Udall of Arizona. Finally, one of McCormack's aides got caught in an influence peddling scheme, and Old John had had enough. He announced his resignation just after a storm of antiwar protests initiated by Nixon's expansion of the war into Cambodia. That same day, construction workers rallied in New York to support the war and an antilabor Republican president. The world was turning upside down.[6]

★ ★ ★

"One day we heard an announcement he [McCormack] was not running for U.S. Congress," Roger Kineavy remembered. "So Joe says, 'We'll make an announcement tomorrow.'" Actually, it was six days later, but Moakley was ready to go. He consulted his closest advisors from past campaigns: his brother Robert, Kineavy, law partner Daniel Healy, and Senate aide Bill Shaevel. There was already a challenger, an antiwar Vietnam veteran named David Houton, but Moakley would be a heavyweight contender. As state senator he occupied the same post that McCormack had before going to Congress. Other possible candidates included Moakley's Dorchester colleague George V. Kenneally, a judge, and three city councilors, all elected at large, whose constituencies were thus larger than that of the 9th Congressional, which included only the North End, South Boston, parts of Dorchester, the South End, Chinatown, Roxbury, Jamaica Plain, Roslindale, and part of the Back Bay. This was an overwhelmingly working-class district, 24 percent African American with a small Latino and Chinese American cohort. The three city councilors mentioned were Thomas Atkins, the first black man elected citywide to the council, John L. Saltonstall, a liberal antiwar Democrat, and most significantly, Louise Day Hicks, who had failed of election to the mayoralty by a mere twelve thousand votes in 1967. Political odds-makers picked Hicks to win.[7]

Moakley declared his intention posed under a picture of John F. Kennedy. He was then forty-three years old and had fourteen years of state legislative experience on his resume. He promised to fight for the same issues in Congress that he had championed as a legislator: "housing, transportation, pollution, recreation, and development of Boston's offshore islands." He attacked President Nixon's priorities, citing a measly allotment of $4 million for water pollution nationally over a five-year period, "when we could use $1 billion in Massachusetts alone . . . [W]hen there is $70 billion for a defense budget, you can't get much back to the states," Moakley declared. In a jab at a potential Hicks campaign focused on busing or crime, he noted that "I don't think anyone is going to win on any one issue." He opposed the war as a waste of resources: "I think the war is draining the lifeblood of our youth and demanding immense financial resources that should be redirected toward solving our urban problems." Observing that he had formerly supported the war, he said, "I'd like to get the troops out of Cambodia and Vietnam without sacrificing troops. We've got to protect our people there." On racial issues, he favored no special programs, but one addressed to the needs of all the poor, and cited his own record on housing.[8]

Moakley established his main office at 487 West Broadway in the Perkins Square neighborhood of South Boston. He might be running districtwide, but Southie was still home. He thus presented himself as he had from the beginning of his career: a neighborhood guy, a nuts and bolts politician, in tune with the progressive concerns of his working-class constituents, a reasonable man on no moral crusade. He said that he had had his eye on the seat for "two or three years"; a signal that he was prepared to assume its responsibilities, was not impulsive, and balanced his ambition against respect for his elders.[9]

Over the next few weeks, the field of contenders took shape. Atkins declined to run. John White, a bearded antiwar Catholic priest from Roxbury, joined the race, asserting that his first act if elected would be to impeach Nixon and Agnew and press for immediate withdrawal from Vietnam. Saltonstall also called for an immediate end to the war and denounced racial violence. His Ivy League background and membership in the ACLU made him the white liberal champion. Atkins's withdrawal opened the door to David Nelson, a black Catholic attorney who served as chairman of the board of Boston City Hospital, and whose key issues were urban reform and opposition to the war.

Last to announce, but clearly the most formidable, was Louise Day Hicks, whose campaign slogan against Kevin White in 1967, "You Know Where I Stand," referred to her opposition to busing. Hicks had left the school committee to challenge White in 1967, but in 1969 she won election to the at-large city council, topping all rivals. She announced on June 8 at the downtown Parker House Hotel, praising McCormack and vowing to continue in his tradition. She claimed to be "neither hawk nor dove" but trusted that the president knew what he was doing when he had invaded Cambodia.[10] By summer, Saltonstall and Father White had dropped out; Houton quit the primary to run as an independent. That left three candidates: Hicks, Moakley, and Nelson.[11]

Once the field was set, the candidates faded back into obscurity. Hicks, the front runner, barely campaigned. She never attended candidates' nights for fear of making a gaffe. Moakley and Nelson dutifully appeared at every neighborhood civic association function and recited the litany of their programs, which differed little, and their accomplishments, in which Moakley's were superior to all. Moakley never contrasted himself to Hicks, fearing a backlash for attacking a woman who wasn't present to defend herself. In a mostly white district, everyone knew that Nelson couldn't win. Moakley, always polite, wasn't very quotable. Hicks, thoroughly unprepared for the job and lacking interest in wider national issues, simply appeared at functions of her loyal antibusing supporters, dispensing lollipops and fans as souvenirs. There wasn't much for reporters to cover.[12]

The 9th District primary had to compete with other campaigns in which the outcome was more in doubt or in which the issues were more clearly drawn. A bitter four-way race was underway in the Democratic gubernatorial primary, pitting Senate president Maurice Donahue, Boston mayor Kevin White, former JFK aide Kenneth O'Donnell, and state attorney general Francis X. Bellotti against each other. Moakley had ties to Donahue and White, and probably to avoid offending either one he went to a meeting for O'Donnell, who didn't have a prayer.[13] Two other competitive Democratic congressional primaries also drew a lot of attention to the war issue. Father Robert Drinan, dean of the Boston College Law School, was challenging Phil Philbin, an old-line McCormack-type, in the 4th District; and Gerry Studds, a liberal history teacher, ran in a field of four for an open seat in the 12th District, the South Shore and Cape Cod. Drinan would become the first Catholic priest to sit in the Congress, and Studds, then "in the closet," would become the first openly gay congressman. Both these campaigns were fought along the political lines that were tearing the country apart in the streets.

That was not the case in the 9th District. Moakley distributed a campaign brochure, "Nine Reasons That You Should Vote for Joe Moakley," which identified his concerns, in order, as housing, pollution, health care, minority groups, consumer protection, crime, the economy, Vietnam, and transportation. It cited his impressive record on the first two issues, and declared his general desire for a single-payer health-care system. He supported bilingual education, and declared that there was no room for hatred in Boston. He called for improved mass transit at the expense of highway construction. "Vietnam" was buried as issued number eight. Hicks also barely mentioned Vietnam.[14]

Moakley won significant labor backing from powerful Teamsters Local 25, the National Association of Government Employees, the Metropolitan Policemen's Association, the railroad clerks' union, the bakery and confectionary workers at the South Boston sugar refinery, and others. He thought of his base as consisting of diverse ethnic voters: Irish-Americans, Poles, Lithuanians, Italians, and Jews; Nelson was clearly going to win the black vote. Campaigning in the North End, he met with humorous responses when he called attention to his Italian forebears: "OK, if you're half Italian you get to put up half a sign," one wag commented, and another queried, "Is it true you're half Irish?" In the dog days of July and August, Moakley plugged away, shaking hands on street corners and at MBTA stations.[15]

Moakley scored a point against Hicks when he finally attacked her record on rent control, an issue Moakley was promoting in the Senate. Hicks, by contrast, had voted three times against rent control measures while on the City Council, and lost the votes. Hicks, an absentee landlord herself, owned properties in the Back Bay.[16] Moakley saw Hicks as the high-born daughter of a judge from City Point, while he came from the projects. He had worked hard to master many complex urban issues; she had won attention by agitating only one. He viewed her as a divider, himself as a uniter.

Moakley probably saw the writing on the wall. The final tally was Hicks 24,886, Moakley, 19,656, Nelson, 18,532. He had at least won South Boston.[17] The racial calculus revealed a clear lesson: Nelson's black voters would have voted for Moakley in a two-person race, but Moakley's white voters would probably vote for Hicks if Nelson and Hicks faced off. Had Nelson dropped out of the race, Moakley would have won, but Hicks would have beaten Nelson in a two-person race.

Moakley was emotionally devastated. He took this loss personally, and was depressed for a month. He looked up Beryl Cohen, a former colleague in the state Senate who had lost in the primary for lieutenant-governor. They went to the YMCA on Huntington Avenue, worked out, had a meal, and wondered about their futures. By mid-October Moakley was over it. He had been through this drill twice before, losing his first race for state representative in 1950, his race against Powers in 1960, and now against Hicks—each loss a decade apart. Maybe this one would be followed by a victory too. He consulted his advisors: brother Robert, Kineavy, Shaevel, and Healy. Shaevel recalled, "He was resilient. He said to me, 'How can we get elected?'" Moakley decided to run for city council the following year.[18]

During the course of the 1971 city council campaign, Shaevel looked around for a fresh face to write some position papers. He hit upon Patrick McCarthy, the student who had challenged Tip O'Neill to think more carefully about the war. McCarthy, lean and trim after his service in Vietnam, was completing his undergraduate degree at Harvard and enrolled for Harvard Law in the fall. Meanwhile, he made some contacts among political people, and was writing position papers for state attorney general Robert Quinn. McCarthy was a brash, ambitious twenty-five-year-old who had a rare combination of Irish street smarts and Ivy League academic credentials. He met Moakley and Shaevel in their South Boston law office and agreed to write some position papers on a fee for service basis. There was no talk of Moakley later running for Congress.[19]

Forty-one candidates, including six incumbents, entered the city council race for eighteen ballot spots in a November run-off. Moakley topped the field in September and came in first again in November, a remarkable testimony to his personal appeal and organizational skills.

Media attention focused on Round Two of the Kevin White vs. Louise Day Hicks race. The fact that a congresswoman was running for mayor suggested that Hicks was not happy in Washington. Tom Atkins, the first black man to run for mayor in the city's history, and state senator Joe Timilty ran as well. In September White outpolled Hicks by more than four thousand votes; Timilty came in third and Atkins fourth.[20] In the mayoral final, White trounced Hicks, winning 62 percent of the vote, the second largest margin in city history since Curley lost in 1951. Twenty-thousand fewer people voted for Hicks in 1971 than in 1967. The likelihood is that her voters were moving to the suburbs as the black and Latino population grew; one Roxbury polling station went 909–4 for White. However, no minority candidates were elected to the citywide school committee or the city council.[21]

One newspaper account speculated that Moakley would challenge Hicks for the House seat again. He had won with 92,640 votes. Only 70,226 had voted for Hicks in the mayor's race. She looked vulnerable, but Moakley would still have to solve the problem of defeating Hicks in a crowded field.[22]

Moakley was glad to be back in office, but City Hall, even under a mayor whom Moakley liked, was a letdown after the Senate. First of all was the building—no match for the state Senate's august, tiled corridors. Boston's new City Hall looked like a windowless prison, with a recessed and forbidding entrance that gave onto a dreary interior courtyard. The city council meeting room was a dismal concrete box, utterly charmless in its aspect.

Even worse was the increasingly toxic atmosphere emerging in the city over the busing issue. Under the Racial Imbalance Law, the state would withhold funds from districts that "racially imbalanced," or segregated their schools. The Boston School Committee had done little to comply with the law, and its leaders consistently denounced it. The one step they had made, in 1966, was to build a new school, the Lee, an attractive $8 million structure in a white Dorchester neighborhood, near a black neighborhood. During the five years of construction, the neighborhood changed to be mostly black. To open the building in compliance with the law and receive the state aid, the school committee in August voted 3–2 to assign white children from the nearby Fifield and O'Hearn schools to the Lee. They would walk, not bus, a maximum of four-fifths of a mile. This was the low-impact method of desegregating the schools that the black community advocated.

At a stormy September 21 meeting, hundreds of angry white parents thronged a school committee meeting at the O'Hearn School. School committee member James Hennigan, like all the others an opponent of "forced busing," nonetheless explained the importance of keeping $21 million in state aid if the parents wanted a quality education. Hennigan bravely told the angry crowd that the school committee had abdicated its responsibility by not complying with a state law, and if they didn't, the court would inevitably step in and do its job for it. His prediction turned out to be entirely accurate.

The white parents screamed their defiance, insisting that they would not send their children into a crime-ridden neighborhood. Under this pressure, one school committee member switched his vote, opposing reassignments to the Lee School. Hennigan sent an account of the meeting to his friend Moakley.[23] There would be no desegregation in Boston. White parents preferred to send their children to a segregated school than to send them to a new, integrated, but neighborhood school. The dispute over the Lee School became the decisive tipping point in the battle over desegregation. Black parents had fought in the streets, in the city council, the school committee, and the legislature for an equal, desegregated education since 1950. White opponents of that goal had insisted that their only objection was to "forced busing" of their children out of their neighborhoods. The rage of the white parents on September 21, 1971, showed that their real objection was to desegregation.

★ ★ ★

Within a week after winning the city council seat, Moakley summoned McCarthy to his office again and intimated that he was considering another congressional run, and he asked McCarthy to help him. By chance, McCarthy was dating a woman who knew Joe Casper, Louise Day Hicks's chief advisor, and McCarthy found himself in Casper's office too. Casper had been with Hicks for years. Tall, fit, handsome, he was thoroughly cynical about politics, with a "do what it takes to win" philosophy. He warned McCarthy that Joe Moakley was a nice guy who would waste his time in another primary against Louise. There would be a bunch of candidates in the race; Louise had 40 percent locked up in advance, and Moakley would get creamed. The busing issue was getting more attention this time, and Moakley didn't have much to say about it; Louise did.

McCarthy thought about what Casper said. Then he thought about his grandfather, the former mayor of San Francisco, and that he had once run for office as a labor independent. McCarthy analyzed the results of the general election in 1970. Hicks had won a scant 50 percent of the votes—the rest of the ballots were divided among a Republican, the independent Houton, or were blank. He thought outside the box. What if Moakley ran as an independent?

McCarthy was now at Harvard Law School. One day Moakley drove over and picked him up. As they drove down Storrow Drive toward South Boston, McCarthy raised his idea. The purpose was to get a three-way race with the Republican probably winning 10 percent. "That would be like leaving the church," Moakley said.[24]

He probably meant that literally. People like Joe Moakley felt themselves to be *born* Catholic, Irish, union members, and Democrats. He would catch hell from people he respected—McCormack for one, Tip O'Neill. They'd have to endorse Hicks. But he didn't rule it out. Moakley wanted to go to Congress, knew he would be better at it than Hicks, and that he would have won in 1970 if Nelson had not played the role of spoiler.

There was another wrinkle. The 9th had been redistricted after the 1970 census. For decades it had been configured the same way, because McCormack occupied the seat. But in a redistricting year, the newest member can count on having the district boundary redrawn. A West Roxbury state senator, Robert Cawley, who was on the redistricting committee, also had his eye on Hicks's seat. Cawley shaped the 9th so that it lost a little of Boston (whose population was declining as the suburbs expanded) and added seven suburban towns that were near to his neighborhood: Canton, Dedham, Dover, Needham, Norwood, Walpole, and Westwood.

McCarthy's idea didn't go over well with Moakley's inner circle, but they agreed to conduct a poll for a hypothetical three-way race. They surmised that black people would vote for an independent, but that the district's whites would be fiercely loyal to the Democratic Party, and that the Democrat would win. McCarthy visited Pat Caddell, then beginning what would be a long career as a pollster. Caddell found just the opposite of what Moakley's team had guessed: blacks were hard-line Democrats, whites more flexible. But blacks obviously would not vote for Hicks. Moakley sought out former mayor John Collins and ran the idea past him. Collins thought it might work. The indicators seemed to point to the independent strategy.

McCarthy then came up with an idea to "position" Moakley, prior to his announcement, as an independent of sorts. The national Democratic primary was on as well, and Mayor John Lindsay of New York, once a "silk stocking" liberal Republican, was running in the Democratic primary. McCarthy called Gracie Mansion, got right through to Lindsay, and asked how he'd feel about Boston city councilor Moakley endorsing him, as a fellow "urban mechanic." Lindsay agreed. McCarthy called a news conference for Moakley at a senior citizens' center, and all the media showed up, expecting Moakley to announce his own campaign, only to hear the big news that Moakley was endorsing Lindsay. Nobody cared, and the rest of Moakley's staff began to look at McCarthy as an outsider with little feel for Boston's pulse.[25]

Moakley made a last-ditch effort to get the Democratic primary field to himself. Years later he remembered, "I sat down and tried to get some of the people who were running. I said, Look it, let's take a straw [poll]. Nobody is going to beat her if we put this kind of field out there. Well, everybody had their stairway to the stars and they said, No, no. I said, Okay. So I just stepped out. I ran as an independent." Hicks would be challenged by Cawley, school committeeman Hennigan, and two black candidates, Boston University social work professor Hubie Jones, and Melvin Miller, publisher of the black community weekly, the *Bay State Banner*. Moakley had no chance in a field like that, and neither did anyone else except Hicks. In the September primary, Hicks emerged an easy winner, but with only 21,855 votes.[26]

Moakley voted for Hicks too. Had any of Hicks's four liberal challengers won, he would have no basis for an independent campaign. After

Hicks's victory Moakley established a central office across from City Hall. McCarthy coordinated the campaign from there. They opened a satellite office in Roslindale, near the suburban towns, directed by James O'Leary, who was attracted to Moakley because of his support for public transit. Roger Kineavy worked out of an office in South Boston.

Moakley served as city councilor during the last year of the war in Vietnam, during which George McGovern campaigned against Nixon's carpet-bombing of the whole country. That year another anti-imperialist struggle drew attention, especially from Boston's Irish-American community. In early 1972, British troops in Derry, Northern Ireland, killed fourteen peaceful Catholic protestors on a day that would become known as Bloody Sunday. One of Moakley's supporters, John Burke, brought two friends, Padraig O'Malley, a Dublin Irishman, and Tim O'Neill to seek Moakley's financial help for the victims' families. Moakley persuaded other councilors to contribute to a fund. The trio held a fund-raising concert later in 1972 and they raised a thousand dollars for each family. This was Moakley's first experience with international solidarity. Moakley never spoke much about his Irish heritage, perhaps because he was only half-Irish; he would not have heard about Ireland as a boy the same way that most South Boston politicians did. This incident launched O'Malley on a remarkable career of using civil society dialogue to resolve international disputes, and ultimately to an endowed chair in Moakley's name.[27]

A team of fund-raisers included Ken Lyons, from the National Association of Government Employees, financier Norman Leventhal, John Lynch, an insurance man named Sternhall Spurp, and Evelyn's nephew Stephen Duffy. McCarthy hired both the Jack Connors and Martilla advertising agencies. They produced radio and TV ads, campaign literature, and a jauntily designed teal on blue button. Moakley needed the money this time. At one point McCarthy told Moakley they were out of money: they needed to pay for TV ads, and would lose without a fresh cash infusion. Moakley himself came up with $20,000 over the weekend.

McCarthy had figured the race as a three-way contest with a conservative Republican, improbably named Ronald McDonald, gaining 10 percent of the vote. To McCarthy's concern, a more liberal challenger named Howard Miller defeated McDonald. Miller would be a more attractive candidate in the liberal suburban towns. There was even a Socialist

Workers Party candidate, who, if she won 2 percent of the vote instead of 1 percent, could tip the election to Hicks.

Moakley's candidacy vexed the state's Democrats. Publicly, the state machine backed Hicks, and prominent leaders like McCormack and O'Neill did radio ads for her. O'Neill warned Moakley that he was ruining his career. But as the election drew near, staff members among Hicks's primary rivals began showing up in Moakley's office with donor lists, Mayor White's friends prominent among these defectors from the Democratic camp.[28]

Moakley's supporters worked hard. On one weekend, five hundred hit the streets, dropping a flyer in every home in the district. Hennigan, one of the losers in the primary, announced his support for Moakley, reassuring voters that he was a Democrat temporarily disguised in independent clothing. Moakley campaigned on issues of economic justice, Hicks on her opposition to the Racial Imbalance Law. He ran TV ads, and a full page pre-election day ad in his hometown *South Boston Tribune* announced, under a picture of a smiling, rumpled Moakley, that "Washington might be my next address, but South Boston's my home."[29]

Moakley ran in the black community, and opened an office in Roxbury. He bought full-page ads in the *Bay State Banner*, the black community newspaper, reminding readers who his opponent was. All the leading black political figures endorsed him, and in the pre-election issue, an editorial declared that "Moakley Can Win," opining that he "has not pandered to people's fears and prejudices."[30] On the Saturday before Election Day, Moakley met with members of the black legislative caucus in Roxbury. Moakley needed them—Royal Bolling senior and junior, Mel King, Doris Bunte, Bill Owens—to turn out the vote. The black leaders asked Moakley to open a district office in Roxbury if he won. McCarthy told them that they had already decided to do that. The question of who would staff it came up, and for the first time, Moakley heard the name of James Woodard, the only member of his staff who would work for him throughout his congressional career.[31]

The race went down to the wire. McCarthy stationed Moakley at the John F. Kennedy School in Canton all day on Election Day. Polls showed Moakley losing Canton, but McCarthy thought they could win it. That night Moakley's team watched the results come in at the Statler Hilton in Park Square. Hicks ran ahead in the early returns. It was neck and neck in Boston, and Louise won the city, by 40,810 to 40,618 for Moakley. Moakley carried the black wards, which had some white voters as well, 15,260 to 5,868 for Hicks. Most of the suburban towns were closely divided, but Moakley won Canton by 1,000 votes and Needham, the most middle-class and professional town, by more than 2,000. That was his margin of victory. Moakley was elected with 70,571 votes; Hicks received 67,143, the Republican Miller won 23,177, and the Socialist Workers candidate did better than 2 percent, winning 2,397 votes out of a total of 173, 935 ballots. The final result wasn't determined until five in the morning, and the Moakley camp celebrated not with champagne but by going out for a bleary-eyed breakfast.[32] It was the last close campaign Joe Moakley would ever run.

★ ★ ★

Joe Moakley was clearly the liberal alternative to Louise Day Hicks in the overwhelmingly working-class, Democratic 9th Congressional District. He positioned himself as an antiwar moderate, but all four of Hicks's primary opponents had been more outspoken against the war than Moakley. Hicks was militantly antibusing; Moakley said as little about the issue as he could. Hicks stood not far apart from Moakley on economic justice issues, and both claimed labor support. Neither spoke out for women's rights and both opposed abortion. Although Tip O'Neill endorsed Hicks, Moakley's views on the war reflected O'Neill's. Hicks, when she mentioned the war at all, stood closer to McCormack.

Their real differences would emerge over time, but the stylistic differences could easily be discerned in 1972. Moakley was inclusive, instinctively a uniter who sought consensus, not a polarizer who appealed to white people's fears. By running as an independent, he showed that he could listen, take risks, change. Had McCarthy not proposed the idea, and Moakley not taken him up on it, he would have had a totally different career. He might never have gone to Congress at all.

Moakley won the election, but the tensions that the campaign had delicately surfaced in 1972 would explode over the next decade, exposing Boston as the most violent and racist American city outside the Deep South. Joe Moakley would have some days during the next years during which he could hardly get out of bed.

6

★ ★ ★ ★ ★

The Man on the Barbed Wire Fence

During Joe Moakley's first term in Congress, a lawsuit against the Boston School Committee brought by the parents of black school children initiated the deepest crisis in the city's history. On June 21, 1974, Federal Judge W. Arthur Garrity ruled on behalf of the plaintiffs, finding that the school committee had deliberately allowed the schools to become racially segregated, thus violating the decision in the 1954 *Brown v. Board of Education* case that racially segregated schools were inherently unequal. The judge ordered a remedy adapted from a Massachusetts Department of Education plan that included, among other techniques, the mandatory busing of children across neighborhood lines to achieve desegregation.[1]

Resistance to the plan by white parents centered in South Boston, with echoes in Charlestown, East Boston, Hyde Park, and other neighborhoods. Louise Day Hicks, now a city councilor, state senator William Bulger, and state representative Ray Flynn, a younger man on his way up, led a militant protest movement in their representative bodies, the courts, and the street. The antibusing activists established an organization called Restore Our Alienated Rights, or ROAR, whose symbol was a stuffed lion. They argued for the primacy of the neighborhood school and the irrelevance of racial integration. Moakley also opposed busing, but added another reason. He emphasized on pragmatic grounds that it failed to produce its intended effect—desegregation. In addition, he refused to join the street marches against busing, never joined ROAR, and opposed school boycotts. Moakley believed that such behavior was inappropriate for a U.S. congressman. This quietude on Moakley's part invited the vociferous condemnation of fanatical antibusing advocates, many of them racists, who denounced him in their newspaper, lobbied him in Congress, and marched to his house. To them, he was the man on the fence.

Moakley opposed "forced busing," as everyone in South Boston called it, consistently throughout his congressional career. He fought for a constitutional amendment that would forbid judges from ordering it. Moakley argued his case in a September 1975 letter to President Gerald Ford, in testimony before the Senate Judiciary Committee the following month, and in a speech on the House floor in July 1979.

In these settings Moakley postulated that the judge's order violated the value of community, and defied common sense. He thought it was a waste of time and money to bus children past one school to get to another in an unfamiliar neighborhood. Moakley believed that the neighborhood school was part of the bedrock of a community, along with sports teams, the church, and other institutions that made a physical place feel like "home" and not a group of disconnected houses. Working-class South Boston especially valued community—a place in which children learned and played together in a neighborhood school. To Moakley, the judge's values, which stemmed from an upwardly mobile middle class, were different. The judge prized social mobility regardless of community. In Garrity's view, antibusing activists believed, a person went to school to move up economically, and out, geographically, to the suburbs. Those were individualistic, self-centered, not communal values.

Further, antibusing activists felt that the judge's orders were undemocratically imposed from on high by an appointed official from outside the community. Making his case for a constitutional amendment to ban busing in a speech on the House floor in 1979, Moakley declared that he could not, in good conscience, vote against the opinion of the majority of his constituents on a matter that directly affected them. A city-wide referendum against forced busing had carried by a vote of 13,000 to 2,000. How could a judge substitute his opinion for the clear will of the majority?

Finally, Moakley cited a study by University of Chicago sociologist James S. Coleman that showed that busing caused white flight to the suburbs and defection to all-white parochial schools. The result led to "a highly segregated inner city school system, and perhaps worst of all, no tax base left to buy books, pay teachers, and in general, educate children," Moakley, along with other House colleagues, informed the president.

Moakley pointed out to the Senate committee that Boston's public school system was now 52 percent nonwhite, and Coleman's report showed that the inevitable result would be total white flight now that the "tipping point"—a much lower percentage—had been reached. "Busing is a bankrupt policy whose time never was," he concluded.[2]

Moakley joined with other congressmen, almost entirely Southern Democrats and conservative Republicans, to promote various constitutional amendments to address the problem. Because forced busing was mandated by federal judges, not by legislative bodies, nothing less than the fundamental law of the land must be altered. Moakley properly understood the Constitution's supremacy clause that no ruling by a municipal, county, or state body could overturn a decision by a federal judge.

While busing was widely opposed by white Americans of both parties and all regions, the resistance to it was fiercest in Boston, and especially among the South Boston Irish. There, the judge's order touched mystic chords of memory, to borrow the words of President Abraham Lincoln's First Inaugural. While Judge Garrity was an Irishman himself, nominated at the behest of Senator Ted Kennedy, his ruling echoed the century-old intrusion of Boston Brahmin edicts into the affairs of the Irish village within the city, beginning with the 1850s "Know Nothing" or "American" Party attempts to cripple Catholic schools and block the path to citizenship for Irish immigrants. A surge of Irish-American nationalism arose throughout the city. Shamrocks appeared on every bar, and the Irish tricolor flew from a thousand flag posts. To many antibusing activists, their cause was rooted in the ancient struggle of underdog Irishman against British and Yankee oppressor, the battle of freedom against tyranny.

Not every opponent of busing was Irish of course. The antibusing movement promoted such zealots as Pixie Palladino of East Boston, Avi Nelson, a Jewish radio talk show host, and Dan Yotts, of Lithuanian descent. Joseph Lee, a Yankee school board member, blocked desegregation measures in the early 1970s. Clay Smothers, a black Christian activist from Dallas, came to Boston to announce that blacks opposed busing too. Irish-American activists at once embraced the Irish nationalist aspect of the movement, and insisted, correctly, that most whites were with them.

The antibusing movement also reflected a deep strain of Jeffersonian-Jacksonian populism that had nothing to do with ethnicity. Both these presidents opposed government intervention into national life, and set a template for the libertarian strain in the country. Most Americans believed that the government should leave people alone in their private lives, and schooling was part of that private, or at least local, sphere, that was none of a federal judge's business.

Most antibusing activists resented being called racists. They accused suburban liberals, as the enemy was now identified, of inhabiting lily-white enclaves from which they imposed rules of behavior on them, a virtuous community of hard-working people. The charge especially rankled Hicks, Bulger, Flynn, and Moakley. They weren't racists, and they knew it. Hicks had black friends, and sought to include black opponents of busing in the parades. Flynn had been the only white man on a semiprofessional basketball team. Moakley was the first congressman to locate an office in Roxbury. All four felt the charge of racism to be a cheap shot.

In his own memoir, William Bulger repeated these themes proudly, and felt unconflicted about his stand. From the perspective of twenty years on, he could, with justice, conclude that the warnings of the antibusing group had all proved true. The Boston public schools were, and remain, overwhelmingly nonwhite. Boston, and American society, with the exception perhaps of the military, is still segregated.[3]

Moakley wrote no memoir. The closest he came to doing that was the long interview he granted to Suffolk University scholars shortly before his death. "Oh, it [busing] split people up and many well-intentioned people—some of them are really not able to articulate properly—you know, were labeled as bigots, and then there were other people who wanted to do the right thing, and they were almost thrown out of their homes. It was the worst political time that I have ever gone through in my life. Some days, I just didn't want to get up in the morning and put my shoes on. It was terrible, getting calls all during the night." He recalled a high school girl friend who "just spat as I walked by one day. You know, those things are hard to take for me." He quickly changed the subject. The memory suggests a troubled man, and the phrase about "other people who wanted to do the right thing" leaps out at the reader of these telling lines. To understand Moakley's conduct during the busing crisis we must first look at the situation in Congress and the nation during the time when he took office.[4]

★　★　★

Moakley was sworn in surrounded by supportive family members—Evelyn, his brothers and their families, and some of the campaign aides who would soon become congressional staff members. He entered Congress in a happy mood but worried about the narrowness of his victory and the probability of a rematch with Louise Day Hicks, who in 1974 might be riding a wave of antibusing sentiment to victory. Roger Kineavy assumed the post of district director, assisted by James Woodard. He established a central office at Government Center in the JFK Building, and district offices in South Boston, Roxbury, West Roxbury, and Norwood. Patrick McCarthy, although still finishing Harvard Law School, became administrative assistant, or chief of staff, in Washington.[5]

Moakley's first task was to re-establish his relationship with the Democratic Party, whose candidate he had defeated. His mentor would be Tip O'Neill, who had endorsed Hicks and dispensed to Moakley the conventional wisdom that he couldn't beat her. In January 1973, O'Neill served as majority whip, rounding up votes for a leadership team of Speaker Carl Albert, a diminutive legislator from Bug Tussle, Oklahoma, and Majority Leader Hale Boggs of Louisiana. McCormack's resignation had triggered a complex struggle for the leadership positions, and O'Neill had bested his Washington roommate Eddie Boland of Springfield, among others, in the jockeying for the Whip post. Moakley began to step into the role in O'Neill's life that Boland had played—a fellow working-class Irish Catholic Democrat who could relate to all factions of the party—urban liberals, Southern conservatives, moderates.

The two men did not know each other well. O'Neill, fourteen years older, had been elected to Congress in the same 1952 election that had brought Moakley to the Massachusetts House. O'Neill quickly came to the attention of then–Majority Leader John McCormack, who elevated him to the Rules Committee early in his career. Moakley and O'Neill shared similarly pragmatic sensibilities. Both were "blue collar" liberals, concerned with getting jobs for their district, protecting seniors against inflation, raising the minimum wage, or keeping energy costs down. They were both comfortable having a beer at a veterans' hall. In this sense, they were different from such Massachusetts colleagues as Gerry Studds, Father Robert Drinan, or Michael Harrington of Beverly on the North Shore—"social" liberals who, for example, opposed the Vietnam War on principled grounds—they thought it was morally wrong, not merely unwinnable. Tip O'Neill probably saw in Joe Moakley a younger version of himself.

John A. Farrell recorded Moakley's recollection of their first meeting in Congress: "So Tip is running for majority leader and he's got all the freshmen together and he's growling, getting pledges and all that," said Moakley. "And he makes eye contact with me a couple of times and then moves on because he figures I'm going to kick him right in the balls. But finally we make contact and I put my hand out and say, 'I'm with you,' and his jaw drops.

"I said, 'Listen Tip, I know the game. The ins are in, and the outs are out, and I'm in now.' We became very fast friends."[6]

O'Neill arranged for Moakley's quick admission to the Democratic caucus, and his appointment to the Banking and Currency Committee. This was a position that he coveted because its regulation of mortgage lending affected the housing market, an issue that Moakley had worked on in the state Senate. A second appointment to the Post Office and Civil Service Committee gave Moakley some useful patronage appointments, but that committee was generally regarded as an undesirable post. Moakley had to learn the ropes at his new trade, and he applied himself diligently to the task of meeting his colleagues, learning the issues in Congress, and responding to the demands of his constituents.[7]

In 1973 the country was gradually accommodating itself to peace, and watching the unfolding drama of the Watergate scandal. The electorate in 1972 gave President Richard Nixon an overwhelming second-term victory, and saddled him with a liberal Congress that he loathed. Nixon withdrew from Vietnam totally. Two years later the South Vietnamese regime collapsed, and Beijing-oriented communists in neighboring Cambodia began a mass murder of its middle class. The American public was through with Southeast Asia and no longer cared what happened there.[8]

Also in January, the Supreme Court ruled in a case known as *Roe v. Wade* that states could not outlaw abortion. With the end of the war and the abortion decision, much of the energy of the 1960s dissipated; it is fair to say that "The Sixties" ended in January 1973, the month Moakley came to Washington. The national culture changed. "Acid rock" disappeared, hippies got jobs, disco dominated the airwaves, and men, Moakley among them, could grow long sideburns and wear colorful neckties without appearing to be "anti-Establishment."

Moakley's press secretary, Jack Dooling, churned out a stream of re-
leases on the "meat and potatoes" issues that his boss cared about. He
blasted President Nixon's impounding of Housing and Urban Development funds, criticized cuts in antipoverty programs, and worked to
preserve the Boston Navy Shipyard, which ultimately would close. As
the energy crisis became the big national issue, Moakley insisted that
corporations profiting from the oil depletion allowance be required to
invest in domestic energy production, blaming Nixon for staffing the
regulatory agencies with oil company bigwigs. These themes worked
their way into his maiden speech on the House floor in April. He took
a progressive line on foreign relations: an end to Vietnam War funding; support for Russian Jews and Lithuanian independence; opposition to Portugal, which was then conducting colonial wars in Africa;
and suspicion regarding the CIA-backed coup in Chile on September 11,
1973. Moakley made a fact-finding visit to Israel after the 1973 war. He
voted to defend veterans' benefits, unemployment insurance, and social
security.[9]

The Watergate affair marked the last echo of the 1960s. In his first
term, the vengeful Nixon had abused the power of his office to punish
his enemies. He sent agents provocateurs among liberal, black, and radical groups; the IRS to audit annoying journalists; and so on. In his inner
circle at the White House and the Committee to Re-elect the President,
he arranged for the pointless burglary of Democratic Party headquarters
on the night of June 17, 1972. The burglars were caught and threatened
to spill the beans regarding the instigators of the deed. By May 1973 the
Senate had established an investigating committee; in July a Nixon crony
testified that Nixon had tape-recorded his own Oval Office plotting, and
a struggle to bring the tapes to light led in October to the "Saturday Night
Massacre," in which Nixon fired special Watergate prosecutor Archibald
Cox and two widely respected administration officials resigned in protest. In a separate development, Vice President Spiro Agnew, a scourge
of liberals, resigned when it was revealed that he had accepted kickbacks
while serving as Maryland governor. Congressman Gerald Ford of Michigan replaced Agnew. In 1974 the transcripts of the secret tapes were
revealed, and the House Judiciary Committee voted articles of impeachment. Nixon resigned in August before the full House could vote to bring
charges against him.[10]

Moakley thus was a member of a freshman class of congressmen unique to American history. The 93rd Congress was the only one to orchestrate the resignation of a president. Democrats held large majorities in both houses: 239–192–1 in the House, 56–42–2 in the Senate.[11] Moakley followed O'Neill's lead as an early advocate of Nixon's impeachment. It was O'Neill who, behind the scenes, pushed House Judiciary chairman Peter Rodino to report the impeachment articles out of committee onto the House floor.[12]

Moakley was with O'Neill all the way, coming out early for impeachment. He voted against the nomination of Minority Leader Ford to the vice presidency, not because he didn't like Ford but because he thought Nixon should govern without a vice president, as Lyndon Johnson had done after President Kennedy had been assassinated. Ford was confirmed by a 387–35 vote, and only Moakley, Drinan, and Harrington voted "nay" in the Massachusetts delegation. Moakley instead proposed that a special election for president be conducted if the president was impeached without a sitting vice president. Moakley's Norwood office manager Paul Trayers told an impeachment rally in that suburban town in March 1974 that Moakley would vote for impeachment.[13]

While Watergate dominated the national news, a contest over the House leadership and control of the Democratic Party was also underway. The rising generation that had opposed the war was discontent with the Southern gerontocracy and its seniority system. Moakley followed O'Neill's middle position in the movement for House reform. O'Neill had earlier promoted one significant reform: teller voting, in which a tally board recorded all votes, eliminating anonymous voice votes. Both O'Neill and Moakley developed reputations as builders of consensus.[14]

The struggle for reform in the Congress and Democratic Party was a long process, beginning in 1948 with the election of President Harry Truman. The movement reached an apogee during Moakley's first and second terms. Liberal reformers, organized in a Democratic Study Group, challenged the seniority system that automatically placed the most senior members in committee chairmanships. The Democrats held a majority in both houses from 1933 until 1981 save two, and Southern Democrats became the most senior members. They therefore chaired crucial committees and were in a position to strangle civil rights legislation. Symbol of the sclerotic system was chairman of the House Rules Committee from

1955 to 1967, "Judge" Howard Smith of Virginia, whose committee routinely killed civil rights bills.[15]

As the Watergate scandal, the busing struggle, and reform process played out simultaneously, Moakley worried about a challenge from Louise Day Hicks in 1974. Rumors about her possible candidacy circulated in the press, and in mid-June she announced that her decision to run for Congress hinged on the upcoming ruling in the busing case. Should it be unfavorable, she would stay at her city council post and fight busing there. It was, and she did. Moakley ran unopposed in the primary and general election. That same year, Democrat Michael Dukakis defeated Governor Frank Sargent, and Tip O'Neill's son, Thomas, Jr., was elected lieutenant governor. The congressional delegation turned more liberal as Democrat Paul Tsongas defeated Republican Paul Cronin in the 5th District.[16]

A complex series of reforms led to the Democratic caucus and the Speaker gaining power in relation to the chairmen. One of the changes was that the Rules Committee added two members, to be appointed by the Speaker but confirmed by the Democratic caucus. Albert was still the Speaker, and he appointed Moakley and one other to Rules. The Black caucus wanted Andy Young of Atlanta to be one of the two, so O'Neill expanded the appointments to three, because Moakley would lose if it came to a vote within the caucus. O'Neill thus radically changed Moakley's role in the House, elevating him to a powerful committee ahead of his seniority.[17]

The Rules Committee is the "traffic cop" in Congress. Members serve on only that committee, so that they will not give priority to legislation emanating from their other committees. The Rules Committee schedules bills for floor votes and establishes rules for debate on each bill. It makes rules for amendment, limits time for debate, and determines each bill's relation to similar pending legislation. Ray J. Madden, a liberal from Indiana, had been chairman for one term when Moakley started his job. There was a lot to learn.[18]

While the Massachusetts Senate chamber had been designed to encourage dignified reflection, the majesty of the Rules Committee, and its intimacy, suggested the heavy responsibilities that its members bore. From the domed brown and beige rotunda hangs an ornate rococo chandelier, ringed by filigreed floral and stellar insets in the ceiling's ornamentation. Paintings of mountain meadows, or rooms looking out to the sea, announce the themes of "America the Beautiful"; portraits of previous chairmen remind the members of the large footsteps in which they are following. An anteroom facing the Library of Congress's Madison Building—adorned with fireplace, elegant mirror, and Frederic Remington sculpture of bucking horse and rider—further emphasize the weight of history that comes with the office. For the son of a saloon-keeper and factory worker, membership in the elite House Rules Committee marked the end of one long journey and the start of another.

★   ★   ★

One month after Nixon resigned, school opened in Boston and the city exploded in a storm of white rioting, with some retaliatory black violence. The violence scarred the city for a generation. When the buses rolled into South Boston on the first day of school, a hail of stones, racist epithets, hostile mobs, and a white boycott greeted the arriving pupils. The black students who braved these assaults generally conducted themselves with the same remarkable dignity as the students who had integrated Little Rock High School in 1957. Their parents never gathered to harass the small number of white students who arrived by bus in Roxbury.

Joe Moakley represented these African Americans too. If he disappointed Boston's antibusing hard-liners, he disappointed proponents of desegregation as well. Moakley was opposed to busing but in favor of obeying the law, much like Mayor White. To assess Moakley's conduct, we must consider what the picture looked like to black parents.

The antibusing narrative assigned primary responsibility for busing to the judge. To black activists, this was a self-serving untruth that denied their role as actors. Their struggle went back to 1950 and began in earnest in June 1963. The protagonist in that effort was Ruth Batson, a widely respected activist, built like a fireplug, and blessed with tenacity, insight, and a deep appreciation of the national civil rights movement. As early as 1950, Batson pushed the local NAACP to take up the school segregation issue and fight for genuine equality. She loved Martin Luther King, and tried throughout her career to appeal to the best impulses of white Americans.[19]

From 1963 on, Batson and her allies pressed this issue in campaigns for school committee and city council, by lobbying, and by passing the state Racial Imbalance Law. Other activists included Otto and Muriel Snowden, founders of Freedom House; Ellen Jackson, leader of a voluntary metropolitan busing program called METCO; Paul Parks, a World War II veteran; Elma Lewis, principal of an arts academy; and Ken Guscott and Tom Atkins, successive presidents of the NAACP. Five African American state representatives from Boston played important roles as well: Mel King, Royal Bolling senior and junior, Bill Owens, and Doris Bunte. They backed the Racial Imbalance Act, and decided to seek justice in the federal court after whites rejected the desegregated Lee School in September 1971.

The plaintiffs hired a nationally prominent civil rights attorney who sued on behalf of Tallulah Morgan, her children, and others, charging that her children had been denied the "protection of the laws by the Boston School Committee which intentionally segregated the schools by discriminatory pupil assignments, manipulation of attendance areas, feeder patterns, construction policies," among other methods. The case was known as *Morgan v. Hennigan*, the named defendant being the courageous chairman of the school committee who had voted in the minority to desegregate the Lee. The defendants conceded that segregation existed but denied that they had caused it. Garrity determined the plaintiffs to be right point by point, adding that only 5.4 percent of the teachers, 231 out of 4,243, were black in a system that was 32 percent black, and that 74 percent of those teachers were assigned to segregated schools. The pattern was unmistakable. The school committee had full access to an appeals process and never got anywhere. A report by the Boston Bar Association validated Garrity's finding, and no academic or legal scholar since 1974 has concluded that Garrity's finding was wrong.[20]

More controversial was the remedy Garrity chose. With little time to put it in place, he adapted a state plan that included busing black students into South Boston High School. An earlier state investigation, known as "the Jaffe hearings" for the Harvard professor who led them, had warned against such a move, noting the unusual hatred of black people that was prevalent in that neighborhood. On the first day of school, only South Boston exploded in violent resistance, but its lead would be followed by other neighborhoods in spasmodic eruptions.

The state Racial Imbalance Act of 1965 was a product of the national civil rights movement and the spirit of Martin Luther King. After 1965, however, the climate in Northern black communities rapidly turned to disillusionment. Black America exploded with rage after the assassination of King in April 1968, with the exception of Boston. Into the vacuum left by King's death came a new wave of nationalist leaders who scorned integration. Confronted by an implacable white hostility, black leaders in Boston, even integrationists, began to have their doubts about the wisdom of sending their children into mobs of howling racist adults. Ellen Jackson, confronted with this question on the eve of desegregation, admitted that there was no direct educational benefit to seating a black child next to a white child. By 1974, the times had changed from the hopeful days of 1965.

Sensing this ambivalence in the black community, white antibusing activists pressed their case with marches, rallies, and heated rhetoric. Their target was the Racial Imbalance Act. The activists argued that once this law was repealed, busing would stop. The lawyers among them—including Hicks, Bulger, and new school committee chairman John Kerrigan—knew better, but falsely created that impression to keep the cause alive. Garrity's ruling was based on the U.S. Constitution and would have been the same had the law never been passed. Other federal judges in states without such a law had made similar rulings.[21]

Almost every weekend saw a mobilization of some sort, sometimes in the tens of thousands. On the Monday before school opened, Senator Ted Kennedy went to his downtown Boston office, impulsively vowing to confront an antibusing rally on City Hall Plaza. The crowd spat at him, shouting racist epithets and crying that their daughters would be raped by the animals in Roxbury. They shattered the building's glass. None were arrested. Daily they gathered outside the high school, showering the buses with rocks and bottles.[22]

The violence escalated. In October, a ten-thousand strong rally ended in combat between the police and white youths, and the next night the police tore up a South Boston bar in which they had previously been ambushed. Three days later a Haitian immigrant made a wrong turn, found himself in South Boston, and was set upon by a screaming mob that pulled him from his vehicle and beat him severely with clubs until he was rescued by a heroic police officer. Two days after that the new president, Gerald Ford, encouraged the protestors by declaring his own opposition to busing. Mayor White, and senators Kennedy and Brooke, denounced the president for throwing accelerant on the fire. The mayor, a man with a volatile temper, became "apoplectic." An opponent of busing himself, he particularly resented having to enforce a federal judge's decision in the teeth of presidential opposition. Governor Sargent mobilized but did not deploy the National Guard.

Moakley responded to Ford's statement by writing to him privately. He opposed mobilizing the Guard, worrying that they might open fire on his neighbors. Ultimately, state troopers were dispatched to South Boston to protect the black students. The city was spinning out of control.[23]

Moakley's constituent mailbag overflowed with angry recrimination. "Where have you been?" demanded one letter signed by ten South Boston residents. "You have refused to respect the wishes of the citizens" in their "fight for freedom" against "communistic government." Another, from a woman who knew him personally, was addressed to "Dear Joe." She began, "In God's name—can't you do something about this insane forced busing of innocent kids to the crime jungle of Roxbury?" There were many other such frightened letters from whites, and none from blacks. They didn't know Moakley, and probably felt a congressman to be a distant figure.[24]

Behind the scenes, two sets of secret meetings attempted to bring the contending sides together. State representative Ray Flynn and a black former basketball teammate arranged a discussion among black and white leaders. Accounts of the meeting differed, but the black leaders wanted the whites to issue a statement deploring the violence. The white leaders would not do this unconditionally, and the meeting broke down in discord.

Meanwhile, state representative Mel King and Mattapan state senator Joe Timilty initiated secret meetings at the Parker House Hotel, attended by the mayor, who wanted a unity statement against violence. King was a tall man whose unsmiling demeanor and occasional wearing of a dashiki, caused many whites to view him as an angry black militant. He had a lot to be angry about as he watched the mobs attack black children. Yet King also had a sophisticated understanding of white working-class resentment against the upper class, and a unique appreciation for the nineteenth-century Irish nationalist John Boyle O'Reilly, the rare Irishman who saw the essential brotherhood of black and white against their oppressors. King was looking for that figure to emerge again among the

Boston Irish. This group held five meetings, but those meetings too blew up, when Palladino snarled at Ellen Jackson that the Haitian immigrant beaten in South Boston "deserved exactly what he got. He had no business being over there in the first place." She threatened more violence should busing come to her East Boston neighborhood in the next desegregation phase.[25]

Joe Moakley seemed to be "on the fence" to both groups. He was in the antibusing camp, but not an agitator, and a quiet opponent of rioting and school boycotts. On two occasions, in the fall of 1974, white protestors showed up across the street from his house. He told the first, a large crowd of several hundred, that he approved of their demonstration but wouldn't join it. A smaller crowd in November demanded that he support the school boycott. Moakley knew personally many of the demonstrators. He wouldn't do what they wanted, but he did not forcefully declare his opposition to the violence against black schoolchildren either. There was no Atticus Finch lecture to the lynch mob, as in the book and movie *To Kill a Mockingbird*.[26]

A month later a fight broke out inside South Boston High School, and a black student stabbed a white youth, Michael Faith, grievously wounding him. A menacing crowd of white adults gathered in front of the school, chanting racist epithets, looking for blood. Only a clever ruse involving decoy buses allowed the students to escape. There would be other instances of black violence, including the beating death of a white doctor in Roxbury. All the self-fulfilling prophecies of mayhem would come true in the following years.[27]

After this incident, the racists among the antibusers began a gradual ascendancy. This crowd included the leaders of the South Boston Information Center, Dan Yotts, and Jimmy Kelly, a childhood neighbor of Moakley's and former small-time gangster. They sneered at blacks and Moakley in their newsletter, and defended acts of antiblack violence with crude innuendo and threats. Their hundreds of members echoed American lynch mobs in their behavior, although they never killed anybody. School committee chairman John Kerrigan, a Hicks ally, moved in their circle. He called himself "Bigga," a reference to the size of his penis, and mocked a black news reporter by mimicking a monkey eating a banana. This was the chairman of the school committee.[28]

Moakley never burned his bridges to these people. When they attacked him, he defended his actions with reasoned dialogue. He never publicly denounced them, something that might have undercut their authority. He also might have played a role in the behind-the-scenes negotiations. Moakley did not become the John Boyle O'Reilly figure that Mel King was looking for.

Moakley worked out his busing stance in Saturday-morning meetings in his office. District director Roger Kineavy—a former longshoreman, long-time resident of South Boston, and someone fiercely protective of Moakley—wanted to keep his man in office. Moakley's brother Bob and former law partner Dan Healy agreed. They argued that Moakley had to stake out an antibusing position more like Bulger's but stay away from the issue, focusing on his traditional nuts and bolts themes. Washington administrative assistant Pat McCarthy and James Woodard proposed that the congressman put more distance between himself and ROAR. In this sense, Moakley walked a tightrope. West Roxbury staffer Jim O'Leary, years later, concluded that Moakley would have lost the 1976 election had he urged a peaceful integration of the schools. O'Leary was prob-ably right.[29]

Kineavy's African American assistant James Woodard contributed a thoughtful presence to these meetings. He occupied a unique role in the city's history and remained oddly obscure, as the leading black voice in the inner circle of the congressman from South Boston. "Woody," built like Moakley but shorter, hailed from rural Jefferson County, Florida, where he had been bused past a white school to a two-teacher elemen-tary school with six grades. He attended college at Florida Agricultural and Mechanical University in Tallahassee on a scholarship, participating there in the civil rights movement. Later he served in Vietnam, came to Tufts University on a Woodrow Wilson Fellowship to earn a Master of Arts in Law and Diplomacy, expanding his horizons as an exchange stu-dent in Nigeria. Just shy of his thirtieth birthday, he worked in George McGovern's 1972 campaign and backed Hubie Jones's campaign against Hicks in the Democratic primary. He had an impressive resume.

Woodard interviewed for a job as legislative director for the five Afri-can American state reps, but as an "outsider" in Boston's ingrown black community he didn't get it. The same group vetted him for Moakley's office, and Royal Bolling, Sr., and Ellen Jackson recommended him. Kineavy and McCarthy brought him on board on day one, and Woodard would be the only one of the initial group to work with Moakley throughout his congressional career. Woodard established a standard operating procedure for constituent services in the four regional offices: South Boston, staffed by Al Cataldo; Roxbury, by Carole Ray; West Roxbury by Jim O'Leary; and Norwood by Paul Trayer. He helped shape policy on veterans' affairs, immigration, and social security.

In assessing Moakley's role throughout this crisis, it is important to keep in mind that he broke new ground by hiring Woodard as a key advisor, establishing the Roxbury office, and hiring Deborah Spriggs, an African American, in his Washington office. Moakley attended meetings in Roxbury, did constituent service work personally in the Roxbury office, and kept in touch with Boston's African Americans in the state legislature.

Woodard was in a sensitive situation. He told Moakley that he was on the wrong side of the busing issue. He knew in his bones what segregation was like for a child. He had also worked as a substitute teacher in the schools, and for two days in 1970 he was assigned to South Boston High, where the students gave him the silent treatment and finally hurled bottles at him as he made his way home. He had seen Southern racist violence, and, years later, "Boston was deja vu all over again."[30]

Moakley had white constituents who shared Woodard's views. Michael Faith's mother was one of them. "Whether you agree or disagree with Judge Garrity's decision, you have to accept as a legal fact that there was segregation in Boston," she wrote in the *Boston Globe*. "Segregation is illegal and immoral. I'm against, it," she declared, adding that she too was against forced busing, but recognizing that it wouldn't have happened if the school committee had written its own desegregation plan. The South Boston Clergy Association wrote an "Open Letter" decrying the violence against the black pupils on the buses. There were similar voices in other parts of the city.[31]

Moakley balanced the input of his advisors. He heard Woodard and McCarthy, but he wanted to get re-elected. The likelihood is that a strong antibusing candidate would have emerged in 1976, perhaps Ray Flynn, Hicks, or Joe Timilty, if he had forcefully condemned the whole atmosphere in South Boston. By staking out a role as a quiet opponent of busing, he drew only a weak opponent, a blustering loudmouth called Bob "Peaches" Flynn (no relation to Ray), a favorite of the South Boston

Information Center who fared poorly but carried South Boston in the primary.[32]

These difficult choices kept Moakley awake at night. In 1974 he was still a first-term congressman, and by 1975 his elevation to the Rules Committee would have been challenging enough to master without the chaos of Boston during the 1974–75 school year. At one point he was so depressed that his old friend from the early days, John (Sleepy) Lynch (the uncle of Moakley's successor, Stephen Lynch) drove Moakley up to Gloucester, out of the district, where he wouldn't be recognized. "Joe was really down," Lynch recalled. "[His] neighbors wouldn't talk to him. He was almost having a breakdown." Sure enough, they walked into a restaurant where he was immediately recognized.[33] Washington probably felt like a respite.

There were other prices to pay. In March of 1975 ROAR staged a national March on Washington that targeted Moakley's office, among others. About twenty-five hundred Bostonians boarded buses for the capitol, and fourteen hundred braved a rainstorm to parade through the streets. Many state representatives, city councilors, and other officials participated, despite the inclement weather. The ROAR partisans were a tough breed. They wanted Congress to pass a congressional antibusing amendment. Ray Flynn and James Allen, a Dorchester minister, had drafted one, and other congressmen had their own versions.[34]

The problem for the antibusers was that the House Judiciary chairman, Peter Rodino of New Jersey, represented a majority black district, and a majority of the committee, which included senior black members, opposed the measure. The Massachusetts delegation was solidly opposed to a constitutional amendment. Only Moakley supported it. While few of the other congressmen favored busing, one of them was Tip O'Neill. O'Neill represented one of the most liberal districts in the country, and he echoed Ted Kennedy's opposition to a constitutional amendment. His district also included working-class Charlestown, however, whose "Powder Keg" chapter of ROAR was about to explode too. O'Neill told Ray Flynn's startled delegation that he would urge Rodino to move the resolution, and that he would vote for it if it came to the floor.[35]

By contrast, the ROAR delegates got a stiff rebuff from Senator Kennedy. When the Reverend Allen protested to Kennedy that "[y]ou can't force a cultural pattern by law," Kennedy shot back, "Did you go to a public restaurant when you were here? Did you see blacks eating there where you didn't ten years ago?"[36] O'Neill returned to his former position as soon as the ROAR delegates left. The strong liberals in the delegation, Drinan and Harrington, did not give the ROAR marchers the time of day. The bill stayed where it was in Judiciary, but the ROAR lobbyists returned home, encouraged by their meetings with Southern congressmen like Jesse Helms.[37]

The next act in the congressional drama regarding a constitutional amendment played out in the Senate Judiciary Committee, which held hearings on busing in late October and early November 1975. Moakley appeared on October 29. He emphasized the sharp decline of whites in the school population. In a city that was 81 percent white, the nonwhite school enrollment now had reached 56 percent. Over the past two years, white enrollment in the public schools had dropped by twenty-six thousand students. The number of racially imbalanced schools had increased since busing began, from 61 to 115 of the 165 schools. Whites were fleeing to the parochial schools and the suburbs. Busing had been a complete failure on its own terms, he concluded. Because no other remedies remained, a constitutional amendment to end busing was necessary to "save the Fourteenth Amendment's guarantee of 'Equal protection under the law' and reverse permanent resegregation." Moakley's motivation for the constitutional amendment thus differed sharply from ROAR's, which emphasized local control of the schools.[38]

Moakley was eloquently opposed two weeks later by Massachusetts senator Ed Brooke, a Republican, former state attorney general, and the first black person to serve in the U.S. Senate since Reconstruction. He was likely the most significant proponent of school busing for the purpose of integration in the country. Even Ted Kennedy always emphasized the goal of quality education, not integration. Many black leaders, disgusted by white violence and the increasing apathy among white liberals, were quietly giving up on the idea of integration. Not Brooke. Like Martin Luther King, he was an integrationist who believed that the United States should live up to the theme of the "I Have a Dream Speech."

Brooke asserted that "if busing has become a problem, it is not because of any inherent defect in the constitution. It is not because of any tyranny produced by the federal courts. It is because the political leaders of this country have failed to lead." He rejected the notion that the courts had somehow perverted the intent of the *Brown* decision, reprising Garrity's unchallenged legal conclusions. He even disputed a notion that Kennedy often implied, that busing did not lead to quality education. Brooke declared that this was true but irrelevant—busing was designed to achieve equal opportunity, a constitutionally guaranteed right. He dismissed the idea that judges used only the busing tool to achieve desegregation when better alternatives were available, again citing the many remedies ordered by Garrity and the judge in the Louisville case. A constitutional amendment was an inappropriate remedy that would preclude communities that wanted to use it from doing so. Twenty million children rode school buses to school daily, and millions more took public transit. What was the problem?[39]

Moakley and Brooke, both decent and honorable men, thus posited a similar goal of achieving desegregation but held different appraisals of the means to achieve it. On the issue of a constitutional amendment to end busing, Brooke clearly had the better argument. The very proposal of it admitted that Garrity had correctly interpreted the Constitution. The antibusers never proved in court that busing was unconstitutional. They would have to change the Constitution itself to achieve a policy goal. But the Constitution does not set policies. The Founders crafted a document setting forth modes of procedure, diffusing power among different branches of government and between the states and the newly empowered federal government. It had been amended over the years only to change procedures (the direct election of senators, for example) or to expand the body politic to include African Americans, women, and youth. On the rare occasion that a policy had been made fundamental—prohibition of alcohol sale—the country repealed it within fourteen years. Many people, including the antibusing Chicago sociologist Coleman, to whose statistics Moakley often referred, rejected a constitutional amendment.[40]

If Moakley was wrong on the procedural matter, his case was even weaker than it seemed on the substantive matter. Surely, he did have the facts right. Whites were fleeing to the suburbs. But was busing necessarily the cause? Coleman had his critics, among them Boston University professor Christine H. Rossell, whose database expanded Coleman's time frame. She concluded that "school desegregation has little or no effect on white flight," and presented a chart that showed a steadily declining white population in Boston, about 3 percent annually, beginning long before busing started. Whites would buy suburban homes anyway, even without busing, Rossell posited.[41]

The constitutional amendment made no headway in the Senate. The hearings were most likely a political stunt for Kentucky voters, facilitated by Mississippi segregationist and committee chair James O. Eastland. The Democratic governor of Kentucky was facing a strong Republican challenger, and he needed a national platform on which to play to anti-busing sentiment. Led by Ted Kennedy, the committee voted 8–7 against the amendment.[42]

The constitutional amendment was not dead in the House, however. Mazzoli of Kentucky had rounded up fifty members to force a vote in the Democratic caucus to discharge the Teague amendment from the Judiciary Committee. Moakley's name was the only Massachusetts signature. A discharge petition forces a bill out of committee over the heads of the members. It must ultimately be approved by a House majority. It is very difficult to achieve. Even members who approve of certain legislation will often refuse to sign a discharge petition because they don't want to offend the committee members who have studied and blocked a bill. On November 19, Speaker Carl Albert moved to thwart the discharge petition. The motion carried with only three Massachusetts Democrats against—Moakley, James Burke, and Torbert MacDonald, who joined the white Southerners. Boland, Drinan, Harrington, O'Neill, Studds, and Tsongas and every African American Democrat opposed the move to put a constitutional amendment against busing on the floor of the House. Moakley would be the only Massachusetts member with a 100 percent voting record against busing.[43]

★   ★   ★

Moakley probably felt conflicted about the constitutional amendment. His administrative assistant, Pat McCarthy, opposed it, and asked Moakley not to sign the discharge petition while he was working for him; McCarthy left in the summer of 1975, and Moakley signed only after McCarthy left. This timing suggests that Moakley might have been playing a bit of Kabuki theater; he must have known that the discharge petition wouldn't work.[44] The *Boston Globe*'s congressional correspondent, Stephen Wermiel, knew the score in the House and could see that constitutional amendments facilitated by discharge petitions were very long shots in any horse race. Even should they get through Congress, which wasn't going to happen, they faced lengthy confirmation battles in states that had large black populations. In an article titled "Moakley and the Public Relations Busing Game," he intimated that Moakley knew that the Constitution would not be amended to forbid school busing.[45]

That suspicion among the antibusing racists reached its peak in August, between the ROAR March on Washington and the failure of the constitutional amendment in the 94th Congress. An ultraleftist group had organized a "wade-in" at South Boston's Carson Beach. Blacks certainly had the right to swim anywhere, but under the circumstances this tactic was a foolish provocation that could only lead to violence. It did. During the affray, a motorcycle patrolman ran over a black protestor. Black leaders demanded the officer's dismissal at a stormy Roxbury meeting at which several accused Moakley of betrayal. Woodard, in attendance with Moakley, simmered at the abuse the congressman endured. State senator Bill Owens, a cooler head, hoped that Moakley would take the lead in promoting interracial dialogue to diminish the violence. He didn't.[46]

Dan Yotts of the South Boston Information Center condemned Moakley in his column for attending the meeting in the first place. He enumerated Moakley's other crimes, including his support for the beaten Haitian man the year before. Woodard had helped the man get adequate hospital care and find a new job. Where had Moakley been when Michael Faith was stabbed? Yotts demanded. Moakley wrote back, defending his actions step by step, and Yotts denounced him as an "enemy of your own people," in short, as a traitor.[47]

Violence, threats of violence, and provocative marches continued for years. Hicks, Bulger, and Flynn held demanding legislative posts that required their attention; they gave way to the racist leaders like Kerrigan, Kelly, Yotts, and Palladino. At the supposedly apolitical 1976 Saint Patrick's Day parade, antibusing forces dominated. The U.S. Army contingent at Fort Devens, which traditionally marched in the parade, refused to attend. The previous year, black soldiers had been the victims of epithets and hurled bottles; their commander wasn't going to subject them to that again.[48] The signature incident played out three weeks later. Hicks invited the ROAR crowd to an event at City Hall. Emerging from the building, a gang of hoodlums chanced upon a lone black man, attorney Theodore Landsmark, dressed for business in a three-piece suit. Joseph Rakes lowered the American flag he was carrying and charged, spearing his target as a photographer snapped an iconic photo that ran on front pages around the world. The black community erupted in protest, and finally, the city's political leaders called a massive peace march. Moakley wasn't there.[49]

★ ★ ★

What had happened? Busing failed to desegregate the schools, just as Moakley had predicted. In the next decade, the racist teachers departed, interracial violence declined, South Boston High became virtually all nonwhite. Crime did increase in the minority communities, for reasons that few had foreseen: deindustrialization, the mass marketing of drugs and guns, the defunding of support systems during the Reagan years. The antibusers moved to the suburbs and became Republicans.

There are useful historical frameworks for understanding the white riot in the Boston busing crisis. The fear of outsiders and a dangerous "other" runs deep in human life. European history is full of it. Catholics and Protestants murdered each other in the century following the emergence of Martin Luther, culminating in a Thirty Years' War that devastated Western Europe. In France in 1789, as the revolution began, a Great Fear broke out in the countryside, and peasants, fearing "brigands," murdered their fellow homeless peasants as they scoured the countryside searching for food. And Irish-American Bostonians should have seen that they were playing the role of Protestant Orangemen, with African Americans cast as Catholics during the desegregation struggle.

We have our own, American version of this profound fear of the other, foreigners, the unknown new people. Here it is rooted in the experience of slavery, and the hundred years of oppression of black people that followed it, with its Jim Crow system and century of lynching. Racial violence peaked in the North with the Great Migration to Northern cities after World War I, and the "Red Summer" of violence in 1919. This American "Great Fear" lasted into the 1970s, and the Boston white rioters represented its last gasp. Moakley's position on the barbed wire fence resembled that of moderate white Southerners, whose dilemma the historian C. Vann Woodward, using an analogy borrowed from South Africa, likened to that of "the man on the cliff." Trapped in the middle by fear, he could move neither up nor down.[50] Yet the origins of Boston's 1970 riots run even deeper than that.

There had been hysterical fear of witches in colonial American villages throughout the seventeenth century. Usually the village minister calmed the fears of people who cried that a hostile neighbor was possessed. Much of the witchcraft anxiety was sparked by the status anxiety brought about by the commercial revolution: those engaged in commerce were getting rich while the inland farmers fell behind. These tensions expressed themselves in Salem Town and Salem Village in 1692–93. In that case, however, their minister, feeling the same anxieties, inflamed, rather than calmed, their fears, resulting in nineteen executions. The first person accused of witchcraft was Tituba, the West Indian slave woman.

We all know today that there were no witches. What might have happened if the ministers of South Boston Village had calmed the fears of the villagers? What if those people who knew that there really was little to fear, that busing children a mile or two to the next neighborhood was not really a big deal, and that there actually were social benefits to be gained, had acted? What if the spirit of John Boyle O'Reilly, the nineteenth-century Irish immigrant activist who identified with black aspirations, had reappeared? This failure to lead, as Senator Brooke pointed out, was Boston's tragedy. We study history not to assign blame, but to connect our own experience with that of the past, and, we can hope, to learn lessons.

And what do we make of Joe Moakley during this period? It was not his finest hour, and he knew it. He did not act falsely, but he did not act bravely. In this, he was not alone, and he should not be judged harshly. But when he remembered, at the end of his life, "the people who wanted to do the right thing, and they were almost thrown out of their homes," he was recalling the people who should have been his real constituency. His emotional distress, what his friend Lynch identified as a "nervous breakdown," suggests a deeply conflicted man whose head and heart were not at peace with each other.

Joe Moakley would grow from this experience. For the rest of his life, he would reach out to those people "who wanted to do the right thing," and find his true voice.

7

The Last Days of the Working Class

In the winter of 1976, the antibusing movement split into two camps that mirrored tensions in the conservative wing of the Democratic Party. Louise Day Hicks and her ally Jimmy Kelly supported Henry Jackson, the hawkish "Senator from Boeing," in the upcoming March 2 Democratic primary. Jackson had put forward a measure in the U.S. Senate to compensate Boston for its expenses in the busing battle. Hicks's rival on the city council, Pixie Palladino, and her friends John Kerrigan and Albert "Dapper" O'Neill, backed the openly racist George Wallace, whose verbal attacks on black criminals substituted for his erstwhile defense of segregation. On the Saturday before the voting, both sides paraded together, in a "Men's March," behind a phalanx of American and Confederate flags, urging resistance to busing and a big vote in the primary. William Bulger gave a militant speech and was followed by Kelly, whose denunciation of black society as "a culture with a serious drug problem . . . full of handbag snatchers," was greeted with chants of "Niggers!"[1]

Joe Moakley stayed away from this march, as he did all the others. This one showed how the antibusing movement now had racism, not opposition to a law, as its central theme. The Confederate flag, carried by working-class Bostonians, said it all. Joe Moakley's neighbors were about to vote for George Wallace, who had campaigned before enthusiastic crowds in South Boston in February. Wallace, crippled by an assassin's bullet in the 1972 campaign, tapped into the racism and feeling of powerlessness of the Boston working class. Roosevelt's New Deal was over for them, and they regarded Johnson's Great Society as a giveaway to people they called "Niggers!"[2]

Jackson won the Massachusetts primary, but Wallace ran a strong third. He carried the 9th Congressional District, beating Jackson by more than 4,000 votes there, his best district in the state. Moakley had an anti-busing challenger in that race too, Robert "Peaches" Flynn. Moakley beat him badly, 39,291 to 19,125, but 11,696 blank Democratic ballots were cast, indicating "none of the above," for a total of 30,000 anti-Moakley votes, and Flynn carried South Boston. Even in Tip O'Neill's district Wallace ran well, with more than 12,000 votes, many coming from working-class Charlestown. But in Tip's district one of the liberal candidates, Arizona's Mo Udall, won with double the number of votes he got in Moakley's district. Tip backed his House colleague Udall vigorously; Moakley, as was his custom, lay low in a primary in which he had no stake.[3]

The 1976 primary field included several liberal candidates: Udall, Indiana's Birch Bayh, and Oklahoma populist Fred Harris. With the liberal and conservative vote split, the unheralded former Georgia governor Jimmy Carter, who presented himself as a fiscal conservative and social liberal, a man who had condemned racial discrimination and associated himself with Martin Luther King, won the nomination. On the Republican side, sitting President Gerald Ford faced a challenge from the conservative former California governor and movie actor Ronald Reagan. Reagan ceded Massachusetts to Ford and lost two to one.

In the general election, South Boston voted Republican for the first time, the culmination of a growing storm labeled "reactionary populism" by historian Ron Formisano. Both South Boston wards returned slim Republican majorities while the city and state went overwhelmingly for Carter.[4] Politics was taking a new shape. The white working class was becoming more conservative, expressing discontent as black people began to win a shot at equal education, a job as a bus driver, or a unit in a housing project not in the ghetto. White workers experienced black gains as white losses, and they turned to an almost all-white party that played to their prejudices, rather than join with blacks to defend their eroding standard of living.

In Washington, Tip O'Neill became Speaker of the House upon Carl Albert's retirement. Massachusetts returned ten Democratic congressmen, while Brooke and Kennedy served in the Senate. Moakley's clout on the Rules Committee increased as a result of his alliance with Tip and good working relationships with the next chairmen, Richard Bolling of Missouri and Claude Pepper of Florida. Moakley became chair of the

Democratic Personnel Committee in the new session, which gave him increased patronage power. The reform of the House that had bolstered the Speaker's power led to an expanded leadership team, or Whip organization, and O'Neill co-opted Moakley into it.[5] Over the next six years, Moakley would use his augmented authority to bring the bacon home to his district, embark on his first foray into international relations, and launch a long fight against the tobacco lobby.

At home, the steam went out of the busing issue. Hicks lost her seat on the city council in 1977. Ray Flynn changed his tune and began to focus on issues of economic justice and neighborhood empowerment. John O'Bryant, a black man, and white candidates who accepted busing as a fact, won election to the school committee. The city was moving on.[6] A better period began for Joe Moakley, even as his working-class base became more conservative.

★　★　★

Carter came into Washington promising a new kind of Democratic politics that was foreign to Moakley's instinctive progressivism. Carter had been a centrist governor, and his program prioritized balancing the budget and restraining inflation. Moakley addressed the issue of balanced budgets from time to time in his newsletters, but never with much alarm. A true son of the New Deal, he believed that budgets balanced themselves when people had work, and that if the "free market" produced unemployment, it was the government's job to create demand by putting people to work building the national infrastructure. Moakley spent the Carter administration fighting for jobs and consumer protection, and delivering first-class constituent services.

Speaker Tip O'Neill worked well with Carter in the president's first year, but the relationship was a difficult one for both men. They butted heads over budget and economic stimulus matters, and both could make reasonable cases for their respective positions: O'Neill pushed a water projects bill that looked like a wasteful pork project to Carter. The president likened it to the tax breaks that congressmen gave to local industries in tax bills. These issues, could, and initially were, compromised between the two men, but after a few years the relationship broke down. O'Neill, and Moakley as a lieutenant of the Speaker's, both felt put off by Carter's surrounding himself exclusively with old Georgia hands like Hamilton

Jordan, Jody Powell, and Bert Lance. Moreover, Carter's "born again" Christianity, which he wore on his sleeve, rankled them. Moakley was religious too, but he never discussed his private beliefs in public. O'Neill allowed a series of minor slights regarding personnel issues to get under his skin. In his final interview, Moakley remembered that he "got along with Carter OK," but recalled only the problems.[7]

Carter made a good case on energy policy. He was properly concerned about rapidly rising energy costs that drove inflation and restricted economic growth. A nation that had known cheap gasoline prices throughout the Automobile Age of the twentieth century got its first shock in 1973 when the Oil and Petroleum Exporting Countries (OPEC) combined to raise prices on oil, causing the nation's first gas shortage and spiking prices, which soared from 35 cents to an unbelievable dollar a gallon. Fights broke out at gas stations as long lines formed. The crisis went away as prices stabilized and supply evened out. Carter wanted to move proactively to increase domestic production, transition to renewable alternative sources, and encourage conservation so that the previous upward price cycle would not repeat.[8]

O'Neill worked with Carter to get an omnibus bill through the House that addressed these concerns. Carter, for his part, made several speeches to the nation on energy policy, calling for sacrifice and compromise. Both Carter and O'Neill faced the problem that Democratic majorities in both houses were divided between representatives from energy-producing states such as Louisiana, Texas, and Oklahoma, and the energy-consuming states of the Northeast and Midwest. O'Neill established several committees to direct the legislation, and pushed the Rules Committee to get the president's bill through the House. For many Northern representatives, the bitter pill in the Carter plan was the decontrol of natural gas prices. Carter believed that a free-market approach would encourage small producers to discover new resources if prices could initially rise. Then, with a larger domestic supply, Carter expected that prices would eventually come down. O'Neill didn't like that idea, and when the bill died on a first vote, O'Neill took it out and it passed—a triumph for Carter, O'Neill, and the Democratic Party.[9]

Moakley supported much of this program and showed remarkable foresight on energy policy in general. He was an unusual politician—a working-class guy from South Boston who had also been the only politician to get invited to Harvard's first Earth Day as a state senator in 1970. Congressman Moakley promoted solar power, introducing bills that would provide tax credits to jump-start research and small business solar panel installation. He agreed with Carter's emphasis on conservation. Moakley wanted tax credits for people who insulated their houses, too, and he pushed bills to see that new federal buildings were well insulated and used alternative energy, if possible.

Moakley suspected that the nuclear industry's safety promises were bogus. In a nuanced August 1977 energy statement he accepted further construction of light-water reactors but warned that "more advanced forms of nuclear power may entail significant risks."[10] The following year he introduced a "Radioactive Waste Management Act" that would allow states to prohibit federal agencies from locating disposal sites on their land, and testified in the bill's behalf at a Department of Energy hearing in Boston.[11] Moakley favored clean coal rather than nuclear power. His worries about the industry came nightmarishly true in 1979, when the nation experienced its first major nuclear catastrophe at the Three Mile Island plant in Pennsylvania that effectively ended any new nuclear power development. He expressed similar safety concerns regarding the transport of liquefied natural gas by truck through densely populated urban areas. He urged that LNG be stored in remote areas and be tightly regulated by one central agency.[12]

Moakley opposed any effort to decontrol energy prices. His core constituency consisted of working-class people, the poor, and elderly living on fixed incomes. They were having a hard time paying for the rising costs of home heating oil. Boston had been hit by a record blizzard in the winter of 1978, and home heating costs shot up by 10 percent and then doubled the following year. Homeowners had to buy more fuel to keep warm, busting their family budgets. As the next winter began, Moakley insisted that the Department of Energy open the books of producers, refiners, and shippers so that the cost structures could become transparent to voters. Later Moakley criticized rising oil company profit margins while consumer prices rose. He motivated his support for a windfall profits tax that had passed the House. He successfully sponsored legislation that increased congressional oversight of refined oil exports when he learned that DOE had granted export licenses for shipments to, of all places, Iran. Finally, Moakley fought consistently for emergency energy assistance to the poor and elderly. He helped pass a $200 million measure at the end of 1977 that would aid twenty-six thousand Massachusetts families.[13]

In all of these matters, Moakley maintained a fiercely skeptical attitude toward Big Oil and utility companies, and championed the interests of the most vulnerable. This was the working-class politician Moakley wanted to be.

★ ★ ★

Somewhat by chance, Joe Moakley's first venture into foreign affairs came in an area in which he had limited experience, the Middle East, although he had traveled there after the Yom Kippur War of 1973. When the Arab nations were badly defeated after preparing to strike at Israel, Egypt's president Anwar Sadat began to rethink his position. Egypt was the dominant country in the Arab world, with three times the population of any other Arab nation, and the leading cultural and intellectual nation. Yet it had no oil and was menaced by neighbors Israel, Libya, Syria, and Iraq; it had an uneasy relationship with the Soviet Union. In March 1977, President Carter announced at a town meeting in Clinton, Massachusetts, that he endorsed the idea of a Palestinian homeland. The next month Sadat came to Washington for exploratory talks with the new president.[14]

Over the next several months, a multisided negotiation developed among the many parties to the Middle East conflict. Sadat hoped that a resolution of the various disputes might include a Palestinian state on the West Bank, and a return of Arab lands lost during the 1967 and 1973 wars. Israel, led first by Yitzhak Rabin, and then his successor, the conservative Menachim Begin, hoped for recognition of Israel by an Arab state. Carter and his secretary of state, Cyrus Vance, boldly began to play the role of negotiators. Begin came to Washington, Carter and Vance traveled to Middle Eastern capitals, and the world began to hope for peace.

The U.S. Congress got into the act. O'Neill put together a fifteen-member leadership delegation of ten Democrats and five Republicans, headed by Majority Leader Jim Wright of Texas, to better inform the members directly. Moakley accepted the invitation to join the delegation. Moakley generally disdained junketing, during which congressmen typically attended a state dinner, met with a few ministers, and played golf on the taxpayer's dime. This was different—a potentially major turning point in history.

The delegation arrived in Cairo on November 15 and was briefed by the U.S. ambassador before meeting with Sadat. One of the most difficult issues in dispute was how to represent the Palestinians in negotiation. The Palestine Liberation Organization, headed by Yassir Arafat, did not recognize Israel's existence, and demanded that all territory lost by Palestinians in the 1948 war be returned. Israel would not negotiate with the PLO and insisted that they be barred from any peace talks. When the congressmen met with Sadat, he declared for the first time that he might accept a formula in which individual Palestinians joined an Arab delegation, a major concession. That very day Begin sent Sadat an invitation to address the Knesset. Moakley asked Sadat about the risks of such a trip, for him—both personal and political. "It's the holy thing to do," Sadat replied.

The next day the congressmen flew on to Israel. There they met with Defense Minister Moshe Dayan and other Israeli officials. While Moakley's delegation was meeting with Begin, he announced that Sadat had accepted his invitation. The congressmen rose and applauded. They decided to stay for Sadat's speech, changing rooms at the famed King David Hotel to accommodate the arriving Egyptians.

Moakley was accompanied by Evelyn on this trip. They took in the Old City, ringed by its ancient walls, but for security reasons the group visited Bethlehem without their wives, in case of a terrorist attack. A news photo showed Moakley and Begin posed with an elegant Evelyn, dressed in white, beaming between them. The next day Evelyn and Joe went to the Old City to take communion at the Church of Gesthemane. The priest, aptly named Father Godley, said, "How's my old friend Tip?" Moakley could not avoid his friend and benefactor's shadow.[15]

Sadat's speech opened the possibility of a broad Middle East settlement. It ended the threat of another major war between the great Middle Eastern powers. Moakley told the *Globe* reporter that the speech was "exciting and hopeful, but the issues remain very tough, and Jimmy the Greek couldn't predict the odds on this one."[16] The Camp David Accords of 1978 marked a high point of the Carter presidency and of hope for an enduring peace, a hope that has not been realized.

In the following years, Moakley began to speak out in behalf of Soviet

Jews who were imprisoned for seeking to immigrate to Israel, the "re-fuseniks." While he had protested their treatment as early as 1976, after visiting Israel the matter became more important to him; he issued appeals in behalf of Vladimir Slepak and Ida Nudel, and others in behalf of non-Jewish dissidents, to Soviet officials. He called for linkage of Soviet trade policy to treatment of Soviet Jews, echoing Carter's human rights theme in foreign policy.[17]

Moakley's question to Sadat had proved unfortunately prescient. Sadat was murdered in 1981 by opponents of his peace effort. Moakley was saddened, perhaps not surprised. Moakley grew from this experience. Foreign travel broadens, raises new questions, and changes one's perception of oneself in the world. The fifty-year-old Moakley's trip to Egypt and Israel laid the groundwork for the person he would become in later life.

★   ★   ★

The elusive quest for peace in the Middle East was not just about human rights. American politicians also hoped to achieve a settlement because they wanted a predictable supply of Middle East oil. They never got this, and the price of heating oil and gas would fluctuate unpredictably into the future. Moakley cared about this issue as an economic matter too. Back home, he used his clout on the Rules Committee to pry loose a flood of money for infrastructure development in his district, especially mass transit. He wanted to ease traffic congestion, reduce demand for gasoline, and provide a cheap and efficient way for people to get to work. Moakley won appropriations for the Massachusetts Bay Transit Authority, the commuter rail, and the nascent Amtrak passenger railroad system throughout his career.

After World War II, the United States had let its mass transportation system rot. During the Eisenhower administration, vast sums were allocated to build the first interstate highway system, but at the expense of mass transit. In Massachusetts, authorities governing the commuter railroad system allowed entire lines to close down. Transportation planners built an elevated highway right through the center of downtown Boston, separating the North End from the rest of the city. Plans were developed to do the same in a Southwest Corridor that would slice through minority neighborhoods. South Station, once one of the busiest railroad stations in the country, sank into oppressive decrepitude, becoming a dark, cockroach-infested den. Moakley opposed the Southwest corridor project in the state legislature, favoring mass transit. This stance encouraged the young Jim O'Leary, a mass transit enthusiast, to work for Moakley's early campaigns and serve as his West Roxbury community staffer in the early 1970s before embarking on a career in transit management.[18]

The energy crisis encouraged a re-examination of this broader transportation policy. During the 1970s, Amtrak was created out of the wreckage of the decaying private passenger rail system. Moakley fought to revitalize the Northeast Corridor and its stations. In July 1976 he was floor manager for a bill that appropriated $1.5 million for the renovation of South Station, a small part of a $1.75 billion package in the Railroad Revitalization Act that he promoted along with Republican Silvio Conte of Pittsfield. When the Ford administration dragged its feet on release of the funds, Moakley protested. Two years later, Moakley served as transportation task force cochairman of the New England Congressional caucus, whose twenty-five members all agreed on the necessity for a functioning Northeast Corridor. "We need the trains, but people are not going to ride them unless they are fast and dependable," Moakley reminded Carter's transportation secretary, Brock Adams, when the president's proposed 1979 budget flat-lined rail appropriations. His goal was to get travel time between Boston and New York down to three hours and forty minutes. This target would require electrification of the track throughout the corridor, which took decades to accomplish. Moakley, along with O'Neill, used his clout to redevelop South Station into a modern and inviting transportation hub.[19]

Moakley also promoted the Massachusetts Bay Transit Authority. He delivered hundreds of millions of dollars to knock down the ungainly elevated Orange Line structure that ran along the Washington Street corridor, clacking noisily, casting dark shadows, and depressing property values. An open submerged track transformed that busy section of the black community into a hospitable place to live. He promoted the Silver Line of electrified buses to run along Washington Street, and its extension through South Boston to the airport. Moakley helped find the money for an extension of the Red Line from Harvard Square to Arlington, adding three new stations. The commuter rail system was extended from Framingham to Worcester, and the Old Colony line on the South Shore reopened after Moakley died, but as a beneficiary of his work. Moakley was not a lone visionary on these improvements, but an essential player, as Boston's congressman, in securing the federal funds that put thousands to work building and staffing these additions to the city's life.[20]

Moakley found the money for many other significant infrastructure projects. South Boston's Seaport section languished as a decayed urban wasteland until the 1990s. Moakley worked with colleagues in city, state, and federal government to create a Boston Marine Industrial Park designated as a "foreign trade zone," to facilitate the importation of unfinished goods. This step allowed the GAO to purchase an abutting 167-acre tract from the state for industrial redevelopment, a project that would add eleven hundred new jobs. Next, at Moakley's urging, the House Armed Services Committee appropriated $14.3 million to renovate the Fargo Building. These improvements facilitated the transformation of the port into a modern container facility and center for regional trucking. The following year he secured a $2 million grant to begin reconstruction of the city's fish pier, giving another boost to a troubled industry and adding new construction jobs.[21]

Moakley also had a special interest in historical preservation. He was no history buff himself, but he recognized the potential for tourism and recreation that were unique to Boston as incubator of the Revolution and locus of a magnificent archipelago of unused islands. He testified before the House Subcommittee on National Parks and Insular Affairs that the Dorchester Heights site should be added to the National Historic Park System. This was the South Boston hill from which George Washington and Henry Knox drove the British from the city. Along with Ted Kennedy in the Senate, he introduced a bill that made the Harbor Islands a National Recreation Area, continuing a process that would ultimately change them from dumping grounds into a park system accessible by ferry. He won Interior Department funds to preserve the Historic First Church in Roxbury. He found money to speed up development of the emerging Black History Trail and worked with South End representative Byron Rushing to make Martin Luther King's residence a National Historic Site.[22]

Moakley also encouraged using government power in behalf of struggling industrial sectors and helping manufacturers to secure government contracts. He proudly touted every military contract awarded to the GTE Sylvania plant in Needham as if he had personally secured it. Whenever he could do something to help the district's industry, he did. One such area was in Massachusetts's sagging shoe industry, which was losing ground to foreign competition. The state lost seventeen thousand shoe manufacturing jobs in the decade beginning in 1967, with ninety plant closings. Moakley urged old-fashioned protectionism to keep foreign products out—a stance he would continue fifteen years later when he opposed President Bill Clinton's North America Free Trade Act (NAFTA). Moakley had no grand theory on free trade, but when businessmen who employed people in his district sought his support, he gave it regardless of the consequences for some other sector.[23]

During the late 1970s and early 1980s, Moakley's staff went through the usual shake-ups as people worked in his office for a while and then advanced their careers. In Washington, administrative assistant Pat McCarthy left to work in Tip O'Neill's district. Nelson Hammel succeeded him. John Weinfurter became his press aide, as Joe Dooling moved into a job on the Rules Committee and became administrative assistant when Hammel left. Weinfurter, from a Milwaukee suburb and Jesuit-educated, would hold that position for the longest time of any Moakley Washington aide, from the late 1970s until 1996. His commitment to Moakley lent the Washington office a remarkable stability.[24]

Roger Kineavy played the same role in the district. The son of Irish immigrants, he followed his father into a job as a longshoreman. He had worked for Moakley since his 1964 campaign for state Senate, and, like his chief, he was from South Boston and a Navy veteran, though about seven years younger. He was a gruff character with a good heart, a perfect fit for his job. Kineavy was the guy whose staff got on the phone to the gas company to see if they really couldn't stretch out the widowed Mrs. Doyle's back payments before shutting off the gas. In his first two terms, Moakley placed four offices in the district, in addition to the downtown office, in Roxbury, South Boston, Norwood, and West Roxbury. By 1977 this arrangement proved to be too expensive, and they substituted a traveling van in which the congressman spent a full morning or afternoon holding court as constituents lined up with their troubles and staffers took notes. Every staff member remembered that this was the part of the job that Moakley loved best. In this regard, Moakley descended from pre–New Deal ward bosses like Martin Lomasney who delivered those services directly. After the New Deal and Great Society programs were established, politicians helped their constituents instead to negotiate the new bureaucracies that helped constituents obtain the benefits for which they paid taxes.[25]

He hired people right off the street into his own operation, and recommended thousands of others for the capitol police force, at Amtrak or the MBTA, the utility companies, or at state and municipal agencies. Robert Kevin Ryan, born and raised in South Boston, walked in off the street one day when Moakley was at a Post Office "meet and greet." He was wearing a hockey shirt and a bathing suit. Moakley got him a job in the House Post Office, and a year later he was a legislative assistant on the House Rules Committee, where his job was to boil legislation down to clear paragraphs. This was a young man without a college degree, but Moakley could sense his potential. Was this the best or most fair way to hire people into important positions? Probably not, but in many cases it worked. Ryan earned a master's degree at Johns Hopkins while serving as Moakley's chief of staff in the late 1990s.[26]

Moakley sometimes did constituent service work from his car parked at Castle Island. People came to expect him to be there on a weekend morning. As Ryan noted, Moakley was unusually approachable, answering to "Joe" his whole life, not "Mr. Congressman." An unavoidable consequence of this relaxed operating style was that the normal patterns of Moakley's life brought him into more contact with his South Boston neighbors than people in the black community or the suburbs. Suburbanites needed government jobs less than did urban dwellers. African Americans, through no fault of Moakley's, rarely expected that a congressman would ever do much for them, and the constituent service logs show few black people walking in. Black community leaders rarely referred job applicants to him.[27]

By the late 1970s and early 1980s, with the busing issue quieted down, there were still very few African American workers holding good jobs at the MBTA, on the railroad, the utilities, or in the skilled construction trades. Moakley had placed a lot of people in those jobs, and they were grateful to him. The natural pattern of doing good constituent service work thus tended to reinforce existing hiring practices, and probably explains why some working-class constituents stayed loyal to him but also voted for George Wallace or Ronald Reagan.[28] Critics of congressional patronage point out, with some reason, that legislators should be relieved of their perceived responsibility to help individuals find jobs. Moakley had no theories about this issue. He just helped people who asked him for help, and he never consciously played favorites based on race.

This was a better time for Moakley in his personal life. He had a summer house in Scituate, "the Irish Riviera," right on the water, acquired during the 1960s. He had a boat, the *Evelyn M*, but he rarely took it out past the harbor. He played a little golf, not too well. His brothers would visit with their growing families, and the nieces and nephews became substitute children for Joe and Evelyn. Photos from this period show Joe at the Scituate place, grilling. Unfortunately, Moakley lost the Scituate house in a hurricane that destroyed much waterfront property.

He had an apartment in the Washington area, too. Evelyn decorated everything in modernist white. She had a flair for interior design and lent an air of elegance to this son of a two-fisted saloon keeper, even a cutesy poodle named "Twiggy," named for the fashion model. One photo from the Washington place shows the distinguished congressman entertaining dinner guests by gaily pretending to urinate into a potted plant. Moakley kept a gym in the basement of the South Boston house, but he never worked out in it; his girth expanded with age. Moakley listened to music indiscriminately, sang by himself a lot, and Evelyn took him to Sinatra and Tony Bennett concerts.[29]

★ ★ ★

On Memorial Day 1979 a family of seven—a mother, father, and five children—perished in a Westwood house fire. The blaze broke out early in the morning in their second-floor apartment while the family slept. Both parents were smokers, and one of them had fallen asleep with a lit cigarette that ignited a bed or sofa. There were no smoke detectors in the house; smoke detectors were required in newly constructed homes, but not in existing buildings. Somebody in Westwood came to Moakley and said something about it, perhaps along the lines of, "There oughta be a law."[30]

What law? Wasn't this just a human tragedy caused by human negligence, the sort of daily happenstance that always occurred and always would, the kind you really couldn't do anything about? Moakley had some Washington staffers—Albie Jarvis, Carleton Currens, and later Ellen Harrington—look into it. Maybe you could manufacture a cigarette that went out when you stopped puffing. Moakley wasn't against smoking. He knew people weren't going to stop, even though 300,000 died every year from smoking. Moakley wasn't a moral reformer out to change people's behavior, but the issue he couldn't get away from in this case was the fate of the children. They had not been smokers. Didn't society owe them something?

Moakley was not new to issues surrounding house fires. From his first campaigns in the 1950s, he had run for office with the backing of firemen's unions. Lots of firemen lived in South Boston. In the late 1970s, Boston, and other cities like it, had seen an outbreak of arson. When property values declined, as they did in the 1970s, arson was an easy way to turn a losing venture into a gainer. On many Boston streets in poor neighborhoods, the fire trucks came clanging down the block every night.[31]

Moakley worked with the Symphony Tenants Association, based in the South End near Symphony Hall, and state and city officials, to do something about it. In March of 1978 they secured a grant from the U.S. Department of Commerce to train police and fire departments to deal with the problem. Skilled police work had already uncovered one arson-for-profit ring that included fire department officials, insurance adjustors, and lawyers, but there were others. Moakley, along with Ohio senator John Glenn, introduced a bill that would cause the Department of Justice to coordinate arson programs nationally, keep statistics, and bring the problem under control. By the mid-1980s, a rising economy, improved police work and fire prevention, and community organizing efforts had significantly reduced the problem of arson fires.[32]

Perhaps the same could be done with cigarette fires. Moakley's staffers found that there were nineteen patents for a fire-safe cigarette that would self-extinguish in five minutes, long before the ignition time of twenty to forty-five minutes required for a burning cigarette to set a couch ablaze. Some patents would coat the cigarette paper with a fire retardant. Others changed the tobacco density and eliminated chemical additives.

By mid-October, Moakley called a rare press conference to announce the introduction of HR 5504, the Cigarette Safety Act, which would require manufacturers to market only cigarettes that would extinguish in five minutes, without raising tar and nicotine content. Moakley had with him Boston's fire commissioner; a representative of the Fire Protection

Association; and a fellow from the Shriners Burns Institute, a fraternal association that aided fire victims. Some victims of house fires were horribly disfigured and also faced enormous medical costs, ultimately borne by the entire community through higher insurance premiums. In 1978 there had been seventy thousand smoking-related fires causing eighteen hundred deaths, four thousand injuries, and $180 million in property damages. Moakley believed that he had a simple solution. He blamed the tobacco companies for making the law necessary.[33]

There was more to his argument. The logical regulatory agency for tobacco products was the Consumer Product Safety Commission, established by a 1973 act and signed into law by President Richard Nixon. The tobacco lobby, however, had their products removed from the purview of the commission on the incredible grounds that tobacco wasn't a "consumer product." Later attempts by progressive lawmakers to reverse this were defeated by the powerful lobby, which funneled money to congressional candidates and had most congressmen from tobacco-producing states in their pocket.[34]

The Tobacco Institute, the trade association for producers, had some arguments of its own, as Moakley discovered when he appeared on the television program "Buyline," along with industry representative Anne Browder. She insisted that "there is no such thing as a fire safe cigarette." They could be produced, she acknowledged, but no one would buy them. Two such brands were on the market, she said, but their poor taste limited sales to 1 percent of market share. Finally, she pointed out, the chemicals in furniture were the real problem. Why not change them?

Moakley wouldn't settle for that. "I think the cigarette companies owe it to the people to take care of the product that they put on the market . . . And when you walk through the Shriners Burns Hospital and see children five and six years old with burns . . . Why should they be in the hospital as a result of somebody who does smoke carelessly discarding a cigarette?" This was Moakley at his core. He had walked through the hospital, and he had seen what the tobacco lobbyists wanted to cover up. This fight was classic, early twentieth-century progressivism, the kind embodied by Upton Sinclair's novel *The Jungle*, which had inspired the Pure Food and Drug Act.

Browder pushed back in Boston's tabloid daily. Moakley's proposal was trying to dictate to private commerce that it must take the risk out of life. People cut themselves with knives in their kitchens, so should all knives be turned into butter knives? Smokers who irresponsibly caused fires should not be allowed to penalize the millions of others who didn't. Smokers didn't want their cigarettes to self-extinguish, that's why they didn't buy the ones that did. Once government began to regulate one aspect of smoking, where would it stop? Could it ban them altogether?[35]

These were not specious arguments. The tobacco lobby thought that manufacturers had a right to produce a product without Big Government telling them what to do. Moakley himself had made a similar argument when he tried to change the Constitution of the United States to forbid school busing. Ronald Reagan won the presidency in 1980 by making exactly that kind of argument: "Get Big Government off our back," they said, and let people make their own choices.

After Reagan took office, Moakley rewrote his bill, introducing a new version of it into the next few congresses. HR 1854 would have the Consumer Product Safety Commission study the feasibility of producing a fire-safe cigarette and mandate a performance standard within two years. That, Moakley hoped, would end the bickering between the patent holders and the tobacco companies. Senator Alan Cranston of California introduced a similar bill into the Senate. Moakley felt he was on stronger ground, asking for less.[36]

The tobacco industry had a lot to lose. According to a Tobacco Institute report, U.S. consumption in 1979 was 620 billion cigarettes and about 6 billion cigars. Americans spent $19 billion on tobacco products. The United States was the world's second largest producer, after China, whose population was four times bigger. Tobacco was the country's sixth largest cash crop, grown by 226,000 farms in twenty-two states by half a million farm families, providing 2 million jobs in agriculture, manufacturing, transport, and retail.[37] They were not about to allow some obscure congressman to tell them what to do.

Two months after Reagan was sworn in, his budget team reduced funding for the Consumer Product Safety Commission by 30 percent, as the National Association of Manufacturers cheered and consumer groups booed.[38] The following year Common Cause, a consumer and citizens' advocacy group, glumly observed that "the bill's prospects began to sour early on as the Reagan Administration declared war on the CPSC, threatening to disband the agency entirely."[39] By 1983 a new commissioner (there were five altogether) appointed by the president wrote to John Dingell of Michigan, to whose subcommittee Moakley's bill had been referred: "I am not anxious to encourage enactment of this legislation . . ."[40] The Reagan administration, as it had promised, was starving the beast of Big Government.

The issue came to a head in March 1983 when Moakley and representatives of the Tobacco Institute made dueling presentations before the House Subcommittee on Health and the Environment. Moakley had nothing new to add in his testimony. But the tobacco lobby had, surprisingly, rethought its position and decided that its longer-term interests lay in trying to be part of the solution. They began to pick away at Moakley's support among firefighters' unions by contributing to fire-prevention initiatives. Even with the Reagan administration on their side, they decided that it was better to change their image. They still opposed this bill, but indicated that they took the issue of house fires seriously. They dropped the "free market" solution, agreeing to bankroll fire prevention education and the installation of smoke detectors, but they would not change the cigarettes.[41]

A major cause of the tobacco lobby's reconsideration had to do with similar regulatory action developing in the states. Every manufacturer faces the complex problem of what to do if different states propose different safety standards for their product. House fires caused by cigarettes continued, obviously, throughout the early 1980s, and state legislators began to receive visits from victims, just as they did from the victims of drunk drivers. These bills initially failed, but the tobacco lobbyists concluded that the wiser course for them was to accept weaker national legislation.[42]

Shortly after the 1983 hearings, the lobbyists came to Moakley looking for a compromise. Over the next sixteen months, Moakley's staff and the tobacco lobbyists hammered one out. Moakley introduced an amended version of the bill, as did Cranston and his moderate Republican ally, John Heinz of Pennsylvania. The new bill gave the tobacco lobby a voice at the table, something that was denied them if the CPSC were the final arbiter. A new Interagency Committee was established, with representatives of relevant government agencies, the furniture and cigarette manufacturers, and firefighter groups. They would oversee a Technical Study Group to answer the questions Moakley's earlier bill had addressed. Moakley,

Cranston and Heinz announced the breakthrough in a crowded hearing room on May 3, 1984, and the bill passed later that year.[43]

This did not end the matter. The law mandated only new studies. It was a compromise, and with Reagan running the agencies, the Tobacco Institute correctly felt that it could keep throwing sand in the gears. By 1987 the Technical Study Group found that a fire-safe cigarette was feasible. Two Virginia congressmen introduced a bogus bill, claiming to implement the findings; Moakley introduced a rival bill. But with Republican appointees now dominating the board, the CPSC declined to act. In 1994, Republicans recaptured Congress and blocked further action. After Moakley died in 2001, his colleagues Edward Markey and Republican Peter King of New York introduced a "John Joseph Moakley Memorial Fire-Safe Cigarette Act of 2002" that died in a Republican House.[44]

Although this story sounds like a long, losing, quixotic effort fought against a tobacco lobby juggernaut, it wasn't. In 2004, New York state passed a fire-safe cigarette law. Over the next seven years, all the other states did too. Cigarette-started fires killed forty-nine people in New York in 1997. By 2007, three years after New York's law went into effect, that figure had fallen by almost 50 percent to twenty-seven.[45]

Joe Moakley didn't live to see the results of his twenty-year struggle. His long campaign suggests several lessons. One is that the nation needs strong governmental institutions, in the executive and legislative branches, to stand up to corporate power. The public needs some protection against corporations that market life-threatening products that people buy to satisfy short-term needs. Where that line lies is often in a grey area, but without strong governmental institutions, public safety and health will be endangered. Legislatures, especially, need some institutional memory embodied in representatives committed to public service who stay in office a long time. Sometimes that leads to sclerosis, but sometimes to dogged, persistent struggle that bears fruit over decades.

A second lesson is that labor and professional organizations, especially those concerned with public safety, can and should play vital roles in crafting legislation. Moakley made a consistent effort, from his first news conference, to keep the firefighters' unions by his side, despite the Tobacco Institute's efforts to buy their loyalty. In this case he was successful, but the wider atmosphere in the country ran against labor in the 1980s.

* * *

During the Carter administration, Senator Ted Kennedy watched with dismay the president's failure to encourage the liberal wing of his party. Kennedy gave Carter scant credit for his triumphs—on energy policy, the historic Camp David Accords, an ethics reform in Congress, pardoning Vietnam-era draft resisters, and other matters. Kennedy thought it was time to fight for one big issue—a national health-care system, and Carter wouldn't do it. On November 7, 1979, he announced that he would challenge the sitting president of his own party for the nomination.

This proved to be a colossal miscalculation. While popular within the liberal wing of his own party, the Southern conservatives and centrists strongly disapproved of him. Carter felt that Kennedy was morally tainted by the 1969 Chappaquiddick incident, in which a female staff aide drowned when a probably inebriated Kennedy drove their car off a bridge and later misrepresented his own behavior. His campaign got off to a terrible start. Kennedy in a television interview inarticulately stumbled over his reasons for running. That same day, Iranian fundamentalists took hostages at the American embassy, and the country rallied around its president.

Kennedy's challenge put O'Neill and Moakley in a tight spot. As Speaker of the House, it had been O'Neill's job to carry his president and party leader's program into the people's chamber. As a majority whip, it was Moakley's job to follow O'Neill's lead. Yet Kennedy, as standard bearer for their own political point of view, also had a claim on their loyalty. Carter deftly solved this problem by asking O'Neill, as they sat together at the seventh game of the 1979 World Series, to chair the convention, a role that demanded neutrality. O'Neill accepted. The decision flowed from his own mixed feelings about both men, feelings that Moakley likely shared as well. Moakley spent much of his political career in the shadow of these two giants, Tip O'Neill and Ted Kennedy.[46]

Kennedy's challenge distracted Carter. Meanwhile, Ronald Reagan battled it out with rivals George H. W. Bush, a fellow conservative but not as far right as Reagan, and John Anderson, an Illinois moderate, for the Republican nomination. Reagan finished a very close third to his rivals in the March 4, 1980, Massachusetts primary, garnering 115,334 of the 406,633 Republican votes cast. Kennedy trounced Carter and California governor Edmund "Jerry" Brown in his home state. Moakley ran unopposed in the primary and Kennedy won in the 9th Congressional District too.

As the Iran hostage crisis wore on, Carter's popularity sank. In December 1979 the Russians invaded Afghanistan. There was little Carter could do about either problem. Behind the scenes, Reagan sabotaged Carter's hostage negotiations, promising the Iranians military support in their war with Iraq if he won the election. These international events diminished the Carter presidency.[47]

In the general election, Reagan swamped Carter. The new president came in promising to restore American imperial power, and, in effect, to destroy the Great Society and New Deal. He captured forty-four states, including Massachusetts, by 1,057,631 votes to Carter's 1,053,802, with Anderson, running as an independent, logging 382,539. Two minor leftist candidates won a combined 5,791 votes, larger than Reagan's margin, so Carter would have won the state if they hadn't run, and it is impossible to guess from which party Anderson's votes had come.[48]

The remarkable figure is Reagan's vote total, almost ten times the number he'd won in the primary. Reagan carried both South Boston wards. A white working class that had begun the 1976 election carrying Confederate flags and voting for George Wallace ended up voting Republican in a general election. Moakley could not have foreseen it, but Reagan's escalation of the Cold War would change his life and send it in a direction he never could have imagined.

8

★ ★ ★ ★ ★

Into Foreign Lands

Ronald Reagan's 1980 landslide swept away more Democrats than the unfortunate Jimmy Carter. The Democrats had held majorities in both chambers since the 83rd Congress during the Eisenhower administration. Just as devastating as the loss of the White House was the loss of the Senate, an epic defeat for the Democrats. The 97th Congress elected in 1980 returned a slim Republican majority, 53–46–1, to the Senate for the first time in almost three decades. George McGovern, Birch Bayh, and Frank Church, national figures all, lost their seats, as former segregationists Strom Thurmond and Jesse Helms became powerful chairmen, with Helms at Foreign Relations. Democrats maintained a 243–192 majority in the House but lost 33 members. Moreover, 40 House Democrats formed a "Democratic Conservative Forum," known as the "boll weevils" for the insect that devoured cotton plants in the Southern districts most of them inhabited. Democratic congressmen began 1981 nervously, worried that their votes against the popular president might hurt them in 1982.[1]

As if to punctuate the ending of an era, John McCormack died a few weeks after the election. Joe Moakley had last seen his predecessor on a stormy March day earlier in the year when they both addressed a ceremony transferring the Dorchester Heights Revolutionary War site to the National Park Service. The *South Boston Tribune* reported that McCormack spoke in a "sharp, clear voice" to a large crowd that braved the chilly temperatures in a steady rain. In November Moakley joined Tip O'Neill at his funeral.[2]

Reagan started swinging for the fences on Day One and at first hit everything out of the park. His budget director, David Stockman, launched a frontal assault on the New Deal. During the election campaign, Reagan had presented himself as ambivalent regarding Roosevelt's legacy. He had been a Democrat early in his career, serving as president of the Screen Actors Guild, voting for Roosevelt and Truman, claiming that he had never left the party but that the party had left him. In 1964 he nominated conservative Barry Goldwater at the Republican convention and came into office bearing his imprimatur. In the first six months, Reagan passed budget bills sponsored by Phil Gramm (D-TX) and Delbert Latta (R-OH) that rolled back Great Society programs, and then he signed the Kemp-Roth tax cuts into law. Reagan promised that this "supply side" policy would promote growth by minimizing taxes and government regulation of the private sector, thereby achieving budget surpluses. Vice President George H. W. Bush had lambasted this notion as "voodoo economics" during the primaries, but now even moderate Democrats voted for voodoo. When President Reagan was shot outside a Washington convention hall late in March, his brave, jocular response as he went into surgery made him even more popular.

With Carter out of office and the Democrats a minority in the Senate, Tip O'Neill was now the national leader of his party. As Tip's lieutenant, Moakley found that his stature within the party rose as well. The Democrats were divided into numerous factions ideologically. O'Neill could not command party loyalty and lost vote after vote. Some boll weevils, such as Phil Gramm, bolted the party and joined the GOP, part of a larger realignment in which white Southerners abandoned the Democrats in droves. "He was getting the shit kicked out of him," Moakley remembered of his good friend.[3]

Reagan began to over-reach after his return to health a month later. When budget director Stockman denounced Social Security as a Ponzi scheme, O'Neill struck back, drawing a line in the sand that rallied his caucus and even many wavering Republicans. Social Security forever after became the "third rail" of politics—touch it and you die. Reagan temporarily recovered when he fired thirteen thousand striking air traffic controllers in August. This move initially earned public support but finally awakened the sleeping giant of the U.S. labor movement. The AFL-CIO called a mass march on Washington for the first and only time in its history, in September, in opposition to the Reagan budget, union busting, and the threatened attacks on Social Security. Hundreds of thousands of workers marched behind their union banners in a show of old-fashioned solidarity. The political tide turned against Reagan as growth slowed down and by 1982, the economy was in recession and the budget in deficit.[4]

This was the context in which Joe Moakley faced his first serious opponent since Louise Day Hicks, this time a Republican with a fighting chance. In the national redistricting process, Massachusetts had lost one seat as U.S. population shifted south and west. The state combined the districts of a Republican, Marjorie Heckler of Wellesley, with that of the newest Democrat, Barney Frank, who had replaced Father Robert Drinan in the 1980 election when the Church had ruled that priests could not hold political office. In the process, Republican towns were added to the 9th District. Moakley announced that he was "pleased" that the plan would "enable me to represent the majority of people now in my district" and that he looked forward to representing citizens of the new towns.[5]

The new district dropped some of Moakley's Boston wards and the Republican town of Dover, and added a string of suburban towns extending south of the city but inland from the more Republican-leaning South Shore and Cape Cod district held by Gerry Studds. The new 9th added Lakeville, Easton, Halifax, Dighton, Middleborough, Raynham, Stoughton, Taunton, and Bridgewater. On the map, the new district looked like a squat two-legged beast with Boston at the head, and it was promptly dubbed "the dragon district" by headline writers. Moakley's remaining twelve Boston wards still constituted 45 percent of the district (formerly Boston had made up 60 percent) and registered Democrats outnumbered their rivals 51 to 13 percent, with the rest registered as independent. Commenting on the map, Moakley observed, "I've bought new Nikes."

In the changed political climate brought on by the Reagan Revolution, Republicans thought that they might pull off an upset. They felt that it was still "Morning in America," and their leaders convinced an unheralded state representative from Dedham, Deborah Cochran, to run for the seat. Despite the Democratic majority in the new district, the Republicans knew that many of them had voted for Reagan along with the independents. Their poll found that 44 percent of the district's voters self-identified as "conservative" and only 29 percent as "liberal."

Moakley knew this too, and he was careful to present himself appropriately. "I'm neither liberal nor conservative," he declared. "On the whole I'm a moderate." The *Boston Globe* duly noted that he had opposed busing and abortion, and that he was increasingly outspoken on the threat of budget deficits brought about by "Reaganomics." On the liberal side he was a vigorous proponent of government jobs bills, public housing, defense cuts, including elimination of the B-1 bomber and the MX missile, and a supporter of the popular nuclear "freeze" that would halt production of new nuclear weapons.[6]

Cochran's problem was that she had to cater to the same public, which was temporarily turning against Reagan in the normal pattern of biennial correction by which the president's party usually loses congressional seats. Moreover, she was inexperienced and poorly versed on national issues. She had a hard time distinguishing herself from Moakley, agreeing with him on social security, student loans, and the nuclear freeze. Busing was no longer an issue. Cochran emphasized that she was a fiscal conservative. That wasn't enough to dent Moakley's popularity, and Cochran went very negative on Moakley, charging him with cutting the phone lines to her office, for example, again with little effect.[7]

Cochran's low road in the campaign signaled a new turn in national politics that would make this tone the new normal. The Massachusetts Republican Party had been more liberal than the Democrats on social issues, and more upright on matters of probity, during the 1960s and 1970s. It had produced models of rectitude such as Henry Cabot Lodge, Leverett Saltonstall, Eliot Richardson, John Sears, Frank Sargent, and Ed Brooke. But during the 1960s and 1970s, national Republican figures like Goldwater, Nixon, and Reagan pursued the white Southern vote, and got it. Segregationists like Strom Thurmond and Jesse Helms, and scores of lesser figures, joined the Republicans. Increasingly shrill younger politicians, like Newt Gingrich, who had never been Democrats, broke the Solid South as it gradually turned Republican. The Northern moderate Republicans occupied narrow ground within their own party.

Moakley ran against Reagan, not Cochran. His newspaper ad asked, "What have you got against Reaganomics?" and answered, "You've Got Congressman Joe Moakley." His campaign picture showed a distinguished-looking man whose visage conveyed the calm, mature look of a statesman, now graying at the temples. He was running in a new district and worked hard to get acquainted with it: on one day his machine put fifteen hundred volunteers on the street. He touted his record of bringing home the bacon and putting people to work, listing all the projects he had successfully sponsored. He outspent his opponent. Moakley visited every town, wading through cranberry bogs while joking about his urban upbringing.[8]

Moakley won by a 64 to 34 percent landslide. He never again faced a serious challenger. Joe and Evelyn celebrated with a large crowd at Dorchester's Freeport Hall. He won 78 percent of the Boston vote, and most of the new towns, scoring especially well in Taunton, the only other city in the district. "My opponent accused me of being a clone of Tip O'Neill, while she was more in line with Reaganomics," Moakley said. "Then when she saw Reaganomics going down the drain, she tried to get further and further away from it." In the other state elections, Mike Dukakis and running-mate John Kerry were elected governor and lieutenant-governor, Ted Kennedy was re-elected, and Barney Frank bested Heckler in the one close congressional race. That left one lone Republican in the delegation, Silvio Conte, who was as liberal as any Democrat. After the wipeout two years earlier, Massachusetts Democrats finally had something to celebrate.[9]

★ ★ ★

During this campaign, three of Moakley's new constituents, the Charles Fiske family of Bridgewater, were fighting a battle of far greater consequence. Daughter Jamie, born in November 1981, showed a jaundiced skin color a few months after her birth, a sign of biliary atresia. Jamie's liver bile ducts were blocked, and unless she got a liver transplant she was going to die. Only two hospitals in the United States performed liver transplants in 1982, one in Pittsburgh and one in Minneapolis. Nor was there an organized manner in which to obtain a liver. The United States did not have an organ donor system in place. The possibility therefore of obtaining an appropriate organ for Jamie Fiske was very small.

Charley Fiske, a financial officer at Boston University, and his wife did whatever they could, hoping against hope. They reached out to physicians' associations, politicians, and the media. Moakley, not yet Fiske's congressman, assigned a staffer to work and strategize with Fiske. Jamie's struggle for survival was a dramatic story, and the American Academy of Pediatricians agreed to let Charlie Fiske speak to them. He did, eloquently, and sang "Please Don't Take My Sunshine Away" at the end. The speech showed on television; there were only three networks in those days, and millions of Americans saw it. Among them was a family in Alpine, Utah, whose eleven-month-old child died in a car crash a few days later, just as Joe Moakley became Charley Fiske's congressman. When the call came in about the available organ donation, Charley immediately booked a flight for Minneapolis. Moakley called at 8:30 that night, offering too late to arrange a free flight. But Jamie had the surgery and survived.

A few months later, in April 1983, Moakley introduced the Fiskes to congressional subcommittee hearings chaired by little-known Congressman Al Gore of Tennessee. They testified about their experience and urged the creation of a national organ donor network. An appropriate bill passed the House. Senators Ted Kennedy and Orrin Hatch, representing the recipient and donor state, cooperated across party lines to establish the network. The Reagan administration was opposed on ideological lines, arguing that this was inappropriate for government and should be done in the private sector, but Reagan's quirky surgeon general, C. Everett Koop, pushed back, and Reagan signed the National Transplant Act of 1984.[10] Moakley couldn't know it at the time, but his efforts on behalf of the Fiskes would one day save his own life as well.

★ ★ ★

Five weeks after his election, Moakley's office got an unusual letter from a group of ten Jamaica Plain residents concerned about the growing problems in Central America and requesting a meeting for early January. The signers included representatives of the Jamaica Plain Committee on Central America (JPCOCA) and representatives of leftist Catholic and Hispanic groups. The meeting was scheduled for January 28. That day changed the course of his life.

Jamaica Plain was an odd place in the 9th Congressional District. "JP" as Bostonians know it, was an old Irish and German neighborhood in the southwest of the city, graced by Jamaica Pond, whose ring path invites joggers and strollers; and the Arboretum, a hilly refuge for naturalists and lovers. In the 1970s, when the antiwar protestors from the baby boom generation graduated from Boston-area colleges, many gravitated to the neighborhood. By the 1980s these people were in their thirties, well into careers in human services or teaching, and starting young families. Their equivalents in Tip O'Neill's district were far more numerous and had pushed O'Neill into anti–Vietnam War positions. Moakley had to go to Cambridge in those days to find them. Now he had one community of these young committed activists in the district, and Moakley paid attention to every constituent.

Five activists showed up in his office: Carol Pryor, Chicago-born, a thoughtful, determined woman with an advanced degree in history from UC Berkeley; Virginia Zanger, a former anti–Vietnam War activist with a doctorate in education—both from JPCOCA; Ed Crotty, a lively, articulate Yale graduate in Latin American studies who had served in the Peace Corps in Brazil, representing the liberal Citizens for Participation in Political Action (CPPAX); Felix Arroyo, a leader of the Puerto Rican community, soon to be the first Hispanic elected to the city council; and Miguel Satut, a Cuban immigrant and the executive director of Oficina Hispana. While the group was properly attired and carefully prepped for lobbying, Crotty sported a bushy mustache, and Arroyo and Satut wore beards. Only Crotty was born in the Boston area. Moakley's predecessors, McCormack and Hicks, would have regarded these people as weird. By their places of birth, education, and personal history, they were outsiders, and Jamaica Plain itself was becoming a foreign land to the Irish-American residents who began departing for the suburbs as these people moved in.

They had a big stack of petitions signed at tables staffed in Jamaica Plain, urging upon their congressman a peace agenda: no military aid to El Salvador; no military aid to Honduras and Guatemala; strict congressional oversight of any funds allotted to Central America; support for regional peace initiatives; and granting of Extended Voluntary Departure (EVD) status for Salvadoran refugees. The petitions had been drawn up by a larger lobbying group, Crotty's CPPAX, and the Jamaica Plain activists had no special interest in any particular demand. Carol Pryor recalls that she and Zanger did not expect much. Moakley seemed to them to be what he said he was, a "meat and potatoes" Southie politician more comfortable with the Veterans of Foreign Wars group that was scheduled for a visit after their hour was up. Central America was not meat and potatoes; it had never been raised in the 1982 campaign. It was the kind of issue that came up in other districts, in which people had college degrees and traveled abroad, like Newton or Cambridge.

Moakley ticked off the list point by point and told them he was with them on each one. He said he wasn't really up on the subject, but that he trusted Gerry Studds, among the most outspoken congressional opponents of Reagan's policy, and followed his lead. Then he came to the last issue, about refugees. He didn't know what that Extended Voluntary Departure legal status was. Neither did they. To Pryor's surprise, Moakley picked up the phone and called his young aide Jim McGovern in Washington and asked him to call Studds's people. Sometime during the meeting, Satut spoke movingly about how lucky he was to have immigrated to the United States and how Hispanics contributed to American society. After a few minutes the phone rang. Moakley listened, and then told his visitors that McGovern said that nobody was doing anything on the EVD status. Moakley said he would take it up himself. Zanger knew that politicians loved to have their pictures taken with constituents, so she posed with a grinning Moakley receiving the petitions from the group. It ran in the *Jamaican Plain Citizen* with an accompanying article in the next edition.

The activists confessed their mutual astonishment to each other as they descended in the elevator. Moakley had just volunteered to defend the Salvadoran immigrants. They had not expected this. That issue hadn't even been their priority. Moakley had picked it off their list himself. They had expected a noncommittal assertion of general agreement with their goals, and then it would be back to business as usual for Congressman John Joseph Moakley.[11]

It wasn't. Something had started to click for Moakley. He didn't like bullies. The big kid beating up the little kid; his father asking him what was the right thing to do. His Old World Italian-speaking grandmother Scappini taking her three American grandsons downtown to the movies, not getting a word of it, a stranger in a strange land. Joe Moakley would look into it.

Gradually the issue of El Salvador would come to dominate Moakley's concerns. Yet he never quite acknowledged this meeting. Asked how his interest in El Salvador began, he sometimes would say that he had been approached by nuns at a post office meeting. Or he transformed Satut and Arroyo into Salvadoran immigrants. It would not quite do for Moakley to admit that a decidedly secular and radical activist group had initiated his interest on the issue, so forever after he repeated the story of the nuns at the post office, or a meeting with Salvadoran immigrants. "Never get too far ahead of your constituents," he would later counsel his aide Jim McGovern, when he first ran for office.

New staffer and press aide Jim McGovern, then twenty-three, a recent American University graduate, became Moakley's early guide into the Central American thicket. McGovern came from the working-class Greendale section of Worcester, where his father ran a liquor store. When Robert Kennedy was killed, his father gathered the family around the table to light a candle and say a prayer. McGovern was Irish (with some Lithuanian and Polish in the bloodline as well), Catholic and Democrat by birth, just as Moakley was. As a junior high school student he was inspired by the 1972 presidential campaign of his unrelated namesake, George McGovern, and became a youthful political junkie. At American University McGovern wrote a thesis titled "American Intellectuals Dissent from U.S. Foreign Policy on Cuba, 1958–1963"; he earned a master's degree in public administration; traveled to Cuba; and interned for Senator McGovern. McGovern joined the Ways and Means staff when the senator lost his seat in the 1980 election. He came on board with Moakley in early 1982 for $13,500 a year, just as El Salvador issues escalated. Earnest, bespectacled, prematurely balding, soft-featured, and slender of build, McGovern had an unassuming manner but felt strongly grounded, like Moakley himself, in his community and political views.[12]

Joe Moakley might have felt that he was looking at the son he never had. Both their fathers had been in the liquor business, an Irish occupation traditionally linked to politics. Thirty years before, Moakley had started out on the same path at the same age. The Jamaica Plain lobbyists didn't realize it, but they had just started both men on a journey that would last to the end of Moakley's days, and on which McGovern would continue after Moakley died.

*　*　*

El Salvador is a small, mountainous country fronting the Pacific, bordered by Guatemala and Honduras to the north and east; it is the only Central American nation with no Caribbean coast. Comparable to Massachusetts in size and population, El Salvador grows coffee, not bananas. Therefore, unlike Honduras and Guatemala, it was never penetrated by foreign capital like the United Fruit Company, nor was it a victim of U.S. intervention because it might be the location for a canal, like Nicaragua or Panama. These circumstances ensured that El Salvador had an autonomous ruling class, known as *Los Catorce*, the fourteen families who owned most of the coffee land, financial services sector, industry and shipping. Its peasantry had revolted once, in 1932, and the military slaughtered thirty thousand of them in a month. For the next forty years, the poor remembered this lesson. They remained desperately poor, inhabiting one-room plywood shacks with leaky tin roofs and earthen floors, with no running water or electricity. Illiteracy and infant mortality were high; life expectancy was short.

By 1972, a political revival was underway. Jose Napoleon Duarte's centrist Christian Democratic Party won the election and shared power uneasily with the military caste that really ran the country. El Salvador's military academy taught its cadets, drawn from the coffee elite, that their first loyalty was to the military, not civilian authority, and instilled in them a special loyalty to their graduating class, or *tanda*. Not every student learned this lesson, and divisions opened in the military. On October 15, 1979, leftist officers ousted their rivals and established a junta with civilians.

This government proved to be short-lived. The right wing quickly struck back. It had a fascist component whose death squads, led by an ousted major called Roberto D'Aubuisson, began assassinating military and civilian rivals. D'Aubuisson appeared on television to denounce "communists," whose bullet-ridden bodies would show up on the street the next day. On February 23, 1980, a Christian Democratic leader was murdered in his home in front of his family after a D'Aubuisson screed.

Prominent among his victims were Catholic parish priests, who had begun to speak out for their parishioners, demanding justice for them in this world. Oscar Romero had not been among these liberation theology priests in his early career, but as archbishop he took up their cause and defended them, calling upon soldiers to disobey orders to kill civilians. On March 24, gunmen who had drawn straws for the honor at a meeting called by D'Aubuisson, shot the archbishop as he celebrated Mass. At the funeral, troops opened fire on a lengthy procession and killed thirty mourners. By the end of 1980, death squads had killed eight thousand; the right regained full control of the government, with President Duarte acting as a fig leaf of civilian rule; and a rural insurrection commenced. Christian Democrats, many facing certain death if they stayed in the capital, San Salvador, bolted their party and joined a center-left coalition known as the Revolutionary Democratic Front, or FDR, its Spanish abbreviation. Five leftist groups merged to form a guerrilla wing, the FMLN, named for the 1932 peasant leader Farabundo Marti.

American ambassador Robert White vigorously denounced these atrocities, following Jimmy Carter's human rights policy, but the administration suspended military aid only temporarily. The Democrats were always afraid that the guerrillas would win, and they didn't want to be blamed by the Republicans for "losing" a country to "communism." During the 1980 election campaign, Reagan attacked Carter for surrendering the Panama Canal and making possible the overthrow of Nicaraguan dictator Anastasio Somoza in July 1979 by the leftist FSLN, or "Sandinistas." Carter therefore restored military aid to El Salvador and cut it off to Nicaragua, despite his personal qualms.

The death squads and their wealthy patrons celebrated Reagan's victory in San Salvador's plush neighborhoods. Now there would be no more talk of "human rights" from the Americans. Reagan's aides warmly welcomed the rightists, while President Duarte got a cold shoulder. On November 27 the maimed corpses of six unarmed civilian leaders of the FDR turned up on the streets. Reagan advisor, soon to be ambassador to the United Nations, Jeanne Kirkpatrick smugly declared that those who lived by the sword would die by the sword. On the day of their funeral, December 2, four American Catholic churchwomen were abducted, raped, and murdered. Kirkpatrick declared that they "weren't just nuns" but actually leftist activists, and Alexander Haig, soon to be secretary of state, surmised that gunfire might have come from their van. One month later, two American labor advisors, from the anticommunist American Institute for Free Labor Development, were gunned down along with a Salvadoran counterpart for the crime of discussing land reform.

Immediately upon taking office, Secretary of State Haig fired almost everyone in the Latin America Bureau and installed people with no experience in Latin America but plenty of experience in Vietnam. The Reagan administration embarked upon an overt plan to defeat the "communist" rebels in El Salvador, and a covert plan to overthrow the Nicaraguan Sandinistas. Haig identified Russia and Cuba as the source of the problem. Reagan wanted to overcome America's "Vietnam syndrome" by scoring an easy win against the communist masterminds in Moscow and Havana. Reagan's wing of the Republican Party reviled Henry Kissinger and Richard Nixon for the Vietnam-era detente with the USSR. Although pragmatic White House advisors James Baker, Michael Deaver, and Edwin Meese restrained Haig's more extreme plans, the Reagan administration increased military aid to El Salvador. Administration hard-liners wanted to get the Democrats on record as voting against the victory they expected to achieve within the year.

Their strategy put Democrats in a quandary. When the State Department produced a white paper allegedly proving that the USSR, Cuba, and Nicaragua were pouring money, men, and supplies into El Salvador, few congressmen bothered to examine its claims. A reporter later discovered that the primary sources it cited showed the opposite. In the Senate, Minority Leader Robert Byrd agreed with Reagan. In the House, Tip O'Neill, supplied with good information from his aunt, a Maryknoll sister, knew what Reagan was up to but calculated that he had to pick his fights—and he didn't pick this one. Many Democrats were with Reagan and Byrd, and the House Appropriations subcommittee approved Reagan's aid request.

A minority of liberals fought back. Among the prominent House opponents were Ben Rosenthal and Stephen Solarz from New York, Mike Barnes of Maryland, David Bonior of Michigan, and Gerry Studds. In March they forged a compromise formula for sending military aid that required the president to come before Congress and certify that El Salvador was making progress on human rights issues that included the investigation and prosecution of the killers of the archbishop and the six Americans.[13]

Moakley usually voted with this group but was not prominently identified with them. He did speak out on the issue, if not quite from the beginning. On the anniversary of the murder of the churchwomen, he acknowledged the arrest of six low-ranking soldiers who had done the deed but decried the lack of progress in identifying their superiors. He called attention to the 9,250 political murders in the first six months of the year in which Reagan came into office. In mid-December 1981, the Salvadoran Army massacred the entire village of El Mozote, killing more than seven hundred men, women, and children, and the story broke in the *New York Times* the following month. Despite this horrific slaughter, Reagan certified that El Salvador was making progress on human rights on January 28, 1982, and a storm of protest erupted. Moakley wrote to the president, opposing the training of Salvadoran troops in the United States and warning of another Vietnam. He issued a press release calling for a suspension of aid until Congress independently verified that what Reagan said was true. Moakley even sent a strong message to a demonstration at

Faneuil Hall in February, calling the Reagan policy "the most tragic diplomatic and moral failure since Vietnam." He declared that the Salvadoran government "lacks respect for the most basic civil and human rights" and called for an end to all military aid. In July he expressed his "outrage" at Reagan's certification of human rights progress in the *Congressional Record*. "Never in my recollection has a previous administration so dangerously combined an ignorance of history with a total misreading of current reality," Moakley insisted. The language might have been Jim McGovern's, but the sentiments were Moakley's.[14]

Moakley and McGovern began to investigate the issue of the refugees. Immigration had emerged as a major concern during the Carter administration and remained a central issue throughout the 1980s. As the Mexican and Central American economies gyrated unpredictably, and the American economy recovered from the recession, millions of Mexicans and Central Americans took up jobs that Americans would not do in agriculture, restaurants, janitorial work, meat-packing, and other industries. The debate about immigration did not follow party lines. Wealthy Republican growers in the Southwest wanted the undocumented immigrants as cheap laborers. Yet nativist Republicans feared that these Hispanics would stay and contribute demographically to a nonwhite majority. Many liberal Democrats, descended from immigrants themselves, welcomed the newcomers, understood that they would adapt to American culture, and wanted to legalize their status. Other Democrats, especially labor officials and some African American leaders, worried that an influx of immigrants would drive down the cost of labor and hurt the people they represented.[15] Moakley understood all these concerns.

The Immigration Act of 1965 boosted immigration by overturning the restrictive national categories established forty years earlier. After 1965, more immigrants could come legally, with admission based on their skills, family connections, or as refugees. Refugees could enter the United States through the long-established principle of political asylum, available to people with a well-founded fear of persecution based on their political views or religion. Still others could come through the category of Extended Voluntary Departure, a temporary status granted to people ineligible for political asylum. Established in 1960, this category was country-specific and available during "temporary" emergencies to refugees who were not being individually persecuted but who were fleeing repressive regimes. Moakley learned that Poles, Cubans, and Ethiopians enjoyed this status. The Justice Department, in consultation with State, determined which nation's refugees were eligible.[16]

The situation in El Salvador was worse than that of most other countries allowed EVD status. There were probably 300,000 to 500,000 Salvadoran immigrants to the United States, almost all illegal. They were fleeing the civil war in which they were trapped between the rebels and the army. The army indiscriminately bombed villages suspected of rebel sympathies, or committed massacres like that at El Mozote. Yet the Immigration and Naturalization Service deported about one thousand refugees a month to this slaughterhouse. Sixteen thousand Salvadorans had applied for political asylum, but only seventy-two of them were granted it. While communist nations like Poland or Cuba were no models of democracy, nothing remotely like those horrors took place there.[17]

Late in April, Moakley joined with Les Au Coin of Oregon in a "Dear Colleague" letter seeking cosigners on an appeal to Attorney General William French Smith. They reminded their fellow legislators that EVD was a temporary status issued only when "compelling humanitarian factors" applied. Eighty-six members requested EVD status for Salvadorans. The State Department released its advisory opinion to Justice a month later, explaining that human rights progress was being made and that EVD status would just encourage economic migration. The *New York Times* ridiculed this conclusion in an editorial titled "Why Poles but Not Salvadorans?" Later in June, Secretary of State George Schultz formally advised Justice of this view, adding that because civil unrest was only local to a few regions, Salvadorans could flee the war zones and go to peaceful parts of El Salvador.[18]

Moakley might have decided at this juncture that he had done his due diligence to the Jamaica Plain activists and could just leave the issue to some other congressman. His fighting spirit was clearly aroused, however, and he partnered with Arizona Democratic senator Dennis DeConcini to introduce a resolution mandating EVD status for Salvadorans. HR 4447, introduced in November 1983, would suspend deportations of Salvadorans pending a study of conditions on the ground in El Salvador by the Government Accounting Office. The House and Senate Judiciary committees would consider the report and pass legislation regarding EVD status accordingly.[19]

To promote the legislation, Moakley sent McGovern on the first of what would be many fact-finding trips to El Salvador. His eleven-day trip uncovered the barbarism and hypocrisy that they would challenge for the next eight years. Moakley's bill never made it out of the House Immigration Committee, chaired by the same Romano Mazzoli of Kentucky who, like Moakley, had been a staunch antibusing partisan.[20] Moakley vowed to try again in the next Congress.

★   ★   ★

Joe Moakley was becoming a citizen of the world. As he rose in the Democratic leadership, Tip O'Neill encouraged this process. Moakley joined a leadership delegation to China in the spring of 1983 for over two weeks. The fourteen congressmen visited the ancient capital of Xian, where they viewed the spectacular life-size army of terra cotta soldiers commissioned by the despotic Qin Dynasty emperor in the late third century BCE. Then it was on to Beijing for a meeting with Communist Party leader Deng Xiaoping. The last stop in China was the emerging port city of Shanghai, and finally the delegates proceeded to the "Asian tiger" city-states of Singapore and Hong Kong.

Most of the congressmen knew nothing of China, but they did know that allegiances were evolving among the USSR, China, and the United States. Only the most rigid reactionaries imagined a mutuality of interests between the Soviets and Chinese based on shared ideological convictions. "I got the feeling they (the Chinese) know we're not an aggressor and they realize Russia is," Moakley told a reporter upon his return. "They would rather be doing business with us than with Russia." Moakley was mindful of the remaining practical problems that soured Sino-American relations, regarding trade and the status of Taiwan, which China argued was integral to the mainland. Moakley was more concerned about exports that threatened to take market share from Massachusetts textile mills.[21]

★   ★   ★

Moakley did not advertise his foreign trips or his work on El Salvador issues. Voters often viewed congressional foreign travel as wasteful, and few were interested in Central America. Moakley did call attention to his opposition to President Reagan's escalation of the arms race and the massive spending that it entailed.

Reagan's partisans can, with some justification, celebrate him as a visionary. He was unlike the three 1980s Democratic presidential candidates in that regard. Jimmy Carter, Walter Mondale, and Michael Dukakis put forward limited goals regarding their fiscal and foreign policy plans. None offered a grand vision. Reagan did. He imagined the fall of Soviet communism, a repressive system that all Americans hated. In 1979 it had been challenged by a workers' movement in Poland called Solidarity that was inspired in part by the elevation of a popular Polish pope. During Reagan's presidency a decrepit gerontocracy presided over the USSR's crumbling economy; three elderly party chairmen died in office. Reagan saw these signs as the beginning of the end of Soviet communism, and he was right.

Moreover, Reagan was impatient with the defense posture into which both superpowers had lapsed—"mutually assured destruction," in which the threat of nuclear annihilation was supposed to restrain rational actors in both Moscow and Washington. Reagan launched a huge military buildup—including Trident submarines, the B-1 bomber, new fighter planes, and the MX missile. Topping off these huge budget busters was a fanciful project, the Strategic Defense Initiative, dubbed "Star Wars," that Reagan promised could shoot down incoming Soviet missiles. This was the brainchild of physicist Edward Teller. Almost all other scientists and even some of Reagan's cabinet secretaries thought it would not work. The defense buildup, however, promised to create tens of thousands of jobs, and few congressmen could resist a contract in their district. Liberals countered with a huge new movement, the "nuclear freeze," that launched mighty demonstrations rivaling those of the Vietnam era.[22]

Moakley instinctively grasped the implications for his constituents. While the collapse of the USSR was a nice thing to think about, Moakley realized that the price tag on Star Wars would cripple the infrastructure, jobs, and social programs he favored. Nor did Moakley believe in voodoo economics, and he started calling attention to the growing budget deficits. After Democrats won their big congressional victory in the 1982 elections, he became increasingly outspoken against the arms buildup. Moakley introduced a bill that would ban space-based weapons. "The amount of money which the Pentagon spends on its space activities now exceeds the entire budget of NASA," he protested in an op-ed. He cited defense officials who said that the United States was already far superior in space weaponry to the USSR, and he estimated the potential cost of Reagan's new buildup in the hundreds of billions of dollars. Rather than waste the money in a spending race with the Russians, Moakley advocated a negotiated agreement with them. The conservative *Washington Times* attacked Moakley as naive, arguing that the Soviets couldn't be trusted.[23]

Moakley didn't like the new F-15 fighter either. It supposedly could shoot down Soviet satellites, but Moakley pointed out that if the Americans built it, then the Russians would do the same thing. Moakley did support the developing satellite information system that was revolutionizing telecommunications and weather prediction. "How can we justify opening up a 'Pandora's Box' of space weapons when America's breadboxes are empty?" he asked.[24]

In the summer, he held a news conference with noted astronomer Carl Sagan and defense expert Richard L. Garwin. If the former sheet metal operator felt a little out of his depth with these experts, he didn't show it, nor was he reluctant to inform his constituents about the educated company he was keeping. He even contributed an editorial to a science magazine devoted to space technology. Just before the 1984 election, he wrote a *Boston Globe* op-ed titled "It's Time to Shoot Down Reagan's Star Wars Proposal." Moakley blasted its $25 billion price tag at a time when the government was running a $200 billion deficit.[25] The country would waste billions of dollars on this useless program, and the Soviet Union would indeed collapse, but skeptics concluded that the USSR imploded as a result of its own internal contradictions, not because of Star Wars.

★ ★ ★

Moakley ventured into another matter of considerable complexity, this time a constitutional question, in the summer of 1983, while the El Salvador refugee and space weapons issues occupied his legislative agenda. On June 23, the Supreme Court ruled in the *Chadha* case that the "legislative veto," a congressional practice initiated during the Depression, was unconstitutional. The ruling restricted the power of Congress in relation to the executive branch. One might suspect that a Democratic congressman might oppose the ruling, both to preserve the prerogatives of his branch and to limit the power of an overweening president. Moakley saw through to the principle of the matter. He had earlier introduced his own legislation to adjust the separation of powers to modern times.

The story had begun when Jagdish Chadha, a Kenyan-born man of Indian descent, studying in the United States but holding a British passport, was threatened with deportation upon the completion of his studies. Kenya, however, had effectively revoked the citizenship of residents born to immigrant parents, and Chadha became a man without a country. He appealed the ruling and won in an immigration proceeding, which is conducted in the executive branch because the Immigration and Naturalization Service, as it was then called, was part of the Justice Department. The House of Representatives however, overturned Chadha's stay of deportation, along with that of many others, by means of the "legislative veto" of an executive branch ruling. Chadha fought his case all the way to the Supreme Court, challenging the constitutionality of the practice.

The case raised deep questions regarding the separation of powers. The legislative veto had emerged during the Roosevelt administration because of the rapid expansion of executive branch powers in a national emergency. Legislators appropriated to themselves the power to check rulings by federal regulatory agencies. The congressmen typically responded to pressure from a commercial or manufacturing enterprise that felt its activities were being too closely regulated. As new concerns over worker health and safety and the environment gained wider public acceptance in the post-Watergate era, conservative congressmen maneuvered legislative vetoes through the House to satisfy the lobbyists who they typically felt were providing jobs in their district.

Moakley was chairman of the subcommittee on the Rules of the House, one of the Rules Committee's functions being to monitor the House's own procedures. On October 7, 1981, he opened hearings to look into the legislative veto mechanism. Moakley didn't like it. He felt that there at least needed to be guidelines, crafted by the courts as a neutral arbiter, for how it should operate. In the absence of judicial intervention, Moakley proposed the creation of a Select Committee on Regulatory Affairs to resolve ambiguities in congressional "veto" and regulatory practices. Basically, Moakley felt that the regulatory agencies should be free to do their work without his colleagues butting in. They were too easily swayed by lobbyists. Naturally, his efforts got nowhere. Ultimately the courts intervened, issuing a sweeping decision in *Chadha* that ended the practice, raising questions about the constitutionality of 210 laws that included legislative veto provisions.[26]

Business groups were worried. Two of them invited Moakley to tell them what he thought it meant. He told the New England Council, Inc., that the legislative veto had been a congressional "power grab" that enabled them to draft vague legislation when defining the mission of executive regulatory bodies. Now Congress would have to delineate their powers clearly, and then leave their hands off, and industry would have to live with the rulings or go to court, not their congressman. He had, for example, voted against a legislative veto of Federal Trade Commission regulations for used-car dealers and physicians, who now would have to be more transparent.[27]

A few months later he told the National Manufacturers' Association that the Supreme Court decision was "a significant one and will force some very fundamental changes in the way our government operates." The legislative veto "was like the small print on an insurance policy. I'd been warning congress for a long time that the practice was unconstitutional. . . . All the great minds said, 'No, it'll never happen.'" Yet his appraisal was nuanced, and he recognized that the world as Congress and business knew it had not come to an end. "In essence, Congress was reversing the rules and allowing the executive agencies to legislate, while reserving the veto power for itself. In this regard the decision should not be viewed as a disaster or as a victory for anyone."[28]

For a man lacking a college degree and educated at a working man's law school, Joe Moakley showed that he had a knack for disregarding contingent circumstances, seeing to the heart of a complex constitutional matter, and stating the fundamental principle in plain language.

★   ★   ★

Boston gradually changed for the better over the next decades. One sign of that transformation was the election of Ray Flynn as mayor in 1983. Flynn, once a leader of the antibusing movement, had put that moment behind him and looked to heal the city's racial divisions. He also promised to focus on the neighborhoods rather than downtown development, as Mayor White had done. When Mayor Kevin White retired after sixteen years in office, a crowded field of contenders vied for the open seat. The field narrowed to two in the September run-off, with Flynn and Mel King emerging as the top vote-getters. The two ran a gentlemanly campaign, showing mutual respect. King, once viewed as an angry black militant by many fearful whites, campaigned throughout the city without incident. Ten years after the height of the busing controversy, it was clear that many of the haters had moved out. Young professionals of the type Moakley encountered in Jamaica Plain now lived in the South End, Allston-Brighton, North End, and Back Bay. The Hispanic population expanded in East Boston, Roslindale, and Hyde Park. Immigrants from other parts of the world lived everywhere. King put together a "rainbow coalition" but won only 34 percent. On election night, he conceded gracefully. Flynn wore a Mel King button.[29] The city was long past the days of James Michael Curley, or even Louise Day Hicks and Pixie Palladino.

Moakley never considered a run for mayor, and, adhering to the traditional wisdom that one should not pick sides among friends, he watched the contest from a distance. On paper, he and Ray Flynn should have been close colleagues. Flynn too was from South Boston, twelve years younger, a basketball star who attended Providence College on a scholarship. Probably the source of the coolness between Moakley and Flynn originated in the busing days. Flynn was in the streets; Moakley wouldn't join him, despite the pressure he was under. "We wasn't close to Ray Flynn," district director Roger Kineavy recalled. "Not that he's a bad guy. We just wasn't close to him."[30]

Flynn shared Moakley's social conservatism and economic progressivism. He championed the concept of "linkage," the idea that developers of urban parcels would in return contribute to affordable housing and urban infrastructure projects. As the national economy recovered from the recession, and the computer boom of the mid-1980s got underway, the Flynn administration traded downtown skyscraper space for money for low-cost housing. He hired a pack of young progressives, dubbed "the Sandinistas" for the Nicaraguan revolutionaries, some of whom came out of tenants' rights groups, like Neil Sullivan from Mass Fair Share, and Peter Dreier from the Mass Tenants' Organization. Flynn loyalist Joe Fisher rode herd on the staff, and by the middle to late 1980s the mayor was enabling grass roots organizers from the Dudley Street Neighborhood Initiative to reinvigorate a multiracial Roxbury neighborhood. Yet Flynn and Moakley had only a businesslike relationship.[31]

★ ★ ★

Several apparently unrelated events in the fall of 1983 and spring of 1984 signaled the beginning of a major change in the national political climate. At the time each seemed to be unrelated to the other, but taken in sequence we can see how they related. Moakley somewhat accidentally presided over the climax. We are still living with the result today.

The United States had stationed a contingent of Marines as part of an international peace-keeping effort in Lebanon. On October 23, a Shiite suicide bomber drove a truck laden with explosives to their barracks and detonated it, killing 243 Marines and wounding many others. The world had seen Muslim extremist terrorism before, but suicide bombing was something new. The nation was horrified. Reagan pulled the Marines out soon thereafter.

Two days after the bombing, President Reagan sent an invasion force to the Caribbean island of Grenada, whose radical leaders had come to power in a 1979 coup. Grenada had a population of 120,000 and a medical school with American students; its major industry was tourism. When one faction overthrew another there, Reagan told the country that he was invading Grenada to prevent the slaughter of the medical students, who in fact were in no danger. The Grenadian Army surrendered without firing a shot. The students returned home and kissed the ground as the cameras rolled. Most Americans concluded that the heroic Reagan had saved the day. His popularity soared. Every international organization condemned the invasion as a violation of Grenada's sovereignty, but to most Americans this merely proved our unique greatness.[32]

Buoyed by his new popularity, the president approved a secret plan to mine Nicaragua's harbors. This was an act of war in international law. When ships entering Nicaragua's waters began to explode, including a Soviet vessel on which several sailors were injured, the administration announced that it had nothing to do with it. The Contras declared that they had placed the mines themselves. The operation had actually been performed by CIA-hired mercenaries and Navy Seals, and the truth soon came out. The UN Security Council condemned U.S. actions by a vote of 14–1. CIA director William Casey reluctantly told Congress that he would notify them in advance of such future actions. Privately he resolved to drive his secret operations further underground. The result would be the Iran-Contra operation uncovered in Reagan's second term.[33]

Moakley disagreed with everything the president did in this period, but could act only as a commentator. He told a Westwood High School assembly that he had disapproved of sending troops to Lebanon in the first place, but he also opposed retreating under fire. In fact, Moakley was at Westwood because one of their recent schoolmates had been a Marine killed in the explosion. Moakley feared that a U.S. troop withdrawal would encourage Syrian intervention into Lebanon, and over the next several years Syrian terrorism drove the country into civil war. A then unknown Saudi Arabian Muslim extremist, Osama bin Laden, concluded from this experience that superpowers, when attacked, would retreat.

Moakley focused most of his remarks on the Grenada invasion, noting that the world community had condemned it. A newspaper headline announced, "Moakley Tells Westwood Students U.S. Is 'Aggressor.'" He didn't buy one line of what Reagan had said. Moakley had spoken to some of the "rescued" medical students, who told him that there had been no threat to their lives and that they all had the opportunity to go home after the coup. "We shouldn't have sent the Marine Corps in," Moakley told the students. "We should have sent the diplomatic corps in."[34]

Language like this seemed treasonous to Republican hard liners. They were now dominant in the Reagan administration, which had fired its pragmatists and elevated shrill warmongers such as Jeanne Kirkpatrick to the inner circle. The war party became ascendant among Republicans in the House. When liberal Democrats who opposed aid to the Nicaraguan Contras sent a letter to Sandinista leader Daniel Ortega, approving and encouraging the fair conduct of elections scheduled for 1984, House conservatives impugned the patriotism of the "Dear Comandante" letter's authors.

The Congress has a practice known as "special orders," during which members may speak from the podium after adjournment to enter remarks into the record. Traditionally, members availed themselves of this privilege to commend local citizens who had done good deeds, a practice to which no one but the concerned parties paid any attention. The new technology of cable television transformed this hitherto insignificant practice. After the "Dear Commandante" letter, Newt Gingrich scheduled free camera time to insinuate that their opponents, O'Neill's friend Eddie Boland in particular, were unpatriotic. Furious, Tip O'Neill quietly ordered that the cameras, previously anchored to focus only on the orator, swivel to show that the speakers were bloviating before an empty chamber. Gingrich lambasted O'Neill, claiming that he had been tricked. Speaking from the floor, O'Neill struck back, calling Gingrich's accusations "the lowest thing that I have ever seen in my thirty-two years in Congress."

By chance, Tip O'Neill's friend Joe Moakley was in the chair. Republicans demanded that the Speaker's remarks be stricken from the record. Moakley turned glumly to the parliamentarian, who advised that the Speaker had crossed the line, and Moakley ruled against Tip, the first time since 1795 that a Speaker had to suffer this indignity.

"I looked at O'Neill and whacked the gavel," Moakley recalled, in an interview with O'Neill's biographer. "He looked back at me and just shook his head. Boy, he could have killed me. For two days he didn't speak to me. He was bullshit. Every once in a while he would look down at me and say, 'My pal Joe.'"[35] Moakley later cracked to a reporter that "I'm leaving for Shanghai in the morning. I just hope it doesn't cost me any strokes on the golf course." Moakley explained that it was a technical ruling based on the parliamentarian's advice, and the incident, dubbed "Camscam" by journalistic wags, did no lasting damage to Moakley's relationship with O'Neill.[36]

"Camscam" did, however, signal deeper shifts in American life and politics. Ronald Reagan was popular with Americans because he restored their sense of self-confidence, reflected their optimism, and personified a classic American congeniality. Reagan lived in a *Readers' Digest* fantasy land in which Americans by definition always did the right thing. He never attacked American opponents personally, and for all his conservatism, he instinctively understood that as president part of his job, like that of a king, was to portray a benign father figure to all of his subjects. He was, after all, a Hollywood actor who understood roles. Reagan had Goldwater's politics but the actor Jimmy Stewart's persona.

Newt Gingrich had none of Reagan's attractive personal traits, was never close to him, and would forever after claim his mantle. Gingrich held a Ph.D. in history yet presented himself as leader of a populist crusade against liberal elitists. First elected in 1978 as part of the realignment that would remove white Southern Democrats from the political landscape, he pursued a scorched earth policy against Democrats and Republican moderates like those who dominated the Massachusetts party. It was not so clear in May of 1984, but the "Camscam" teapot tempest marked the emergence of a new conservative leader. He would rise to the House Speakership in 1994 by polarizing every debate and stigmatizing any hint of comity between the parties. No one since Joe McCarthy would do more to poison the atmosphere of public discourse in twentieth-century America than Newt Gingrich.

"Camscam" was an inside the Beltway nonevent for most Americans. As the 1984 election neared, the economy recovered from recession and people went back to work, especially in Boston, where a building boom, defense contracts, the medical and higher education sector, and an expanding computer software industry combined to revitalize the region. In the state's Democratic primary, Colorado senator Gary Hart, who represented the young urban professionals, or "yuppies," a 1980s neologism, trounced his opponents. Moakley's guy, Senator Walter Mondale of Minnesota, an old-fashioned, labor-oriented New Deal type, captured the nomination. A decent man but an uninspiring speaker, he made headlines by choosing the first female vice presidential running mate, New York's Geraldine Ferraro. Democrats swept all the state's congressional seats in November except Silvio Conte's, and John Kerry, the lieutenant governor, won the Senate seat vacated by Paul Tsongas, who had been diagnosed with cancer. But Reagan won the state too, along with every other except Minnesota. It was the third-biggest landslide in the twentieth century, rivaling Johnson's in 1964 and Nixon's in 1972.[37] For millions of Americans, it felt like "Morning in America" again, and their futures looked bright.

There was a little-noticed nonbinding ballot question in Massachusetts in November. Colleagues of the Jamaica Plain activists asked voters how they felt about Reagan's Central America policies, and if they wouldn't prefer to spend the money for the Salvadoran military and Nicaraguan Contras at home. They voted overwhelmingly for the proposition. This sentiment, which echoed poll after poll, would undo the Reagan administration's second term and pull Joe Moakley's attention, and finally himself, literally, into these foreign lands.

Evelyn Duffy and Joe Moakley, April 28, 1951.
Copyright Suffolk University.

Moakley at meeting in El Salvador, aide Jim McGovern on Moakley's right.
Copyright Suffolk University.

Moakley with
brothers Robert (left)
and Thomas (center),
1930s; Mary Moakley
with her three sons,
1930s. Copyright
Suffolk University.

Moakley at
ribbon-cutting in
African American
community, 1970s.
Copyright Suffolk
University.

Moakley, Tip O'Neill,
and columnist Jimmy
Breslin relaxing,
July 19, 1974.
Copyright Suffolk
University.

St. Patrick's Day Luncheon—Moakley, William Bulger (center),
and Ted Kennedy, 1960s. Copyright Suffolk University.

Moakley, Fidel Castro, Massachusetts congressmen William Delahunt,
Jim McGovern, and Richard Neal on delegation trip to Cuba, 1998.
Copyright Suffolk University.

Thomas Moakley (in suit) and Joe Moakley, Sr., at Moakley's Tavern (Savin Hill, Dorchester), 1940s. Copyright Suffolk University.

Moakley greets John F. Kennedy at Hyannis Airport, 1960.
Copyright Suffolk University.

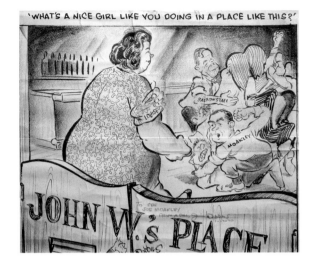

Political cartoon by Jim Dobbins, featuring Louise Day Hicks and Moakley, 1970 Democratic congressional primary. Copyright Suffolk University.

Moakley with fellow Seabee during World War II, 1940s. Copyright Suffolk University.

Moakley and Ambassador Anne Patterson at Santa Marta, El Salvador, November 1997. Copyright Suffolk University.

Moakley with Pope John Paul II on congressional trip to the Vatican, January 2001.
Copyright Suffolk University.

Moakley, Ray Flynn, William Bulger, and others, 1980s.

Joe and Evelyn Moakley, wearing fake mustaches, celebrate Massachusetts Senate victory, probably 1964. Copyright Suffolk University.

Moakley (left), "The Boston Bull," boxing, Miami, 1947.

Moakley waving to crowd, St. Patrick's Day Parade, South Boston, 1960s.
Copyright Suffolk University.

9

* * * * *

A Most Unlikely Hero

oe Moakley's first order of business as the next congressional session opened was to introduce HR 822, a new bill to protect the Salvadoran immigrants. John J. Dooling, a former Moakley aide and now counsel to the Rules Committee, crafted the El Salvador Refugee Act of 1985, a modified, more specific version of its predecessor. This one would establish an El Salvador Refugee Commission in the Government Accounting Office, tasked with settling disputed facts such as the number of displaced Salvadorans, their location and current condition, what happened to returnees, and how their situation compared with that of countries to which EVD status had been granted. The commission would get $800,000 to complete a report within a year. The bill defined the congressional review process, and mandated a temporary suspension of deportations for those entering the United States before October 1984. The last provision was meant to persuade skeptics that the bill would not attract new economic immigrants. Moakley filed it on January 30; it was referred to the Judiciary and Rules committees.[1]

In some ways, the situation in El Salvador had improved since Moakley had last raised the issue. In the presidential election of May 1984, Jose Napoleon Duarte, the moderate Christian Democrat, had, with American backing, defeated Roberto D'Aubuisson, the death squad leader who now headed the oligarchy's political party, known by its Spanish acronym ARENA. Duarte, a former civil engineer, came to Washington to lobby for more military aid. It helped his cause that the enlisted men charged with killing the American churchwomen had been convicted in a Salvadoran court. Despite continued liberal Democratic opposition, Reagan and Duarte got about $200 million in additional military aid.

The money made the situation worse. With their new helicopter gunships, the Salvadoran Air Force began a terrifying round of destroy-ing villages from the air. The AC-47s could fill an area the size of a football field with machine gun fire in seconds. People fled guerrilla-held areas for San Salvador and the United States. Many of those outside the war zone ran away also. A right-wing assembly ended any hope of land re-form, and thousands of peasants were evicted.[2]

Moakley liked Duarte, but he saw the situation on the ground clearly. "For many Salvadorans, this bill could mean the difference between life and death," he announced in a press release. "While the election of Jose Napoleon Duarte may be heartening, it is not realistic to believe that he or anyone else can magically end the civil unrest in El Salvador overnight."[3]

The Reagan State Department's Latin America Bureau maintained its view that Salvadoran migrants to the United States came for economic reasons; that those who claimed they were being persecuted could avail themselves of a political asylum remedy; and that the elected govern-ment of El Salvador was a democracy and therefore not equivalent to communist dictatorships whose fleeing citizens had been granted EVD status. When Moakley requested a review of this opinion, W. Tapley Ben-nett, the State Department's congressional liaison, replied that a poll of Salvadorans showed that 70 percent wanted to immigrate to the United States; surely not all of these people were being persecuted, and clearly the United States could not receive them all. Further, the department averred, people deported back to El Salvador were not victimized. The State Department had interviewed five hundred deportees in El Salva-dor, and none had suffered abuse. The Salvadoran government denied that it pursued deportees, who could easily have been detained at the airport. Finally, the State Department claimed that it was doing what it could to help them.[4]

Civil society opponents of increased immigration expanded upon the State Department's position. Responding to an op-ed by Moakley in the *Christian Science Monitor*, Roger Conner of the Federation for American Immigration Reform argued that because violence against civilians was a global problem, the United States would be acting unfairly to admit some of these victims but not others. Should the Congress adopt Moakley's bill, Conner warned, a flood of immigrants would wash across the border if El Salvador's situation deteriorated.[5]

Duarte's election changed the atmosphere in Congress regarding El

Salvador. Conservative Democrats voted with Reagan in May of 1984 for more military aid. After Reagan's landslide, wavering Democrats became wary of opposing him. Moakley had to win them over, making his case in the *Congressional Record* and the newspapers. In March he read into the *Record* a report by Holly Burkhalter of Americas Watch. She found that death squad killings were down only because the urban populist leaders had all been killed. In the rural departments of Chalatenango, where fifty unarmed people had just been massacred, and Morazan, the army continued to mow down villagers, who fled to the mountains.[6]

In April the Senate Judiciary Subcommittee on Immigration held hearings on Dennis DeConcini's version of the bill (S. 377), known as "Moakley-DeConcini." Morton Halperin of the American Civil Liberties Union introduced his organization's report, which ridiculed the State Department's conclusions. Basing its findings on work by Salvadoran human rights organizations, including that of the Catholic Church, it pointed out that the State Department had confused the political amnesty and EVD categories. Advocates of EVD status did not need to prove that individuals were being targeted—that applied only to the asylum category. They did have to show that violence was endemic and that deportees would be subject to it. The ACLU identified fifty-two murders and forty-seven "disappearances" among deportees; thirteen others had been arrested, including one detained at the airport and tortured. Even the State Department's Elliot Abrams, a hard-line neoconservative, admitted that its information was "flawed" because State had no access to the region in which the war was being fought, the very place from which the immigrants had fled. Finally, the ACLU pointed out that 1.25 million Salvadorans had abandoned their homes since 1980, with half internally displaced and perhaps half a million reaching the United States. That kind of outmigration had to be caused by war, not by some unidentified economic change.[7]

Later in the year, Moakley wrote in the *Los Angeles Times* that Duarte's election had not changed the facts on the ground. Citing a church report, he pointed out that displaced people within El Salvador refused to go home, despite their misery in San Salvador's slums. While death squad killings were down, seventy-seven political murders in seven months was still horrific.[8] In November, El Salvador's Archbishop Arturo Rivera y Damas urged Congress to support Moakley's bill.[9]

Catholics were not the only Christians energized by the problem of the refugees. Some members of liberal Protestant denominations protected refugee families threatened by deportation, granting them "sanctuary." In early 1985, an Arizona pastor and fifteen of his parishioners were indicted after federal agents infiltrated their group. When eight of them were convicted for conspiracy, Moakley criticized the verdict as an "imbalance of justice." The case echoed the days of the Underground Railroad from the time of slavery. Moakley was becoming more radical as he fought for this cause, seeing people who shared his own religious principles now thrown into prison.[10]

Moakley was not becoming some New Age leftist himself. He called each international situation as he saw it, on pragmatic grounds. In April of 1986, Libyan dictator Muammar Qadaffi ordered his intelligence operatives to bomb a West German discotheque frequented by American servicemen, killing one of them. Reagan responded by bombing Libya, targeting the dictator but killing his daughter. Moakley approved. "We had to take a stand to show we won't be pushed around," he said. "I just wish our allies had gotten more involved so we wouldn't be the only kid on the block fighting back."[11] The image hearkened back to the mature man's childhood, and revealed much about the way Moakley thought.

The day after the bombing raid, rumors swirled about a possible reprisal aimed at the U.S. Capitol. Moakley supervised the hiring of Capitol police through his position on the Personnel Committee, and fretted about the reduction of the force because of budget cuts. "Just think of the explosive power of all the gasoline in the cars parked in our underground garages if someone planted a high-powered bomb in some of the autos," Moakley said.[12] His worries prefigured the terrorism of the following decades.

In the fall of 1986, Moakley sent McGovern to El Salvador on his second fact-finding trip of the year, this time an extended journey of eleven days. He met with Maria Teresa de Canales, thirty-eight, a member of the Mothers of the Disappeared. In addition to losing her son, her husband was murdered in 1980. Two years previously she had been awarded the prestigious Robert F. Kennedy prize for human rights work. Incredibly, the State Department regarded her as a threat to national security, so she was denied a visa. Shortly after her meeting with McGovern she was abducted by the dread Treasury Police, a death squad in uniform, tortured, and thrown into Ilopango women's prison. In a *Boston Herald* opinion piece, McGovern pointed out that the United States had spent $2 billion on aid to El Salvador, 85 percent of it on military hardware and training, and the country still had this sort of brutality as its human rights record.[13]

Moakley used McGovern's findings in a new appeal to the State Department to change its policy, which would moot the need for legislation. Moakley praised Salvadoran president Jose Napoleon Duarte as "a man committed to peace and democracy" but pointed out that little had changed with the military still in control behind the scenes. "There appear to be abuses of human rights by the Salvadoran military and . . . violence against civilians by the guerillas is on the rise." Moakley was no apologist for the revolutionaries, who responded to the military's attacks with a wave of kidnapping, seizing Duarte's daughter in September 1985. The State Department would not change its position.[14]

A few weeks after Moakley made his appeal, the Reagan administration received a staggering blow. On October 6, 1986, a young Nicaraguan soldier shot down a cargo plane laden with arms and ammunition for the Contras. The sole crash survivor was an American mercenary who began to talk freely. Ironically, Eugene Hasenfus's plane was called *The Fat Lady*, and the CIA's illegal support for the Contras was about to unravel as the fat lady sang. In 1982 and 1984, Massachusetts congressman Edward Boland, chair of the Intelligence Committee, had sponsored and passed two amendments to appropriations bills that limited administration support to the Nicaraguan Contra rebels. The Boland amendments specifically made this CIA covert action illegal. When the funding source of the operation—Iran—was revealed, the public was astonished as the "Iran-Contra" saga unfolded on television in 1987.[15]

Just after the CIA plane was downed, Moakley's bill passed the House by a close 199–197 vote. It was subsumed into the Alan Simpson–Romano Mazzoli Immigration Reform Act of 1986, which addressed issues such as border control, new national quotas, and paths to citizenship for immigrants who had entered the country illegally. That bill would now have to go to a conference committee. "Simpson has publicly made a statement no way it will stay in," Moakley told reporters, "but we're working on it. I'm still cautiously optimistic."[16]

Behind the scenes, the Reagan administration set its sights on Moakley's provision. It would be a major embarrassment for them to have to admit that after six years of war, they were still backing a brutal military dictatorship with a civilian president acting as a cover for its crimes. "Meese called up [Peter] Rodino, who was the chairman; he said, 'Look it, if Moakley's amendment goes through, the whole bill is dead,'" Moakley recalled years later. "So Rodino said, 'Joe, what am I going to do? There's a lot of good stuff in here for the Irish, the Italians . . . and even some Hispanic.' I said, OK, I'm not going to kill the bill, but I want to be sure that I'm the first one out of the box the next time this immigration comes up."[17]

Moakley had lost for a second time. He was not discouraged. "I will be back," he told reporters, flanked by representatives of religious and human rights groups. This time, the bill had passed the House. He had extracted promises from Judiciary chairman Rodino to move it quickly through his committee next time, and from Simpson, who opposed the bill, not to block it. "My amendment raised important questions relating to our responsibilities morally and under international law to those who have sought safe haven here from the dangers attendant to wars for which we as a nation have more than a passing responsibility," he declared.[18] In this final scene of the second act, Moakley showed far-sightedness, patience, and resolve.

★ ★ ★

As global technology began to change with new developments in computers and satellite communications, the American military sought to upgrade its capabilities in the crucial areas of command and control of its troops, and communications between allied armies. Two rivals from the military-industrial complex bid for a $4–5 billion telecommunications contract that would allow twenty-six divisions of American Army troops to talk securely with their European allies. The industrial giants were Rockwell International, which partnered with a British firm, and GTE, which had a French partner. Defense Secretary Casper Weinberger would decide who got the contract.

GTE, headquartered in Rosslyn, Virginia, had a significant operation in Massachusetts, and they planned to site its facility in Taunton, the one place that Moakley had a field office. The old mill town had a 15 percent unemployment rate. Its mayor, Richard Johnson, had been a staunch Moakley ally in the 1982 campaign. A new factory would radically alter the region's economic landscape. Moakley sent his administrative assistant John Weinfurter to Europe to learn about the troops' needs first-hand. Rockwell meanwhile got Britain's prime minister, Margaret Thatcher, to prevail upon her friend Ronald Reagan in behalf of the British firm allied with Rockwell.[19]

The army and Weinberger stalled, so Moakley finally went over to Speaker O'Neill's office. Moakley told O'Neill that the project would produce a thousand jobs, and O'Neill called the Defense Department while Moakley sat in his office. "You're not playing politics with this fucking thing!" O'Neill bellowed into the phone. GTE was the low bidder, and it won the contract.[20]

GTE hired five hundred skilled engineers, designers, and scientists, and five hundred production workers, cutting unemployment in Taunton to below 4 percent and sparking an economic renaissance in the region. Ocean Spray, the country's largest producer of cranberry-related products, relocated its headquarters to the neighboring Middleboro-Lakeville region. Moakley joined Governor Michael Dukakis and local officials in a traditional ground-breaking ceremony before a sign announcing "Future Headquarters of Ocean Spray."[21]

It would be the last time that Moakley could call on his good friend. O'Neill retired after thirty-four years in the House, ten as Speaker. He had been Ronald Reagan's great antagonist, successfully fending off his attacks on the New Deal's safety net, while losing as the president cut taxes for the rich (although he raised taxes eleven times), reduced social programs, spent lavishly on the military, and left huge budget deficits for future generations. The two men dominated the decade's political life and set the terms of debate, if not the tone, for all that followed. Beneath the battles over principle, the President Reagan and Speaker O'Neill, on ceremonial occasions at least, presented a picture of bonhomie, good humor, and mutual regard. Reagan participated in O'Neill's farewell ceremonies, declaring with unalloyed sincerity that he was proud to call him "friend."[22]

"A lot of times we would take credit for things in our district that we couldn't have gotten without the Speaker," Moakley told a reporter. "We will miss him." His Massachusetts colleagues echoed his sentiment. One of O'Neill's legacies was to leave a powerfully placed state delegation. Silvio Conte, Ed Boland, and Joe Early of Worcester served on the

Appropriations Committee; Brian Donnelly on Ways and Means; Studds on Foreign Affairs and Merchant Marine and Fisheries; Barney Frank on Banking; and Ed Markey on the Telecommunications Committee. As the new Congress opened in January 1987, Nicholas Mavroules of Peabody lost a bid for the chairmanship of the Armed Services Committee. "Nick would have had a better chance with O'Neill [still in office]," Moakley said. "There are a lot of chips he could pull in." The scramble to replace O'Neill went to Joe Kennedy, Robert's son. Nationally, the Reagan Revolution was running out of steam and the Democrats recaptured the Senate and increased their House majority. Jim Wright of Texas replaced O'Neill, continuing the "Austin-Boston" axis of Democratic House leadership.[23]

Tip O'Neill's retirement was overshadowed by the explosive scandal that began with the downing of the CIA resupply plane in Nicaragua. In Massachusetts even that news got lost in the epic defeat of the Red Sox in the 1986 World Series, when the home team lost despite having the New York Mets down to their last strike. As journalists pieced together the Central America story, a Lebanese newspaper reported that the United States was secretly selling arms to its enemy, Iran, to achieve the release of American hostages in Lebanon. Iran used the antitank weapons to turn the tide of battle in the Iran-Iraq War. The United States then used the illicit money to supply the Contra rebels against the elected Nicaraguan government. The country watched, aghast, as congressional hearings reveled a rogues' gallery of international arms dealers and shady businessmen-contractors who detailed the secret operation. At the conspiracy's center was the National Security Council's John Poindexter and his aide, Marine officer Oliver North.[24]

Moakley had always opposed aid to the Contras, as did the entire Massachusetts delegation. Despite the Boland amendments' ban on military aid, Reagan managed to wring small amounts of "humanitarian" aid to them from Congress. Moakley voted against those bills as well. "With all the scandal, we should have an accounting before we put any more money down there," he grumbled when Reagan came looking for $40 million in 1987. He voted to withhold the money.[25]

By 1988, El Salvador had faded from the news. Its civil war was overshadowed by the Iran-Contra scandal, the October 1987 stock market crash, and events in the USSR, where a new reform leader, Mikhail

Gorbachev, had succeeded the last aging Soviet oligarch. The Congress grudgingly allocated small amounts of military aid, hedged around with restrictions on its use. The military had already killed most of its enemies in San Salvador. Death squads and bombings had claimed nearly sixty thousand lives, but the resilient guerrillas still enjoyed the support of desperately poor peasants in the rural departments. However, President Duarte maintained the support of U.S. congressmen, who saw him as a thin reed of democracy against the military and the revolutionaries.[26]

Events in the Soviet Union changed Central America's destiny. Mikhail Gorbachev's policies of *glasnost* and *perestroika* ended the Soviet posture of hostility to the United States. He made Reagan's war policy in Central America seem anachronistic. Gorbachev reduced Soviet support to Cuba, which gave up on exporting revolution. He extricated the USSR from its war in Afghanistan, and yielded to the challenge from the Polish working class, whose Solidarity trade union demanded freedom, democracy, and workers' rights. Global tensions relaxed.

In this context, Moakley modified the El Salvador bill, now HR 618, for the new Congress. This time he included Nicaraguans in the EVD category. Barney Frank and Rules Committee chairman Claude Pepper of Florida suggested this change to Moakley. While at first glance the addition of Nicaraguans might seem to limit the bill's support by expanding the number of temporarily legal immigrants, it had the advantage of appealing to conservatives who had voted for Contra aid. How could they vote against a bill that protected refugees from the Sandinista regime?[27]

In reality, Nicaragua had held a more democratic election than El Salvador's in 1984. It imprisoned some opponents but never killed any. The only Nicaraguan civilians who had to flee for their lives ran from the Contras, who staged hit and run attacks on civilian targets in northern zones. In one case they murdered a gentle young American volunteer, Ben Linder, a civil engineer.[28] Granting EVD status to Nicaraguan refugees was therefore silly as a matter of international judgment, but for Moakley's purpose it helped the cause of the Salvadoran refugees to include the Nicaraguans, so he did.

Moakley held hearings on the measure in his own subcommittee during May and June. Salvadoran officials, including President Duarte, urged congressmen to pass the bill, but not for Moakley's reasons. Duarte even sent a letter to President Reagan, declaring that the immigrants to the United States were economic migrants, but that El Salvador would collapse without their remittances home. Moakley acknowledged this in his opening remarks but insisted that his motivations were different. Duarte's letter placed Moakley in the contradictory position of having a powerful ally on his side, but one whose motivations hindered the winning of their common goal.[29]

Immigration and Naturalization Service director Alan Nelson restated the administration's position on the Salvadoran refugees. He argued that there were forty wars raging in the world, all generating their refugee populations, and that the Moakley bill would open the door to all of them. Georgia congressman Patrick L. Swindall added that the El Salvador death squad toll was down to 251 in 1986, a huge decrease from the early 1980s. He cited a Congressional Budget Office cost estimate of $500,000 to $750,000 should the bill pass.[30] Moakley was unimpressed. He had heard it all before. "I am tired of the double talk, I am tired of the politics and I am tired of the games," he announced. "The bottom line on this issue is the protection of human life. And, quite frankly, it is unconscionable that this administration and this Congress have yet to offer protection to these refugees."[31]

Moakley introduced two compelling witnesses during these hearings. The first was David E. Evans, a Marine Corps Vietnam veteran, a volunteer for Medical Aid to El Salvador. He had lost both legs in Vietnam to a land mine. Evans came from Charlestown, West Virginia, where he fashioned prosthetics for veterans and coal miners. He first went to El Salvador in 1985 as a member of a Vietnam Veterans delegation led by Dr. Charles Clements. During the trip, they visited a veterans' hospital. Evans moved so comfortably on his artificial legs that the Salvadoran amputees didn't notice that he was an amputee. Sizing this up, Evans stuck his fingers in his mouth and whistled, drawing the attention of the wounded veterans. To their amazement, he plopped down on a bed, removed his prostheses to show his condition, reattached them, and dashed up the stairs, demonstrating to the wounded that they too might walk again. The Salvadoran soldiers cheered, whistled, laughed, and cried.[32]

"Joe Moakley called me and I flew up to Washington," Evans remembered. "To me, that was like a summons." The Vietnam Veterans' trip to El Salvador showed that the group was humanitarian, not partisan. They offered real help to wounded soldiers on both sides. "In El Salvador," Evans told the committee, "I am able to replace arms and legs, and finally be the Marine I should have been in 1970."[33] Evans's testimony about conditions there differed entirely from the picture painted by the Reagan administration.

The day after Evans appeared, his employer, the J. E. Hangar Company, fired him for taking an "unauthorized leave." Hangar was doing prosthetic work on a "one size fits all" basis, cutting corners on a government contract, and Evans had pointed that out as well. Moakley was ripping mad, but all he could do was dispatch a letter of protest to the Charleston, West Virginia newspaper. "When I was a young boy, my mother used to tell me to count to ten before venting my anger," he wrote. "I am through counting and ready to start writing," and proceeded to unload his fury.[34]

The other witness was Dr. Segundo Montes, a Spanish Jesuit, now a professor at the University of Central America (UCA) in San Salvador. Montes bore an imposing resume. He held degrees in theology, philosophy, and sociology. He had studied in Austria and Ecuador, acquired his doctorate at the University of Madrid, and written eight books. A photograph taken at the university showed a man of sober mien with a long face, close-cropped graying beard, aquiline nose, and widow's peak hairline, not unlike Cervantes's Don Quixote.

Montes's testimony showed that he was a careful scholar. He had conducted his own study of displaced people in El Salvador, and cited the work of an MIT doctoral candidate whose dissertation title directly addressed the issue before the committee, "Economic Migrants or Refugees from Violence?" Their studies of refugees in the United States and in rural El Salvador showed the mixed motivations of the displaced. In El Salvador, the repression went on. From September 1985 through August of 1986, 121 labor leaders had been detained, with many "disappeared." In the countryside, the UCA researchers found, thousands of young men fled conscription into the army. Among those who reached the United States, 47.12 percent of Salvadoran immigrants said that they had left for political reasons. They worked mostly as domestics, in restaurants, or as janitors. They sent home an average of $106 a month. So, did that make them economic or political immigrants? Clearly, both poverty and repression had caused them to flee, but, Montes concluded, "The Salvadoran situation was caused by war and violence."[35]

Moakley's hearings ran at the same time as the Iran-Contra hearings, which began in May and stretched into August, overshadowing the issue of El Salvador. With the administration reeling, Attorney General Ed Meese granted Nicaraguans a stay of deportation from the United States. This move was designed to make the Sandinistas look reprehensible. Moakley was not appeased. "The Reagan administration is playing politics with people's lives," he said. "To ignore any mention of El Salvador is to turn a cold and callous shoulder on refugees who have fled a violent civil war."[36]

The changed international situation and the addition of Nicaraguans to the bill produced a better result this time. The full House Judiciary Committee approved it 20–15 and moved it swiftly onto the floor. President Duarte personally lobbied wavering House members by telephone; Moakley read Duarte's appeal to his colleagues on the House floor. "The temporary safe haven is the single most important initiative the U.S. can now take to help my nation," Duarte said. He was dying of cancer, and he felt that his country's economic fate was at stake. In late July the bill passed the House by a large majority, 237–181, with 33 Republicans voting in favor.[37]

"This was not a squeaker vote," Moakley declared in reference to his two-vote margin in the previous session. DeConcini's version passed the Senate Judiciary Committee by a 9–3 vote, with Ted Kennedy urging strong support. Moakley sensed victory. "The bill makes no political statement. To a child pulled out of an American grade school and deported to his homeland only to have his leg blown off by a landmine, it is of small difference whose landmine it is."[38]

The debate would now move to the full Senate, where a representative of the national American Civil Liberties Union had testified before the Judiciary Committee in behalf of the bill. Wade J. Henderson, associate director of the ACLU, wrote to the *Boston Globe*, urging them to consider editorializing on its behalf. Henderson recapitulated the bill's history:

> A lot has changed in the last three years. As you know, several members of Congress have spoken eloquently about the plight of Central American refugees. Many members of the Massachusetts delegation were among the leadership of congressional efforts to protect these refugees more effectively. However, one member in particular stands out because of his unique commitment and perseverance

with the issue. The fact that he's from South Boston only adds to the rather strange mix of considerations. Rep. Joe Moakley is a most unlikely hero on human rights measures in Central America.[39]

Meanwhile, with Tip O'Neill gone from the scene, a surprising figure emerged as the face of Massachusetts on the national stage. This was its governor, Michael Dukakis, a hard-working, fiscally prudent technocrat with little charisma. Dukakis was Greek-American, had grown up in Brookline, and as governor he rode the Green Line to the State House, the symbolic opposite of Reagan's limousines. He was a pragmatist with no particular vision, socially liberal but determined to balance the nation's budget, which was awash with red ink after eight years of voodoo economics. He had no close allies among the predominantly Irish politicians or labor leaders in the state. Nobody gave him the proverbial snowball's chance in hell of winning the nomination in a large field. Colorado senator Gary Hart enjoyed much better national recognition, and had a more vibrant physical presence. Ideologically there was not much to choose between them.

Dukakis worked hard. On Saint Patrick's Day, 1987, he walked the whole six miles of the South Boston parade, and the crowd cheered on the hometown, soon-to-announce candidate with surprising enthusiasm. At the annual corned beef and cabbage joke fest traditionally hosted by the South Boston state senator, Dukakis gamely presented Senate president Billy Bulger with a case of "Dukakis Draft Beer." This was another sign that the city had healed; Dukakis, an integrationist, might have been driven out of the neighborhood during the bad old days.

Moakley was an early skeptic but eventually came around. "Hart certainly is the front runner right now, but he's like a band leader with nobody behind him. . . . I realize now [that Dukakis's] chances are as good as anyone else's. He's a bright guy and a representative of the industrial state with the lowest unemployment average." Not exactly a ringing endorsement, but probably typical of the sentiments of the state's political leadership, all of whom would be happy to have a Bay Stater in the White House.[40]

Then the Hart campaign imploded in an instant in May, when the senator was discovered to be having an extramarital affair and dropped out of the race as the nation, still reeling from the Iran-Contra scandal, watched, bewildered that anyone so smart could be so stupid. The feminist revolution had changed gender relations in the United States, but Hart seemed to think he was still living in the days of Jack Kennedy and Marilyn Monroe. Steady Mike Dukakis plugged away against remaining rivals Jesse Jackson and Jerry Brown, reminding detractors that a campaign was a marathon, not a sprint, and headed toward the Atlanta convention a sure winner.

The 1988 campaign revealed changes internally within the Democratic Party that left old sailor Joe Moakley a little at sea. His anchor had been Tip O'Neill, now out of service. The party establishment had been pitched overboard during the reforms of the 1970s, only partially restored later with the creation of "super delegates" at the convention, a category reserved for elected congressmen, governors, and DNC members, giving them 15 percent of the vote. Labor played less of a role in the party now, as did big city machines. The major candidates—Dukakis, Hart, Jackson, and Brown—reflected a party whose base now consisted of suburban liberals, African Americans, Hispanics, women, and the young. Even George McGovern was shoved aside. Dukakis gave a speech to the Atlantic Council, assuring them he was "not another George McGovern." Someone in Moakley's office, perhaps the Dakotan's namesake, scrawled on the news clipping, "The Dukakis people should lay off McGovern."[41]

Moakley missed O'Neill, not just personally, but the world they had both inhabited, in which politicians met their constituents face to face and in which individual loyalties fostered power. "If you needed a bridge built here, Tip's clout got it," he told a reporter the year after O'Neill retired. "It's like a manager closing a sale at an auto dealership."[42] Moakley appeared content with his own career a month later: "Well, at one time everybody would like to be Speaker," he reflected. "In every corporal's knapsack is a major's baton." However, Moakley declined to contend for a leadership position, now occupied by Speaker Wright, Majority Leader Tom Foley of Washington, and Whip Tony Coelho of California. As Dukakis wrapped up the nomination, Moakley sounded an ambivalent note to a reporter. "He'd make a great president. I just don't like the word admire. I would say I would be an O'Neill admirer."[43]

Moakley worried that voters might reject Dukakis because of his limited military and foreign affairs experience. He hoped that the governor would choose Senator John Glenn of Ohio, the former astronaut-hero, or Sam Nunn of Georgia, a defense expert, as running mate, and later touted fellow congressman Lee Hamilton of Indiana. He was surprised at Dukakis's choice of Texas senator Lloyd Bentsen, a former Treasury secretary. "I guess it shows you don't have to love a guy to have him as vice president. Jack Kennedy showed that," Moakley mused. For many older Massachusetts convention delegates, the comparison was natural, and reminded them of their youth, when Kennedy had selected Lyndon Johnson as running mate, another Massachusetts-Texas ticket.[44]

★ ★ ★

Moakley expanded his concerns regarding Central America during the presidential election year. In El Salvador, the war remained deadlocked. With the war stalemated and their adversary Duarte in office, El Salvador's death squads set out to kill labor leaders. By law, the U.S. trade representative was supposed to monitor labor relations in nations, such as El Salvador, enjoying special status; Reagan's appointee turned a blind eye. Moakley got fifty-five colleagues to demand an administrative review of these murders, but Reagan ignored their remonstrance.[45] He protested a spiteful action by the Reagan administration when it blocked the importation of Nicaraguan coffee processed in third countries.[46]

As the presidential election moved into its final lap, Reagan's war against the Sandinistas went down to defeat. Costa Rican president Oscar Arias revived the peace process that Reagan had sabotaged. Nicaraguan president Daniel Ortega encouraged Speaker Jim Wright to participate in the final negotiations. Most of the Contras were giving up, although a rump group pressed on with hit and run attacks against civilian targets. Wright derided the CIA's pouring money into Nicaragua's opposition parties, and Newt Gingrich vowed to destroy Wright for his peace efforts; later he would do it. Now he carried a fake machine gun onto the House floor and accused Wright of handing it to America's enemies: the implication was that Wright had committed treason by working for peace.[47]

Meanwhile, the Moakley-DeConcini bill languished in the Senate, even with a Democratic majority. The 1986 Simpson-Mazzoli bill had not provided enough visas for Irish and other European temporary workers. Moakley joined his fellow Irish-American Massachusetts colleagues Brian Donnelly and Ed Boland in successfully promoting a bill that added ten thousand visas for northern Europeans. Ted Kennedy partnered with

Simpson to win an 88–4 vote for the bill in the Senate. Reagan, who promised to veto the El Salvador bill, indicated he would sign the bill for the Irish.[48]

While Alan Simpson had promised not to oppose the El Salvador bill, Majority Leader Robert Byrd of West Virginia became an obstacle this time. Byrd was reluctant to oppose a president on foreign policy. The final session of the 100th Congress was scheduled to adjourn October 7 before resuming as a postelection lame duck, and in mid-September Byrd had not scheduled the El Salvador bill for a vote. Moakley told a Jamaica Plain delegation that he still hoped Byrd would schedule a vote.[49] Byrd did nothing. Moakley had little leverage with him. The Senate, Moakley complained, "virtually ignored" the issue, showing a complete "lack of will." He still wasn't giving up. "The Salvadorans and Nicaraguans who fled the wars in their homelands deserve and are entitled to protection. And I will be back next Congress to fight for them."[50]

Moakley was angry, especially at Reagan as his second term closed, with the scandal of the Iran-Contra affair lingering in the atmosphere. "It was our bombs, our guns and our mines that made these people refugees," he told *Boston Herald* reporter Tom Squitieri. "We should be responsible for their safety . . . The White House is playing a cynical and duplicitous game with the lives of the refugees, valuing human life only if it fits into its geopolitical plans . . . I find it particularly disheartening that President Duarte's unusual and compelling appeal was virtually ignored." Moakley left no doubt that his fighting spirit was up on this issue; Squitieri noted that "Moakley is angry and ready to step out of the shadows and knock some heads together."[51]

Nor could Moakley's mood have been lightened by the results of the presidential election. Dukakis, who had portrayed himself as a centrist and declined to be identified as a liberal, lost the election by 54 to 46 percent to George H. W. Bush, who promised a "kinder, gentler" brand of conservatism whose differences from Reagan's free market variety were never identified. In Massachusetts, all the incumbents won, and Richard Neal, the former mayor of Springfield, replaced the retiring Ed Boland. Moakley ran unopposed.

There was some negative fallout inside the state congressional delegation afterward. Chester Atkins in the 5th District, Joe Kennedy, and Connecticut's Bruce Morrison all contended for a seat on the powerful

Appropriations Committee. Committee assignments typically first went through regional party caucuses, which made a recommendation to the Democratic Steering and Policy Committee. Atkins was personally friendly with Moakley, who became dean of the state delegation upon Boland's retirement. A personnel decision that might have been resolved by a smoke-filled room compromise went to a vote in the regional delegation. The winner needed a majority. Kennedy won the first round 8–6–3, one vote short, but lost on the second round when Morrison withdrew. What should have been a gentlemanly contest among friends turned bitter. Moakley publicly rued the absence of O'Neill, who, he allowed, would have decided the matter behind closed doors and saved the other congressmen from a difficult vote. The incident further suggests tension between Moakley and Ted Kennedy, who lobbied behind the scenes for his nephew, the junior man among the three. The whole episode, an inside the Beltway brouhaha, probably raised Moakley's old feelings, going back to the 1962 Ted Kennedy–Eddie McCormack primary, that the unwritten rules of climbing the ladder through seniority did not apply to the high-born.[52]

★ ★ ★

Later in his career, Moakley would burnish his credentials as a "regular Joe" by remarking that before he got involved with the El Salvador issue, his idea of foreign affairs was to go to East Boston to get an Italian sub. The remark had ironic overtones on several levels. He was ethnically just as Italian as he was Irish, a fact to which he rarely referred. He had already traveled to Israel, Egypt, Ireland, Yugoslavia, Portugal, Morocco, China, Singapore, and Hong Kong. And East Boston was changing too in the 1980s. The old Italians were dying off, or moving out to Everett, Revere, or Saugus, and new immigrants were moving in. By 1990, about twenty-five thousand Salvadorans lived in Boston—most of them near Logan Airport in East Boston. It was harder to get an Italian sub there now, but easier to get a "papusa," El Salvador's version of the same dish.

10

★ ★ ★ ★ ★

The Jesuit Murders

Joe Moakley greeted the new Bush administration warily. "I don't think we can afford a honeymoon," Moakley told a reporter. "Bush comes into office as a former congressman who knows the Hill, who didn't run against Congress . . . We're not going to beat him to death, but face [the problems] with hands joined," he promised. Bush faced skeptical Democratic majorities in both houses. George Mitchell of Maine replaced Byrd as majority leader in the Senate; in the House Jim Wright, Tom Foley of Washington, and Tony Coelho of California occupied the leadership positions. Later in 1989, *RollCall*, the congressional newspaper, assessed the Massachusetts delegation as the seventh most powerful, and the Americans for Democratic Action scored it the most liberal. Moakley showed up ready to work, announcing that his priorities in the new session would be to increase protection for the handicapped, safeguard Social Security, continue his campaign on fire-safe cigarettes, and achieve Temporary Protective Status (TPS), a variant of the extended voluntary departure protection, for Salvadoran immigrants.[1]

There was real hope for the latter issue this time. Despite the new international climate, the war in El Salvador wouldn't go away. In January, Moakley called on Bush to solve the problem with a stroke of his attorney general's pen. "There are at least half a million Salvadoran people living in this country who are afraid to go back to their homeland because they know they will be incarcerated, beaten or even killed," he told Central America activists at the venerable Cambridge Old Baptist Church, headquarters for a dozen leftist organizations clustered in its basement. "There is support from the Bush administration and I will meet with Attorney General Richard Thornburgh to appeal the matter directly to him." Moakley told the audience that Jim McGovern had just returned from El Salvador and had found it "a place where fear is running through every mind. It is a country that could explode at any moment."[2]

Moakley added Chinese immigrants to Nicaraguans and Salvadorans in the new version of the bill, HR 45. In the spring of 1989, Gorbachev's campaign for *glasnost* and *perestroika* found an echo among Chinese youth, who gathered in the capital's Tiananmen Square. The world watched in horror as Chinese troops mowed down the protestors. Moakley filed the new bill before that final confrontation, but what conservative could vote against granting Chinese students in the United States Temporary Protective Status? "HR 45 is supported by the government of El Salvador, leaders of the Nicaraguan and Chinese exile communities, and hundreds of religious, civil rights, ethnic, voluntary, labor and local government groups nationwide," Moakley's talking points emphasized.[3]

Unhappily, there was trouble in the House as Moakley pushed for the refugee bill. In December 1987, Gingrich brought charges against Wright for financial improprieties regarding a book he had published. The Ethics Committee investigated and found that Wright's aides had connived with lobbyists to arrange bulk book sales, thus violating House rules, and that he had improperly received $140,000 in gifts from a Fort Worth businessman. Democrats liked Jim Wright, and those on the Ethics Committee faced a tough vote. "It's a very difficult situation," Moakley said, regarding those committee members. However, he added, "I just think that Jim Wright has got a decent defense to a lot of those charges."[4]

Moakley hoped that lawmakers could reach a compromise in the Wright case, but acknowledged that "we're living in the worst type of political climate that I've seen in Congress." Wright stepped down in June. That was the last of the "Austin-Boston Connection" that had dominated the Speakership since the time of the New Deal, from John Nance Garner to Wright. The overthrow of Wright destabilized the New Deal coalition and hastened the flight of white Southern Democrats to the Republican camp. Gingrich's victory taught him that aggressive partisan tactics worked.[5]

Gingrich made personal vilification the new normal. Majority Leader Tom Foley, a lugubrious-looking man with a basset hound's countenance, ascended to the Speakership, and Richard Gephardt took Foley's place as majority leader. Republican operative Lee Atwater immediately generated rumors that Foley was gay. The Republicans compared Foley's votes with Barney Frank's, suggesting that there was some hidden "gay agenda." In 1989 most gay congressmen preferred to keep their sexual preferences private. Foley wouldn't dignify the rumors with a response, and the feisty Frank threatened to name closeted gay Republican colleagues if the Republicans didn't drop the issue. They did, and President Bush privately rebuked Atwater.[6]

By coincidence, Claude Pepper, the eighty-eight-year-old chairman of the Rules Committee and the oldest sitting congressman, died in the midst of the Wright affair. Moakley was next in line for the chairmanship; that position was determined by seniority. "I just saw him at the hospital last Thursday," Moakley said. "He was in great shape; very much alive. I told him we are keeping the seat warm for him on the Rules Committee. He said, 'I'll be back Tuesday.' We all expected this, but when it happens, it really hits you between the eyes." Pepper had been Moakley's mentor on the intricacies of the Rules Committee. The Miami congressman had made elderly affairs his life's work, and Moakley had brought him to South Boston to visit senior residences a few times. Moakley said that "he had the heart of a giant—a heart that felt the pain of a world where children go to sleep hungry and where the old die alone." That was the kind of congressman Moakley aspired to be.[7]

Foley and Moakley thus rose in authority together at the beginning of June 1989. Both were viewed as being fair-minded builders of consensus. "I plan to run it [the Rules Committee] in the same style and mood as Senator Pepper—to be fair to everyone." First up for the Rules Committee would be a bailout bill for the Savings and Loan industry, whose reckless lending practices had produced a real estate bubble that burst. The House approved it by a huge margin later in the month.[8]

Meanwhile there had been important developments in both Nicaragua and El Salvador. Chairman Gorbachev's cutting of aid to Nicaragua, and the growing storm of protest in Poland and East Germany against Soviet rule, now made "communism" seem less threatening. The Bush administration agreed to send only nonlethal aid to the Contras in Nicaragua. The Sandinistas, battered by a decade of war, agreed to move up the date of national elections to February 1990. Contra violence would reappear sporadically, but the war was clearly in its final phase. In El Salvador, ARENA candidate Alfredo Cristiani defeated Christian Democrat Jose Napoleon Duarte in the March 1989 elections as the Salvadoran economy contracted. Cristiani represented El Salvador's business class, and he had no association with death squads. Leftist candidates ran this time, atrocities declined, and the U.S. Congress voted an additional $90 million in military aid, with no conditions.[9]

Thus it was an improvement in the Central American atmosphere that framed Moakley's management of the debate on Salvadoran, Nicaraguan, and Chinese refugee status on October 25. Moakley proposed a closed rule that precluded amendment, so that countries could not be deleted or added to the "Central America Studies and Temporary Relief Act of 1989." Despite Republican objections, the rule passed by a big margin.

Moakley opened the debate himself. "Mr. Speaker, seven years ago, I met with a group of Salvadoran refugees in Boston. That meeting, in large part, resulted in my introducing legislation to offer them temporary safe haven. Their testimony . . . [has] weighed heavily on my conscience." This was a touch of blarney, but effective for dramatic purposes. He then adduced the list of strange bedfellows who backed the combined legislation: El Salvador's Archbishop Rivera y Damas, President Cristiani and his opponent Duarte, Nicaragua's Contra leader Adolfo Calero and anti-Sandinista presidential candidate Violetta Chamorro, a Chinese student leader, and Holocaust survivor Elie Wiesel. This list could mollify wavering conservatives.

Moakley's colleagues addressed Republican objections. Bruce Morrison noted that many people felt some degree of sympathy for these immigrants, all of whom were in the country illegally but who had all arrived under duress. The new legislation would remove them from their shadow life and bring them into the sunlight—temporarily. Bill Richardson of New Mexico, a prominent Hispanic member, argued that the bill provided some standard way of classifying which country's immigrants qualified for TPS in a currently haphazard system. Barney Frank granted that the United States could not admit immigrants from every repressive regime but postulated that in cases in which American action had precipitated the immigration, "the compassionate thing for us to do is to welcome these people for an indefinite period."

It would be simplistic to conclude that congressional Republicans did not have legitimate concerns. Moakley rose throughout the debate, answering objections by mentioning endorsements from individuals or groups that assuaged Republican concerns: big city mayors prepared to bear the burden of accepting the newcomers, labor leaders who no longer worried about losing jobs, humanitarian activists pressing the moral obligation. He delivered an eloquent summary, praising the level of the debate yet appealing for his opponents to reconsider: "To those of you who argue that this bill will simply create illegal or uncontrolled migration—I say you've got your facts backwards. It is war and oppression which creates exiles and refugees—not this bill. And I hope that we can work together to help resolve the root causes of flight." Moakley knew he had the votes. Some version of it had passed in two previous sessions, and this time he won 258–162–13 on the final tally. He would still have to sweat out a fight in the Senate and a conference committee if he won. But he could not have known on October 25, 1989, the day that the Moakley bill passed, that his involvement with El Salvador was only just beginning.[10]

★ ★ ★

The very next week Moakley received an award from the Central America Refugee Center for his service. Honored along with him was Segundo Montes, the Spanish Jesuit at the University of Central America who had testified at Moakley's hearings two years previously. Things were not going so well in El Salvador, Montes told him. With a weak economy, the trade unions mounted demonstrations for the first time in many years. The night before the award ceremony, the union headquarters was bombed. And the Jesuits were getting death threats.[11]

Meanwhile the world watched the incredible spectacle of the collapse of communism. A new chapter in world history was beginning. Poland held a free election and the communists lost, elevating Lech Walesa's Solidarity Union to power. A similar process unfolded in Hungary, and then the Hungarians opened their border with East Germany, inspiring a flood of migrants. In late October, Gorbachev announced that the USSR would no longer intervene in Eastern European affairs. On November 9, jubilant throngs took sledgehammers to the Berlin Wall. Over the following months, the communist tyrannies in Eastern Europe dissolved. "All that is solid melts into air," Marx had written in the Communist Manifesto, but this was not what he had expected.[12]

Two days after the historic destruction of the Berlin Wall, FMLN guerrillas in El Salvador launched what they hoped was a "final offensive." Only a fraction of these rebels were communists, and even they were not fighting to replicate a Russian-style regime in the Americas. They took the Salvadoran military by surprise, capping two years of planning with a well-coordinated attack that gave them control of the poor neighborhoods in the eastern part of the capital, San Salvador, and penetrated the wealthy neighborhood of Escalon. There they captured the Sheraton Hotel, which housed Green Beret military trainers. The Salvadoran Army counterattacked, surrounding the hotel, and President Bush mobilized a Delta Force rescue team to evacuate the trapped soldiers. A backdoor negotiation resolved the deadlock; the Americans went free and the guerrillas escaped the cordon disguised as pajama-clad guests. The offensive shook the high command to its core. They rocketed and strafed the poor districts, killing innocent civilians. Meanwhile, they met around the clock at military headquarters.

The guerrillas gambled that their supporters in the city would rise up. They sensed the end of their international support, with the cut-off of Soviet aid to Nicaragua. It was now or never; even if they had to retreat, they would at least force the military to negotiate.[13]

The high command responded by raiding every religious, labor, and humanitarian organization and targeting the Jesuit-run University of Central America in the southern sector of the city. On Monday night, November 13, Father Ignacio Ellacuria, the philosopher-theologian editor of the magazine *Estudios CentroAmericanos*, returned from a European journey to what was now a war zone. Tanks patrolled the Jardines de Guadelupe neighborhood outside the campus. Half an hour after Ellacuria's return, an army detachment searched the campus thoroughly. Meanwhile, radio broadcasts on the government-controlled media denounced the Jesuits as traitors. Ellacuria, Montes, and their colleagues were the most prominent nonpartisan advocates of a negotiated settlement to the war. They had international contacts in the Jesuit, Catholic, wider Christian, academic, media, political, and diplomatic communities. Ellacuria reassured his colleagues that, with the army having found no weapons, they were safe, despite the death threats.[14]

★ ★ ★

At dawn three days later the gardener, Obdulio Ramos, discovered the corpses of Ellacuria, Montes, and their colleagues Ignacio Martin Baro and Amando Lopez. Following a trail of blood, Ramos peered into a small room where his wife, Elba, and fifteen-year-old daughter, Celina, slept. They lay in each other's arms, their bodies covered in blood and his wife's brains splattered against the wall. Nearby were the bodies of Fathers Juan Ramon Moreno and the seventy-one-year-old Joaquin Lopez y Lopez. Ramos ran and told the rector, Miguel Francisco Estrada. Estrada found Father Jose Maria "Chema" Tojeira, provincial of all Central America's Jesuits, who was shaving, and told him what had happened. The surviving Jesuits, clad in their nightclothes, covered the bodies of their friends and prayed together. Catholic leaders, including Archbishop Rivera y Damas, military intelligence, and the media hurried to the campus. The story broke on the morning news.[15]

Jim McGovern was awakened by an early phone call. It was Sylvia Rosales, a human rights worker for CARACEN, a Salvadoran group. "They killed them! They killed them all!" she sobbed into the phone.

"Who?" McGovern asked. "Who killed who?" A few minutes later McGovern called Moakley. He was stunned, and angry.[16]

The American embassy staff got the news at its morning meeting. Ambassador William Walker, a veteran diplomat in his mid-fifties with reddish-blond hair and mustache, denounced the crime in the strongest possible terms to reporters, calling it "a barbarous act that has not only brought shame to El Salvador, but will leave a gaping hole in this country's intellectual and academic communities."[17] Walker was a professional with experience in the region, but he was viewed suspiciously by liberal opponents of Reagan's Central America policy.[18] Coincidentally, Walker bore the same name as the most reviled gringo in Central American history, a proslavery Mississippian who in the 1850s had led a band of mercenaries to Nicaragua, briefly declared himself president, and later was captured and executed.

President Bush, speaking at a rally for a Republican candidate in Chicago a few days later, was interrupted by hecklers who demanded to know why the United States was killing priests in El Salvador. Flustered by the angry interruption, the president denied the charge, praised Salvadoran president Alfredo Cristiani, and mocked the protestors as security guards escorted them out. "Look at this guy!" he sneered at one of them. There was no hint of remorse in the president's remarks regarding the murdered priests.[19]

The Salvadoran military reported on its radio station that the perpetrators may have been the FMLN, motivated by their opposition to Christianity. A spray painted sign on the campus gate claimed FMLN responsibility. Bullet casings at the scene of the crime showed that a Russian-made AK-47 was used to kill the priests, a weapon used only by the guerrillas, not by the American-armed military. "Whoever did this," Ambassador Walker declared, "was doing the work of the FMLN." Salvadoran president Alfredo Cristiani immediately met with three Catholic leaders, Tojeira, Rivera y Damas, and Bishop Gregorio Rosa Chavez. He assured them that the military had nothing to do with the murders and that an inquiry by the Special Investigations Unit would get to the bottom of it.[20]

The Jesuits already knew otherwise. There had been a witness, unknown to the military, a janitor named Lucia Cerna, who slept in a room just south of the college grounds. She had seen much of the entire operation from her window, including the murder of some of the victims. It was conducted by men in camouflage uniforms. She heard the trucks coming and going, and the rifle fire. She immediately told Father Tojeira, who arranged for her to testify before the country's attorney general and the investigating judge, and then to be flown to safety in Miami immediately afterward with her husband and child. To the dismay of Cerna and her Jesuit protectors, she was subjected to an interrogation in Miami by FBI agents and the head of El Salvador's Special Investigations Unit (SIU), a part of the army. Fearing that she would be deported and killed, she panicked, changed her story, and failed a lie detector test. The episode inflamed the already hostile relationship between the Jesuit order and U.S. authorities.[21]

Congressional opposition to U.S. policy flared up as well. A Senate subcommittee chaired by Chris Dodd opened hearings on November 17, during which Senator Patrick Leahy questioned what all the military aid over the past decade had bought. Even the State Department's secretary for Latin American Affairs, Bernard Aronson, a former Democrat, declared, "My gut tells me they were killed by the right." Congressman Ron Dellums of Oakland, California, a former Marine and strong antiwar voice, introduced a bill calling for a complete end to military aid. That didn't pass, but on November 20 the House did pass a resolution denouncing the killings. The Senate followed suit the next day.[22]

The global human rights community sprang into action, with the Lawyers Committee for Human Rights leading the way. They had represented the families of the American churchwomen slain in El Salvador in December 1980. Chaired by Michael Posner, the group included on its staff Martha Doggett, whose office in El Salvador was in touch with the Catholic Church's human rights monitoring office, Tutela Legal. They wrote to Secretary of State Baker, conveying information gleaned by Doggett that implicated the military and strongly suggesting that the government of El Salvador was going to cover it up.[23]

The Bush administration had a major public relations disaster on its hands. Ambassador Walker, operating in an atmosphere of swirling rumors, began echoing the Salvadoran military's line, hinting that the FMLN was responsible. He downplayed the murders, suggesting that they were similar to the U.S. internment of Japanese-Americans after Pearl Harbor, an understandable over-reaction to an enemy's provocation.

The new Speaker of the House, Tom Foley, convened a meeting of the Democratic caucus. Gerry Studds, among the most vociferous opponents of U.S. military aid to El Salvador, proposed the formation of a Speaker's Task Force on El Salvador whose job it would be to monitor the investigation of the Jesuit murders and report on the human rights climate in the country and the progress of peace negotiations. On December 6, Foley named nineteen Democrats to the body, including long-time Reagan critics such as David Bonior and Studds, and moderates such as David McCurdy of Oklahoma. At Studds's urging, the chair of the new committee was to be John Joseph Moakley of South Boston.[24]

Years later, Moakley told filmmaker Esther Cassidy that when Foley called, "I said, Mr. Speaker, if you put an ad on the bulletin board looking for people to serve on the committee, 434 out of 435 would sign up, and my name wouldn't be on it."[25] He would repeat this story again and again, along with the self-effacing line that his idea of foreign affairs was to go to East Boston to get an Italian sandwich. Moakley doubted his ability to lead such a delegation. Foley warned him that the whole enterprise would be like walking through a minefield; even the Democratic caucus was split on aid to El Salvador. Yet Moakley had been working on this issue for years. A month earlier he had given the emotional appeal on the House floor to protect the immigrants from deportation. He had seen Montes two weeks before his murder. Moakley wanted the job, and he had suspected a cover-up from day one. His only hesitation was whether or not he had enough foreign policy experience to lead the group.[26]

Studds and Foley made the perfect choice. Moakley had been Tip O'Neill's friend and was widely respected among the House leftists and moderates on El Salvador. Moakley's religious affiliation would naturally connect him to the wider American Catholic community, and to the Jesuits in El Salvador. Catholics also constituted the largest denomination in the House and even for the fervent anticommunists among them killing six priests and two women would be inexcusable.

Moakley wrote to Salvadoran president Alfredo Cristiani a week later, informing him of the appointment of the Task Force and praising him for his public declaration that he would see that justice was done. He kept El Salvador's ambassador in the loop as well.[27] Throughout the Task Force's investigation Moakley always assured Cristiani and Walker of his support for their efforts. He knew that they would have to work together, but that their political agendas would necessarily diverge. Their job was to win the war against the guerrillas, a task that was not necessarily advanced by solving the crime. Moakley's job—to monitor the Salvadoran investigation—might result in El Salvador losing its military aid.

Moakley's committee heard from Lucia Cerna a week before Christmas, this time accompanied by an experienced attorney. Moakley asked her about the traumatic events of November 16. While she couldn't be sure that the men doing the killing were army soldiers, the congressmen could have little doubt. They already knew that the whole area had been cordoned off by the military. The campus was near to military headquarters and the military academy. The army maintained a strict 6:00 p.m. curfew. But why had she told the FBI and Salvadoran SIU a different story in Miami? Congressman Pete McCloskey pressed her. Cerna replied that when she asked her interrogators if she would be returned to El Salvador, they had answered that "it depends on your declarations."[28] A janitor had little to gain by inventing a story that damned the Salvadoran military.

Moakley's behind the scenes work in December played out against the backdrop of another gathering storm. President Bush was preparing to invade Panama, for reasons that seemed obscure to the public. Panama was governed by a bouncy thug with a pock-marked face, Manuel Noriega, who had come into power following the mysterious plane crash of his predecessor, Omar Torrijos. Noriega had been on the CIA's payroll for many years, and he enhanced his personal profits by smuggling drugs and weapons to the Contras based in Costa Rica. Noriega at first agreed to allow the United States to keep bases that were supposed to revert to Panama in 2001 under the terms of the Carter-Torrijos Treaty. When he later refused to do this, the CIA backed his pro-American opponents, and Noriega called off an election that they seemed likely to win. The United States then staged a series of minor provocations and swooped in with overwhelming force on December 20. Americans never saw the devastation wreaked on Panama, and they thrilled to the narrative that portrayed the heroic President Bush rescuing innocent civilians from an evil dictator. Bush's popularity soared. This drama dominated the news for the next month. El Salvador and its murdered priests were forgotten.[29]

As the Panama invasion began, Moakley and McGovern met with a mysterious exile in Washington who was to become their guide through the Salvadoran thicket. Rick Swartz of the National Immigration Forum arranged a meeting of the three men at his house. The Salvadoran was Leonel Gomez, then forty-nine. He had been the Central American motorcycle racing champion and a sharpshooter on the El Salvador national rifle team. He came from Santa Ana, the country's second largest city, in a coffee growing center. Gomez had gotten involved with the land reform movement in the 1970s, supporting an agricultural cooperative endeavor of small businessmen-farmers. Gomez worked with Rodolfo Viera, who became head of the Institute for Agrarian Reform; Viera was the man assassinated with the two American labor advisors in 1980. Gomez himself had survived several assassination attempts, and Viera's death won him political asylum in the United States. "Walker helped save Gomez's life," McGovern recalled. "They respected each other."[30]

Gomez was blunt-spoken and skeptical about whether Moakley meant business or whether this was to be another fake attempt to cover Washington's ass. "I want to smell you to see if this fucking thing is going to be any different," Gomez said. Every sentence Gomez spoke had a swear word, which suited Moakley just fine. "We couldn't have done this without Leonel," McGovern later said.

Gomez had contacts at various points on the political compass. He claimed Ambassador Walker as a friend. Walker quietly put out the word in El Salvador that nothing should happen to Gomez, or the consequences would be big. In Washington, Gomez introduced Moakley and McGovern to a former death squad killer. On McGovern's first trip for the Task Force to El Salvador, Gomez arranged a meeting with Roberto

D'Aubuisson, who was rumored—maybe by the CIA, to take the heat off the military—to be the mastermind behind the Jesuit assassinations. D'Aubuisson could honestly say that he had nothing to do with this one. Gomez had contacts among the FMLN too. "We called him El Gordo," Ferman Cienfuegos, leader of the Resistencia Nacional group, recalled affectionately of the rotund Gomez. He didn't have to be told to stay under the radar.[31]

Meanwhile, the U.S. embassy and State Department shifted into denial mode, with Walker telling Moakley and his staff on January 2 that the military was not involved. "[A]nybody can get army uniforms," Walker reminded them, retailing the army's theory about the case.[32] The good publicity from the Panama invasion may have strengthened their sense that Salvadoran military involvement could not be proven. "The State Department came in with maps, charts, props," McGovern told filmmaker Esther Cassidy. "Their bottom line: the rebels killed the priests. . . . It was damage control, damage control."[33]

Then in mid-January came a major break in the case. President Cristiani revealed that "some elements of the armed forces" were behind the killings. Moakley told the *New York Times* that he was "very happy about the announcement," and that Cristiani "knows that Congress is serious about reviewing American aid if these killings are not solved, with the right people indicted and sentenced." While praising Cristiani, Moakley added that "the responsibility goes extremely high."[34]

McGovern heard the news as he boarded a plane for El Salvador to plan the delegation's visit. A few days later indictments were delivered against nine soldiers, including a colonel, Guillermo Alfredo Benavides Morales, and three lieutenants. Although the Salvadoran Special Investigations Unit and attorney general's office were investigating the murders, the names of the accused were chosen and announced by a military honor commission. This obvious usurpation of the function of the judicial system by the military showed the farcical nature of the proceedings from the start. The likelihood is that the military leaders had promised to take care of the defendants' families, and secure an innocent verdict or a light sentence for them in exchange for their silence.

American military advisor Major Eric Buckland provided the crucial information. His Salvadoran colleague Carlos Aviles told him that he knew who had done it. Aviles told Buckland that Colonel Benavides, the head of the military academy, had confessed to Manuel Rivas of the SIU; that Rivas was not sure if he was allowed to indict an officer, because no officer had ever been indicted during the last decade of mass murder; and that this story had leaked to him, Aviles, through another party. Buckland then had a nervous breakdown. He was unsure where his loyalties lay. Aviles was his friend; if Buckland told his American superiors, Aviles might get killed. Moreover, Buckland had absorbed the ethos of the military high command, which was that the priests were traitors who deserved to die. Finally, on January 2, Buckland confessed what he knew to his superior. It was the same day that Walker was in Washington, telling Moakley's staff that the military probably had nothing to do with it.[35]

Meanwhile, Moakley's committee had been doing its own digging in closed door hearings. One of those testifying was Frank Smyth, a journalist who had been in El Salvador since February 1988. He painted a stark picture of a nation whose political center had collapsed and whose president was marginalized. The country was really being run by Air Force general Juan Rafael Bustillo and Vice Minister of Defense Juan Orlando Zepeda. Cristiani's friends were fleeing the country or moving their money offshore. Bustillo and Zepeda were old associates of D'Aubuisson. They knew that the November offensive strengthened the hand of Cristiani's wing of ARENA, which was contemplating negotiations with the rebels. The priests were the most prominent advocates of negotiation, and the military sent a message by killing them. In this scenario, Colonel Benavides was a risk-averse officer who had always deferred to the leader of his military class, or *tanda*, a Colonel Rene Emilio Ponce. Benavides was a mid-level fall guy, not the instigator of the plot.[36]

Moakley suspected the higher-ups almost immediately. On January 27 he gave a speech to a closed door meeting of Boston's Clover Club, an Irish-American version of a Brahmin gentleman's club, at a downtown hotel. Moakley lit into the Salvadoran government in his trademark straight-shooting style, speaking from the heart. He told how he had decided to take the assignment: "I was shocked into it. And you should be shocked as well." He described the brutality of the murders, and his own acquaintance with some of the victims, and his certainty that the church was a target. "El Salvador's Attorney General, Mauricio Eduardo Colorado . . . wrote a letter to Pope John Paul II asking for the removal of priests who promote 'the questionable ideology of the church of the poor.' That's what my priest does," Moakley told them. Moakley reassured his audience that he condemned the guerrilla offensive, recognized that they had committed atrocities as well, and was not picking sides in Salvadoran politics. But, he added, "Our embassy people characterize church figures as subversives . . . Such careless words get people killed." He again praised Cristiani for the detention of the suspects but warned that "this is not the final curtain—it's only the first act . . . Those who ordered or otherwise consented to the crime must also be brought to justice." His stirring conclusion left no doubt about his intentions: "My friends, let us not allow these fallen Jesuits to have died in vain."[37]

The U.S. Congress was not the only concerned body monitoring the investigation. The Jesuit Order, and especially the U.S. section of it, was determined to see the true perpetrators brought to justice. The American Jesuits had their own college and university association, and they sent a delegation of prominent college presidents to El Salvador just before the congressional delegation arrived. Their members were not impressed by what they heard, and sensed the investigation grinding to a halt. None of the military leaders spoke frankly to them. Log books of troop movements had already disappeared. The U.S. Jesuits channeled the suspicions of their Salvadoran colleagues.[38]

President Cristiani arrived in Washington a few days later, as Moakley prepared for his committee's visit to El Salvador. After a meeting with President Bush, Cristiani spoke with Foley, Majority Leader Gephardt, and Moakley. Moakley "let him know what our people are thinking about the Jesuit case," reminding the president that "votes for El Salvador aid have been diminishing over the years."[39] Cristiani was in a very difficult position. He probably shared Moakley's suspicions, distrusted the general staff, and feared a coup if he helped expose them.

Moakley ran into a dead end with the Bush administration as he tried to find out what they were doing. He requested the cable traffic from the State Department, and information from Secretary Richard Cheney at Defense about the American training of the Atlacatl Battalion, which had surrounded the UCA on the night of the murders. He got delays and prevarications. State planned to monitor the congressional delegation's visit and accompany Moakley. "The day before we left," McGovern told Esther Cassidy, "Moakley called State and told them, 'Unless we get the material we asked for, I will personally throw your guys off the airplane. They're not coming.' The next day six guys from the State Department showed up with boxes containing all the information we asked for."[40] This incident showed another reason Foley had chosen wisely with Moakley. He was tough, and wouldn't take no for an answer.

Five Republicans appointed by Minority Leader Robert Michel joined ten of the nineteen Democrats serving on the Speakers Committee. Moakley's delegation included long-time opponents of military aid to El Salvador like Gerry Studds and George Miller of California among the Democrats, and hawks like Robert Dornan (CA) among the minority party. Their Marine aircraft touched down on February 11 at San Salvador's Ilopango Airport, where they were met by Ambassador Walker and escorted to the Camino Real Hotel. Over the next three days they met with President Cristiani, leaders of the general staff, the Jesuit leaders and the archbishop, the investigating authorities, and FMLN defectors.

The congressmen started at the scene of the crime. Fathers Tojeira and Estrada led the entire delegation to the places where the bodies had been discovered. "You'll show us the place where the bullet marks are?" Moakley asked, clad in a tropical shirt on a hot morning. They did. The walls were dotted with bullet holes, and not all the blood had been removed, three months after the crime. Jesuit offices had been firebombed and presses destroyed. The congressmen viewed gory photographs of the corpses laid out on the campus lawn, and the mother's and daughter's bodies huddled together. The Jesuit fathers frankly told them they didn't believe the murders began with a decision by Benavides.[41]

"I am not an emotional type of guy, but it was hard not to get choked up as we walked on the very ground where these holy men were so brutally killed," Moakley later told a Boston audience. "I kept asking myself, 'How could one human being do this to another?'"[42]

Later the congressmen crammed into an auditorium at headquarters for a briefing by generals Ponce and Zepeda. The delegates pressed them about a November 15 meeting of the high command at which they speculated that some general or generals had given Colonel Benavides his orders. The generals claimed to know nothing and couldn't figure out why Benavides would order such a stupid move. "I just couldn't believe it," Moakley told author Teresa Whitfield a year later. "I mean they open up with . . . how much they pray before every meeting. I just thought some of the things they said were right out of Hollywood." While the generals were talking, the auditorium lights went out. "I just wish you'd put your hands together and pray for light from above right now," Moakley cracked.[43]

Moakley was not coy with the generals during this first trip. He told them straight out that he didn't believe them, and that they had better tell the truth or they were going to lose their military aid. The committee's investigations already had disclosed that Benavides, head of the military academy, had been granted operational command of his sector, which included the UCA, during the offensive. Nothing in his previous career indicated that he was capable of making a historic decision to murder six prominent priests. The entire area around the UCA had been cordoned off, the log books of the Atlacatl Battalion had disappeared, and the high command had met on the night of the murders. "You can't bullshit an old bull-shitter," Moakley told them. "I'm a general," one of them replied. "You can't talk to me like that." Moakley laughed and told them they should try coming to a meeting in South Boston and listen to his constituents talk to him.[44]

Not every military official was on board with the official line. One night, Moakley slipped out of the hotel into a vehicle defended by armed security guards and sped down back roads to the home of another colonel. The colonel told Moakley that people in the high command had ordered the murders, and Moakley saw the fear in the man's eyes. Throughout the investigation, others would come forward in secret as well, typically officers from other graduating classes. Each class in the military academy was taught that loyalty to each other, not to the law, was the highest virtue. Ponce was the leader of the biggest class, and his clique was in power now. In April, Colonel Sigifredo Ochoa would appear on the "60 Minutes" television show and voice the same suspicions.[45]

Moakley had to be tricky as well as tough. He found out that Buckland had given Salvadoran general Ponce a written statement regarding his conversation with Aviles, who had, understandably, denied that he had told Buckland anything. Moakley wanted the embassy's copy. Walker had to check with Cheney at the Defense Department. The document was classified; Moakley couldn't see it. Moakley couldn't believe it. He told Walker, "Lookit, this is part of the investigation . . . I need that letter." Walker had his orders. Moakley and McGovern stormed out, and went straight to the office of the Salvadoran investigating officer. Moakley inquired about the Buckland letter, mentioned that he'd left his copy at his hotel, and asked the officer to Xerox a copy, which he did. Moakley felt that the administration handled everything that way. They wanted Congress out of the loop.[46]

The following day the entire delegation met with President Cristiani. Over the course of a two-hour meeting, the Democrats generally tried to reassure him that they did not doubt his veracity, but they made it clear that they were not satisfied with the course of the investigation, or with the human rights situation in general. Their other concern was to push Cristiani to end the war by negotiating with the FMLN. Even Bob Dornan, among the most militant right wingers in Congress, told Cristiani that he had met the night before with peasants from a village in Chalatenango that had been bombed by the air force, which had denied the event. Cristiani replied that the FMLN would not negotiate. Matthew McHugh of New York reminded Cristiani that the FMLN's Joaquin Villalobos was changing his mind about that.[47] Given the subsequent developments—that Cristiani did accede to negotiations—it is likely that this meeting gave him the sense that time was running out on U.S. support for his military. The murder of the Jesuits ratcheted up American pressure against the Salvadoran war party.

Moakley delivered a businesslike statement as the CoDel prepared to depart from the Camino Real Hotel. The whole delegation, Republican and Democrat, stood behind him as he read it. Moakley pulled no punches, pointing to "reports which suggest that the intellectual authors of the murders may not have been identified and suggestions that there may have been a cover-up of this crime by some in the armed forces. We note in this connection that Colonel Ponce told us that no one person in the military—not one—came forward to report to him the complicity of any member of the Army in the murders." Moakley raised further questions about the human rights climate, and called for negotiations to end the war. The message was unmistakable: Congress had had enough.[48]

Moakley left El Salvador with a working theory that he couldn't prove. Proving whodunit wasn't his job; the Task Force was monitoring, not conducting, the investigation. But a confidential staff document summarized Moakley's conclusions. "There is a general consensus that . . . Benavides . . . is either innocent, a scapegoat, or was following orders from his superiors: a crime of such magnitude . . . could not have been conceived of as implemented by a single officer, much less a circumspect man like Bena-vides. [Yet] President Cristiani . . . said, 'There is no evidence that sug-gests the involvement of other military officers in the assassinations.'" The staff report then listed "key Salvadoran officers possibly related to the case"—that is, the real authorities who Moakley suspected gave the order. First on the list was Air Force general Juan Rafael Bustillo, who had been forced out of office after a December 1 visit by U.S. Southern Command general Maxwell Thurman. Bustillo was an advocate of total war against the rebels, without regard for collateral damage to civilians. His chief ally was Colonel Juan Orlando Zepeda, vice minister of Defense and former commander of the U.S.-trained Atlacatl Battalions. Bustillo had been replaced by General Ponce, who was closer to Cristiani in the internal ARENA power struggle. The report named seven others.[49] Most of them had been present at the November 15 staff meeting, and it made sense to suppose that afterward, when no minutes were being taken, some men in this circle, all superior to Benavides, gave him his orders.

Meanwhile, events in Nicaragua lent energy to the notion of ending the Salvadoran war. On February 25, 1990, Nicaragua held a presiden-tial election that the Sandinistas were widely expected to win. They had held massive rallies, while their moderate opponents could muster only hundreds at public meetings. Yet Violetta Chamorro, widow of the edi-tor whose murder by the Somoza dictatorship had sparked the revolu-tion over a decade earlier, won the election. The Sandinistas accepted the result and handed over power peacefully, an outcome that the Rea-gan administration had postulated was inconceivable because the San-dinistas were totalitarian Marxists. In the following months, Chamorro herself would find, to her chagrin, that no one in the United States cared about Nicaragua anymore. When she was invited to address the U.S. Con-gress, a rare honor, congressional aides had to be summoned to fill up the empty House chamber. Her government got very little economic aid. Ni-caragua was no longer a piece on the Cold War chessboard.[50]

Moakley came back from El Salvador determined to use U.S. aid to reassert civilian control over the military, end the human rights abuses, prosecute the intellectual authors of the Jesuit murders, and bring about negotiations that would end the war. Moakley partnered with Pennsyl-vania congressman John P. Murtha to craft legislation that conditioned further aid upon achievement of those objectives, with an up-front 50 percent aid cut to start. Murtha was a blunt-spoken former Marine who sat on the Defense Appropriations Subcommittee that doled out billions in defense contracts. His Marine background made it tough for hawks to paint him as a peacenik. Murtha and Moakley made a perfect team in that regard. At the outset of the Salvadoran war, the Reagan administration had been forced to certify "progress" toward such constraints, and Reagan simply lied about the realities in biannual reports to the Congress. Now it was ten years later. Nothing had changed in the Salvadoran military. The Bush administration never saw Central America as crucial to its foreign policy agenda, the way Reagan had. The economy was wobbling, and foreign aid was never popular with the public, especially the idea of giving guns to people who were killing priests. This was the background to the Moakley-Murtha legislation as their staffs worked out its details in March and April.[51]

After an April staff trip to El Salvador, Jim McGovern, Studds's staffer Bill Woodward, and Leonel Gomez toiled late into the night to draft a detailed Interim Report of the Speaker's Task Force on El Salvador. Despite its over one hundred page length, the report wasted few words in backing up its principal assertions. "The murders of the Jesuits reflect problems within the Salvadoran armed forces that go far beyond the actions of a particular unit on a particular night," its summary began. The report praised good police work in El Salvador, but noted that without the intercession of the American major there might have been no indictments at all. Yet no one higher than Benavides had been charged, and "preparations for prosecuting the case have come to a virtual standstill," which made it "less and less likely that full justice will be done." The body of the report put together an accurate account of the crime itself—but could not say who gave the orders. All nineteen members signed it.[52]

The Interim Report sealed the beginning of the end of the Salvadoran military dictatorship. The House vote on military aid for the coming fiscal year arrived three weeks later. Republicans proposed to restore military aid. Unfortunately for the minority, their chief antagonist now chaired the Rules Committee and had recently visited the scene of the crime where people he knew personally had been murdered. The vote would be held under the "King of the Mountain Rule," whereby the Republican plan sponsored by William S. Broomfield could pass and still lose if the Democratic bill passed last. The Moakley-Murtha bill matched a parallel effort in the Senate by Chris Dodd and Patrick Leahy that would cut military aid by 50 percent. Moakley-Murtha had been refined to include restoration of money if the FMLN launched attacks on civilians—thus motivating both sides to maintain a cease-fire. To get any military aid, the government of El Salvador would have to ensure progress on judicial reform, freedom of the press, reform of the military, and report on investigations into all political murders.[53]

"Enough is enough," Moakley declared in debate. "The time to act has come. They killed six priests in cold blood. I stood on the ground where my friends were blown away by men to whom the sanctity of human life bears no meaning." The bill passed the House by a 250–163 vote, a huge margin that sent a plain message to the Bush administration. The bill passed the Senate in October and was attached to a foreign aid measure that Bush approved of, so he signed it. Military aid was cut from $85 million to $42.5 million in the next fiscal year. Bush would later temporarily invoke an escape clause when the FMLN violated the terms of the law, but the writing on the wall was clear.[54] The United States was getting out of the business of paying for the Salvadoran military's attack helicopters.

The Interim Report and the passage of Moakley-Murtha encouraged those elements in the Salvadoran military that were looking forward to a postwar El Salvador. They began to talk. In mid-August a Task Force staff delegation, including McGovern and Bill Woodward, conducted a new round of interviews in El Salvador. On August 11 an unidentified military leader confirmed Moakley's suspicions regarding the military staff meeting just before the murders a few hours later. He said that Air Force general Bustillo had told a group of his officers that a decision had been made to kill Ellacuria and leave no witnesses. General Ponce was among the plotters, and later told his officers that the decision to kill the priests was his own. Benavides was ordered to do the deed. He in turn told Lieutenant Colonel Camilo Hernandez and his men that he "had received the green light to go after the UCA." Hernandez arranged to use a Russian AK-47 as the murder weapon. Later, the military leaders told President Cristiani through his brother-in-law, General Vides Casanova, not to investigate. Only the communication by Colonel Aviles to Major Buckland foiled the plan, which otherwise would have remained a "mystery," like all the other murders. Benavides, who was being "imprisoned" at a beach resort, had been promised a few years in jail, if he were convicted as fall guy.[55]

Should the August 11 source testify publicly, he would probably have been killed, and perhaps the judge with him. He did tell Cristiani what he knew in private. A few weeks later Cristiani came to Washington to lobby against the Dodd-Leahy aid cutoff in the Senate. Moakley met with Cristiani three times during his visit. One meeting was in private in Moakley's office. Shortly afterward, Jim McGovern told author Teresa Whitfield what Moakley said. "I know who did it and you know who did it. So what are you going to do about it?" According to Whitfield, "The president said not a word."[56] The likelihood is that if Cristiani spoke out and the attorney general indicted the high command for the murders, it would have precipitated a coup. Few civilian presidents have faced more stark dilemmas.

Secrets were kept on the American side as well. A few weeks later, in mid-October, Moakley learned from a source he would not identify that Major Buckland had declared in his January FBI interrogation that he had prior knowledge of the murders, and then retracted the statement in a later interview. A low-level embassy official discovered the FBI information in the embassy files in late September as Buckland returned to El Salvador to testify under rules that excluded questions about Buckland's FBI testimony. Buckland was clearly an unstable, self-aggrandizing character, and Moakley doubted Buckland's "prior knowledge" statement. It could not, however, be ruled out. To this day, no one knows for sure when Bustillo and Ponce (the latter died in 2010) decided to kill the Jesuits. There were five days between the FMLN offensive and the murders. Moakley thought that Americans should not decide that Buckland's incriminating statement could not be heard by the Salvadoran court. The discovery of the Buckland statement meant that the State Department, the embassy, Buckland's military superiors, and the FBI all knew potentially key information that they deliberately hid from Moakley and the Salvadoran court.

Moakley, according to McGovern, "went ballistic."[57] He fired off angry letters to all the offending parties, demanding from Bernard Aronson at State that all the relevant FBI transcripts and other documents be forwarded both to him and the judge in El Salvador. "I have given the Administration and the Embassy every possible break in reporting this stuff," he wrote. "We could have gone after a lot of things—but we decided not to. I really feel betrayed on this one." Moakley issued a press statement on

October 18, just as the Senate aid debate opened. "The bottom line is not whether the Buckland statement is true or false," Moakley said. "The fact is that American officials withheld from Salvadoran authorities for more than ten months a statement that I believe is of obvious relevance." The State Department now had no choice but to comply, and the Salvadoran judge confirmed receipt of the transcripts a few days later.[58]

★ ★ ★

While Moakley was jousting with the State Department and the FBI, the Senate was completing its deliberations on the immigration bill whose House version contained TPS provisions for the Salvadorans. Senator Kennedy had worked hard to include 200,000 new visas for European, especially Irish, immigrants. Moakley and his colleague Brian Donnelly from Dorchester had supported this too, and the bill was especially popular with Irish-American organizations. However, the Senate bill omitted the Salvadorans. A conference committee would debate each section of the bill to determine its final shape.

Moakley arrived prepared to win or block the pending legislation. The atmosphere in the conference room was tense. Moakley recalled that "there were about a hundred fifty people in the room. The theater was great. The senators were on one side, the house members on the other. So Jack Brooks was in charge of the House members and Alan Simpson was in charge of the senate members." Simpson read out the House version and announced that the Senate wouldn't accept the Salvadoran provision.

Moakley remembered what happened next: "I said, 'Well, if you're not going to do it, you're not going to have a bill.' He says, 'You wouldn't do that, would you?' He says, 'A lot of good stuff in here for the Irish.' I says, 'Yeah. I know it, but there's no stuff in there for the El Salvadorans.' He says, 'You'd jeopardize the bill?' I says, 'You bet your ass.'"[59]

Everybody knew that Jesse Helms of North Carolina, the most virulent anticommunist in the Senate, one of the few who even opposed land reform in El Salvador, was prepared to filibuster the bill if Moakley's provision were included. Kennedy said, "I know the enormous frustration that Joe Moakley has, but I do not believe that this measure with that amendment on it would be able to go through the Senate." Kennedy called; he wanted Moakley to drop the El Salvador issue for the greater good of a sound immigration bill that protected illegal Irish immigrants. McGovern remembered that Moakley told Kennedy, "I know, but I'm not convinced if you sent an Irishman back to Dublin he's going to get shot." This time the blood of the slain Jesuits was on the ground, and this time Joe Moakley was chairman of the Rules Committee. "[F]or five years I've been sweating and thinking about this thing," he told an attentive chamber. "You say seven killings a month isn't a lot," he continued, addressing the argument that death squad activity had declined. "But in Massachusetts, which has roughly the same population, if seven people were killed each month for political reasons that would be a lot."

Moakley had engineered a high stakes showdown. "If it [the Salvadoran issue] goes, then there'll be no fucking bill," Moakley warned. Simpson's people got on the phone with President Bush. The Senators huddled, and Paul Simon of Illinois suggested an eighteen-month stay of deportation, instead of thirty months. Moakley took it. Simpson folded his hand, and a few weeks later the bill was signed into law.[60]

★ ★ ★

Joe Moakley was no longer just a "nuts and bolts" politician with only a domestic agenda. The Jesuit murders were one of the great crimes of the twentieth century, but their significance was obscured by the fall of the Berlin Wall and the Panama invasion. It was Moakley, and his aide McGovern, who challenged his congressional colleagues, and the wider American public, to recognize that it was American policy, and money, that placed the murder weapons in the killers' hands. For the rest of his life, Moakley would act on this new understanding. He was changing and growing in a way that he could never have anticipated when he first entered the Massachusetts legislature in 1953.

11

* * * * *

"Wellcom Senador Smoklin"

oakley's fight for the Salvadoran immigrants and his investigation into the murder of the Jesuit priests constituted two
major contributions to justice for Salvadorans. He could have
dropped his interest in the country at this point, but he didn't. He was
hooked. In 1991 he would on his own initiative venture out into the Salvadoran countryside to meet real people, a very different experience from
confronting generals. By doing so he would encourage the peace process
in El Salvador, his third major contribution to the country to which he
was becoming attached.

Peace was gradually breaking out in El Salvador, the last great battle of the Cold War. Sensible combatants on both sides of the civil war
came to the conclusion that they had nothing to win and everything to
lose by continuing the military conflict. In the March 1991 elections for
the Constituent Assembly, the leftist Democratic Convergence won eight
seats; none of its campaigners were killed in the process. A peace party
appeared among the ARENA civilians; they were exhausted by war but
satisfied that there was not going to be a Cuban-style leftist victory in El
Salvador. The FMLN leaders knew this as well. They had never received
direct Soviet aid, but now, with their Sandinista allies voted out of office,
what little aid they received from Nicaragua was diminishing. Even if
they won a military victory, an impossible outcome, they would be economically isolated. On the ARENA side, Oscar Santamaria, a tall, suave,
former business associate of President Alfredo Cristiani, led a team that
negotiated a preliminary peace accord that was signed on April 25, 1991,
in Mexico City.[1]

The U.S. administration was heartened by this process. President
George Bush had a much more realistic assessment of the situation in

Central America than had his predecessor, who had lived in a Cold War fantasyland. Bush's secretary of state, James A. Baker, while serving as Reagan's chief of staff, had tried unsuccessfully to mitigate Reagan's opposition to any peace initiatives. Reagan, however, wanted military victory in both Nicaragua and El Salvador and viewed the region as the front line of the Cold War; he didn't care how many people got killed to achieve his objective. Baker appointed a former Democrat, Bernard Aronson, as undersecretary of state for Latin American Affairs; he was a study in contrast to his hawkish predecessor, Elliot Abrams. Baker understood that communist subversives were not about to attack the United States from El Salvador. He saw Central America as a minor distraction.[2]

Ambassador William Walker could read these tea leaves. He and Moakley had had a cautious relationship so far. Ambassadors represent their government, not congressional majorities, to foreign powers. They typically have little room to maneuver if their instincts don't match those of their superiors. While the Jesuit case had sometimes found Moakley and Walker pursuing separate agendas, the peace process did not. Walker aligned U.S. interests with the new direction of ARENA's civilian leaders. This crystallized a power struggle among the generals, with General Ponce adhering to Cristiani's camp, and General Bustillo leading the irreconcilables linked to former death squad organizer Roberto D'Aubuisson. Yet all the generals had everything to lose by an end to the war. They could not accede to their own prosecution and conviction. Walker had to balance this reality against the need to get the generals to accept a peace agreement. "Deep down," Jim McGovern later concluded, "Bill Walker did not want to believe that the military was implicated in the Jesuit affair, but deep down, he also wanted justice."[3]

Meanwhile, Moakley had to navigate these currents as well. In December 1990 Jim McGovern and Congressman Gerry Studds's aide Bill Woodward made another trip to El Salvador. They prepared a memorandum that directed congressional attention to the problem, revelatory from the beginning, that the indicted soldiers had been identified not by the prosecutor's office but by the military Honor Commission. Their superiors had never been questioned by the Special Investigations Unit. That crucial fact suggested a cover-up directed by the military. As the peace negotiations proceeded in the spring of 1991, President Cristiani tried to discredit McGovern's memo by hiring a Washington public relations firm, Hannan and Connor, to produce a counter-report. They sent two hostile representatives to visit McGovern, questioning his qualifications to make the judgments he had made. McGovern told Moakley about it. By chance, Moakley ran into one of the firm's representatives in the men's room at a Washington reception. Moakley pulled the guy aside and warned him to back off. "I don't like the shit you're pulling," was how McGovern recalled Moakley's account. "If you continue this, if you have a client with a bill before the Rules Committee, I'll fuck it up." Hannan and Connor backed off.[4]

A little later, Moakley urged the head of the U.S. Southern Command to pressure Ponce to testify, and he did. Ponce got the message, and was interviewed by the court. Moakley kept plugging away on the Jesuit case in obscurity while the world watched Operation Desert Storm, the U.S.-led war to drive Saddam Hussein's forces out of Kuwait.[5]

Leonel Gomez was working quietly behind the scenes, too. He facilitated a meeting between Moakley and one of the guerrilla factions. Gomez's wife came from a small village on the Honduran border in Cabanas province called Santa Marta. That village was now under guerrilla control. Santa Marta's military leader was a man called Raul Hercules, a member of the Resistencia Nacional faction of the FMLN and formerly a leader on the crucial Guazapa front. Hercules's *comandante* was Ferman Cienfuegos, a wiry, bespectacled intellectual whose strategy was to negotiate a settlement of the war. Early in the war, Cienfuegos had sought out Dr. Charlie Clements, a Vietnam veteran who had volunteered as a medic on the Guazapa front in 1982, trying to learn more about Americans and their government. By 1991, Cienfuegos had negotiated the preliminary peace accord in Mexico City. A meeting of one of his lieutenants with Moakley was right up his alley. Gomez believed that a visit by Moakley to Santa Marta would send a powerful message to the FMLN that the Americans wanted a lasting peace that included a role in governance for them.[6]

Still, Gomez faced a difficult dilemma. The State Department didn't like the idea. Secretary of State James A. Baker called Moakley and tried to dissuade him. Years later, Jim McGovern remembered that Moakley replied, "I want to see for myself what's going on in this country—and that means not only traveling all over, but it also means meeting with everyone—no matter what their politics."[7] Previous to the signing of the peace accord, such a meeting would surely have been seen as a hostile act. It would have been like a British Member of Parliament visiting Virginia during the American Civil War. The military had killed the Jesuits precisely because they advocated dialogue. The April 25 preliminary accord did not include a ceasefire, and both sides were still at war. It could not be ruled out that Gomez's guerrilla contacts were suckering him, and that Moakley would be kidnapped.[8]

While Gomez worked on the Santa Marta visit, Moakley and several liberal colleagues implored President Bush to withhold military aid still in the pipeline. Anticipating a final peace accord, they wanted to use the money for the transition period instead.[9] This was a reasonable request, but should the aid money be released, Moakley's leverage would be diminished. He met with Aronson two days before his departure for El Salvador and learned that the money was on its way. That, Moakley told McGovern, "was the stupidest thing this administration has done."[10]

Moakley arrived in El Salvador disappointed with the administration and determined to go ahead with his trip to Santa Marta. Because the State Department could not allow Moakley to conduct a private negotiation with a guerrilla leader, Walker decided to come along, and brought a *Washington Post* reporter. This development probably caused Raul Hercules, the FMLN representative, to leave town.

The night before they left, Jim McGovern dined at an embassy reception and woke up sick to his stomach and running a fever.

"I can't go," he told Moakley.

"I can't do this without you," Moakley worried, but McGovern insisted, and Moakley took off without him. To McGovern's surprise, the whole convoy turned around and Moakley begged him one more time. "Let me go upstairs and be sick again," McGovern replied. Then he downed some medication, and, feeling better, got in the vehicle.[11]

So Moakley set off in a convoy, accompanied by Walker, Gomez, and McGovern, armed security guards from the embassy, and journalists. Departing from the congressman's luxurious surroundings at the Camino Real Hotel, the caravan proceeded east through the city's worst slums to the Pan American Highway, then just a pot-holed, two-lane affair that stretched past the industrial and military zones of Ilopango and Soyopango, where rural El Salvador began. The road wound eastward through dusty market towns like San Martin and Cujutepeque, until the route forked north toward Ilobasco, bending east again to San Isidro and the hilly provincial capital of Sensuntepeque. Moakley got off somewhere along the way and joined some teenagers playing basketball, launching a shot that clanged off the rim. During the journey Moakley could see the full panoply of life unfolding along the roadside: impassive gnarled women walking upright to a river bearing loads of laundry balanced on their heads; tough old men working in corn fields with machetes dangling from their belts; people carrying chopped firewood on their backs, straining silently under the burden; skinny, stunted children scurrying barefoot alongside their elders. They continued north toward Victoria, where the landscape became mountainous and expansive rural vistas opened up. After Victoria the paved road ended and a perilously rutted downhill dirt track began.

This was guerrilla territory. Here the palm trees receded, mountain forest appeared, and glimpses of an extinct volcano on the Honduran border came into view. Teenaged warriors manned checkpoints along the last ten kilometers, bearing RPGs and assault rifles. Moakley regarded them with wry humor and wary apprehension. "I anticipated there'd be armed guards," he told a reporter. "I mean, you don't expect it to be Broadway, South Boston." It had been a rough three-hour trip.[12]

The procession halted at the outskirts of town and Moakley, dressed in a guayabera-like tropical shirt with twin breast pockets, got out and walked in. Santa Marta's three thousand inhabitants mobilized to greet him. A sign reading "Wellcom Senador Smoklin" probably caused him to chuckle. A man with a bullhorn blared *Viva el Congresista y el Ambajador!* while a string band serenaded the dignitaries. Moakley could see right away that the village was dirt poor. There was a little electricity from the single generator that powered the town's only television. There were no phones, doctor, or adequate school building. The houses were wattle and thatch single-room affairs with tin roofs and smoky wood stoves for cooking and heat; no child had his own bed. The town was inhabited by women, children, and the elderly, for the young men fought with the guerrillas.

Joe Moakley connected with them immediately. He had not ever been among people like this before. As he had observed, this was not South Boston, where people had their problems, to be sure, but Moakley immediately grasped that these farmers faced basic challenges of survival every day. He came bearing gifts, and strolled through town dispensing coloring books, crayons, and soccer balls to the kids, and Gillette razors from the South Boston factory to the men. The children loved him. He was now a stout and ruddy old grandfatherly type, and he looked like Santa Claus without a beard. Moakley told *Washington Post* reporter Lee Hockstader, "I felt I really couldn't get a complete picture of what El Salvador was about until I came to a place like Santa Marta where people are living in very tough conditions." Moakley mixed up *buenos dias* and *muchas gracias* with one town leader, whom he told through his translator, "Little by little, my life is becoming entwined with El Salvador."[13]

After a while, Moakley retreated to the home of Carlos Bonilla Aves, who was born and raised in Santa Marta and by age fifty was a village elder. Among his colleagues who met Moakley that day were Enrique Otero, a man Bonilla's age; Geraldo Arturo Leyva; and Luis Rivas, who looked a little younger. Maria Ida Hernandez, a tall, striking war widow, cooked for the men, and told Moakley that her husband had "disappeared." The farmers told Moakley that in 1981, when the guerrillas established themselves in their midst, the army began to rain mortar shells down on them from their base in Victoria, and the town became unlivable. The inhabitants fled across the border to UN refugee camps in Mesa Grande, Honduras. There they remained until 1987 as virtual prisoners, refugees from a town that no longer existed because the army burned everything in it after they left. They literally scorched the earth.

By 1985 Santa Marta's inhabitants voted to return. They were only 1,008 people, but they were well organized, well led, and universally determined to work together. After a two-year negotiation with the United Nations and the Salvadoran Ministry of the Interior, a deal was struck and the people boarded UN buses to go home. With a few hand tools they rebuilt their houses and planted new crops of maize, sorghum, and beans, enough to stay alive and even sell at market. Sometimes the army fired down into the village, but not often enough to drive them out. Moakley listened to their story. He gobbled everything on his plate while the still wobbly McGovern shuddered at the impending consequences.

The villagers presented Moakley with a petition asking for electricity, financing for a better latrine system, and an end to the sporadic attacks. There was not much Moakley could directly promise, but Walker vowed to get U.S. AID money for corn silos. Twenty years later, Enrique Otero recalled that Moakley had "said something I will never forget. He said: 'I have my heart in Santa Marta. I am your friend.'" They knew that he meant it, and they knew he had power. "He had a big love for our community," Otero remembered. "He was like a prophet for the peace negotiations."[14]

Moakley went outside and the children approached to sing a song. Something deep in the old Boston Irish politician's veins responded. A century earlier John F. Kennedy's fabled grandfather, Mayor John F. "Honey Fitz" Fitzgerald, had swept into office by serenading his constituents. Moakley broke into "If You're Irish, Come into the Parlor." An old woman in the crowd sang something back. Moakley responded with "Redhead," and finally the spirited "Southie Is My Hometown." Gomez told McGovern, "This is fucking huge." Moakley probably could have been elected mayor.[15]

Not everyone was impressed. This was FMLN territory, and there were skeptics about Yankees. "This visit is worth nothing," one resident told a reporter. He said that nothing would change until the United States stopped funding the military. The reporter told Moakley what the man had said, and he shrugged, "If it was that simple to solve in one meeting, this thing would've been solved a long time ago."[16]

This first meeting between Americans in official positions and friends of the FMLN changed the atmosphere on the FMLN side and furthered the peace process, which at this point was still in a preliminary phase. McGovern recalled meeting FMLN leader Joaquin Villalobos in New York during the next phase of negotiations. "You know, Santa Marta was a turning point," Villalobos said. "That's when we realized that the United States was getting serious about peace. When Moakley came to our turf—and stayed for hours—it showed us respect—something that no American official had shown us—we realized that now was the time to negotiate an end to the war."[17]

Just as important for the future of El Salvador, the meeting changed Joe Moakley. Moakley recognized in these tough villagers the dignity and pride of people who might be materially impoverished but whose sense of community made them spiritually rich. They recognized in him their first powerful American friend: *El Congresista.*

The Jesuit case, meanwhile, was still stalled. Back in the capital, Moakley confronted Ponce in a private meeting, accompanied by McGovern and an embassy official who translated. Moakley demanded to know if

Ponce thought he had an institutional problem on his hands, because now Colonel Benavides was in the dock and yet no one in the military had voluntarily come forward with any information. Ponce gave terse answers, and the embassy translator elaborated at length. Moakley and McGovern realized that the official was putting the best face on Ponce's responses by telling Moakley what he wanted to hear. Moakley reamed the guy out in the parking lot. "Don't forget, you work for the United States, not the fucking Salvadoran military," Moakley barked at him. "If you ever do that again, I'll do what I can to see that you're fired." The guy realized he'd been caught, and clammed up after that.

Moakley and McGovern headed from that meeting to the UCA, where Moakley was scheduled to make an important speech, arranged by the Salvadoran and U.S. Jesuits. Father Jon Sobrino, a slender, gentle intellectual whose absence on the night of the murders had saved his life, was to make a formal response. McGovern and Bill Woodward had worked on the speech back in Washington, and McGovern refined it to accuse Ponce publicly. "Do you really think this is OK?" Moakley asked McGovern, who reassured him. "Yeah, well, that's easy for you to say," Moakley protested as he headed on stage.

The meeting was held in the auditorium, a modern brick building with a raised roof that allowed for natural air circulation. Now it was named for Father Ellacuria. Three to four hundred people packed every hard metal seat. The entire diplomatic corps attended. The presence of television cameras and radio microphones added to the excitement. The audience waited expectantly to hear Moakley's oration after Father Miguel Estrada finished his introduction.

Some of the Jesuits still were perplexed about Moakley. Father Jose Maria Tojeira was especially curious. The revolutionaries may have trusted Gomez, but the Jesuits did not because of the latter's connection to Walker. Tojeira, a lanky, good-natured man with twinkly eyes and an informal manner, had been born in Galicia, a northern region in Spain but had lived in Honduras, where he worked with a campesino-oriented radio station. In 1985 he was posted to El Salvador and became Jesuit provincial in 1988.

Tojeira deeply distrusted Walker. After the murders, Walker had told him privately that the embassy thought some part of the military was culpable, while publicly suggesting that it might have been the FMLN.

Walker defended his aide Richard Chidester, a hard-line right-winger who the Jesuits thought had facilitated the ill treatment of witness Lucia Cerna. Finally, Walker had knowingly plied two aggressive prosecutors with false information that the FMLN was planning to kill them. Now Moakley's man Gomez sat together with Walker as the congressman approached the podium, stage right beneath the UCA's cross-and-owl coat of arms.[18]

Moakley began on his usual note of self-effacing humor, including a nod of respect toward the ambassador. But he quickly came to the significance of the Jesuit case, pointing out, "Every one of us is entitled to our rights; and every one of us is entitled to justice when those rights are violated." While all the victims of the past decade were equally important, the prominence of the Jesuit victims had made them symbolic of all the others. "In this one case," Moakley insisted, "we demand the truth . . . [f]or if El Salvador, with all the international pressure, cannot bring those who murdered the Jesuits to justice, how can anyone expect justice the next time a labor leader or a teacher or a campesino is killed?" He briefly reprised the salient inconsistencies in General Ponce's account of the crime and concluded: "General, believe me, you have got an institutional problem. . . . I am convinced that, at a minimum, the high command of the armed forces knew soon after the murders which unit was responsible for the crimes." Would any verdict in this case satisfy him? he asked rhetorically, and insisted again that only the full truth would suffice. Then he came to the stirring peroration: "There is no such thing as half justice. You either have justice or you don't. There is no such thing as half a democracy. You either have a democracy in which everyone—including the powerful—is subject to the law or you don't." He concluded with a ringing appeal to both sides to stop the violence, advance the peace process, and demand justice for the downtrodden. "So in closing, I say let us pray that God will grant us the strength, with the memory of those martyred heroes always present in our minds, to fulfill this duty each and every day of our lives."[19]

The audience exploded with enthusiastic applause. McGovern's crafting of the speech echoed Jack Kennedy's address to the nation during the Birmingham demonstrations of 1963, and it concluded with Lincolnesque cadences reminiscent of the Second Inaugural. The somber nature of the occasion, and the uncertainty borne by many auditors such as Father Tojeira, sent a powerful message to all. The speech broke down any lingering doubts about Moakley's resolve among any skeptics. "This really had an impact," Tojeira recalled. "There was a dinner afterward that was a catharsis for all of us." A feeling of mutual regard opened between Moakley and the Jesuits of the UCA that would last to the end of Moakley's life.[20]

Ambassador Walker departed with a sour feeling. He told Moakley that the direct address to Ponce was "unnecessarily sarcastic," and he felt miffed because he had not received an advance copy of the speech. After Moakley returned home, Walker griped about Moakley to a visiting American Jesuit and a Senate delegation. Word of this got back to Moakley, and relations between the two men cooled again. Moakley always praised Walker in public, but the diplomat, who had been doing the bidding of Republicans Reagan and Bush for many years, never reciprocated.[21]

Moakley later paid a surprise visit to two of the accused prisoners. Playing the role of soft cop, he told them that he knew they had acted under orders and were therefore less culpable than the men who gave the orders. One of them said, "Congressman, you have given us a lot to think about," but they both concluded it was wisest to say nothing. Moakley suspected that the fix was in, and that they both knew more about the murders than he did.[22]

Moakley also met twice with President Cristiani to discuss the Jesuit case. He insisted that there should be no amnesty in the event of a conviction. He meant what he had said at the UCA by "There is no such thing as half justice." Cristiani replied that only the legislature, not the executive, could grant an amnesty. Moakley pressed the president to make a public declaration that he was personally opposed to an amnesty. Cristiani demurred.[23]

Once again, events in the Soviet Union drove the Salvadoran drama. In August, Communist Party militants launched a coup against Gorbachev while he vacationed in the Crimea. Moscow party leader Boris Yeltsin theatrically climbed onto a tank to denounce the coup; within three days in late August the plot had collapsed, and with it Russian communism. Gorbachev's authority crumbled too. He dissolved the Communist Party and granted independence to the Baltic states. By Christmas, Gorbachev would resign from office.[24] Anticommunism, the bogey man driving U.S. foreign policy since the end of World War II, had lost its *raison d'etre*.

Both sides in El Salvador understood this. Few FMLN leaders had been Marxists or ideological dogmatists, American propaganda to the contrary. At the UN-sponsored round of talks in New York, a second agreement was signed on September 25. Cristiani agreed to cut the size of the military in half and to establish an ad hoc commission to purge the military of human rights violators. The officer corps had lost its morale. The FMLN accepted that they would not be integrated into the military, but rather into a new civilian police force. Only the terms of the cease fire remained to be negotiated.[25]

The Jesuit murder trial began the next day. The court moved up its schedule for political purposes, to clear the military's name and get the issue behind the country. All eight defendants were charged with the murders of all eight victims, and additional counts of terrorism; each faced thirty years in prison. The charges did not bear any relation to who had given orders or who killed whom. One soldier had confessed to killing the two women, for example, but was not charged that way. Jim McGovern joined a delegation of Spanish parliamentarians, representatives of the U.S. Jesuits, including Father J. Donald Monan, president of Boston College, and members of the press, in the audience. The trial lasted a mere three days. The defense never attempted to prove that any individual had not committed the crimes. Instead, they praised their clients for defending the fatherland. Several of the men had confessed to killing particular individuals, but the confessions were not admissible. Outside, a raucous demonstration of military wives and their friends threatened the Jesuits with further revenge; their chants could be heard inside the courtroom. The five-person civilian jury, which included an employee of the Supreme Court, decided on eighty separate counts in five hours. Only Colonel Benavides and Lieutenant Yusshy Mendoza were found guilty, Mendoza for the killing of Celina Ramos, even though another soldier had confessed to that. The international observers sat stunned in speechless revulsion as the jury delivered its incomprehensible verdicts.[26]

Moakley blasted the whole proceeding two weeks later in the *Washington Post*. He acknowledged that, yes, as the State Department lamely crowed, officers had for the first time been convicted of a human rights violation. However, the authoritative parties had not even been charged. With the trial over, Moakley let some of his cats out the bag. Salvadoran officers had told him in advance how the verdict would go. They predicted that the jury would have to convict Benavides to continue getting U.S. aid, and surmised that he had probably been promised amnesty after a brief stay in jail. "A terrible injustice has been done," Moakley concluded in regard to the failure to indict the perpetrators and substitute a fall guy. But given the disappointing outcome, there were still a few possibilities for further action. First, he proposed an investigation into the report that one defendant threatened to talk if he was convicted. That man had walked free. He urged President Cristiani to dismiss all the defendants from the military, the State Department to bar General Bustillo from the United States, that no amnesty be granted the two convicted men, and that new, lesser charges be brought against officers who had obstructed justice. Finally, he called on President Bush to suspend further military aid to El Salvador, because a professional investigation into the murders had not taken place. The headline writers picked up on Moakley's wail, "Where is the outrage? Where is the leadership?"[27]

Moakley issued one final statement in his capacity as chairman of the Speaker's Task Force, on the second anniversary of the murders. He was still in a very delicate situation. He had information given to him—in confidence by people whose lives were in danger if they came forward—that implicated the high command. Two officers who knew what had happened had already been killed under mysterious circumstances.[28] When the Bush and Cristiani administrations celebrated the verdict with "case closed, let's move forward" statements, and a mysterious outfit called the Central American Lawyers Group (perhaps a creation of Cristiani's public relations firm) issued a voluminous rebuttal to Moakley's allegations, Moakley decided to issue a six-page memo that detailed his theory.

According to Moakley's sources, Air Force general Juan Rafael Bustillo convened a meeting of four other commanders at the military school on the afternoon of the 15th. They included General Ponce, then chief of staff and now minister of defense, Colonel Benavides, General Juan Orlando Zepeda, and Colonel Francisco Elena Fuentes. Bustillo proposed to murder the Jesuits and his colleagues had acquiesced. The Atlacatl Unit assigned to do the deed were issued new uniforms without insignias. The log books of their movements were later destroyed. Benavides, the officer who organized the murders, told his subordinates that "he had received the green light," a clear indication that higher-ups had given the order. Bustillo and Ponce later told other colleagues that they had organized the murders, before the arrest of Benavides and his subordinates. Bustillo and Ponce then covered up the evidence, and likely would have succeeded had it not been for international pressure, good police work facilitated by President Cristiani, and the belated testimony of military advisor Eric Buckland (whom Moakley did not name). He offered that "I personally find this version of events more credible than the alternative, which is that Col. Benavides acted on his own."[29]

Moakley cautioned *Boston Globe* reporter Pamela Constable that, while he stood by his statement, "I wouldn't put my hand on the Bible. This is circumstantial information, not evidence." The State Department, rather than congratulating Moakley for his diligent work, used the fact that his informants would not come forward to diminish its significance. Their unidentified spokesman (the *Globe* guessed it to be Aronson) scoffed that "it's hard to understand why they would wait until the second anniversary of the deaths and release that evidence to the media rather than turn that evidence over . . . to the judge." But Aronson knew that the judge himself had fled El Salvador, fearing for his life, the day after the verdict was declared. Bush's spokesman John Sununu trumpeted the verdict as "a triumph for human rights." President Cristiani praised Moakley's intentions but noted that "unfortunately he has used information that is not confirmed, that is rumor." The *Globe*, commenting editorially that it found Moakley's theory "convincing," expressed its skepticism about the administration. "Nor is it a surprise that Bush administration officials are still tangled in a decade's worth of moral evasions."[30]

Meanwhile, Moakley moved in Congress to shut down the military pipeline once and for all. The war might be waning, but it wasn't over. McGovern worked with the staffs of several colleagues to craft a bill that would give Congress control of any future allocations and to close down presidential loopholes. It proposed that further U.S. aid to El Salvador be channeled through the United Nations or other multilateral agencies.[31]

Even that bill's purposes were rendered nugatory by the next dramatic turn of events. The guerrillas announced a unilateral cease fire, the final step that would trigger implementation of the accords signed in Mexico City and New York. At first the government responded by moving troops into guerrilla territory around the Guazapa volcano. Then they shifted course, and by December 16 talks had resumed in New York at the United Nations. Secretary General Javier Perez de Cuellar wanted to finalize an agreement by the end of the year, when his term expired. The sides agreed, and ended the war on New Year's Eve. In an emotional ceremony held on January 16, 1992, at Mexico City's Chapultepec Park, President Cristiani came down from the dais at the final ceremony ending the war and shook hands with the leading FMLN *comandantes*, some of whom had tears in their eyes. Dr. Charlie Clements, the Quaker medic attending as a special guest, choked up as well. In San Salvador, the government and guerrillas held massive celebratory rallies in nearby public squares. On this high note of expectation the last battle of the Cold War ended. Joe Moakley had contributed significantly to its arrival.[32]

The murderers of the Jesuits had avoided prosecution, but now their power was about to be shorn and their true place in history fixed. Moakley's report on the second anniversary of the murders was covered by the world press. Bustillo appealed to Moakley in a confidential letter, sticking to his story and daring Moakley to come to El Salvador and try to prove what the courts could not. He denied attending a meeting at the Military Academy but acknowledged attending a meeting at military headquarters the day before the murders. This was "indictment by innuendo" Bustillo charged, and affirmed that "I categorically deny each and every allegation in your report," which constituted a "libelous charge."[33] Ponce, a smooth operator, struck a chummy tone in a letter to Moakley, noting that it had been a pleasure to see him while accompanying President Cristiani on a Washington lobbying trip in April. He maintained that he had been at his post at the military headquarters, not at the Military Academy, and he insisted that Moakley withdraw the charges against him, since they were based on anonymous sources.[34] Moakley had nothing more to say to these men.

The peace negotiations also stripped the Salvadoran military of its power. The ARENA civilians agreed to a rapid diminution of the army's size and its removal from police functions. The final agreement incorporated demobilized FMLN combatants into one national civilian police force, replacing the three units that had formerly served as death squads. In addition, an ad hoc commission was designated to review the military officer corps and remove human rights violators. When the State Department dragged its feet on cooperating with the ad hoc commission, Moakley and his colleagues urged the State Department to comply with their requests for documents. In the end, Cristiani, despite opposition by his military, acceded to a far-reaching purge of more than one hundred officers. Cristiani and his colleague Oscar Santamaria showed remarkable resolution in this affair, placing the reconciliation of the country over the careers of their fellow ARENA party members.[35]

Another blow against the military fell with the release of the UN Truth Commission report titled "From Madness to Hope" on March 15, 1993. The commission was assembled in July 1992 and was mandated to complete within six months a report on human rights violations during the civil war. Chaired by Alvaro de Soto, it charged D'Aubuisson with orchestrating Romero's murder. On the Jesuit case, the commissioners refined Moakley's allegations. The report found that Bustillo and Ponce had proposed the murders at a meeting at military headquarters, where they both admitted to being. Benavides departed from that meeting to the Military Academy and dispatched the hit squad, protected by the Atlacatl Brigade, to the scene of the crime. Reporting on the commission's work to the U.S. Congress, Commissioner Alvaro de Soto declared that it was the Moakley Task Force that had laid the groundwork for its conclusions. Documentary filmmaker Esther Cassidy's camera found Jim McGovern, who had done so much to achieve this outcome, standing quietly against a rear wall, far out of the spotlight, as de Soto spoke.[36]

Joe Moakley and Jim McGovern had played a crucial role in ending the war and bringing to light the truth about human rights abuses during El Salvador's civil war. Now the UN Truth Commission had recorded the names of the perpetrators of those crimes for all time. The Jesuit murder case, along with the murder of Archbishop Romero and the four American churchwomen, ranks among history's most notorious assassinations.

★   ★   ★

Moakley had been dealing with one other Salvadoran problem as the war wound down. On January 2, 1991, guerrillas killed two captured Americans whose helicopter had crashed in their territory: Lieutenant Colonel David Pickett and enlisted man Ernest Dawson, Jr. The guerrillas on the ground claimed that these were mercy killings of men who were almost dead from the crash, and for whom they had no medicine. Their commanders, who included Anna Guadalupe Martinez and Joaquin Villalobos, insisted that they had given orders by radio not to shoot the Americans because they were prisoners of war, protected by the Geneva

Convention.[37] Speculation mounted that President George Bush would use an escape clause in the Moakley-Murtha bill to renew $42.5 million in withheld aid.[38]

"When I heard this, I went sick," Moakley told a reporter for *Newsweek* magazine. If the reports were true, he continued, "[t]he guerillas and their commander should be tried for murder." Moakley was now the congressman to whom national reporters turned for reaction to Salvadoran events. Moakley's tabloid hometown newspaper, the *Boston Herald*, demanded that Moakley pursue justice in this case as fervently as he had in the Jesuit case.[39]

The FMLN detained the two guerrillas, announcing that they would try the men under their own authority. In a letter to Moakley months later, the FMLN explained its reasoning. "We would like to turn them over to the Salvadoran judicial system, but we can't trust that there would be a fair trial." The guerrillas reminded Moakley that the FMLN tried to be strict about not engaging Americans, recalling the FMLN capture of the Sheraton Hotel in November 1989, with a dozen Green Berets trapped inside. The FMLN had deliberately negotiated their release. Meanwhile, the Bush administration announced that it would seek an indictment of Villalobos, who had been nowhere near the scene of the crime, and resume the suspended military aid.[40]

The murders of Pickett and Dawson opened Moakley to attacks by prowar critics. The *Boston Herald* used the incident to suggest that Moakley used a double standard of justice when his friends committed war crimes. Their argument was wrong on a number of counts. First, Moakley urged the FMLN to turn the perpetrators over to Salvadoran or U.S. authorities over the next fifteen months, and they finally did that. In addition, Moakley, who had been assigned to head the Jesuit investigation, was under no special moral obligation to resolve every subsequent case of injustice in El Salvador, but in this instance he volunteered to do so. Third, the circumstances of this case contrasted sharply with those in the Jesuit case. There was only one similarity: in both cases defenseless victims were murdered. The difference was that in the Jesuit case, the perpetrators acted under the premeditated orders of their superiors and killed men pledged to nonviolence, along with two innocent witnesses. The intellectual authors of that crime, recipients of U.S. aid, then obstructed justice. In the Pickett-Dawson case, two soldiers wounded in battle were wrongly executed in a mercy killing, against the orders of their superiors, who brought the details of the crime to light. Finally, Moakley's critics themselves were highly selective in their indignation. Two weeks later, Salvadoran soldiers massacred fifteen peasants, including a fourteen-year-old girl whose throat they slit, in the village of El Zapote near the Guazapa volcano. That story got little coverage and drew no cries of outrage from the Bush administration.[41]

Little progress was made on the Pickett-Dawson case until late October 1991, when Moakley sent a "Dear Colleague" letter, signed by eighty members, and addressed to five FMLN leaders. He urged them to turn the accused men, who Moakley said had committed "cold-blooded murder," over to U.S. or Salvadoran authorities. The lack of justice in other cases should not prevent the FMLN from doing the right thing in this case, Moakley reminded them, in a clear reference to the Jesuit case. He insisted that they set a higher standard of behavior, and suggested that a resolution of the case would build confidence in the FMLN's commitment to peace.[42]

In December 1991, Villalobos, in New York for the UN peace negotiations, told McGovern that they were prepared to hand the accused combatants over on the condition that there would be no death penalty.[43] He asked for a meeting with Moakley. McGovern sent Moakley two memos suggesting how to proceed. The first advised Moakley to push for a handover to U.S. rather than Salvadoran officials, with Moakley himself guaranteeing safe passage by his own presence. McGovern had already checked with the Defense Department, which was prepared to send a plane, but the State Department objected. "You are the only guy the FMLN trusts," McGovern pointed out. A second memo reflects McGovern's impatience with foot-dragging on the FMLN side. Moakley should remind Villalobos that "I personally feel betrayed. I am told that one of your field commanders is holding it up. I can't believe that." Moakley should say that if they couldn't resolve the issue, the peace process and reconstruction aid would be jeopardized, "and all of you will look like shit. Already the State Department has told me that I've been 'used' by the FMLN. I want to prove them wrong."[44]

Moakley never met with Villalobos because he had a minor surgical procedure on December 12. He had a lesion on his kidney removed at the Brigham and Women's Hospital. Told that he would make a full and complete recovery, he cracked, "Yeah, but can you say the same about the economy?"; it was now in recession.[45]

Leonel Gomez convinced the guerrillas to accept a simple hand-over arrangement. Moakley got a prominent Washington attorney to pre-pare a legal document by which both sides agreed that the two suspects would surrender to Moakley and be granted a fair trial. Unfortunately, the embassy and FBI came up with a ridiculous plan that Gomez and the guerrillas found unacceptable. The FBI proposed that the suspects be de-livered to a hotel in Honduras, where the FBI would claim to have cap-tured them. "No one in Central America in their right mind would trust a scheme like that," Leonel Gomez later told a reporter.[46] In March 1992, two months after the signing of the peace accords, the men surrendered to Salvadoran authorities, were tried, found guilty, and quickly freed in the general amnesty that Moakley had opposed.[47] By his actions in the Pickett-Dawson case, Joe Moakley showed that he believed in dispassion-ate principles of justice that applied to all.

★ ★ ★

These dramatic events in Joe Moakley's life were overshadowed by politi-cal events at home. In a crowded field of Democratic contenders for the nomination, the young, charismatic governor Bill Clinton was emerg-ing as a front-runner, challenging former Massachusetts senator Paul Tsongas in the New Hampshire primary. Clinton was a political phe-nomenon—brilliant, hard working, handsome, and backed by a promi-nent wife who acted as a colleague to her husband; this was a modern marriage that challenged traditional sensibilities regarding gender rela-tions. As the primary neared, another aspect of the marriage exploded into the news as a former Clinton girlfriend told all to a tabloid news-paper for a huge payout. The night of the Super Bowl, both Clintons appeared together in a television interview, with Hillary Clinton stick-ing up for her husband and rescuing his reputation. The public loved it. Clinton, a "comeback kid," ran well in the primary and went on to win the nomination in a campaign marked by a third party challenger, the bizarre Texas billionaire Ross Perot. President Bush, hindered by a fail-ing economy, looked out of touch in a series of October debates. The youthful Democratic president and his running mate, Al Gore of Ten-nessee, celebrated at the Inaugural Ball to the tune of the saxophone-playing Clinton's rocking theme song, "Don't Stop Thinking about Tomorrow."[48]

There were a few changes in the Massachusetts congressional delegation that year. The state lost Brian Donnelly's Dorchester district to redistricting. Two Republican challengers, Peter Blute in the 3rd District and Peter Torkildsen in the 6th, defeated Democratic incumbents; John Olver, a Democrat, was elected to his first full term in the 1st District after the death of Republican Silvio Conte, and Marty Meehan, a Democrat, won fellow Democrat Chester Atkins's seat in the 4th District. Moakley faced token opposition in an expanded district that now included a part of Brockton. Nationally, Democrats maintained control of the House and Senate.

Joe Moakley had good reason to face the New Year and new administration with renewed political optimism. He had done his work in El Salvador, and imagined he could now focus his attention on his own city and state. But the visit to Santa Marta and the new friendship with the Jesuits of the University of Central America had changed him forever. He had promised them that he'd be back. He little realized that the road he had embarked upon would take an unexpected turn in the new Clinton administration.

12

★ ★ ★ ★ ★

Death and Resurrection

J oe Moakley relished the inauguration of President Bill Clinton. He
had served in Congress for twenty years in January 1993, only four of
them under a Democratic president. Unlike Jimmy Carter, Clinton
came into office without having run against a corrupt Washington establishment, and he appointed former representatives like Leon Panetta to
important offices that worked closely with the Congress. Moakley liked
Clinton's style too. He recognized the new president as a gifted politician
who, like himself, came from modest circumstances. The president easily
rubbed shoulders with ordinary working people, and yet he had studied
at Oxford.

Clinton enjoyed majorities in both houses of Congress. Fifty-seven
Democratic senators could do business with Senate Republican leader
Bob Dole, a pragmatist who knew how to compromise. In the House,
Speaker Tom Foley, Majority Leader Dick Gephardt, and Whip David
Bonior led 258 Democrats of varying political hues. Moakley worked eas-
ily with this leadership team and Republican leader Bob Michel. When
Clinton took office the Cold War was over and the Soviet Union was of-
ficially dead. Central America was at peace. Moakley and his colleagues
tingled with optimism.

Moakley also had reason to be wary. Clinton associated himself with
the Democratic Leadership Coalition (DLC), or "New Democrat" centrist
group within the party that had formed in 1984 after the defeat of Walter Mondale. The New Democrats respected, but distanced themselves
from, the New Deal legacy. They accepted the notion that a conservative mood predominated among the electorate and wanted to "bend the
curve" of increasing budget deficits. Emphasizing the limits of energetic
government, they sounded compassionate themes regarding the dispos-

sessed. More vociferously, they distinguished themselves from New Politics Democrats of the 1960s and 1970s such as Eugene McCarthy and George McGovern, who had led the opposition to the war in Vietnam.[1] Moakley was an instinctive New Dealer who believed in stimulating demand through government-sponsored jobs programs and cutting taxes on the middle class. In addition, by fighting against the murderous Salvadoran government, he had also taken on "New Politics" issues himself. Jim McGovern had chosen George McGovern as a mentor, as well as Moakley. So Moakley and the DLC did not see eye to eye.

The new president was confronted by a much bigger deficit problem than he had anticipated. This was the result of the "voodoo" economics derided by candidate George Bush in 1980, the "supply side" policy that cut taxes and hoped that resultant economic growth would lead to budget surpluses. After several difficult policy meetings with an economic team that included Wall Street insiders like Bob Rubin and Larry Summers, the president opted to reassure bond traders that the federal government would move toward meeting its obligations; this in turn down-sized every appropriation. The Democratic congressional leadership reluctantly accepted fiscal reality; as Dick Gephardt prophetically pointed out, congressmen faced election every two years, the president every four years, and the benefits of budget cuts might not show up in two years.[2]

Moakley agreed in general. He was part of the leadership and a loyal party man. "We're in an era of pay more and get less," he acknowledged. "Now comes the time when the credit cards are piling up in front of us and we have to finally pay the bill."[3] The bill included an energy consumption tax promoted by Vice President Al Gore, a leader on the issue of global warming who wanted to reduce carbon emissions. The energy tax was universally opposed by Republicans and some Democrats, especially those from rural districts whose constituents drove long distances to get to work.[4]

When the budget bill came to the floor, some Democrats in swing districts worried that if they voted for the energy tax, they would be voted out of office. Moakley imposed a closed rule on the energy tax; he wouldn't give the Republicans a chance to strip it away. To offset anticipated price hikes, the legislators had been promised federal heating aid to low-income voters. House Republican leader Bob Michel naturally criticized the rule, noting that "Joe and I are good friends," as did ranking Rules Committee Republican Gerald Solomon, who opposed the rule in a gentlemanly fashion.[5] The 103rd Congress would be the last American Congress in which this traditional comity would be the norm.

The dealing began, with Clinton and Gore working the phones. Moakley did too. "You do whatever you have to do," he told a reporter. "Clinton can't afford to lose." Reporter Joe Battenfeld noted, "The sixty-six year old man was in a near zombie state yesterday, operating on only three hours sleep."[6] All the Republicans voted against, thirty-eight Democrats defected, and the bill passed on a narrow 219–213 vote. However, the Senate stripped away the energy tax, and a conference committee substituted a gas tax increase, along with a higher tax on incomes over $200,000. When the final version came back to the House in August, it squeaked through on a 218–216 vote, with Republican hecklers taunting the last Democratic balloter that she would be defeated in 1994. The mood in the House was getting uglier.[7]

During the budget debate, Moakley still kept fighting for necessary earmarks for his district. A case in point was the clean-up of Boston Harbor, mandated by a federal court in the 1970s. To clean up the mess, the Massachusetts Water Resources Authority charged home-owners the highest water and sewer rates in the country; they had tripled over the past seven years. When voters elected a moderate Republican governor, Bill Weld, in 1990, President George Bush couldn't turn down his requests for relief; the state got $100 million a year from the feds.

This still wasn't enough. The rates shocked homeowners and businessmen and threatened to keep the region mired in recession. In February, Moakley, Gerry Studds, Joe Kennedy, and Ed Markey sent a letter to the president asking him to double the grant to $200 million. Later that month Moakley told a packed crowd of businessmen at Lombardo's function room in Randolph, "It'll be a tough fight to even get the $100 million. . . . I'm beginning to feel what people need is not a congressman but a Roto Rooter man." A few months later, the Clinton administration, perhaps calculating Moakley's value as Rules chairman, came through with the $100 million.[8]

This problem highlighted minor tensions running through the state delegation, and the wider issue that underpinned the harbor clean-up. Moakley hoped for a full-court press by the entire delegation, which he didn't get. The new delegation now included two Republicans, Peter Blute and Peter Torkildsen, and two independent-minded Democrats, Martin Meehan and Joe Kennedy. Meehan at first gave Moakley fits. The town of Southbridge, in Richard Neal's recession-strapped Springfield district, had lobbied for months to be the site of a Pentagon accounting facility. Meehan pressed for a site in his district, without consulting Moakley. "If we come out with more than one site from Massachusetts, we stand a good chance of losing it," he fumed. "You just don't go stomping in someone else's territory." Meehan stood his ground. "I was elected by the people in the 5th District, not Joe Moakley," he countered.[9] Coming from within his own party, this challenge represented to Moakley a breakdown in party loyalty, and an "every man for himself" sensibility that seemed to be emerging more generally in American life. By May 1994, with Ted Kennedy's support, Southbridge got the Pentagon accounting facility.[10]

Meehan made a better case on a procedural question that reflected generational differences in Congress. Peter Blute, the Worcester Republican, cosponsored a bill that would make public the names of congressmen who signed discharge petitions. A discharge petition moved a bill that was pending consideration in a committee onto the floor, regardless of the committee's deliberations. Meehan joined him. Moakley disagreed. He disapproved of discharge petitions because they short-circuited the deliberative process. He knew that the petitions were often the tools of special interest groups seeking a special dispensation for their industry. Revealing the names of the petitioners would alert the lobbyists to those who had not signed and cause them to descend with threats upon the holdouts; a bad business, Moakley thought. He and Meehan joined a public debate in the newspapers, arguing for their respective views. To Moakley's dismay, the ground was shifting beneath his feet on this issue. The public responded readily to broadside denunciations of "government insiders" and the bill passed the House 384–40, with the entire state delegation abandoning their dean. Moakley and Meehan later improved their relationship, after getting off to a difficult start.[11]

Moakley was a little jealous of Kennedy's inside track with President Bill Clinton. The resentment came to a head over Clinton's appointment of an ambassador to Ireland. Moakley promoted his former colleague Brian Donnelly of Dorchester, who had championed the cause of Irish immigrants in the House. Kennedy, who had worked hard on the Irish peace process, promoted his sister Jean Kennedy Smith, who got the post. The pro-Republican *Boston Herald*, always eager to play up internal Democratic rivalries, billed the dust-up as a "donnybrook," but Moakley held no lingering antipathy toward Kennedy. In fact, the two were moving closer together as their prolabor stances put them on the same side of the barricades during the Clinton administration.[12]

The big test of Joe Moakley's relation with his president and members of the delegation came over the North American Free Trade Act (NAFTA). NAFTA was born during the George Bush presidency. The idea was to reduce tariff barriers and promote the free flow of capital and commodities to Mexico. Its mostly Big Business supporters saw NAFTA as a "win-win" proposition that would grow the American economy while giving Mexican consumers access to cheaper American-made goods. Its detractors, mostly in the labor movement, saw the plan as a job-killer that would encourage capital flight to low-wage Mexico. What made the debate interesting is that people took sides on it across class and party lines. Clinton, the New Democrats, and Republicans were for it; billionaire businessman Ross Perot mobilized working-class support in 1992 by proclaiming "that giant sucking sound you hear is your job going to Mexico." NAFTA's effects would vary district by district, depending on matters such as whether a district had export-dependent industry, or had a powerful labor movement. Joe Moakley's district had both. House Speaker Tom Foley, who represented Seattle, and hence Boeing Aviation, supported the bill, but Majority Leader Dick Gephardt and Whip David Bonior represented Rust Belt districts with strong unions that were militantly opposed.[13] The battle was joined. Moakley stayed diplomatically silent.

The matter came to a head late in October when Clinton visited the Gillette factory at the edge of South Boston to sell his plan. Gillette's enormous sign signaled its global ambitions: "World Shaving Headquarters" meant they wanted to sell razor blades everywhere. Its chairman predicted that NAFTA could allow his company to triple its sales in Mexico. Gillette gave Clinton, whose oratorical gifts soared when he was bullish on America's opportunities, a chance to pitch the free trade message to workers assembled inside the factory. Moakley introduced the president; journalists observed that the congressman looked uncomfortable.[14]

Moakley was publicly undecided, but he quietly opposed NAFTA. "Just because I'm introducing him doesn't mean I endorse his sermon," Moakley told a reporter. Moakley's friends in the labor movement threatened to picket, but the congressman dissuaded them. "I'd rather the president come to my district to talk about health care. But he is my president and I don't want him to be embarrassed in my district." The workers applauded Clinton's speech. They were well-paid and nonunion, a perfect audience for the pro-NAFTA side. The president was joined by Republican governor Bill Weld, a big promoter of Massachusetts industries seeking global markets.[15]

Moakley got fifty calls a day, almost all anti-NAFTA. Moakley heard it from the administration side too. Clinton urged Moakley to support NAFTA as they sat in the back of the presidential limo; he got calls from Secretary of State Warren Christopher and Secretary of the Treasury Lloyd Bentsen; Secretary of Labor Robert Reich praised Joe Kennedy for doing so.[16]

To mollify the president, Moakley invited him to a South Boston bar during his visit. Patrons of the Cornerstone Restaurant on West Broadway got a hint that something was up when Secret Service men came by the night before. "Bill Bellies Up to the Bar" made a perfect headline the next day, an appropriate riposte to President Reagan's visit to a Dorchester tavern a decade earlier. "The president loves to be among the working people," Moakley declared. "He's a man of the people."[17] The moment perfectly captured Moakley's political skill. He stood up for the president while diplomatically opposing one of his key policies.

The complexity of the situation only grew when Clinton visited the Kennedy Library and used the occasion to remind his audience of President Kennedy's support for free trade. Ted Kennedy, who was still undecided, laughingly grabbed his own necktie and yanked it above his head, indicating that Clinton was killing him. Yet Congressman Joe Kennedy was in favor. "Some of us are not convinced," Moakley said of Clinton's speech. Ted Kennedy told a reporter that he might be for NAFTA if Moakley backed it, a sign of Kennedy's respect for Moakley.[18]

The vote neared in November, and no one could predict how it would come out. Moderate opponents like Moakley came under increasing pressure from both sides. Boston business leaders met with Moakley and argued that economists predicted job growth of 12,600 in the region should NAFTA pass. Representatives of the International Brotherhood of Electrical Workers Local 103 doubted the figures and wondered what kind of jobs those would be. Trade unionists in their work boots and Irish scally caps protested NAFTA on the Taunton Green, near Moakley's office. Jim McGovern told reporters about his boss: "He thinks some of the concerns raised by the unions are legitimate: that Mexican wages will stay down and drag down U.S. wages."[19]

President Clinton and Vice President Gore worked the phones as voting began. The Massachusetts delegation split. Five congressmen—Kennedy, Markey, Meehan, Studds, and Republican Torkildsen—voted in favor. Five voted against—Frank, Moakley, Neal, Olver, and Republican Blute. "I didn't see the protection for the working man that should have been in there," Moakley remarked.[20] The lineup cannot be explained by ideology or party affiliation. Members with declining industrial bases and strong unions voted against. They represented, respectively, New Bedford, Boston, Springfield, Pittsfield, and Worcester. The other districts typically included high-tech, nonunion industries such as software, medical services, or biotech whose jobs wouldn't be going to Mexico under any circumstances.

Moakley urged labor leaders not to campaign against Democrats who voted for NAFTA. The bill passed the House 234–206, with 132 Republicans and 102 Democrats making up the winning coalition, an unusual cross-party margin. Moakley, despite his opposition to NAFTA, admired the way Clinton got the bill through and hoped that his misgivings might prove wrong. "Clinton just pulled the damn thing out and really showed his mettle."[21] He was relieved that Clinton didn't try to buy him off, as so many other votes had been purchased during the horse trading. What if Clinton had offered to pay for the whole Boston Harbor clean-up? Moakley's big issue in 1993, a reporter asked. "I voted my conscience and I think I did the best thing for the working man," Moakley replied.[22]

The following January Tip O'Neill died. Moakley gave an emotional eulogy to his best friend and mentor. "A reporter once asked me what kind of congressman I wanted to be," Moakley told the hushed mourners in Tip's North Cambridge neighborhood. Crowds gathered outside in the snow at St. John the Evangelist Church on Massachusetts Avenue, a modest beige brick building whose north tower gave it an unbalanced look. "I said I wanted to be a Tip O'Neill type of congressman. . . . He cared about everyone, and he wasn't particularly impressed with those with power." He and Evelyn had shared Thanksgiving dinners with Tip and Millie for years at Tip's place on Cape Cod. The two congressmen had been very similar in style and sensibility; two lunch-bucket Irish Catholic pols whose old gangs stood by them.[23]

The great disappointment of Clinton's first term was his failure to pass the Health Security Act that would have achieved universal health-care coverage and brought down the rapidly rising cost of health care. Clinton had run on the issue during the election campaign. Many Americans sensed the need for action. Political scientist Alex Wadden noted, "In 1960 national health care expenditures accounted for 5.1 percent of U.S. GDP . . . and had already reached 13.4 percent by 1992." Almost 40 million Americans, about 15 percent of all, had no health insurance. Critics of the unique American system pointed out its strange defining characteristic: it was employer-based, putting a major drag on the economy. Something did have to be done. At the outset of 1993, Democrats believed that they had an ally in the pragmatic House Republican leader Bob Michel, and they probably did at that point. Hillary Clinton chaired a blue ribbon panel that held numerous public hearings and finally produced a lengthy report.[24]

This centrist proposal was dubbed "managed competition," and it was explained by candidate Bill Clinton in 1992 as including "personal choice, private care, private insurance, private management, but a national system to put a lid on costs, to require insurance reforms, to facilitate partnerships between business, government, and health care providers." In line with the New Democratic appraisal of the conservative public mood, the plan relied on a private sector solution. It differed from the single-payer approach that decoupled health insurance from employment, and made health care a government-run program like the popular Medicare program for seniors. Some liberals therefore gave only lukewarm support to Clinton's program.[25] Bill and Hillary "personally delivered our health care legislation to Congress," Bill Clinton recorded in his memoir. "Many House Republicans had praised our efforts," Clinton remembered. He expected the bill to pass.[26]

So did Moakley. "It's a big, big project," he declared. "This is probably bigger than Social Security. All the chairmen, they believe in the concept. But turf is an awful precious thing up here." Moakley quietly had his reservations about assigning the crafting of the bill to an extracongressional body headed by the president's wife, but he was a team player with a key role in moving the bill through the process. Moakley spoke once a week with either the president or Hillary Clinton. The tone, he said, was, "Hope you can make this one fly." Ultimately, the bill would have to be reviewed by seven House committees. Hillary Clinton held her first news interview on health care in Moakley's office. Moakley predicted that the legislation might be introduced gradually, "with the simple things handled first." David Bonior, who also served on the Rules Committee, assured a reporter that "Moakley is the guy to get them [the committee chairmen] to work together."[27]

Conservatives in the Democratic Party advanced an alternative plan. This was the brainchild of Jim Cooper from Tennessee, which promised to add only 60 percent of the uninsured to the insured category by means of market-based incentives. Cooper contrasted his bill as a bipartisan alternative to the leftist measure cooked up by the Clintons.[28]

By summer, Joe Moakley saw trouble ahead. He gave a passionate speech to four hundred ophthalmologists, urging them to lobby their own congressmen to get everybody covered.[29] He felt the gathering storm on the Republican side. "The minority are much more militant now than they used to be," he told a reporter. "The days of Tip O'Neill and Gerry Ford and Bob Michel, who'd fight a bill to the death and go out and play golf the next day—that just doesn't happen anymore," he noted ruefully. Moakley was ready to play hardball too and signaled that there would be a closed rule should a bill come to the floor.[30]

The Republican enemies of health-care reform calculated that any gain for the nation was a loss for them in the November election. Using this zero-sum approach that treated compromise as treason, Newt Gingrich and Dick Armey dragged out the debate as the Democrats splintered. Meanwhile, the insurance companies unleashed an effective advertising campaign that sank popular support for health care reform by 20 percent. Moakley felt frustrated. "They don't want to give the president a victory," he groused. Moakley praised Clinton for tackling the health care, crime and welfare issues, and complained that "people started walking away from him. I've never seen a president so besieged."[31] The bill stalled in the Senate, and by August health care was effectively dead. Joe Moakley never got to play his expected role of carefully guiding it through the House. "Every year it seems to get worse and worse," Moakley glumly told a reporter as gridlock crippled a Democratic-controlled Congress. The worst was yet to come.[32]

Minority Whip Newt Gingrich seized control of the Republican agenda in the midterm election by devising a national platform, called the "Contract with America," for Republican congressional candidates. Congressional candidates usually emphasize what they have done or will do for their district. Gingrich's gambit made the campaign a referendum on Clinton and the Congress. Clinton biographer Nigel Hamilton observed the odd similarities between Gingrich and Clinton—brilliant sons of doting mothers and disapproving step-fathers, they both became draft-avoiding college professors whose careers would be characterized by adulterous relations with women. Both were very ambitious. Gingrich touted his affinity with Ronald Reagan, but there was one big difference. Reagan had a sunny disposition, but Gingrich could never quite hide the dark side that made him look like the villainous Richard III in Shakespeare's play. On September 27, the day after Senate Majority Leader George Mitchell announced that health care was dead in the 103rd Congress, Gingrich assembled a host of Republican congressional candidates on the Capitol steps to announce the common platform. The Contract with America was a mean-spirited compendium whose ten points included a balanced budget, limited welfare benefits, rigorous application of the death penalty, an increased defense budget, more social security, and cutting taxes. How this was all supposed to be paid for remained unaddressed. It was deja voodoo economics all over again.[33]

Moakley didn't face much of a race in 1994; he hadn't since 1982. This time his opponent was Michael Murphy, a moderate African American who served on several corporate boards but had never won elective office. The state Republicans offered Murphy little support; Murphy turned his frustration on Moakley, who, perhaps uncharitably, declined to debate him.[34]

The bigger story was Jim McGovern's venture into electoral politics. Peter Blute, the Worcester Republican, had been a particular thorn in Moakley's side, and it looked to some like this was Moakley's revenge— Batman sending Robin to defeat the Joker in his deck. That was not the case. McGovern was a young man, harboring his own ambitions, seeing an opportunity in a traditionally Democratic district to beat a fluke Republican. Unfortunately for McGovern, five other Democrats had come to the same conclusion, and he lost the primary to a state representative. However, McGovern ran a strong race for a rookie, finishing second in a field of six with 13,603 votes to the winner's 17,619. No one else tallied in the five figures. Moakley's policy was that staffers who left could not come back, but for McGovern he made an exception. "Moakley told me I was too stiff," McGovern remembered. "He called, he said, 'What the hell happened? I thought you were gonna win!' and I said something like, 'How about, nice race?' but he was right. I needed to learn to tell some jokes."[35]

All eyes in Massachusetts were on the Senate race, a battle of dynasties. Ted Kennedy faced a serious opponent in moderate millionaire Mitt Romney, the son of the former Michigan governor. Kennedy found Romney's weak spot as a venture capitalist business consultant whose real forte was ruthlessly down-sizing foundering businesses and collecting huge sums for his advice. It looked like a tight race; Kennedy campaigned in the final days with Moakley and Bulger at his side in South Boston. Kennedy won, as did all the other Massachusetts incumbents, including Republican governor Bill Weld; Moakley won his by a landslide.[36]

Moakley held his victory party at the International Brotherhood of Electrical Workers hall in Dorchester. "We knew there'd be some losses, but we didn't expect to lose the House," congressional aide Sean Ryan remembered. "Moakley went out and made his speech; we were feeling very good about that. But then we started watching television, and as the returns came in, and we saw that we had lost the House; that was like a kick in the stomach."[37] It was a historic reversal, as Democrats lost the Senate too. Now Gingrich was poised to become Speaker of the House.

Massachusetts Democrats looked to Moakley for answers. In February after the election he gave a speech at the McCormack Institute on the University of Massachusetts campus to reflect on the debacle. He praised Clinton for his accomplishments, now mostly forgotten: a family medical leave bill, the deficit reduction package, a crime bill, an education measure, and creation of a domestic service corps based on a Boston area youth program. Perhaps Congress should have banned lobbyist gifts, or passed campaign finance reform, he mused, noting the anti-incumbent mood. But Democrats should not conclude that the country had shifted to the right, and that the party should follow them.

The attacks by Gingrich "were so outrageous that we often never responded to them," Moakley pointed out. He warned about growing economic inequality despite economic growth. The top 20 percent had done better, but the rest of the population had seen its real income decrease, and they took that out on the party in power. Democrats therefore had to return to their base, not drift to the right. He dismissed the balanced budget amendment to the Constitution as "stupid" and reminded his audience of an old saying from Speaker Sam Rayburn, that he had heard Tip O'Neill repeat: "Any jackass can kick down a barn—but it takes a real carpenter to build one." Moakley offered four themes for Democrats in the new Congress. They should promote a jobs program through incentives for new technology industries and by rebuilding the aging physical infrastructure; a national health-care plan that would cover all Americans (the Republican plan was "take two tax breaks and call me in the morning"); a plan to cut crime through drug and alcohol rehabilitation programs; and a return to civility in public discourse.[38]

Moakley thus reaffirmed the principles of the New Deal, updated for current conditions. He still saw an active role for government to stimulate the economy and protect society's weakest members. Notably absent from his list of accomplishments was NAFTA, which he saw as a business-inspired antilabor arrangement. Moakley's plan was for the Democrats to regroup, campaign on their own terms, and win the next election. Clinton would draw the opposite conclusion and attempt to conciliate the Republican House majority.

"Every year it gets worse and worse," Moakley had moaned in August about Congress. Now life was about to get a lot worse, in more ways than one, and all at the same time.

* * *

Evelyn had been in declining health for several years. In July 1993 her doctors noticed a lesion on her lung; she had been a heavy smoker, and the doctors ordered her to quit. Later in the month she had it removed. Joe stayed with her throughout the ordeal.[39] At first it looked as though the operation had eliminated the cancer, but in the next year Joe came home one day and found Evelyn motionless on the floor. Doctors discovered a brain tumor. Evelyn began a series of radiation treatments that she endured with courage. "Sometimes she gets blue, sometimes she's not—she's a strong girl," Moakley told a reporter in May. They both knew she was dying. "This thing is never all over. A woman and cancer, it's a deadly foe."[40]

Evelyn had not signed up to be a politician's wife. He was just a state representative when he married her. They had wanted to have children, but they couldn't; she had wanted at least a normal life. District director Fred Clark remembered once picking up his boss at Logan Airport and Moakley's insisting that he drive really fast back to South Boston. When they got home, Moakley rushed to take out the garbage. The story suggests a woman who sometimes felt abandoned, and who wanted her husband to take out the trash like every other guy on the block.[41]

She was a private person, and more interested in her husband, Joe, than the latest infighting on the Appropriations Committee. She stood by his side on election nights but never hit the campaign trail with him. "When I decided to run for office," Jim McGovern recalled, "Evelyn called my wife and told her to talk me out of it."[42] Lisa McGovern worked as a congressional aide like her husband; she came from the feminist generation of women who expected to have careers and be equal partners with their spouses. Evelyn and Joe had grown up and shaped their identities in the 1940s, when the expectation was that women would be housewives. They conducted their marriage through changing times.

Then Joe's health declined even more rapidly than Evelyn's. His hip was killing him. "I may need hip replacement surgery," he announced. "My wife Evelyn urged me to go public with this information because it will be the first time in a long time that the word 'hip' and the name Joe Moakley have been used in the same sentence."[43] Moakley was feeling tired all the time, and thought that the hip was the problem. He was using a cane, and bumped into Congresswoman Carrie Meeks on the floor, who was using one too. He tapped her cane with his. "Ready for the hockey game?" he joked.[44]

Moakley's doctors told him that the fatigue was not due to his hip. His liver was failing, and if he didn't get a transplant, he was going to die. Moakley also had contracted hepatitis B from a blood transfusion. The doctors gave Moakley a beeper and told him to wait. He told the press, who asked if he had heard from former Yankees center-fielder Mickey Mantle, an alcoholic who had just gotten a transplant. Moakley, resiliently jocular, said he hoped that they didn't give him Mantle's old liver. He went into a hospital room adjoining Evelyn's at Massachusetts General Hospital; Jim McGovern remembers watching the Fourth of July fireworks from the hospital window. The operation would have to be in

Charlottesville, Virginia, the only East Coast hospital that did liver transplants for patients with hepatitis.[45]

A week later the beeper sounded around 11:00 p.m. There was a certain poetic justice in this: Moakley's good deed in establishing a national organ donor network during Jamie Fiske's emergency had come back to help him. McGovern's phone rang next; he was to join Moakley immediately on a flight to Charlottesville from the Norwood Airport. McGovern called his driver and the two men got lost in the dark as Moakley waited on the runway. Good naturedly, Moakley gave McGovern hell and the plane flew off into the night. The next day Moakley endured a twelve-hour operation. For the next seven days he was very weak and couldn't even speak, but the transplant was working. "I told him his wife sends her love, and his eyes lit up," McGovern said.[46]

Moakley spent the next six weeks recuperating. He did a lot of thinking. The chances that a transplant recipient with hepatitis would survive for five years were 50 to 60 percent. Evelyn probably didn't have much time left. She came down to visit between radiation treatments. They thought about their lives together. McGovern thought about his future too.

When he got back on his feet, Moakley made an appearance in South Boston, campaigning for young city council candidate Michael Flaherty. He looked like an old, sick man. He hobbled about on a cane and was taking a lot of medication. He had lost about thirty pounds, looked gaunt, and had grown a white beard. A few weeks later he called a press conference, and word went out to the media that he was going to announce his retirement.[47]

An hour before the press conference in Washington, Evelyn called Joe from Boston. She knew the only thing that he really loved to do was his job. The two of them could make a deal. Joe would work a shorter Washington week and spend more time with her. Every Boston outlet with a reporter in Washington came to the news conference, as did several of his colleagues. They were all stunned. "I was prepared just an hour ago to announce that I'm not going to be a candidate for re-election, that my wife deserves my presence. . . . But when I told her what I was going to do, despite her loneliness and despite her physical condition, she said, 'Joe, I just think that you're going too far.'" Moakley wasn't dropping out. His press secretary, Karin Walser, had told reporters that Moakley had a retirement speech in his hands, "but we don't know what he will say once he gets up there."[48]

The rambling news conference delivered lots of human interest; the media gave the story more coverage than Moakley had ever gotten before. "In an extraordinary turn of events, Representative John Joseph Moakley, the most powerful New England Democrat in the House, decided yesterday to end his twenty-three-year-old congressional career. And then he didn't," the *Boston Globe* story began.[49] No one quite knew what to make of it. One political cartoon showed pall bearers hoisting Moakley's casket toward an open grave as a hand reached out from within and a startled priest heard a voice cry out, "On second thought!"[50] Newspaper columnists divided over it. One, Peter Gelzinis, in a tribute to the heart of a fighter, lauded the gritty courage of the old man as he battled against the odds.[51] Another, the acerbic Howie Carr, kicked Moakley when he was down, scoffing at the "whacko" television appearance by a man who "seems to have one foot in the grave and the other on a banana peel."[52] Eileen McNamara, an admirer, thought Moakley should have retired to spend time with his wife.[53]

Moakley did look old and disoriented. He later acknowledged to a reporter, in a confessional interview, that he was heavily medicated at the time of the news conference, looked terrible, and probably shouldn't have gone public.[54] Yet, by October, he was recovering quickly and looked like the Moakley of old, although his hip was still giving him pain. Moakley fought through it; he had an incredible ability to work despite pain, his aide Sean Ryan later pointed out.[55] Back from the political grave, the next unexpected big adventure of Joe Moakley's journey was about to begin. He was sixty-eight years old.

★　★　★

Two years earlier, in April 1993, a few months after Clinton's inauguration and one month after the release of the UN El Salvador Truth Commission report, Moakley's newest friends threw him a birthday party. These were the leaders of the American Jesuit educational establishment. They had conspired with his old Boston friends to endow a chair at the University of Central America in his name. A thousand guests paid a thousand dollars each, and the champagne flowed. The Boston political establishment came down and stole the show from the holy men; to the Washington press corps, this was a great chance to see the rare birds of America's most unusual political aviary in full springtime song. Tip O'Neill returned to Washington; and Moakley even got Ray Flynn and William Bulger to join him in warbling "Southie Is My Home Town." Bulger told a few jokes: "Moakley and I want to be buried at St. Augustine's cemetery because we want to remain politically active," after which he repaired to the Dubliner Pub, at which he performed a James Michael Curley imitation. Against this competition even Bill Clinton's appearance got buried in the story, and few could remember that Miguel Francisco Estrada, president of the UCA, had announced that he would confer an honorary degree upon Moakley.[56]

The following year, in February, Moakley went to El Salvador for a brief third trip. In his speech at the UCA, Moakley sounded a new theme: the need to rebuild El Salvador. He had already made three signal contributions to the tiny nation: defending its immigrants to the United States, unearthing the truth about the Jesuit murders, and winning the peace. For the rest of his life he would remain committed to this fourth goal; he would often say, "We spent five or six billion dollars destroying the place, and we ought to spend at least as much to rebuild it." At the UCA he declared: "For most of this century the U.S. has ignored Central America except in times of war. And in those cases our objective has not been economic development, but rather, to help one side in a conflict defeat another side."

At the university ceremony, Father Estrada pointed out that Moakley had made "an extraordinary contribution to uncovering the truth in this most painful case involving the martyrs of this university." Since the signing of the peace accords two years earlier, political violence had largely, but not entirely, subsided; two dozen leftists had been gunned down over the past two years. The Jesuits stood squarely for peace and Christian forgiveness; they had accepted the verdict of the court and the amnesty decreed by President Cristiani as his price for the UN Truth commission. Moakley was for peace too, but he had never agreed with the amnesty. Moakley, still dissatisfied with the final adjudication of the Jesuit case, echoing the words of Father Ellacuria, reminded the audience, "The killings will not stop, and the intimidation will not stop until those who perpetuate these crimes realize that there is a price to pay."[57]

If there was no justice to be had in the Salvadoran courts, Moakley at least believed in "naming and shaming," Jim McGovern remembered. Moakley, accompanied by McGovern, district director Roger Kineavy, and former rebel leader Ana Guadalupe Martinez, made an extraordinary visit by helicopter to the site of the El Mozote massacre to say a prayer for the victims. El Mozote, located in northern Morazan province, was the forgotten horror of the war. In early December 1981, elite troops of the American-trained Atlacatl battalion massacred 767 unarmed men, women, and children in that peasant village and about two hundred others in neighboring hamlets. The United States pumped another $5 billion of ammunition into the hands of the killers over the next decade. In the months before Moakley's visit, Mark Danner reported in the *New Yorker* on the UN's forensic investigation of the massacre, which unearthed the bodies. Moakley's visit symbolized his commitment to the memory of the victims.[58]

★   ★   ★

A year and a half later, while Moakley was recovering from the liver transplant, Jim McGovern approached him with startling news. Moakley recalled: "McGovern walks over to the office. He says 'Castro wants to talk to you.' I said, 'I don't need any couches.' He said, 'Not that Castro, the Castro in Cuba.' I said, 'What's he want to talk to me about?'" Despite Moakley's humorous, self-deprecating account, he knew.[59]

Fidel Castro had heard of him through one of the Salvadoran guerrilla commanders, Joaquin Villalobos, whose associate was the woman who accompanied Moakley to El Mozote. Villalobos was reassessing his own past; so was Castro. The collapse of Soviet communism cut off Cuba's economic lifeline. Of all the cultural shotgun marriages in the world, that between the Russians and the Cubans was the world's most unlikely. Russia was frozen, brooding; its cultural markers were Dostoevsky, chess, and Shostakovich. Cuba, whatever its problems, was warm and festive; its cultural markers were rum, cigars, salsa music, and baseball. The Cubans missed Russia's financial support, but probably nobody, Fidel Castro included, missed a particular Russian "friend." Fidel Castro reached out to Joe Moakley because of his work in El Salvador.

If the end of the Cold War left Castro in a tough spot, it also left U.S. policy toward Cuba in an illogical time-warp. The United States had recognized the USSR since 1933 and never withdrew its ambassador, not even during the purge trials conducted by Joseph Stalin; arch anticommunist president Richard Nixon had visited China, which the United States continued to recognize even after the Tiananmen Square massacre; and in 1993 the United States, prodded by senators John Kerry and John McCain, both Vietnam veterans, recognized Vietnam. Cuba had never fired a shot at the United States, and while Cuba had a bad human rights record, Castro never did anything that approached the records of Stalin or Mao, both of whom he reviled. Cuban troops never fired into peaceful demonstrations, as had U.S.-backed regimes in Nicaragua and El Salvador. Yet the Cuban-American exile community, clustered in the crucial swing state of Florida, blocked any discussion of ending the trade embargo that helped strangle the Cuban economy, and denied Americans the right to travel there. Extending diplomatic relations was not even on the agenda. President Clinton, mindful of the 1994 drubbing he had just taken at the polls, was tacking right to "triangulate" his position with the congressional Republicans. No progress seemed likely on Cuba policy, despite its foolishness.

Moakley held a safe seat in Congress, and he was maturing as a statesman on Latin America. In April 1995 he sent a letter to President Clinton, urging an end to the embargo. He argued that the embargo "strengthened the sentiments of nationalism in Cuba, provoked an increase in immigration to the United States, and it has provided Mr. Castro with the perfect excuse to justify the failure of his system." He noted that former president Nixon, Pope John Paul II, conservative columnist William F. Buckley, the United Nations, and the U.S. Chamber of Commerce had all said pretty much the same thing. Nor were all Cuban-American groups uniformly supportive of the embargo. Moakley drew the obvious conclusion that exposure to American people and products would further, rather than retard, the democratic process in Cuba. A veteran diplomat, Elizabeth Shannon, wrote an op-ed the following month that included an apposite remark by a European diplomat: "Castro could probably defend Cuba against 100,000 Marines. There is no way he could defend it against 100,000 tourists."[60]

So Castro invited Moakley to meet him in late October when he was in New York for the UN General Assembly session. President Clinton and every other U.S. politician shunned Castro during his three-day visit. Moakley, accompanied by McGovern, braved an angry exile picket line and attended a buffet reception at the Cuban mission to the United Nations, along with two hundred foreign dignitaries. Castro embraced Moakley warmly, kissing him on both cheeks. Moakley thought, "Hope that picture doesn't get into the *South Boston Tribune!*" They spoke twice, for a total of forty minutes, as Castro worked the room. "We talked about human rights, we talked about commerce, we talked about trade," Moakley told one reporter. Castro invited Moakley to Cuba. "Fidel is not my hero. He screwed up the country, but this is 1995 and we've come to terms with Vietnam, China and Russia. . . . He seemed to understand that the onus was on him now. He knows human rights in Cuba have to change." Moakley also told Castro that he hoped President Clinton might ease restrictions on commerce and travel in his second term.[61]

Moakley wasn't flying under the radar, either. He wrote an op-ed for the *Boston Globe*, arguing, "Change in Cuba will come only through dialogue. We should be talking to Castro and Cuban citizens about both trade and human rights." He would be going to Cuba with a business delegation, including executives from Gillette, Reebok, GTE, biotech companies, banks, and hotel chains. America's business class wanted in on a Cuban market that was already doing $2.5 billion worth of business with America's less blinkered European rivals.[62]

Meanwhile, the Republican Congress was heading down the opposite path. Representative Dan Burton of Indiana and Jesse Helms, the North Carolina former segregationist who now headed the Senate Foreign Relations Committee, were preparing the Cuban Liberty and Democratic Solidarity Act, which would punish foreign businessmen who invested in Cuba by exposing them to litigation in U.S. courts. Secretary of State Warren Christopher warned Speaker Gingrich that he would advise a veto of this bill, sure to be condemned in every European and Latin American capital.[63] Republican congresswoman Ileana Ros-Lehtinen of Florida, a Cuban-American, wrote to President Clinton asking him to deny Moakley a visa to Castro's "slave economy."[64]

Clinton allowed the visas but threw a bone to the hard-liners by waiting until the last minute to do so, and hemming the trip around with restrictions. Clinton was already by this point taking his guidance from the cynical consultant Dick Morris, and was careful not to inflame conservative sensibilities. "In fact, the State Department didn't want to let us go," Moakley recalled. They told him: "So then if you go there . . . you can't tour the tobacco companies. So I said, 'Okay.' We didn't tour them. We visited them."[65]

Moakley and his staff accompanied a dozen New England–area business leaders hoping to get in on their share of the Cuban market. They visited factories and farms and met with government economic ministers. Moakley and McGovern pressed human rights issues at a private meeting with Castro. "I politely suggested he make some sort of move around politics and human rights reform if he wanted to avoid a still harsher embargo and set the stage for improved relations," he reported. Castro said he would "seriously consider" the idea.[66]

Meanwhile, the State Department hectored the delegation while it was in-country, insisting that Moakley bring dissidents to meetings with Cuban government officials. Moakley compared that gambit to "bringing all your former girlfriends to a marriage proposal. . . . They really screwed us around." Moakley met with seven prominent oppositionists in public, at the stately Hotel Nacional, an extraordinary occurrence, with Cardinal Jaime Ortega, and with Jewish members of a synagogue.[67]

Moakley's trip suggested the possibilities of communication with the Cuban government and with members of civil society. At another late-night meeting with Castro, Moakley presented the former baseball pitcher with Red Sox memorabilia, a cap, a watch, and a pen. "Are these Red Sox communists?" Castro joked, referring to the team color.[68]

This was feigned ignorance; before the revolution the Red Sox had scouted him. Yet there was probably more to this visit than Moakley might care to admit. Fidel Castro liked him, and Moakley at least understood Castro. They were both military veterans, almost exactly the same age. They shared a common tough virility and instinctive warmth toward the working man. This is not to suggest that Moakley was going soft on communism. But he saw in Castro not a rigid ideological Marxist, which in fact Castro had never been, but an aging dictator who was nevertheless a human being open to change. What happened next represented the tragedy of that lost possibility.

During the same January that Moakley visited Cuba, two separate sorties by private airplanes departing from the United States dropped anti-Castro leaflets over Havana. On February 24 the planes returned, and the

Cuban Air Force shot two of them down. Should Cuban airplanes have penetrated American airspace, the likelihood is that they would have been shot down too. Yet this was a monumental blunder on Castro's part if he was serious about improving relations; he unleashed all the conservative political furies in the United States. The House passed Helms-Burton 336–86, and the Senate passed it 74–22. Clinton signed the bill on the day of the Florida primary. The rest of the world rejected this extraterritorial restriction of their economic rights virtually unanimously. The European Union and a fourteen-member group of Latin American states decried a law that threatened private trade with Cuba by legal actions in an American court. One newspaper pointed out that the United States should have prevented the anti-Castro planes from taking off; the failure to do so had allowed "radical exiles to hijack U.S. policy toward Cuba." As for Moakley, he denounced the shooting down of the planes and the Helms-Burton Act. Clinton wrote him a cheese-paring, conciliatory letter explaining away his action. The opening that Moakley had sensed was now shut down.[69]

★ ★ ★

When Moakley returned from Cuba, Evelyn's health was failing, and on March 16 the brain tumor took her life. Moakley was at her side in the final weeks. She had made enormous sacrifices for him. She might have insisted that he retire and spend her final days alone with her, but she didn't. She knew his life would have to go on without her, and she gave him that gift. Meanwhile her friends and his staff looked after her. "She kept him grounded," Fred Clark remembered. "We never heard them say 'I love you' to each other, but they did. It just wasn't their style." They were more like George Burns and Gracie Allen, reporters gleaned from staffers, gruff, bantering, warm-hearted, funny. "Politics deprived her of a lot of time with him, but he was incredibly devoted to her," Sean Ryan said years later.[70]

Moakley had lost his best friend. "She was the president of my fan club and my number one critic. . . . She was the life of every party—and she was the love of my life," Moakley said. Jim McGovern offered a warm tribute at the final ceremony; he recalled her throwing a party for the hospital staff and ordering Chinese food for the nurses. "Throughout the illness, there was no self-pity, no why me?" he said. The guests were startled to notice that among the floral gifts from family, friends, and colleagues, one of them was from Fidel Castro.[71]

★ ★ ★

Moakley threw himself into his work, and soon he was back to the congressional grind. He worked successfully with Gerry Studds to make the Boston Harbor Islands part of the National Park system, bringing full circle a vision he'd had since his days as a state senator. He and Studds partnered with Clinton to shake another $50 million loose from Congress to continue the Harbor clean-up.[72] Studds was retiring; Gingrich had abolished his committee, and a close primary contest began for the open seat. Moakley faced another weak candidate who had never held elective office, a Medfield surgeon who didn't stand a chance. The big news was the Senate race between Governor Bill Weld and Senator John Forbes Kerry; the headline-writers dubbed it "the battle of the Brahmins." Weld had to get some Irish working-class votes, and he proposed that the new Northern Avenue Bridge just up from South Station, for which Moakley had acquired much of the $29 million, be named for Evelyn. Running to the center, Weld admitted that he had once voted for Moakley. Moakley felt humbled. "I'm proud to say for most of my life Evelyn was my road home . . . Now literally over this bridge she will bring me home," he said.[73]

The real thrill of the campaign season for Moakley was Jim McGovern's challenge to Peter Blute. McGovern had been thinking about running again while he nursed Moakley in the Charlottesville hospital. It would be easy to get the nomination this time—no one wanted to challenge a two-term incumbent. But the seat had been traditionally Democratic, and a reaction against the Republicans was setting in after they shut down the government in late 1995. Just as important, McGovern had learned a thing or two from Moakley. He was looser, he'd learned some jokes, he remembered people's names, he mastered the candidate's craft as he had mastered the policy-maker's. No one gave him a chance, but he won, the old-fashioned way, with shoe leather and a ground game, taking 53 percent of the vote. John Tierney defeated Republican Peter Torkildsen in the 6th District, and Bill Delahunt, after edging out his rival in a primary that required a recount, took Studds's seat. Kerry beat Weld, and Clinton beat Senate Majority Leader Bob Dole, a forward-looking candidate defeating a backward-looking candidate. The day after the election, Moakley joined McGovern in Attleboro in the street to thank passing motorists. The 1996 election was a clean sweep for Democrats in Massachusetts.[74]

In December, Moakley got the hip replacement surgery. He felt like a new man immediately. Joe Moakley was back from the grave.

13

★ ★ ★ ★ ★

Return to Santa Marta

A month after his hip replacement surgery, Joe Moakley celebrated Bill Clinton's second inauguration and the swearing-in of freshmen Jim McGovern, Bill Delahunt, and John Tierney in the new Congress. During this session, Moakley would return to El Salvador, where he was hailed as a hero in Santa Marta. In Cuba he would participate in a historic papal Mass, and meet Fidel Castro again. As they took their oaths, no member of the 105th Congress could imagine that they would conclude the session by voting on the impeachment of a president.[1]

★ ★ ★

Moakley's primary concerns always lay in his district. Two days after the inauguration, Paul P. J. Rakauskas, a teenager from the Old Colony project, died of a drug overdose. Over the past decade, South Boston had lost about two hundred young people to a plague of guns, drugs, and suicide. This wasn't supposed to happen in South Boston, a neighborhood that prided itself on family values and neighborhood solidarity.[1]

Some version of P. J.'s tragic story had been taking place in working-class communities across the nation since the 1980s. A wave of deindustrialization reduced the number of good jobs that formerly made home ownership attainable for millions. In the Boston metropolitan area the Framingham auto plant, the Quincy and Boston shipyards, and a plethora of midsize machine shops closed their doors. Sheet metal work was no longer a path to a good union job. Some young people reoriented their careers toward the new industries in high-tech manufacturing, software development, or the medical services that had made the region prosperous in the 1990s. Many young men got good jobs on the construction projects—the Big Dig, the downtown skyscrapers, or the new Orange Line—

that were reshaping the face of the city. Thousands of South Boston and Dorchester residents moved out to suburban towns and started happy families. Others did not, and some of their kids felt as though they had no future; the phrase became a slogan for a generation of punk rockers.

South Boston, however, had an additional problem that its equivalent neighborhoods did not have. Its resistance to busing in the 1970s had been predicated on the notion that it was a uniquely virtuous community of hard-working people, living by honest moral values. Their resistance to busing intensified the feeling that one couldn't trust outsiders, who didn't understand them. A bunker mentality set in, especially among those who felt abandoned by even their own politicians. South Boston tried not to notice that teenagers like P. J. Rakauskas were killing themselves. It didn't fit the narrative.

South Boston's drug trade had another unique wrinkle. The leader of its criminal underworld pretended to be the man who kept drugs out of the neighborhood. In fact, he made his money by extorting drug dealers. This was James "Whitey" Bulger, whose younger brother, William, was the state Senate president. Joe Moakley and his brothers knew Jimmy and Billy as boys; even as young teenagers they could see that the elder brother was dangerously violent. James Bulger was sent to Alcatraz in the 1950s, and after a long stint in prison he returned to Boston and became the leader of the Irish mob; their antagonists were the North End–based Italians. By the early 1980s, people who crossed Bulger started getting killed, or disappearing. People whispered that the powerful good brother was somehow protecting the bad one.

The truth turned out to be much worse. James Bulger had taken into his camp an FBI agent, John Connolly, a Southie kid who had looked up to him as a boy; Connolly in turn convinced his boss to sign Bulger up as an informant against the Italian Cosa Nostra. This was the ultimate story of neighborhood loyalty trumping the principles of law; under the FBI's protection, Bulger committed nineteen murders. When the scheme finally unraveled, the newspapers reported the unbelievable—"Whitey" Bulger had been an FBI informant, as he fled one step ahead of the state police, whose investigations the FBI had stymied for decades. Bulger wasn't caught until 2011. The story ranks among the worst scandals in FBI and U.S. law enforcement history.[2]

Joe Moakley had seen the same pattern in El Salvador, whose military caste was taught to be loyal to itself first, not to civilian authority. They too conceived themselves to be a virtuous community under siege by outsiders, and they closed ranks to justify the murder of priests and unarmed peasants. Moakley had seen American advisors, like Eric Buckland and the embassy translator who had attempted to deceive him, drawn into the criminal circle. The corrupt Boston FBI agents were just like these men; the dynamic was the same. Moakley knew the dark side of closed communities that viewed a diverse society with suspicion.

The spread of drugs, youth suicide, and criminal violence in Boston, and South Boston especially, was painful to Moakley. His own home had been burglarized in the early 1990s, and the thieves had gotten away with loot that included a championship ring given as a gift from Red Sox star Carl Yazstremski. Mayor Flynn, a neighbor famous for listening to the police scanner, showed up so fast that Evelyn and Joe kidded each other that he was in on the job. "The wave of suicides disturbed him enormously," Sean Ryan, an aide at the time, recalled. "He was so proud of what his own generation had accomplished, and to see young people giving up on life made him sad. He was very involved in the community response. He helped secure money for substance abuse programs, and Pop Warner [youth football] leagues." Beyond that, Moakley was careful not to tread on the toes of local officials who had primary responsibility for law enforcement, rehabilitation, and recreation programs. Moakley stayed loyal to William Bulger too, whose critics alleged that he had forced the retirement of a state police officer who was on his brother's tail. Moakley called Bulger and offered to take him out to dinner somewhere in public; Bulger, perhaps sensing that Moakley was trying to protect him, never took him up on it.[3]

South Boston still had to deal with lingering racial resentments from the busing period. The city's public housing projects remained segregated because the entry lists were neighborhood-based. Because of economic disparities, the majority of people on the lists were nonwhite; but the city's Housing Authority assigned people by neighborhood. Mayor Ray Flynn courageously took this issue up, and explained to two hostile South Boston audiences that the federal and state government would eliminate subsidies for the projects if the city did not comply with the legal guidelines—there had to be one citywide list for public housing. "Forced housing!" Flynn's critics jeered, an echo of "Forced busing!" and wrote him off as a traitor. This was the mayor's finest hour; his stand helped transform the city. Flynn won every ward in 1987 except the two in South Boston.

When Ray Flynn took the post of ambassador to the Vatican, City Councilor Thomas Menino, a Flynn ally cut from the same cloth as his predecessor, was appointed acting mayor. Menino was the first Italian-American to serve as mayor. After Menino's election to a full term, Moakley came to his aid on a controversial South Boston development issue.

The New England Patriots football team owner, Robert Kraft, decided to relocate its stadium from Foxboro, a suburb halfway between Boston and Providence, to South Boston. The new venue would also host rock concerts and soccer matches. Kraft promised to attract more than a million visitors a year, who would spend money in restaurants and stay at hotels. This project had the enthusiastic backing of Governor William Weld; his appointed head of Massport, Peter Blute, the former Worcester congressman; and both newspapers. Kraft, Blute, and Weld had not bothered to hold public hearings in South Boston, whose various civic associations were studying the project with a rising sense of disfranchisement. The land transfer would be made by Massport, not the city or state directly, and no legislative vote or mayoral decision could stop what looked like a fixed deal between Kraft and Weld.

South Boston had a long history of suspicion against any outsider-driven change in the neighborhood. A new problem was the neighborhood's growing traffic congestion. The Big Dig highway construction was in progress; to avoid traffic jams, commuters would abandon the expressway and cut through South Boston. The new stadium would aggravate that problem. Finally, a football stadium would transform what might be a pedestrian-friendly waterfront district into a noisy center for tail-gate partiers. Football stadiums and densely populated urban neighborhoods don't mix, especially when the neighbors don't want it. Every South Boston community group and politician united against the stadium, but no one knew what to do about it.[4]

Moakley found the fly in Kraft's ointment. The proposed twenty-seven-acre stadium site required the transfer of a small army property that the Kraft plan needed for a parking lot. Moakley called the army and asked them not to transfer the site. Perhaps the army figured that one day Moakley would be Rules Committee chairman again and they would need his help; it's not likely that army chief Togo West concluded that five acres in South Boston was vital to the defense of the United States. The army wouldn't sell, and the deal was off. Moakley, ever the class act, invited Kraft to announce his decision not to build in South Boston at a news conference in his office. This allowed Kraft to look like a good guy rather than a ruthless businessman, and he graciously backed down.[5]

"That night I walked into the Farragut House to eat," Moakley told the Globe's David Nyhan. "Everyone stood up and applauded."[6] Joe Moakley was back.

★   ★   ★

A few months later, the Jesuits at the University of Central America in San Salvador invited Moakley to give a speech on the anniversary of the slaying of their colleagues.[7] Moakley was glad to accept. He had been following events in El Salvador, and he had added a new aide, Stephen LaRose, a slender and diligent young man, to take McGovern's place as his international relations staffer. LaRose had joined the team right after college at Villanova, assisted McGovern during his final years with Moakley, and so had the appropriate training to take over this important job.[8]

El Salvador had made some significant steps forward in the years since Moakley's 1994 visit. There had been five years of peace. In March 1997 the elections returned a strong cohort of FMLN delegates to the assembly; they had a working majority through a bloc with smaller parties. The president was an ARENA businessman; the army played no role in governance. In San Salvador and Santa Ana, FMLN mayors struggled to upgrade city services. Moakley also had a very good relationship with President Clinton, the State Department, and new ambassador Anne Patterson during the second Clinton administration; he communicated to them anytime he had his own information or opinions.[9]

LaRose made an advance trip and reported the situation back to his boss. He advised Moakley not to be snowed by the good macroeconomic figures brought about by ARENA's business-friendly policy, which had privatized government utilities such as the telephone company. GDP was up, but income disparities were growing. "The poverty is horrifying. People are literally starving to death," he wrote. Another big problem was crime. The police forces had improved but possessed no modern technology, couldn't keep records, and some judges were still corrupt.[10]

Moakley and McGovern returned for five days in mid-November, setting up headquarters in the familiar Hotel Camino Real. They both felt upbeat. Moakley gave a personally revealing speech to a large crowd at the University of Central America. They filled the Ellacuria Pavilion, with people having to stand at the back; television cameras and radio microphones recorded the speech. Moakley recounted the passing of his wife, his own health problems, and his commitment to El Salvador. He told about visits he had received since the Peace Accords from Salvadoran politicians; formerly military enemies, they were now political opponents learning to work together. Moakley cited his continuing concerns—the need to reform the judicial and electoral systems, the crime problem, and the deportation of Salvadoran immigrants from the United States. He noted the partial progress on human rights and land reform, and the fair election conducted the previous March. Moakley proudly introduced McGovern, once his aide and now his colleague.[11] This was a moment of triumph and a renewal of vows.

"The trip after the liver transplant, we wondered, what could he eat?" Father Jose Maria Tojeira recalled. "It turned out he could eat anything, and he even had a few beers." After the speech, Moakley and McGovern celebrated with their old friends in the Jesuit residency, eating, drinking, and singing together. Father Jon Sobrino, the priest who had escaped assassination only by being away the night of the murders, sang a song, and other Jesuits told stories about their fallen colleagues. Moakley gave his rendition of "Redhead," an old show tune. The following night Moakley and McGovern attended a moving midnight Mass in honor of the Jesuit martyrs. Ambassador Patterson came too; her presence marked a new Salvadoran-American relationship.[12]

Then the congressmen embarked on a busy schedule that broadened their relations with Salvadorans, deepened their understanding of the country, and tested their endurance. One of the key issues they studied was crime and the drug trade, which had now spilled into the United States through violent transnational gangs. Moakley and McGovern met with San Salvador's mayor and police chief; a Salvadoran news photo showed the quartet as two matched pairs, the stout and bearded Mayor Hector Silva and slender police chief Eduardo Linares mirroring their North American guests. The congressmen and Salvadoran officials arranged a police training session in Boston, which had reduced crime by working with community leaders. Later they met with the legislature's Foreign Affairs Committee to discuss an extradition treaty so that Salvadoran criminals in the United States who fled to El Salvador could be prosecuted in the U.S. They held another meeting with victims of bank fraud perpetrated by an oligarch whose cement factory had recently received a big loan from the World Bank.[13]

The human rights situation in El Salvador had improved dramatically but was still unsatisfactory. Moakley and McGovern had campaigned successfully before their trip to maintain the UN's monitoring office and the national human rights ombudsman. The congressmen met with Benjamin Cuellar, director of the university's human rights program, and with the widow of an FMLN candidate who had been murdered before her eyes three years earlier. Two gunmen had been arrested but one escaped, probably through the collusion of prison officials. They met with a group of labor leaders and dined with Ruben Zamora, a former FDR leader whose brother had been murdered during the repression.[14]

The following day old friend Leonel Gomez arranged a whirlwind trip by helicopter to the countryside. After a brief stop at Cujutepeque, where they met with Villa Victoria mayor Adolfo Blandon and other community leaders in the town square, they flew off next to Santa Marta, returning to the mountain village in Cabanas that had sealed Moakley's commitment to El Salvador. The whole town assembled as the helicopters touched down on the dusty soccer field. "There were signs welcoming him, the children put on a play, and there was music," Steve LaRose remembered: "Moakley sang 'If you're Irish, Come into the Parlor' again and the people absolutely loved it. I mean, they were cheering . . . We were out in this field, and they started singing . . . it was surreal."[15]

Santa Marta had been rebuilt by this time. Many people now had electricity and running water, and the mud and thatch huts had mostly been replaced by more durable cinder block structures. The streets were still unpaved, but the physical infrastructure was clearly improved. Now the town had elected an FMLN mayor, and the people felt they had power. When the former military commander of the district, a man the villagers called the "Butcher of Cabanas," tried to attend the festivities, the town leaders told him to stay away. Carlos Bonilla, a Santa Marta leader whom Moakley had met on his first trip, had visited Moakley in Washington in 1996; this was a warm reunion for both men. "I consider him someone who was in solidarity with us," Bonilla remembered, "because, through his words and actions, he encouraged us." The two men were very much alike—tough, grounded in one place, yet men of the world. Moakley always remembered the day as a highlight of his life. Through Moakley's visits the people of Santa Marta learned to make strong connections abroad in the following years.[16]

After a few hours the helicopters took off for one more stop, at the village of La Mora, a scene of much fighting during the war, located near the larger center of Suchitoto, a lovely town located on a lake, so beautiful that both sides protected it during the war. There, under a mango tree in a junglelike setting, Moakley participated in a ceremony finalizing plans for a health clinic; Moakley drank *ocheta*, a local fermented sesame drink, with leaders including former guerrilla Javier Martinez, who would later be elected mayor of Suchitoto. "They gave him a *cuma* [a sickle]," Ana Maria Menjivar remembered. "He had a real human sensibility, he was approachable." Menjivar, a local community leader from a campesino background, had lost relatives in the war; she was proud that the clinic had a picture of Moakley.[17]

"Now I know how McArthur felt coming back to the Philippines," Moakley told a reporter when he got home.[18] While the imperious general and the warm-hearted former sailor could not have been further apart in temperament, the analogy was apt. In a sense, Moakley had helped to liberate the country—in his case, from the Americans. McGovern too could fairly summarize: "I'm very proud to have played a role in identifying the murderers . . . The United States spent six billion dollars in taxpayers' money supporting that regime."[19] The embassy report concluded that the trip generated much goodwill.[20] Both congressmen wrote to U.S. AID and the Office of Management of the Budget praising the work of Ambassador Patterson but pointing out the disparity between the wartime military aid and the parsimonious $36 million appropriated for aid to El Salvador in 1997.[21] This paltry contribution disappointed Moakley to the end of his days; he and McGovern would pepper the administration and the Republican congressional leadership with requests to increase aid to El Salvador. Twenty years after the peace accords, the total U.S. aid to El Salvador would not equal half the $6 billion spent to destroy it.

★　★　★

Moakley spent two months at home and in Washington, then joined 150 Massachusetts "pilgrims" to attend the historic visit of Pope John Paul II to Cuba in late January. Fidel Castro's revolution now faced a perilous hour. Economic conditions on the island had only gotten worse since passage of the Helms-Burton Act. Castro signaled that he could liberalize some aspects of Cuban life by inviting the pope to visit. For its part, the Vatican opposed the U.S. embargo, shared Castro's disdain for material success as the purpose of life, and hoped to end the repression of the church and improve human rights in Cuba. Again, the moment seemed pregnant with change.[22]

The whole world was watching this "clash of the titans," as *Time* magazine played the story. Two decades earlier Pope John Paul II had helped inspire the Polish people to overthrow its Soviet oppressor. In Cuba the standard of living was arguably lower than it had been in Poland, but the Castro dictatorship was home-grown, had a broader base of support, and was historically rooted in the Latin American struggle against Yankee imperialism. Cubans were poor, but there was a safety net in place: enough to eat, housing for all, free education, and a national health service protected Cuba's poorest. "People keep asking me who wins . . . Castro or the Pope, as if this was some kind of tug of war between two world leaders," Moakley told the *Boston Herald*'s Peter Gelzinis before leaving for the island. "Ultimately it's the Cuban people who stand to win." Moakley was hopeful, as he had been on his first trip. The pope's visit, he told Gelzinis, will do "more in a few days than all our diplomatic efforts of the last twenty-five years." He blamed the embargo as "Castro's greatest excuse for a lousy economy."[23]

The Massachusetts delegation included fifty-one priests and nuns, a host of businessmen, and political officials, distinguished by the presence of four congressmen. Moakley, Richard Neal, Jim McGovern, and Bill Delahunt, an Irish quartet, formed a merry company. On their first day they met with Cuba's vice president and attended a Mass celebrated by Boston's cardinal Bernard Law, who was pre-eminent among American cardinals on Cuban relations. The congressmen visited an Oxfam-sponsored farming cooperative, strolled around Havana at liberty, and observed Cuban life as Moakley had not been able to do on his first visit, when he had been the center of attention.[24]

The key moment of the trip came to Moakley by surprise, and had nothing to do with the pope or Fidel Castro. The congressmen were touring the William Soler Pediatric Hospital when their guide, a doctor, introduced them to a toddler who had endured months of uncomfortable treatment that could have been avoided for want of a simple medical shunt unavailable because of the embargo. Moakley became furious. "I told that doctor—no, I promised him, that we'd get back to him . . . There's no justification for that. A child suffering needlessly? It's not right," he told a reporter.[25]

That night they attended the papal Mass in Revolution Square, an unforgettable spiritual moment for all the pilgrims. Later Cuban National Assembly president Ricardo Alarcon hosted a cocktail reception for the small Massachusetts group and their aides as well as a few Cuban parliamentarians at an old Havana mansion. Alarcon hectored the Americans, stressing the damage done to the economy, which Moakley took as boilerplate rhetoric. Moakley replied that "as long as you don't change your human rights policy, nothing's going to change on the embargo," LaRose remembered.

At eleven o'clock *El Presidente* Fidel Castro stopped by unannounced to see his old friend, *El Congresista* Joe Moakley. The Massachusetts group had a heads-up from the American interest section that Fidel might show up, and LaRose remembered that the congressmen could observe the Cubans looking over their shoulders before his arrival, so they weren't taken totally by surprise. After a while the group formed a seated circle, with Moakley and Castro at focal points. "Castro started pontificating on a variety of subjects," LaRose recalled, "economics, human psychology, physics, and it went on for a while through his translator." Moakley put in a few words again on the need for the human rights situation to change. Castro was trying to get back the spotlight stolen by the pope; he was used to bloviating endlessly as acolytes soaked up the words of wisdom. "So after a while Moakley just jumps up and yells, 'OK, this has been fabulous! Steve, you got everything? Let's go!'" Castro wasn't used to people walking out on him. "Everyone in the room was shocked," LaRose recalled, "but it was actually a funny moment, and Castro, to his credit, didn't get angry." By good naturedly cutting Castro off, Moakley had delivered a simple message: skip the blather and reform your system, or there won't be any deals.[26]

The congressmen summed up for reporters the next day. "He was pretty mellow, and he said he thought the pope's visit was a good thing and would cause all religions, not just Catholicism, to grow," Moakley said. Delahunt told another reporter that the genie of religious freedom was out of the bottle; Neal jokingly invited the former altar boy Fidel to take communion with them the next morning. "He [Fidel] could talk a cat off a fish truck," McGovern wryly observed.[27]

The congressmen boarded the return flight laden with boxes of forbidden Havana cigars as gifts. As the plane neared the airport, it dawned on Delahunt that they wouldn't be able to get the cigars past customs. He expressed this concern to Moakley, who just chuckled. "So Joe, Richie, Jimmy and I get off the plane," Delahunt recalled, "and we get to customs, and all the guys just go, 'Hiya Joe,' and wave us through." Former attorney general Delahunt had inadvertently joined a jovial gang of smugglers, but his retrospective account reveals much about the political success of all four men. They all really thought of themselves Bill, Joe, Richie and Jimmy, perhaps four kids on their way to a hockey game, not as "Mr. Congressman."[28]

Moakley and his colleagues beseeched the administration to ease up on some restrictions on Cuban-American relations in which the administration had some discretion. They urged the administration to allow direct flights, end the ban on family remittances, license humanitarian health and nutrition programs, and lift restrictions on the sale of food and medicine. Clinton met Moakley half-way a few months later. Moakley wrote to Fidel urging the release of political prisoners too; he had bent Castro's ear on that subject at the cocktail party. Fidel released about three hundred political prisoners, not because of Moakley but under pressure from the Vatican.[29] The papal visit might have broken a logjam, but once again, as had happened so often in his career, more significant events overwhelmed the narrative of Joe Moakley's journey.

★ ★ ★

"On January 21, the *Washington Post* led with the story that I had had an affair with Monica Lewinsky, and that Kenneth Starr was investigating charges that I had encouraged her to lie about it under oath," Bill Clinton laconically recorded in his memoir.[30] This story did seem unbelievable, and to millions of Americans, inconsequential even if true. The origin of the story lay in a now familiar chain of events: during the first Clinton administration, when Democrats held a congressional majority, Clinton assented to a special prosecutorial investigation into alleged financial misdeeds in a real estate transaction he had made while governor of Arkansas. The first prosecutor retired without completing the report and was replaced by the conservative bulldog Kenneth Starr, who found nothing for several more years until Monica Lewinsky fell into his clutches. The young intern had been sexually intimate with Clinton, although they had not had intercourse, and she had been secretly recorded by a deceiving confidante as she poured out her frustration. Starr bullied the young woman into testifying, and used her confession to catch Clinton in his web.

Hillary Clinton's first public appearance as this bombshell story exploded across the front pages was to be at the celebration of Joe Moakley's silver anniversary in Congress. She had done one interview previously, on the day of the State of the Union address, telling an NBC reporter that the charges against her husband were part of a "vast right-wing conspiracy" against her husband, whose fidelity she did not doubt. At Boston's Copley Plaza Hotel on a rainy January night, Hillary paid tribute to Moakley and brought down the packed house with a joke about how nice it was to get out of Washington because things were so boring there. Along with the humor, she showed the same steely resolve as her husband had at the State of the Union address. "We will not be intimidated. We will not give up. We will finish the job that we went to Washington to do," she vowed.[31]

Earlier in the day Moakley had enjoyed a tribute at Faneuil Hall addressed by state officials; Moakley told a reporter there that he and neighbor William Bulger had come a long way from the Old Harbor Village housing project, but at heart they had never left. "The politicians when I was a kid . . . put oil in your cellar, put food on your table, helped you get a job, helped you get to school, a politician was . . . like a priest," he said. This concept really hearkened back to the days of ward boss politics, an approach that Moakley had reconfigured by delivering first-class constituent service. The previous morning a television reporter accompanied Moakley to the Galley Diner on P Street in South Boston, Moakley's favorite local breakfast joint.[32] Moakley's simple tastes and lack of pretension reminded people that public service could be an honorable calling. These character traits also explained why Moakley rarely appeared in the larger regional media outlets like the major broadcast networks or *Boston Globe*. Less flawed than outsized figures like Clinton, Moakley didn't generate any controversy in his transparent personal life or gentlemanly conduct of public affairs.

Moakley stood with Clinton all the way through the unfolding impeachment process. For Moakley, Newt Gingrich was the villain of the story; Gingrich was the only figure in his long career whom he viewed with contempt. "Gingrich came in with a war-like attitude," he told the television reporter at the Galley Diner. He recalled the pre-Gingrich days of bipartisan comity, when Tip O'Neill and Minority Leader Bob Michel socialized and negotiated legislation amicably. "Now if somebody on the other side invited me to dinner, I'd have to take a [food] taster with me."[33] He was disgusted by the way Gingrich orchestrated his party's response to Clinton's State of the Union address, noting that the Republicans applauded only when Gingrich did, while "the rest of the time they sat down there like they had lost their hearing aids." As for the Lewinsky matter, Moakley scoffed that "it is still in the rumor stage. If you look at the source of the information . . . it is funded by extreme right-wing organizations."[34]

Gingrich was Moakley's opposite in every way. Moakley could smell the Machiavellian personal ambition that was rooted in the Speaker's personal insecurities. Gingrich ran his caucus with an iron hand, riding roughshod over even his own committee heads and rooting out any hint of bipartisanship among members. He flaunted his intellectual pretensions as a former history professor, selectively invoking quotations from the Federalist Papers to justify his own ideological predilections, which were actually incoherent and rankled true conservatives. After two years even his own faction rebelled, rebuking the Speaker, and the House voted to reprimand him, imposing a hefty fine for lying to the Ethics Committee regarding financial improprieties.[35] The moderate rank and filers next assigned an ad hoc Ethics Review panel, on which Moakley served. Gingrich simply dissolved it as it prepared to issue its report. "In my twenty-five years here I have never seen such a display of arrogance," Moakley expostulated.[36] A few months later Gingrich pushed through a bill that weakened ethics strictures, on a partisan 225–184 vote, leaving Moakley to complain, "What began as a bi-partisan effort to improve the ethics process has disintegrated into one more political sham."[37]

Moakley even suggested to Minority Leader Dick Gephardt that the Democrats expose Gingrich's use of House subpoena power to harass opponents. In June 1998 Gephardt released a report entitled "Politically Motivated Investigations by House Committees 1995 to the Present" that identified fifty-five such travesties, costing $17 million, not counting the $40 million for the Starr report, none of which disclosed anything. Moakley told *Boston Globe* columnist David Nyhan that Gingrich's strategy was to poison the atmosphere and financially bankrupt his opponents; Nyhan adduced Gingrich's claim that Clinton operated "[t]he most systematic, deliberate obstruction of justice . . . seen in American history"; Nyhan wondered if the history professor remembered Watergate.[38]

In August, with the long-awaited Starr report looming, Bill Clinton finally confessed to his wife and to the public that he had in fact had an inappropriate sexual relationship with Lewinsky, and that like most adulterers, he had lied to his wife to protect her from his own failings. Millions of the president's supporters, Moakley included, felt betrayed. "He wasn't contrite enough," Moakley grumbled. "He misled us. They all feel like me in the House. It's a terrible situation. But in the end, we are the jurors. We'll be . . . deciding on whether it's censure or impeachment. So people want to wait until the facts are in."[39] The next day, Clinton met a less ambivalent response at Worcester's Mechanics Hall, where McGovern and Moakley welcomed the president to a rousing reception by the faithful. Clinton stuck to his subject, school safety and police work, and got three standing ovations. "This is not a city of fair-weather friends," McGovern told the president.[40]

Moakley condemned the Starr report when it was finally released in September. It was supposed to be about the Whitewater real estate deal, and turned out to have nothing to say about it. "It's all Monicagate," Moakley sniffed. "It looks like he [Starr] wrote a sex book for $40 million."[41] Moakley was similarly angered by the Republican majority's release of the report without granting the president a customary ten days to review it first. Moakley knew a frame-up when he saw one, and like most Democrats, realized that Clinton was guilty of committing a personal indiscretion and had violated a legal technicality in the process of hiding the "affair" from his wife. The Republicans had turned the real estate investigation, which found nothing wrong, into a fishing expedition that they used to tar the administration for partisan purposes.

That effort did not succeed. In November the Democrats gained five House seats, a surprising confirmation of the notion that the public felt the Republicans had over-reached. In Massachusetts, Democrats held all ten House seats, with Michael Capuano of Somerville taking the seat from which Joe Kennedy had resigned after a decade. Acting Governor Argeo Paul Cellucci, who had assumed the office when Weld resigned, defeated former state attorney General Scott Harshbarger in the governor's race. Moakley felt encouraged. "The feeling is that the Republicans will wrap up their impeachment hearing by the end of the year. It won't be dragging on and on," a prospect that many Democrats had feared.[42]

Moakley got more than he imagined a few weeks later. Upset by the defeat, and by Gingrich's imperious conduct, his own caucus forced his retirement; offstage whispers hinted that Gingrich's affair with a staffer would be made public if he didn't step down. In December he resigned from the House too, but not before bringing an impeachment, rather than censure resolution, to the House floor. Why impeachment? Clinton aide Erskine Bowles asked Gingrich. "Because we can," Gingrich replied. Impeachment was Newt's revenge, one last fouling of Congress before the old professor headed off into the sunset, never to be heard from again, many congressmen hoped.[43]

The irony ran even deeper. Clinton had indeed tacked toward Gingrich's positions after the 1994 election, worrying liberals like Moakley. With Republican backing, Clinton had passed a welfare reform bill in 1996 that Moakley voted against because it included no money for job training and education.[44] Moakley opposed presidential "fast track" trade negotiating powers, another Republican and New Democrat idea, the following year, citing the failure of NAFTA to protect American jobs.[45] Clinton's triangulation brought about a rapprochement with Gingrich that worried the real conservatives in the Republican Party; for them, Gingrich seemed too cooperative with Clinton, and too much like him.

Moakley would have voted for censure. "In my district, ninety per cent don't want impeachment," he told a reporter. "You know what they're doing? They're un-electing a president that was elected twice."[46] Moakley spoke once during the floor debate in December, correcting several Republicans who justified impeachment rather than censure by asserting that Speaker Tip O'Neill had pushed for Nixon's impeachment. Moakley reminded his colleagues that O'Neill was not then the Speaker and that

Nixon had resigned before an impeachment vote had come to the floor. On party lines, the House voted two articles of impeachment.[47]

In January the Senate failed to approve the articles, deadlocking fifty-fifty on the obstruction of justice charge. The new Congress elected J. Dennis Hastert of Illinois, an affable former high school wrestling coach, as Speaker; his first request was for both sides to bury the hatchet. The nation's second long national nightmare had come to an end.

14

* * * * *

Man of the Century

When Moakley returned from Cuba in January 1998, moviegoers were flocking to a new film set in South Boston starring two young actors, Matt Damon and Ben Affleck, called "Good Will Hunting." Both played typical working-class young men, but Damon's character, Will, an adopted child, was a math genius. Will wouldn't leave South Boston to cross the river to Cambridge where he might have gone to the Massachusetts Institute of Technology; but through the efforts of his buddy, a girlfriend, and a quirky psychologist, Will learns to confront his inner demons and realize his potential. The film surfaced one of the great themes in American fiction: the talented lad from an insular community that views ambition with suspicion and social climbing as disloyalty. Joe Moakley's great skill was to balance these contrasting values of ambition and community loyalty.

In the last years of his life he made a significant contribution toward physically transforming his neighborhood, much the way Will transformed himself; and to play out his role on the world stage. Moakley would cross the seas to El Salvador, Cuba, and the Vatican, and come home to South Boston a hero. No one else could champion the cause of foreign aid to Salvadoran farmers, negotiate with Fidel Castro, and yet win the admiration of South Boston. Moakley was that rare politician of provincial origin whose empathy grew throughout his career.

* * *

In the early 1990s, Moakley put forward a new vision for the Seaport District of South Boston, located across the channel from the downtown Fort Point neighborhood and northeast of the residential end of the peninsula above Summer Street. There a series of disused piers jutted into the Boston Inner Harbor, facing Logan Airport, and a tangle of railroad tracks and parking lots cluttered the landscape. Its sole attractions were the World Trade Center office complex, set on the Commonwealth Pier, two neighboring fancy restaurants—Jimmy's Harborside and Anthony's Pier Four—and a charming relic called the No Name, where working-class diners could get a good cheap fish chowder. Moakley had moved his office to the World Trade Center in the 1980s. He could look out at the Fan Pier, named for the shape of the railroad tracks now overgrown with weeds.

A decade earlier, far-sighted officials in the state and city administrations pondered a much bigger urban planning problem. Highway 93 sliced through downtown Boston on giant stanchions, separating the North End from downtown, casting malignant shadows and rendering much of downtown generally unappealing. The highway choked with traffic during rush hours, sending impatient motorists onto already clogged city streets. During the 1980s, Governor Michael Dukakis and his transportation secretary, Fred Salvucci, boldly resolved to depress the Central Artery and add a third tunnel to Logan Airport. A project engineer for what later became known as the "Big Dig," more formally as the Central Artery/Third Harbor Tunnel Project, remarked that the construction challenge was akin to performing heart surgery on an ambulatory patient. The attendant political and financial problems would vex planners and politicians for a generation. Moakley joined a succession of governors, his House colleagues, and senators Ted Kennedy and John Kerry in shaking loose $13 billion from federal and state coffers to complete the most expensive construction project in American history.[1]

Meanwhile, federal judges in the District Court and Court of Appeals chafed at lodgings they felt to be inadequate to handle the region's growing caseload. Located in a twenty-two-story 1933 building just off Boston's Post Office Square, justices led by Stephen Breyer, Douglas D. Woodlock, and Moakley's 1970 primary campaign rival David Nelson began pressing city and state officials for a new location, and the General Services Administration for a new building. A flow of communications began among all three levels of government, all three branches of the federal government, and a variety of neighborhood civic associations. The downtown business groups and Mayor Flynn advocated a site near New Chardon Street and the Government Center.[2]

Moakley literally had his eye on the Fan Pier, which he could see from his window. He argued that for security purposes, a free-standing building bounded by water would be best. The justices liked the idea. The Fan Pier was a potentially magnificent location. Moakley secured the money for a feasibility study, and by November 1990 he, Kennedy, and Kerry won a $184 million appropriation, pending a final site selection to be determined by the GSA. The GSA picked the Fan Pier site, and within two or three years an architectural firm had won a bid and construction got underway.

"There's a tendency to view Joe Moakley as a mechanic, not a big vision guy, but, going back to his days in the Massachusetts Senate, he had a vision of the Harbor," aide Sean Ryan pointed out. "Over a long period of time, he put the pieces in place that made the vision come to life." Moakley saw the emerging Seaport District as "the hottest part of town" for responsible, mixed-use development. The Federal Courthouse would be the magnet.[3]

The architects proposed an L-shaped, ten-story brick structure facing the sea, graced by a welcoming curved glass atrium on the water side, with a harbor walkway and grassy area. Deficit hawks squawked. "Judge Breyer and the Taj Mahal," nationally syndicated columnist Jack Anderson harrumphed. The now $218 million project "would make Donald Trump blush," Anderson charged, and suggested that Moakley had fixed the site to benefit his friend Anthony Athanas, owner of the nearby restaurant, and from whom Moakley had previously rented a beach cottage. As Republicans criticized government spending during the 1994 campaign, even some Democratic senators challenged Judge Breyer to justify the cost at his Supreme Court nomination hearing.[4]

Cost-consciousness must be part of all planning decisions. Building Shah Jahan's marble Taj Mahal, an Islamic mosque in poverty-stricken Hindu India, did contribute to the collapse of the Mughal Dynasty in the seventeenth century, but the analogy was faulty. Building the Federal Courthouse stimulated the Massachusetts economy, then just emerging from the Bush recession. Two decades later no one complains about its cost, and its statement about the majesty of the justice system is generally celebrated. The project put a thousand construction workers to work, with bricklayers setting almost 2 million bricks. The architecture critics loved the building, marveling over its "weighty and grand" aspects that were balanced by its "open and inviting" characteristics. Moakley, caught up in the congressional crush of work as the nation stumbled toward the possible impeachment of the president, couldn't attend the opening ceremony but sent a taped message: "Once upon a time, as a state representative and as a state senator—I dreamt of one day bringing life to these forty acres," he said. The courthouse was only a first step.[5]

One of the objections to siting the courthouse in the Seaport had been that it was not near a rapid transit stop. The closest was at South Station, a long walk away. Moakley proposed a transit link initially called the South Boston Piers Transitway, whose configuration underwent several iterations during the planning phase. Meanwhile, transportation planners decided to install an electric bus as a replacement for the relocated Orange Line; the new route was dubbed the Silver Line, a hybrid concept that ran along Washington Street, through Chinatown, to South Station. Fred Salvucci also planned a more direct public transit route to the airport; most travelers were required to take a discouraging three subways and a connector bus to reach their terminal. Ultimately, Moakley's South Boston Piers Transitway merged with Salvucci's Silver Line, using the same silent electric bus to run along the seaport's length and out to the airport. "Joe got $600 million for that extension," Sean Ryan, who held Moakley's transportation portfolio, remembered. "It was really a Joe Moakley project." Moakley did not live to see its completion, but this second aspect of the Seaport's development was crucial to everything else.[6]

Related to the Seaport development process was a controversy about whether or not to build an additional runway along Logan Airport's southwest border, facing the Seaport. Heavy traffic caused airplanes to circle the field waiting for runway clearance. Boston's Chamber of Commerce, the construction unions, Governor Cellucci, and Moakley's old nemesis, Massport director Peter Blute, favored the plan. East Boston and South Boston residents, who would bear the burden of additional noise pollution, said no. Moakley told a boisterous rally at the State House in March 1999, "I'm going to do everything in my power to stop the construction of Runway 14-32." This won easy cheers of, "Way to Go, Joe," but runway opponents had to do a little better than chant "Not in my backyard." Moakley and McGovern pushed for expansion of Worcester's Airport as an alternative, and over the next decade the Manchester, New Hampshire, and Providence Airports would expand their schedules and accessibility as the Boston metropolitan area grew. Moakley brought Federal Aviation Administration chief Jane Garvey to Boston. In January 2000 she sent the Logan expansion plan back to the drawing board, citing the unanimous opposition of local political leaders. Moakley's "No" position wasn't absolute; he just wanted the noise pollution issue addressed, but it wasn't, and the runway was never built.[7]

Moakley committed one faux pas during the airport dispute when Blute resigned and Cellucci appointed Virginia Buckingham, a thirty-three-year-old campaign aide who had no transportation experience, to replace him at Massport. "Sure, just pick some girl in an office down the hall," Moakley huffed, viewing Buckingham as a rubber stamp for the governor. Lieutenant Governor Jane Swift pounced on Moakley's characterization of Buckingham as sexist, which it was, and the septuagenarian Moakley couldn't quite get his foot out of his mouth on this matter.[8] Yet he had identified the bane of state politics—the persistent patronage dimension of too many appointments that should be made by professional commissions rather than by politicians. The entire American political system is infected by cronyism, and the public sometimes pays a price for the appointment of campaign staffers to positions for which they are not qualified.

★ ★ ★

In November 1998, Hurricane Mitch pounded the Caribbean coast of Central America, crossing the isthmus to the Pacific and tracking south through El Salvador, where it dumped seventy-five inches of rain, mostly in the southeastern portion of the country. Guatemala, Honduras, and Nicaragua bore the brunt of the damage; the storm killed eleven thousand, another eleven thousand went missing and presumably died, and 2.7 million people were left homeless in a disaster of epic proportions. In El Salvador, the southeastern region was hardest hit, with crops and livestock destroyed, eighty-four thousand left homeless, and half a million temporarily evacuated from their homes. Moakley and McGovern wrote immediately to President Clinton, who mobilized $250 million in emergency aid; Hillary Clinton journeyed to the stricken region to indicate U.S. concern.[9] The disaster struck just as citizens of the United States were riveted by the unfolding drama of the possible Clinton impeachment, diverting attention and possible charitable contributions from this urgent humanitarian crisis.

Moakley and McGovern monitored the situation throughout 1999, and in mid-November returned to El Salvador to visit the affected areas on a trip funded by the Association of Jesuit Colleges and Universities. As they planned their departure, the State Department and congressional Sergeant at Arms office warned Moakley that there had been a threat against his life. Moakley went anyway, convinced that it came from a bitter individual spouting off, not from a man with an operational plan.

The congressmen immediately met with Ambassador Anne Patterson, with whom they had corresponded on excellent terms since her appointment. That night they joined their old friends at the Jesuit University of Central America for dinner. It was the tenth anniversary of the Jesuit murders, a somber occasion, but appropriate for taking stock of the country's long journey since that fateful night. Even after the devastation wrought by the hurricane, Moakley sounded an optimistic note in his speech, seeing "a country moving forward, a country with hopes and dreams." He observed that the March elections had been free and fair. Poverty and crime still stood out as the main problems; Moakley noted that Salvadoran police officers had come to Boston where they learned about community policing techniques. Moakley fondly recalled his visit to Santa Marta in 1997, and concluded by invoking the spirit of the martyred Jesuits and his friendship with the survivors.[10] He might have mentioned as well the improved relations between an El Salvador at peace and a North American administration that was sending some minimal humanitarian aid rather than military aid to a dictatorship. This was indeed a new era.

The next day, Moakley and McGovern set off for the flooded regions in the Rio Lempa basin. They traveled by jeep, Moakley, Ambassador Patterson, and LaRose in one and McGovern and his staff riding in another. The vehicles bounced along pot-holed roads. "At every bump, Moakley would yell 'Jay-zus!'" Stephen LaRose recalled, mimicking Moakley's Southie accent with a chuckle. He was, after all, a seventy-four-year-old man with a lot of spare parts in his body. At the first stop, the village of San Faustino in the Zacatecoluca region of the La Paz department, Moakley met with about fifty community leaders whose corn, squash, and sesame crops had been completely wiped out. Some five thousand farmers had suffered the same fate, and while they were receiving U.S. aid, their situation was precarious. At La Canoa, on the Rio Lempa, it was the same story, but the congressmen observed 220 solar panels installed by a campesino organization. In all, 136 villages had been hit, 60 percent of the roads damaged, and fifteen major bridges destroyed in the region.[11]

Back in the capital the next day, the congressmen met with the president, leaders of the assembly, and FMLN leaders. These included San Salvador mayor Hector Silva, who had impressed Moakley greatly on his last trip; Moakley thought Silva would make a good president. "Moakley wasn't thrilled by the level of U.S. aid after Hurricane Mitch," LaRose remembered, but without the pressure brought by these advocates for Central America, the funding probably would have been much less.[12]

Moakley worked throughout this period on a number of related Latin American issues. He campaigned to close the Army School of the Americas (SOA), located at Fort Benning, Georgia. The opposition to the school originated with Father Ray Bourgeois, a Maryknoll priest, and was taken up by Central America activists around the country. Congressman Joe Kennedy insisted on closing the school during his decade in Congress. When Kennedy stepped down in 1998, Moakley found a Republican colleague, Joe Scarborough of Pennsylvania, to cosponsor bills calling for the school's closing or a reduction in its funds.

The putative mission of the SOA was to teach military professionalism to Latin American officers, but it really devolved into a counterinsurgency training school in which the soldiers learned to suppress their own nation's dissidents. As Moakley often pointed out, the school's graduates never fought against Cuban or Soviet invaders. Its notorious graduates included nineteen of the officers implicated in the Jesuit case, two of the men who assassinated Archbishop Romero, and some of the officers in the case of the slain American churchwomen. Ten graduates conducted the El Mozote massacre of unarmed civilians in El Salvador. In Guatemala, SOA graduates murdered Archbishop Juan Jose Gerardi in 1998 after the Church released a damning report on atrocities committed by the military against Mayan villagers. "Put simply, the SOA has trained some of the most brutal assassins . . . the Western Hemisphere has ever seen," Moakley said.[13]

Moakley and Scarborough won a House vote to close the SOA in late July 1999; fifty-eight Republicans joined the Democrats in a 230–197 vote. Later that year, on the tenth anniversary of the Jesuit slayings, ten thousand demonstrators protested at the school. The Clinton administration, needing the military's support for the war in Kosovo, threatened to veto the measure and it died in conference committee. Finally the army closed the school, but reopened it under another name. The happy ending really unfolded in Latin America itself, whose nations gradually elected center-left governments over the next decade and brought their militaries under civilian control.[14]

Moakley worked on a number of other human rights cases from Latin America. He helped win the release of a constituent, David Carmos, from a Mexican prison on fake charges of drug trafficking; this was a fifty-year-old alternative medicine healer with no history of drug involvement.[15] He appealed to President Clinton to have the Honduran government investigate the disappearance of an American priest there in 1983.[16] Moakley was furious when he learned about the murder of Guatemala's bishop Juan Jose Gerardi, and threatened the nation's president with economic reprisals should the assassins not be brought to justice; some of the plotters were convicted a year later.[17] He had the same reaction when the killers of the American churchwomen in El Salvador admitted that they had acted under orders, not on their own initiative; and at the same time it emerged that two powerful Salvadoran officials from that period were living legally in the United States.[18]

★ ★ ★

Just after Moakley got back from El Salvador, a dramatic story from Cuba broke into the headlines. A tiny craft overloaded with refugees capsized in the sea, and fishermen encountered the wreckage off the Florida coast. Only one couple and a six-year-old boy survived, the child miraculously clinging to life by floating in an inner tube. This touching story that might have stimulated a thoughtful discussion about the tragedy of Cuban-American relations instead provoked a bitter debate about the boy's future. It turned out that Elian Gonzalez had been effectively kidnapped by the estranged mother of the boy's father, and she, with her new boyfriend, had recklessly loaded the child onto the rickety vessel without the father's knowledge. The father wanted his son back. Miami's Cuban community took the boy into its custody, boarding him with relatives of the mother; Cubans in Havana and Miami mobilized on opposite sides of this twenty-first-century version of the Dreyfuss case or O. J. Simpson trial.

Moakley met with the boy's father and two grandmothers, all of whom came to the United States demanding the boy's return. To Moakley, this was a simple case of family reunification in which politics should play no role; that was the position of the Catholic Church as well. As President Clinton's term drew to a close, however, Vice President Al Gore, the presumptive Democratic presidential nominee, with his eye on the Florida vote in the 2000 election, reversed his earlier position and decided that the best course was to offer the boy and his father permanent residency in the United States. The father, however, had no desire to leave Cuba. Moakley, a Gore supporter, was mightily disappointed in him. "Gore is wrong, dead wrong," he declared. "It's kidnapping. If another nation did it, we'd scream bloody murder. It's all about the Cuban-Americans. If this kid was from Haiti he would be a blip on the radar screen." In June, federal courts ordered the boy's return, and Attorney General Janet Reno organized a predawn rescue that reunited the boy with his father, who promptly returned to Cuba.[19]

While the Elian Gonzalez case developed, Moakley and McGovern quietly planned a venture that would help bring the people of Cuba and the United States together. Steve LaRose, working with Jeff Thale at the Washington Office on Latin America, organized a trip to the island for forty-nine Massachusetts university presidents and other higher education leaders.[20] Moakley, worried that the trip might be misperceived, explained the idea to Peter Gelzinis, a friendly journalist from the *Boston Herald*. "I know I'm a lone wolf on this Cuba thing . . . My point is this: As long as Cuban-Americans can dictate our diplomatic policy . . . then Castro has nothing to worry about. His people will continue to suffer. And he will continue his total grip on that island." Gelzinis called the Castro-Moakley relationship "an intriguing tango." While Castro had invited Moakley to dance, the congressman needed his constituents to know that he was leading. "Of course he [Castro] understands what my ultimate objective is. It's the liberation of the people on that island. Still, he and I have this relationship, I guess. It's hard for me to explain, but we seem to understand each other."[21]

In mid-April Moakley and McGovern set off on another adventure together, this time with a planeload of college presidents. Their goal was to initiate exchange programs and promote dialogue, according to college specialty. The University of Massachusetts at Dartmouth hoped for an exchange program in maritime studies with the islanders. The Massachusetts College of Art wanted to host Cuban artists; Lesley University had a new writing program that might gain attention with a Cuban writer-in-residence; the Harvard contingent included the dean of the Education School and the executive director of Latin American Studies. The Schepens Eye Research Institute at Harvard arranged to send fifty postdoctoral scholars to Cuba. The visitors even provoked a public debate between Castro and Abel Prieto, the Cuban minister of culture. International exchange programs are inimical to authoritarianism, and Castro probably knew what Moakley was up to.[22]

The Bay State scholars stopped off at the Martin Luther King Memorial Center, an independent Afro-Cuban cultural center, in Havana. Miren Uriarte, a Cuban-American based at the University of Massachusetts at Boston, had helped its director, a Baptist and noncommunist, to open the center during the mid-1990s with financial support from Canada, Norway, and the Netherlands. African American congressmen visiting the island routinely stopped there.[23] The King Center exposed the foolishness of America's isolationist policy. Most African Americans, whose great hero was a radical Christian, had no opportunity to share their life experiences with Afro-Cubans, fellow inhabitants of the African diaspora. Did the Cuban-American hard-liners really believe that a few thousand African American visitors to Cuba would return as communists? Or wasn't it more likely that African American jazz musicians, intellectuals, journalists, politicians, scientists, and religious leaders would open up civil society in Cuba?

The trip had another unusual dimension for Moakley. William Bulger had been eased out of politics and appointed to head the University of Massachusetts by Republican governor William Weld. Bulger was a surprising choice for this job, but it worked. He became a perfect emissary to the state legislature, a hands-off administrator who let the education people do their jobs, and a model to the state's working class that higher education was a good thing in and of itself, not merely as job training. Moakley and Bulger led busy professional lives and rarely saw each other; in Cuba, of all places, they sat together on the tour bus, joked and reminisced. "Bulger was great in the meetings," Steve LaRose remembered. "He quickly got right down to the point every time."[24] Moakley and Bulger made a strange sight as two South Boston politicians leading a posse of professors to communist Cuba. They could not have predicted such an outcome for themselves as boys walking on Carson Beach a half-century earlier, contemplating their futures in the millennium year.

★ ★ ★

Moakley worked on development of the Seaport throughout the late 1990s, as the New Boston emerged from the recession. He was one player among many, and tried to be careful not to impose his weighty authority as congressman on issues that should be settled at the municipal level. Yet the development plans were soon ensnared in a complex contest of competing agendas. One of them involved rival proposals by developers, the Pritzker Group, which ran the Hyatt Hotel chain, and Frank McCourt, a local builder. Pritzker had been a partner of restaurant owner Anthony Athanas, who owned much of the Fan Pier; Athanas and Pritzker had a falling out that led to a bitter lawsuit that Athanas lost. Moakley tried to work with all parties throughout the courthouse land acquisition period and on the building of the Seaport Hotel and adjacent office buildings afterward. "Joe actively assisted McCourt in terms of roadway configuration, sidewalks, lighting, Silver Line, etc.," district director Fred Clark remembered, "but he did not really get deep in the weeds in regards to condominiums, versus retail versus office/commercial space." Staying out of the weeds was a wise decision; the vast project gave every city and state official, from urban planners to environmental regulators, fits. Moakley did not pick sides between developers, but he was impatient with all the bickering that accompanied the project. "It's time to put a hole in the ground and get something going over there," he sighed to a reporter, when the Pritzkers finally accepted a scaled-back plan. "It's not perfect. But this is a real step in the right direction."[25]

Moakley viewed the Northern Avenue pedestrian bridge that crossed the Fort Point Channel just down from the Evelyn Moakley Bridge as another obstacle. "It's an ugly thing," Moakley protested. "It's absolutely an eyesore." Then the Boston Landmarks Commission voted unanimously to designate the 1908 bridge as a historic landmark; Mayor Menino overruled their decision, but later agreed to a compromise that left the structure as a pedestrian bridge. Moakley didn't see the point of that, since pedestrians could walk over the new one. He and Clark went over to the two bridges and counted thirty paces between them, but the bridge stayed up as preservationists raised a hue and cry. Moakley was a preservationist himself; he was meanwhile securing more money for the old African American Meeting House on Beacon Hill, but this was a round that Moakley lost.[26]

The most contentious of all development issues around the Seaport concerned new housing. New housing always raises issues regarding property values and rents for neighbors, and the vexing issue of what type of people will inhabit the new units. South Boston was already changing. Old-timers sold their increasingly valuable property to young professionals as they left for the suburbs or assisted-living units. By the mid-1990s, Volvos were parked where once there had been Chevrolets. Moakley considered change as inevitable; he knew that the world of shamrock-adorned shot and a beer joints could not last forever. In this regard he was like Good Will Hunting; he, in his mid-seventies, was ready for his beloved peninsula to change with the times and grow. Yet he respected the point of view of his neighbors whose slogan seemed to be, "OK, but not so much and not so fast."

The housing issue was connected to a plan to locate a vast new convention center at the edge of South Boston and Downtown, a plan that neighborhood leaders might have been expected to oppose just as they had the football stadium. They didn't. Negotiating behind closed doors with the mayor, state senator Stephen Lynch, state representative Jack Hart, and City Council president Jimmy Kelly wrested a "Memorandum of Understanding" that gave South Boston a big disproportion of linkage funds that might have gone to other neighborhoods. When Kelly wouldn't clearly answer a reporter's question about whether South Boston might restrict the new tenants to a "whites only" clientele, Moakley insisted that "I am not with those guys."[27]

Moakley did want new housing in the Seaport, however. The City Council and Menino pressured the South Boston leaders to reconsider the linkage funding ratios; the entity through which money should be appropriated; and the availability of new units to all residents. Unfortunately, this dispute strained relations between Moakley and Mayor Menino when Menino challenged a real estate developer whom Moakley had nominated to chair the South Boston Development Trust; as with many Boston projects this one snarled in clashing political agendas and simmering rivalries. Moakley "was very happy about the courthouse and with the development associated with the World Trade Center," Clark remembered, "but he was very frustrated with the lack of development in the seaport area otherwise." To this day, a certain corporate sterility mars the district, whose lack of residential housing makes it vibrant by day but desolate in the evening.[28]

Moakley enjoyed a series of personal triumphs in the millennium year that matched his feeling of accomplishments locally and internationally. He felt rejuvenated physically. Despite the obstacles, he could see South Boston and Boston rebounding from the recession of the early 1990s. Moakley had not had the best relations with Flynn or Menino, but both mayors presided over the city's rebirth. Racial tensions had long since receded, new immigrants from all parts of the world revitalized every neighborhood, and the Big Dig and Seaport construction energized blue-collar workers, while new computer and biotech industries stimulated the high end of the economy. Moakley had even been upbeat about El Salvador's prospects after the hurricane.

One sign of the city's growth was the expansion of Suffolk University, at which Moakley served as a trustee. Its law school was adding faculty and staff, and a magnificent new building on Tremont Street opened in 1998. Two years later the university named the law library at Sargent Hall for Moakley at a grand ceremony attended by Senator Kennedy, Father Charlie Currie of the American Jesuit Universities, Jim McGovern, and a host of leading legal lights and alumni. Moakley stayed humble. "The only two places I never visited when I was a student here were the ladies' bathroom and the Law Library," he wise-cracked.[29]

Perhaps the highlight of the Millennium Year for Moakley was his selection as Person of the Century by a South Boston committee that organized a neighborhood reunion in September. Moakley shared the honor with the late Cardinal Cushing, whom he had greatly admired as a tolerant, ecumenical leader of the Catholic Church. Ray Flynn was chosen as South Boston's greatest athlete, along with another man. Moakley hung out and gabbed with thirty-five hundred former and current residents, relishing the affection of his neighbors. "Any affirmation of his good work by the people of South Boston was very important to him," Fred Clark said. "When he lost South Boston to Bob 'Peaches' Flynn [in the 1976 primary] it cut really deep." He had once told a reporter, after his liver transplant and confusing "retirement" news conference, that he wanted it written on his tombstone that he represented his district and neighborhood well; the respect of his friends and neighbors mattered more to him than any honorary doctorate.[30]

A final accolade came with the release of a Public Broadcasting System documentary "Enemies of War," produced and narrated by actor Martin Sheen and directed by Esther Cassidy. Cassidy followed Moakley and McGovern on their mission to investigate the murder of the Jesuits in El Salvador, and traced the country's progress toward democracy afterward. It was a fitting tribute to the dedication of both congressmen over many years.

A few months after the South Boston celebration, Moakley campaigned for a fifteenth term against a Republican talk show host, Janet Jeghelian, who had no hope of winning. Elected officials in Massachusetts were solidly Democratic, except for the governor. Many independent voters now commonly split their tickets, voting for a Democratic state representative and a Republican governor because they feared the corrupt practices that often accompanied one-party rule; in the following years Massachusetts would see three Democratic House speakers forced out of office for questionable practices. Moakley sailed to victory with 77 percent of the vote, the highest percentage among all ten returning Massachusetts Democrats; Ted Kennedy swept into a seventh term against a weak rival. A conservative columnist penned a mournful requiem, "Last Rites for GOP in Bay State?"[31]

Moakley held his victory party at a veterans' post in Randolph; not many people attended because there had been no contest. Moakley came out, thanked his supporters, and went back to the TV set, watching in astonishment as the Florida vote came in. Over the next month Florida election officials presided over a catastrophe of "butterfly ballots" and "hanging chads," until the Supreme Court ended the recount process and awarded the election to George Bush.[32]

Moakley was philosophical and hoped that Bush would work with a minority party whose standard-bearer had won the popular vote. "We're not lying in the woods, waiting for him to make his first mistake," Moakley said. "But we're going to wait and see what happens. We'll go half-way on things, but we won't go all the way." Moakley was further disappointed by the failure of Democrats to reclaim the House, and their loss of five Senate seats, leaving them only a tenuous one-vote majority.[33]

★ ★ ★

In early January, Moakley, Speaker Dennis Hastert, and a few other congressmen boarded a plane for Rome to present the Congressional Medal of Honor to Pope John Paul II. Hastert had invited Moakley to represent the minority party. The two men didn't know each other well but treated each other with respect throughout; Moakley deferred to Hastert's rank in all the trip's minor decisions.[34]

In Rome, the congressional delegation was joined by Republican senators Susan Collins of Maine and Bob Smith of New Hampshire. The presentation was to take place in the Apostolic Palace's frescoed Clementine Room, a magnificent setting. As he entered the chamber, Moakley's thoughts went back to Havana, when he had attended the papal Mass. The Americans could feel the spiritual intensity of the frail, seated pontiff as he received the medal from Hastert, with Moakley looking on. Each member of the delegation approached the pontiff individually; a photographer captured Moakley and the pope conversing together. "Being a Roman Catholic, what greater delight could I have than being in the presence of the Pope? Even with his frailty, you could feel the strength that exudes from him," Moakley said.[35]

Accepting the medal, the octogenarian pontiff, showing the signs of Parkinson's disease, was gracious but tough. He read a three-paragraph statement in English that criticized American materialism. "You are the wealthiest nation in the world," LaRose recalled him saying, "so you have responsibilities to the poor." The fifteen Americans listened, intent. When the audience had concluded, the pontiff rose from his chair, relying upon his cane, and moved deliberately toward the exit. Then he stopped, spun around, raised his cane, and fairly shouted, in English, "God Bless America." For Moakley, it was an unforgettable moment. "This is the cap of my political career, to kneel down and kiss his ring."[36]

Moakley meant that sincerely. His fight in El Salvador had been motivated by his own Catholic beliefs. He never attempted to take political advantage of his piety. While he shared the Church's social conservatism, he never trumpeted his opposition to abortion. Nor did Moakley concern himself with internal Church disputes. The El Salvador Jesuits were part of the "liberation theology" tendency within the Church whose inclinations were to the left of John Paul II; Moakley respected both sides.

The congressmen laid a wreath at the American cemetery in Rome, visited the Leaning Tower of Pisa, and headed off to Camp Bondsteel in Kosovo. There the Americans led a NATO mission to protect the Kosovars against Slobodan Milosevic's Yugoslavia. Moakley and LaRose joined the mess line and dined with Massachusetts soldiers. They proceeded on to Morocco for a friendship meeting with King Mohammed VI. Moakley told the king that he had met his father twenty-two years earlier on a delegation with Tip O'Neill. After a week's journey, the Americans returned to Washington just before the inauguration.[37]

Moakley watched Bush take the oath of office under a cold, raw drizzle. The next day, January 21, the *Boston Globe* noted that Moakley had met Martin Sheen earlier in the week. Sheen, the producer and narrator of "Enemies of War," now played a fictional president on the popular television show "The West Wing." He wanted Moakley to make an appearance, playing himself. He told a Moakley aide, "He's my hero."[38]

The television appearance never got written. It should have been a funny sketch, like the one that featured Tip O'Neill on "Cheers," the popular comedy set in a Boston bar. Moakley would have liked that, but he was feeling a little tired and short of breath, and he had an appointment for a check-up out at Bethesda Naval Hospital that day. Otherwise he was feeling pretty good, and he wasn't worried about a thing.

NOTES

Oral Histories denominated as "OH" in notes were recorded by Robert Allison, Beth Bower, Joseph McEttrick, and colleagues.

1. CHRONICLE OF A DEATH FORETOLD

1. "Moakley Has Cancer, Won't Run Again," *Boston Globe*, February 12, 2001, 1; "Resolute Moakley Confronts Fate," *Boston Globe*, February 13, 2001, 1; "Feb. 12, 2001 Press Conference," Moakley, John Joseph Papers, John Joseph Moakley Archive and Institute. Suffolk University, Boston, MA. Series 100.01.01, Box 2, Folder 67. All archival sources hereafter, unless otherwise noted, are from this collection, and are denominated with a 100 prefix at Suffolk University. Hereafter cited (in order) by series, box, and folder. Moakley identified as JJM.

2. Fred Clark, author interview.

3. 09.02 #137, JJM Video Archive.

4. "At White House, Moakley Given a High Honor," *Boston Globe*, March 14, 2001, 1; "House Resolution 559," 01.01, 2, 66.

5. "JFK Library Tribute Video," March 16, 2001, JJM Video Archive 09.02 #144. The video shown was the "Clark Booth Tribute Video," #133. Joe Moynihan, author interview.

6. "Teases, Tributes: S. Boston Breakfast Serves Jabs, Salute to Moakley," *Boston Globe*, March 19, B1.

7. Fred Clark-JJM Oral History 20, hereafter "OH."

8. "Courthouse Dedicated to Moakley," *Boston Globe*, April 19, 2001, 1.

9. "A Din That Drives out Sorrow," by Joan Vennochi, *Boston Globe*, May 1, 2001; "Joe Moakley Park Dedication Sunday," *Boston Globe*, April 29, 2001, 01.01, 2, 56.

10. Edward Del Tufo, author interview.

11. "People's Legislator Moakley Dies," *Boston Globe*, May 29, 2001, 1.

12. Kevin Maguire to JJM, March 13, 2001; Ana G. Franco to JJM, March 12, 2001, 01.03; 7, 62; others in Folders 56–61.

13. Fidel Castro Ruiz to Honorable Congresista Joe Moakley, April 23, 2001, 03.06, 9, 93.

14. JJM to Fidel Castro Ruiz, May 24, 2001, 03.06, 9, 93.

15. Fred Clark, author interview.

16. Fred Clark, author interview; "Statement of Intention for Funeral, April 12, 2001," 01.04, 1, 55.

17. "People's Legislator Moakley Dies," *Boston Globe*, May 29, 2001, 1; Padraig O'Malley, *Boston Globe*, May 30, 2001, 19.

18. Edward Del Tufo, author interview.

19. *Boston Globe*, May 29, 31, 2001, 1.

20. "Honoring a Life," *Boston Globe*, June 2, 2001.

21. James McGovern, author interview.

22. "Honoring a Life," *Boston Globe*, June 2, 2001, 1; Channel Five News Videotape #156, JJM Video Archive; William Bulger, OH-014.

2. SOUTHIE WAS HIS HOMETOWN

1. Manifest of Alien passengers for the U.S. Immigration Officer, Ship *Cambroman* October 31, 1903, from Boston Passenger and Crew Lists, 1820–1943; on ancestry. com.

2. U.S. Census 1910, on ancestry.com.

3. Author interview, Thomas Moakley.

4. U.S. Census, 1930, viewed on ancestry.com.

5. Photograph in JJM Archive.

6. U.S. Naturalization Records Indexes, Petition #12422, on ancestry.com.

7. Thomas H. O'Connor, *The Hub: Boston Past and Present* (Boston: Northeastern University Press, 2001), 193–94.

8. *Boston Globe*, February 18, 1919, 12; Massachusetts Death Certificate for Ilario Scappini, Volume 10, page 245. Elario's name appears in official documents with both spellings.

9. Jeri Rhodes posting on ancestry.com; Rhodes e-mail to author, February 5, 2011; Boston City Directory 1900, 1905, 1910; Thomas Moakley, author interview.

10. U.S. census 1910; Boston City Directory 1900, 1905, 1910.

11. U.S. Census, 1910.

12. Death certificate, Bridget Moakley, Volume 70, page 311, Massachusetts State Registry; Jeri Rhodes posting on ancestry.com. Family informants claim she was hit in the head by a golf ball while on vacation.

13. Marriage certificate #3549 in Massachusetts State Registry, 1926.

14. Thomas H. O'Connor, *South Boston My Home Town: The History of an Ethnic Neighborhood* (Boston: Northeastern University Press, 1994), 173.

15. Ibid., 172. A check of the Boston marriage registry for 1926 supports this observation.

16. Thomas Moakley, author interview; Thomas and Robert Moakley, OH-003.

17. Thomas and Robert Moakley, OH-003.

18. Thomas Moakley, author interview.

19. Jack Beatty, *The Rascal King: The Life and Times of James Michael Curley (1874– 1958)* (Boston: Addison Wesley, 1992), 461–62; John Joseph Moakley, OH-001.

20. Thomas Moakley, author interview.

21. JJM, OH-001; Thomas and Robert Moakley, OH-003, JJM; Thomas Moakley, author interview; William Bulger, author interview.

22. O'Connor, *South Boston My Home Town*.

23. JJM, OH-001; JJM High School transcript.

24. William Bulger, OH-014.

25. JJM, OH-001.

26. Ibid.; Robert O'Leary (son of the history teacher) to author, February 20, 2011, e-mail.

27. JJM, OH-001; Service Record "Moakley, John Joseph," National Archives and Records Administration; "Seabee Units History," and "Seabee History: Formation of the Seabees and World War II," no author given, from Cruise Book "Memories on CD," National Seabee Museum.

28. Boston City Directory, 1946; High school record.

29. Headmaster Harry Lynch, e-mail to author, April 5, 2011.

30. JJM, OH-001; Tom Moakley, author interview; Jack Moakley, author interview; JJM Photo Archive.

31. E-mail, University of Miami Registrar Lois J. Bauer to author, March 29, 2011; JJM Photo Archive.

32. William Bulger, author interview.

3. FROM CURLEY'S BOSTON TO KENNEDY'S AMERICA

1. Joe Moakley, OH-001.

2. Nigel Hamilton, *JFK: Reckless Youth* (New York: Random House, 1992), 703–4; 732–33.

3. Jack Beatty, *The Rascal King: The Life and Times of James Michael Curley (1874–1958)* (Boston: Addison Wesley, 1992), 470–96; quotation, 489.

4. JJM, OH-001; Tom and Robert Moakley, OH-003.

5. *South Boston Gazette*, September 8, 1950, 1.

6. Robert and Thomas Moakley, OH-003; John Lynch, OH-011.

7. *South Boston Gazette*, September 8, 1950, 5; Election Statistics, Commonwealth of Massachusetts, 1950.

8. JJM, OH-001; Joe Moynihan, author interview; Duffy Family Scrapbook, Box 6.

9. Marriage Certificate, City of Cambridge, V. 39, 1942; Photo, Christmas card, 1946; Honorable Discharge; Ernest Buckley to "Dear Mom," January 29, 1945; Telegram, General Dunlop to Mrs. Buckley, January 12, 1945; Oversize Box 6, MS 100/11.04; Personal Photographs, 11.03.02, Box 1.

10. Thomas Whalen, *Kennedy versus Lodge* (Boston: Northeastern University Press, 2000), 42–51; Beatty, *The Rascal King*; 389–96; Garret Byrne, Joseph A. DeGugliemo, Oral Histories, John F. Kennedy Library, Boston, MA.

11. *South Boston Gazette*, August 29, 1952, 1, 5; September 5, 1, 5; September 19, 1; Massachusetts Election Statistics, 1952.

12. "State House of Representatives Political Complexion (1867–present)," www .mass.gov.

13. Beryl Cohen, author interview.

14. "Boston's Political Times," unidentified clipping, 11.01, 1, 1.

15. Murray B. Levin, *The Alienated Voter: Politics in Boston* (New York: Holt, Rinehart and Winston), 1960.

16. "Boston's Political Times," 11.01, 1, 1; *South Boston Gazette*, September 3, 1954, 8; September 10; Election Statistics, Commonwealth of Massachusetts, 1954.

17. David Sargent, OH-016.

18. Jeanne M. Hession, OH-015; David Sargent, OH-016; James F. Linnehan, OH-065.

19. JJM, OH-001; Personal Photos, 11.03.02, 1, 17; marriage certificate.

20. Thomas H. O'Connor, *The Hub: Boston Past and Present* (Boston: Northeastern University Press, 2001), 213–19.

21. William Shaevel, author interview. Shaevel was Moakley's legislative aide in the Senate during the late 1960s, when Moakley focused on the statewide aspect of the problem, the "snob zoning" housing law.

22. Thomas P. Coston, Richard K. Donauhue, Garrett Byrne oral histories, JFK Library; William Shaevel, author interview.

23. William Shaevel, author interview.

24. Beatty, *The Rascal King*, 12.

25. Beryl Cohen, author interview; William M. Bulger, *While the Music Lasts: My Life in Politics* (Boston: Houghton Mifflin, 1996), 62–64, 75–77, paints a similar picture of Thompson.

26. Levin, *The Alienated Voter*; Thomas H. O'Connor, *The Boston Irish: A Political History* (Boston: Northeastern University Press, 1995), 99, 228; quotation, 230.

27. Tom and Robert Moakley, OH-003. For Moakley's filing, see unidentified clipping, 11.01, 1, 10.

28. Bulger, *While the Music Lasts*, 41.

29. *South Boston Gazette*, September 7 and 15, 1960, 1; Tom and Robert Moakley, OH-003.

30. Bulger, *While the Music Lasts*, 53.

4. THE INVISIBLE, THE BLIND, AND THE VISIONARY

1. Death certificate, Mary Moakley.

2. Tom Moakley, author interview.

3. William H. Shaevel, author interview.

4. William H. Shaevel, OH-017.

5. "A Distinguished American," *South Boston Tribune*, March 16, 1966, 1.

6. Adam Clymer, *Edward M. Kennedy: A Biography* (New York: Harper Perennial, 2009), 35–42.

7. For a comical story about the campaign, see William M. Bulger, *While the Music Lasts: My Life in Politics* (Boston: Houghton Mifflin, 1996), 91–102. Roger Kineavy, author interview.

8. J. Anthony Lukas, *Common Ground: A Turbulent Decade in the Lives of Three American Families* (New York: Alfred A. Knopf, 1985), 115–38; quotation, 122.

9. Lukas, *Common Ground*.

10. See the *South Boston Gazette*, March 1950 issues, and *South Boston Tribune*, March 19, 1964, 1; Lukas, *Common Ground*, 384.

11. *South Boston Tribune*, April 30, 1964, 1, 5.

12. Ibid., August 6, 1; August 27, 1, 11; September 3, 1; September 10, 9; September 17, 1; November 5, 1; all 1964.

13. See, for example, Robert Weisbrot, *Freedom Bound: A History of America's Civil Rights Movement* (New York: Plume, 1991), 127–53; and Harvard Sitkoff, *The Struggle for Black Equality 1954–1980* (New York: Hill and Wang, 1981), 188–97.

14. Ronald P. Formisano, *Boston against Busing: Race, Class and Ethnicity in the 1960s and 1970s* (Chapel Hill: University of North Carolina Press, 1991), 33–35.

15. *Boston Globe*, April 15, 1964, 1, 10; Lupo, quoted in Formisano, *Boston against Busing*, 34.

16. *Boston Globe*, April 22, 23, 24, 1965, 1; Beryl Cohen, author interview.

17. *Boston Globe*, August 11, 16, 18, 1965, 1.

18. Beryl Cohen, author interview; *Boston Globe*, August 18, 19, 1965, 1; Commonwealth of Massachusetts *Journal of the Senate* 1965, 1523–26, 1532, 1581.

19. Commonwealth of Massachusetts, *Journal of the Senate* 1965, 1523–26.

20. "Black Senator or Bust," *Bay State Banner*, February 8, 1968, in 11.01, 2, 4; Mel King, author interview.

21. Election Statistics, Commonwealth of Massachusetts, 1966, 1968.

22. Roger Kineavy, author interview; Lukas, *Common Ground*, 585–97.

23. *Boston Globe*, November 15, 1967, 44; Jack Moakley, author interview.

24. Bill Shaevel, author interview; "Senatorial District of Negroes Urged," by Tom Gallagher, *Boston Sunday Herald*, in 11.01, Box 1, Folder 22; "Black Senator or Bust"; "Solon against Police Residence," unidentified clipping, June 28, 1967, 11.01, Box 1, Folder 22; "Senate, House Keep Death Law," unidentified clipping, February 28, 1967, Box 1, Folder 22.

25. "Rep. Haynes Blasts Slow City Officials," *Bay State Banner*, March 26, 1966, 11.01, 1, 14; Mel King, author interview.

26. "Senate to Consider Bill for Eviction of Tenants," April 18, 1968, 11.01, 2, 27; Bill Shaevel, OH-017; Bill Shaevel, author interview.

27. Hillel Levine and Lawrence Harmon, *The Death of an American Jewish Community: A Tragedy of Good Intentions* (New York: Free Press, 1992).

28. "The Harbor Islands," prepared for the Massachusetts Senate Harbor Islands Commission by a Massachusetts Institute of Technology study group, in 03.03 Box 9, Folder 132; Moakley speech to Senate for Bill 5581, press release, August 7, 1969, 11.01, 1, 7.

29. See, for example, Vina M. Aylmer to JJM, August 13, 1969, for direct quotation; legislative cochairmen Alfred Edwards, Joseph M. Magaldi to JJM, March 3, 1969, in 11.01, 1, 7, which is thick with such protests.

30. Bill Shaevel, OH-017; author interview.

31. "Will Gov. Sergeant Go for the Fair?" *Boston Globe*, April 8, 1969, in 11.01, 2, 27.

32. "Moakley Spells Out Opposition to World's Fair," *South Boston Tribune*, April 10, 1969, 6.

33. "'Distinguished American' Award to John Joseph Moakley," *South Boston Tribune*, March 13, 1969, 1.

34. "The Harbor Islands" prepared for Boston Harbor islands Commission by the Harbor Islands Study Group," (MIT) April 16, 1969, in 03.03, 9, 132.

35. Unidentified clipping, "New Approach to Aircraft Noise Problem," February 29, 1968, Folder 25; "Hub Solon Assails Boston Edison Company," *Salem News*, March 26, 1969, Folder 31; "Senator Seeks Ban on Gasoline Cars," *Patriot Ledger*, October 3, 1969, all 11.01, Box 2, Folder 37.

36. "Birth Control Measure Advanced by Senate 29–11," *Springfield Union*, April 28, 1966, in 11.01, Box 1, Folder 14; Bill Shaevel, author interview.

37. "Senate, House Keep Death Law," unidentified clipping, February 28, 1967; "Gang Killings Tied to Loans, Board Told," *Boston Record American*, March 21, 1967, in 11.01, 1, 22; Mark S. Brodin, *William P. Homans Jr.: A Life in Court* (Lake Mary, FL: Vandeplas, 2010), 208–27.

38. "Municipal Budgets Sinking Hospitals," *Springfield Union*, March 13, 1968, Folder 26; "Hospital Bill Is Killed," *Boston Record American*, May 10, 1968, 11.01, 2, 28, Folder 28; Clymer, *Edward M. Kennedy*, 82–85.

5. MOAKLEY VERSUS HICKS

1. "The Congress: Mr. Speaker," *Time* magazine, January 19, 1962; Anthony Champagne et al., *The Austin/Boston Connection: Five Decades of House Democratic Leadership, 1937–1989* (College Station: Texas A&M University Press, 2009); *Boston Globe*, May 21, 1970, 1.

2. John A. Farrell, *Tip O'Neill and the Democratic Century* (Boston: Little Brown and Company, 2001), 207–8.

3. While the literature on Vietnam is vast, among the best volumes are Stanley Karnow, *Vietnam a History: The First Complete Account of Vietnam at War* (New York: Viking, 1983); and George C. Herring, *America's Longest War: The United States and Vietnam 1950–1975* (New York: Alfred A. Knopf, 1979).

4. Among the many very good books on the peace movement are Melvin Small, *Antiwarriors: The Vietnam War and the Battle for America's Hearts and Minds* (Wilmington, DE: Scholarly Resources, 2002); and James Miller, *Democracy Is in the Streets: From Port Huron to the Siege of Chicago* (New York: Simon and Schuster, 1987).

5. Farrell, *Tip O'Neill and the Democratic Century*, 204–35.

6. Champagne et al., *The Austin/Boston Connection*, 130–47; "McCormack Will Retire This Year," by Martin E. Nolan and S. J. Micciche, *Boston Globe*, May 21, 1970, 1.

7. "Would-Be Successors Queue Up," by David Nyhan, *Boston Globe*, May 21, 1970, 1.

8. "Moakley Seeks Bigger Platform for Programs," by Gloria Negri, *Boston Evening Globe*, May 26, 1970, 3.

9. "Moakley Will Be Candidate for Congress," *South Boston Tribune*, May 28, 1970, 1.

10. "Mrs. Hicks Initiates Campaign for Election to Congress," *South Boston Tribune*, June 11, 1970, 1.

11. "Atkins Drops Bid for Congress, Says He May Run for Mayor," May 22, 1; "Priest Joins Race for Congress Seat, " May 28, 6; "David S. Nelson Announces

Candidacy for Congress," May 28, 5; all *Boston Globe*, 1970; unidentified clipping, "Boston's Congressional Fight," by Stanford Stoane (pseudonym of former Saltonstall aide) in Oversize Box 38, Item 622, Series 09.03 "Memorabilia Scrapbook."

12. "Political Circuit: Hicks the Issue, No Matter What," by Robert Healy, *Boston Globe*, n.d.; "Most Exciting Race in U.S.," by Christopher Wallace, *Boston Globe*, n.d., in Moakley campaign scrapbook. The body of Wallace's article belies the headline.

13. Beryl Cohen, author interview.

14. "Nine Reasons Why You Should Vote for Joe Moakley," 05, 1, 4.

15. "Uneasy Role of Underdog," by Carol Liston, *Boston Globe*, August 6, 1970; "These People Think Joe Moakley's a Winner," campaign ad, all in 09.03, in Memorabilia Scrapbook; Moakley, OH-001, Robert and Tom Moakley, OH-003.

16. "Moakley Charges Hicks against Rent Payers"; "Mrs. Hicks' Lead Trimmed," by Thomas C. Gallagher, unidentified clipping, in Memorabilia Scrapbook.

17. Commonwealth of Massachusetts, Public Document 43, Year 1970; *South Boston Tribune*, September 17, 1.

18. Beryl Cohen, Bill Shaevel, author interview.

19. Patrick McCarthy, author interview.

20. "Moakley Tops Boston Council Vote," by Robert A. Jordan, *Boston Globe*, September 15, 1971, 1.

21. "Mayor White Sails to 62–38% Victory"; "Vote Reflects Changing City," by Robert Healy, *Boston Globe*, November 3, 1971, 1.

22. "Moakley Tops Vote in Boston, Five Incumbents Returned," *Boston Globe*, November 3, 1971, 14; William Bulger, author interview.

23. "Boston School Committee Hearing Transcript 9/21/71," James W. Hennigan to Moakley, SUA/003.004.

24. Patrick McCarthy, author interview.

25. Ibid.

26. JJM, OH-001; Massachusetts Public Document 43, 1972 Primary.

27. Padraig O'Malley, author interview.

28. Patrick McCarthy, author interview; Farrell, *Tip O'Neill and the Democratic Century*, 319–20.

29. "Moakley Campaign for Congress Accelerates in Past Week," September 28, 1; "Mrs. Hicks Heads Citizens Seeking Signatures on Imbalance Law Repeal," October 5, 1; "Hennigan Backs Moakley," October 5, 8; "Moakley Announces Fourteen Point Program to Restore Confidence in Economy," October 12; ad, November 2, all in *South Boston Tribune*, 1972.

30. "Moakley Can Win," *Bay State Banner*, November 2, 1972, 4.

31. Patrick McCarthy, James Woodard, author interviews.

32. Patrick McCarthy, author interview; Massachusetts Public Document 43, 1972, General Election.

6. THE MAN ON THE BARBED WIRE FENCE

1. Ronald P. Formisano, *Boston against Busing: Race, Class and Ethnicity in the 1960s and 1970s* (Chapel Hill: University of North Carolina Press, 1991) is an excellent

scholarly history. Jon Hillson, *The Battle of Boston* (New York: Pathfinder Press, 1977) is an antiracist activist's account.

2. JJM to President Gerald R. Ford, September 19, 1975, Series 04, Box 6, Folder 60; "Moakley Rips Busing before Panel," October 30, 1975, in Series 7.1, Box 2, Folder 70; JJM speech on House Floor, typescript July 24, 1979, Series 04, Box 6, Folder 63.

3. William M. Bulger, *While the Music Lasts: My Life in Politics* (Boston: Houghton Mifflin, 1996).

4. JJM, OH-001.

5. Roger Kineavy, author interview.

6. John A. Farrell, *Tip O'Neill and the Democratic Century* (Boston: Little Brown, 2001), 320; JJM, OH-001.

7. JJM, OH-001; Steven S. Smith and Christopher J. Deering, *Committees in Congress* (Washington, DC: CQ Press, 1990), 61–75, 97–98.

8. George C. Herring, *America's Longest War: The United States and Vietnam 1950– 1975* (New York: Alfred A. Knopf, 1979), 252–72.

9. "Moakley Acts to Block Rent Hike for Public Housing," n.d.; "Congress Should Investigate Chilean Coup for CIA Involvement," September 12, Folder 1; "'Independent' Moakley Seated as a Democrat, Opposes War as First Act," January 3, Folder 10; "Moakley Works to Block Shipyard Shutdown," July 10, Folder 14, are typical. All 1973, Series 07, Box 1.

10. Norman L. and Emily S. Rosenberg, *In Our Times: America since World War II* (Upper Saddle River, NJ: Pearson, 2003), 205–15.

11. Roger H. Davidson et al., *Congress and Its Members*, 12th ed. (Washington, DC: CQ Press, 2010), A3.

12. Farrell, *Tip O'Neill and the Democratic Century*, 361–82; quotation, 363.

13. "Agnew Affair Worries Moakley," October 16, 1973; "Line of Succession," November 5, 1973; "Drinan, Moakley, Harrington Vote against Ford," December 7, 1973, all *Patriot Ledger*; Folder 41; "Nixon Fares Poorly at Impeachment Rally," by Kathy Salzburg, March 11, 1974, *Patriot Ledger*, Folder 42, all Series 7.1, Box 2.

14. Farrell, *Tip O'Neill and the Democratic Century*, 383–414.

15. Julian E. Zelizer, *On Capitol Hill: The Struggle to Reform Congress and Its Consequences, 1948–2000* (New York: Cambridge University Press, 2004), 156–76.

16. Patrick McCarthy, William Bulger, author interviews.

17. Zelizer, *On Capitol Hill*, 156–76; Patrick McCarthy to author, e-mail May 24, 2012.

18. Davidson et al., *Congress and Its Members*, 247–52; Smith and Deering, *Committees in Congress*, 88–90.

19. Ruth Batson, author interview. (This interview was conducted in 1996, not for this book.)

20. John F. Adkins et al., "The Boston Orders and Their Origin: Desegregation," a pamphlet by the Boston Bar Association Committee on Desegregation, August 1975. The pamphlet is endorsed by forty-five attorneys.

21. Formisano, *Boston against Busing*, 1–65.

22. Adam Clymer, *Edward M. Kennedy: A Biography* (New York: Harper Perennial, 2009), 217–19.

23. "Moakley Says Guard Not Needed," *Herald American*, October 16, 1974, in 04, 6, 66; Formisano, *Boston against Busing*, 75–80.

24. Ten South Boston residents to JJM, September 31, 1974; J. A. White to JJM, October 19, 1974, 04, 5, 52.

25. "The First Year of Boston School Desegregation," *Boston Globe*, May 25, 1975, 7.1, 2, 64; Mel King, author interview.

26. "400–700 March in S. Boston against Busing," unidentified clipping, n.d., 04, 6, 66; "Busing Opponents Plan Charlestown Rally," *Herald Advertiser*, November 3, 1974, 04, 6, 66.

27. Formisano, *Boston against Busing*, 81–82; "Eyes on the Prize," PBS documentary film.

28. Formisano, *Boston against Busing*, 55–58. Formisano argues convincingly that Hicks and Kerrigan were allies.

29. Roger Kineavy, author interview; James O'Leary, OH-068.

30. James Woodard, author interview.

31. "School Integration Must Be Achieved, but Problem Is to Find Best Way to Do It," by Lorraine Faith, *Boston Globe*, October 6, 1975, in 04, 6, 68; "Open Letter," South Boston Clergy Association, n.d., 04, 6, 67 (1975 file); Formisano, in *Boston against Busing*, focuses on exactly those voices.

32. Public Document 43, Commonwealth of Massachusetts; James Woodard, author interview.

33. John Lynch, OH-011.

34. "Strong Showing by Bay Staters in Busing Trek," *Boston Globe*, March 20, 1975; "Marches on Nation's Capitol Usually Futile Endeavors," *Boston Globe*, March 21, 1975, 04, 6, 67.

35. Farrell, *Tip O'Neill and the Democratic Century*, 521–25.

36. "O'Neill Offers to Help Boston Busing Foes in Amendment Battle," *Boston Globe*, March 5, 1975, Series 04, Box 6, Folder 67.

37. "ROAR Gets Aid Pledge in D.C.," by Thomas Southwick, *Patriot Ledger*, n.d.; "Congress Misses Target on Busing, Southwick," n.d.; "O'Neill's Stand on Busing a Question Mark," all *Boston Globe*, n.d., in 4, 6, 67.

38. "Testimony of John Joseph Moakley before the Senate Judiciary Committee," October 29, 1975, 04, 6, 60.

39. "Testimony Opposed to Constitutional Amendment," Senator Ed Brooke press release, November 11, 1975, 04, 6, 60.

40. "Coleman Opposes Constitutional Ban on Busing," by Stephen Wermiel, *Boston Globe*, October 29, 1975, 04, 6, 68.

41. "The Effect of School Desegregation on White Flight," by Christine H. Rossell, *Political Science Quarterly*, Winter 1975, 04, 6, 64.

42. "U.S. Senate Hearings on Busing Amendment in Last Day," by Stephen Wermiel, *Boston Globe*, October 29, 1975; Grace Bassett, *Herald American*, November 12, 1975, 04, 6, 68.

43. "Democrats to Vote on Busing Ban," by Stephen Wermiel, *Boston Globe*, October 18, 1975, Folder 66; "Democratic Caucus Roll Call petition to Table Albert Motion," *Boston Globe*, November 19, 1975, 04, 6, 60.

44. Pat McCarthy to author, e-mail, May 24, 2012.

45. "Moakley and the Public Relations Busing Game," by Stephen Wermiel, *Boston Globe*, n.d., 04, 6, 68.

46. "Officials, Community Leaders Seek End to Violence," by Leah Fletcher, *Bay State Banner*, 04, 6, 68.

47. "South Boston Information Center News," by Dan Yotts, August 21, October 9, 1975, 04, 6, 67.

48. Forest F. Rittgers, Commandant Ft. Devens, to Arnold McGee, Chief Marshal, January 20, 1976; James Woodard to JJM, February 23, 1976, 04, 6, 61.

49. Massachusetts Black Caucus to JJM, April 20, 1976; JJM to Black Legislative Caucus, May 7, 1976, 04, 6, 61; Formisano, *Boston against Busing*, 150.

50. C. Vann Woodward, *The Strange Career of Jim Crow*, 3rd ed. (New York: Oxford, 1974), 111–47.

7. THE LAST DAYS OF THE WORKING CLASS

1. Jon Hillson, *The Battle of Boston* (New York: Pathfinder Press, 1977), 214–16.

2. Jefferson Cowie, *Stayin' Alive: The 1970s and the Last Days of the Working Class* (New York: New Press, 2010).

3. Commonwealth of Massachusetts, Public Document 43, 1976; John A. Farrell, *Tip O'Neill and the Democratic Century* (Boston: Little Brown, 2001), 444.

4. Ron Formisano, *Boston against Busing: Race, Class, and Ethnicity in the 1960s and 1970s* (Chapel Hill: University of North Carolina Press, 1991), 193–99.

5. John Weinfurter, OH-055.

6. Formisano, *Boston against Busing*, 193–97.

7. Ibid., 71–73; Farrell, *Tip O'Neill and the Democratic Century*, 514–19, 535–36; JJM, OH-001.

8. Farrell, *Tip O'Neill and the Democratic Century*, 91–124.

9. Ibid., 463–71.

10. Untitled August 4 Energy Statement, 07.02, 3, 67. Footnotes hereafter until otherwise noted are from this series.

11. Press release, n.d., in July 1978 Folder, "Moakley Introduces Major Legislation Giving States Veto Power over Nuclear Installations," Box 4, Folder 79; "Moakley Testifies on Nuclear Waste Disposal," 4, 81.

12. "GAO Accounting Office Audits of LNG Transportation and Storage Impacts Boston," July 31, 1978, 4, 79.

13. "Moakley Calls for Definitive DOE Action to Curb Home Heating Oil Price Increases," Box 4, Folder 86; Fall 1979 Newsletter, Box 1, Folder 17; "Moakley Hails Passage of Fuel Assistance Legislation," December 18, 1977, news release, 3, 71.

14. See, for example, Nadav Safran, *Israel: The Embattled Ally* (Cambridge: Harvard University Press, 1981), 599–622; Ian J. Bickerton and Carla L. Klausner,

A Concise History of the Arab-Israeli Conflict (Upper Saddle River, NJ: Prentice Hall, 1998), 197–203.

15. News release, "Moakley to Embark on House Leadership Tour of Mideast," November 9, 1977, in Folder 70; typescript for newsletter, in Folder 73; "Rep. Moakley—A Witness to History," *Boston Globe*, November 21, 1977, 21.

16. "Rep. Moakley—A Witness to History," *Boston Globe*, November 21, 1977, 21.

17. News release, "Moakley Condemns Conviction of Slepak and Nudel," June 29, 1978, 4, 79; news release, "Moakley Responds to Action for Soviet Jewry Survey," October 31, 1978, 4, 83.

18. James F. O'Leary, OH-68.

19. Press release, "Moakley Announces Funding for South Station Renovation," July 2, 1976, 2, 53; "New England Caucus Prods Secretary of Transportation on Completion of New England Rail Corridor," February 6, 1978, 3, 73.

20. News release, "Moakley and O'Neill Announce $300 million for MBTA Project," 2, 61, n.d., in January 1977 Folder; "Moakley Announces Major MBTA Grant," May 6, 1977, 3, 64; "Moakley Announces Major Federal Underwriting of MBTA Purchase," May 15, 1978, 4, 78.

21. "Port of Boston Selected as Foreign Trade Zone," March 15, 1977, 2, 62; Untitled news release, April 21, 1977, Box 3, Folder 63; untitled news release, July 29, 1977, 3, 66; "Moakley Announces EDA decision to Renovate Boston's Fish Pier," 4, 81.

22. News release, March 13, 1978, 4, 75: "News from Congressman Joe Moakley," Summer 1978, 1, 14; news release, July 7, 1978, 4, 79; Byron Rushing, OH-062.

23. On government contracts, see, for example, "Moakley Announces Major Defense Contract Awarded Needham Firm," August 1, 1977, 3, 67; news release, "Moakley Urges President to Adopt Quotas on Shoe Imports," n.d., in January 1977 Folder, 2, 61.

24. John Weinfurter, OH-55.

25. Roger Kineavy, author interview; see Fred Clark OH-020, or John Weinfurter, OH-55, for reflections on Moakley's constituent services; John and Molly Hurley, OH-019.

26. Robert Kevin Ryan, OH-027.

27. James Woodard, author interview; see series 06.04, Box 3 for constituent service logs.

28. There is a very large body of scholarly literature on white prejudice within the working class. See, for example, Noel Ignatiev, *How the Irish Became White* (New York: Routledge, 1995); and David R. Roediger, *The Wages of Whiteness: Race and the Making of the American Working Class* (London: Verso, 2007).

29. Photos in 11.03.02, "Photos Personal," Box 2; Fred Clark, author interview.

30. "Westwood Fire Blamed on Smoking," by Shelley Corkum, *Boston Globe*, June 5, 1979, in 03.03, Box 17, Folder 244.

31. Peter Medoff and Holly Sklar, *Streets of Hope: The Fall and Rise of an Urban Neighborhood* (Boston: South End, 1994), 2, 12, 30–33, 68.

32. "Moakley and O'Neill [Lt. Gov. Thomas O'Neill II] Announce Major Federal

Effort to Combat Arson in Boston," March 31, 1978, 4, 75; JJM to John Glenn, May 4, 1979, 4, 92.

33. Memo to JJM from Albie Jarvis, October 11, 1979; "Statement of Representative John Joseph Moakley," October 12, 1979, 4, 98.

34. "Cigarettes and Sofas: How the Tobacco Lobby Keeps the Home Fires Burning," by Becky O'Malley, *Mother Jones*, in 03.03, Box 18, Folder 245. Footnotes hereafter are from this series.

35. Transcript from TV show "Buyline," January 28, 1980, cover letter, Carole Khan to Albie Jarvis, 18, 253; typescript, "Quotes from the Tobacco Industry on Fire-Safe Cigarettes," 20, 307.

36. JJM to "Dear Colleague," February 26, 1981, 17, 254; Extension of remarks, *Congressional Record*, February 17, 1981, and *Congressional Record*, March 4, 1981, 17, 255.

37. "Tobacco Industry Profile 1980," Tobacco Institute, 17, 258.

38. "CPSC Begins Struggle for Life as Hill Panel Mulls Agency's Future," by Lilah Lohr, *Washington Star*, March 5, 1981, 18, 265.

39. "Chances for Safe Cigarette Go Up in Smoke," *Common Cause*, April 1982, 22, 324.

40. Terrence Scanlon to John Dingell, May 27, 1983, 18, 266.

41. "Testimony by John Joseph Moakley before the Subcommittee on Health and the Environment on the Cigarette Safety Act," 22, 324; "Statement of Horace R. Kornegay on HR 1880," 22, 325. An excellent analysis of Tobacco Institute Strategy appears in E. M. Barbeau et al., "From Strange Bedfellows to Natural Allies: The Shifting Allegiance of Fire Service Organizations in the Push for Federal Fire-safe Cigarette Legislation," *Tobacco Control* 2005; 14, 338–45.

42. "Proposals' Target Is Cigarette Fires," *New York Times*, December 19, 1982, 19, 282.

43. JJM to Henry Waxman, May 9, 1984; news release, "Fire Safe Cigarette Legislation Passes Congress," October 3, 1984; both 21, 319.

44. Barbeau, "From Strange Bedfellows to Natural Allies," 342.

45. Firesafecigarettes.org.

46. Adam Clymer, *Edward M. Kennedy: A Biography* (New York: Harper Perennial, 2009), 283–310; Farrell, *Tip O'Neill and the Democratic Century*, 532–36, for Carter, see 530–32.

47. Nigel Hamilton, *American Caesars: Lives of the Presidents from Franklin D. Roosevelt to George W. Bush* (New Haven: Yale University Press, 2010), 326–36.

48. Public Document 43, Commonwealth of Massachusetts, 1980.

8. INTO FOREIGN LANDS

1. John A. Farrell, *Tip O'Neill and the Democratic Century* (Boston: Little, Brown, 2002), 542–46; Congress website.

2. *South Boston Tribune*, March 13, 1980, 07, 7, 159.

3. Farrell, *Tip O'Neill and the Democratic Century*, 552–62; quotation, 557.

4. Ibid., 573–93; Lou Cannon, *President Reagan: The Role of a Lifetime* (New York: Simon and Schuster, 1991), 263–69, 496.

5. "Keverian Spreads out Redistricting Map Today," by Chris Black, *Boston Globe*, n.d.; untitled typescript; both in 04 9, 98.

6. "In the Ninth, It May Be a Test for Moakley," *Boston Globe*, July 5, 1982, 05, 25, 536.

7. "Dear Friend" letter from Deborah Cochran, October 15, 1982; "Cochran Trying to Paint Moakley as a Big Spender," by Robert Burns, *Enterprise*, n.d., 005, 25, 536.

8. Campaign ad; "Deborah Cochran: Is She Giving Voters a Good Reason to Change, or Is She a Desperate Candidate?" by Michael Kramer, *Enterprise*, October 26, 1982.

9. "Moakley Sweeps to Victory over Cochran," by Michael Kramer, *Enterprise*, November 3, 1982, 005, 25, 536.

10. Charles Fiske, author interview; "Jamie Wows 'Em in Washington," *Boston Herald*, April 15, 1983, in 07, Box 8, 196.

11. Virginia Zanger, Carol Pryor, Fran Price, Ed Crotty Oral Histories, 5–8; "Briefing on US Policy toward Central America for the Jamaica Plain Delegation to Congressman Joe Moakley"; JPCOCA letter to JJM, December 13, 1982; "Residents Lobby Moakley about Central America Issues"; *Jamaica Plain Citizen*, February 3, 1983, in MS 103 (JPCOCA), Box 1, documents filed by title, JJM Archive; Carol Pryor, Fran Price, Ed Crotty, author interview.

12. Jim McGovern, author interview.

13. William M. Leogrande, *Our Own Backyard: The United States in Central America, 1977–1992* (Chapel Hill: University of North Carolina Press, 1998), 3–103; Cynthia J. Arnson, *Crossroads: Congress, the President and Central America 1976–1993*, 2nd ed. (University Park: Pennsylvania State University Press, 1993), 23–82; Kevin Murray, *Inside El Salvador* (Albuquerque, NM: Resource Center Press, 1995), 3–7.

14. "Who Murdered Four American Women in El Salvador?" JJM speech in *Congressional Record*, December 8, 1981; JJM to President Ronald Reagan, February 1, 1982; "Moakley Condemns Reagan's Decision to 'Certify' Conditions in El Salvador," February 3, 1982, press release; typescript, "Moakley Statement Written by Jim to Be Read at Rally"; July 28, 1982, *Congressional Record*; in 03.04 1, 1; Mark Danner, *The Massacre at El Mozote* (New York: Vintage, 1994).

15. Nicolaus Mills, ed., *Arguing Immigration: Are New Immigrants a Wealth of Diversity . . . or a Crushing Burden?* (New York: Touchstone, 1994).

16. Les Au Coin and Joe Moakley to "Dear Colleague," June 2, 1983, 03.04, 1, 15.

17. Les Au Coin to Jim McGovern, May 10, 1983, forwarding his *Congressional Record* speech, 03.04, Box 1, Folder 10; see Leogrande, *Our Own Backyard*, 155, 254, for El Mozote massacre.

18. Les Au Coin and Joe Moakley to "Dear Colleague," June 2, 1983; "Why Poles but Not Salvadorans?" *New York Times*, June 1, 1983; George P. Schultz to William French Smith, June 23, 1983, all 03.04, 1, 15.

19. "Bill Filed to Protect Salvadoran Exiles," unidentified clipping, November 18, 1983, 007, 8, 203.

20. Howard Wolpe to Romano Mazzoli, August 3, 1984, 03.04, 1, 19.

21. "Moakley Optimistic about US and China," by Bob Ferri, April 19, 1983, *Taunton Daily Gazette*, 007, 8, 192; Farrell, *Tip O'Neill and the Democratic Century*, 661–62.

22. Nigel Hamilton, *American Caesars: Lives of the Presidents from Franklin D. Roosevelt to George W. Bush* (New Haven: Yale University Press, 2010), 358–62; Cannon, *Ronald Reagan*, 310–33.

23. JJM, "US, Russia Should Ban Weapons from Space," *Boston Globe*, February 3, 1983; "Freeze in Space," *Washington Times* editorial, February 16, 1983; 007, 8, 194.

24. "Moakley and 76 Others Challenge Administration to Halt Space Weapons," *South Boston Tribune*, February 17, 1983, 007, 8, 194.

25. JJM article in "L5 News," September 1983, 007, 8, 201; JJM, "It's Time to Shoot Down Reagan's Star Wars Program," *Boston Globe*, November 1, 1984, 007, 8, 205; "Space Weapons Ban," Summer 1983, JJM newsletter 07.02, 1, 25.

26. Barbara Hinkson Craig, *Chadha: The Story of an Epic Constitutional Struggle* (New York: Oxford, 1988), see, esp., 178–84 for Moakley.

27. "Moakley Says Court Ruling May Help Better Congress," *Taunton Daily Gazette*, July 2, 1983, 07, 8, 198.

28. "Death of 'Legislative Veto' Seen as a Threat to Industry," by Michael M. Kramer, *Sunday Enterprise*, September 18, 1983, 07, 8, 201.

29. Pierre Clavel, *Activists in City Hall: The Progressive Response to the Reagan Era in Boston and Chicago* (Ithaca, NY: Cornell, 2010), 55–58.

30. Roger Kineavy, author interview; Weymouth Mayor Sue Kay, author interview, contributed helpful insights into congressional relations from a mayor's perspective.

31. Clavell, *Activists in City Hall*, 59–85; Peter Medoff and Holly Sklar, *Streets of Hope: The Fall and Rise of an Urban Neighborhood* (Boston: South End, 1994), 129–31.

32. Gordon K. Lewis, *Grenada: The Jewel Despoiled* (Baltimore, MD: Johns Hopkins University Press, 1987).

33. Leogrande, *Our Own Backyard*, 326–40.

34. "Moakley Tells Westwood Students U.S. Is 'Aggressor,'" *Daily Transcript*, n.d., 8, 203.

35. Farrell, *Tip O'Neill and the Democratic Century*, 628–36; quotation, 635; Leogrande, *Our Own Backyard*, 340–42.

36. "O'Neill Takes Floor, Is Ruled Out of Order," by Eileen McNamara, *Boston Globe*, May 14, 1984; "Moakley Says Tip's Remarks Insulting," *Taunton Daily Gazette*, May 16, 1984, 07, 8, 205.

37. Commonwealth of Massachusetts, Public Document 43, 1984, Presidential Primary and General Election Results; "Presidential Elections," in James L. Roark et al., *The American Promise: A History of the United States* (New York: Bedford St. Martins, 2005), 34–36.

9. A MOST UNLIKELY HERO

1. John J. Dooling to Jim McGovern, December 11, 1984, 03.04, 2, 22; HR 822 in Folder 23.

2. William Leogrande, *Our Own Backyard: The United States in Central America, 1977–1992* (Chapel Hill: University of North Carolina Press, 1998), 237–59.

3. JJM news release, January 30, 1985, 03.04, 2, 23.

4. W. Tapley Bennett, Jr., assistant secretary of state for legislative and intergovernmental affairs, to JJM, December 13, 1984, 03.04, 2, 22.

5. Roger Conner, letter to the editor, *Christian Science Monitor*, February 27, 1985, 03.04, 2, 22.

6. JJM, *Congressional Record*, March 6, 1985, 03.04, 2, 23.

7. ACLU report by Morton Halperin et al. for the Senate Judiciary Subcommittee on Immigration, April 22, 1985, 03.04, 2, 22.

8. JJM, "Salvadoran Refugees Deserve a Temporary Haven Here," *Los Angeles Times*, August 18, 1985, 03.04, 2, 23.

9. Archbishop Rivera y Damas to Members of Congress, November 15, 1985, 03.04, 2, 26.

10. "Smugglers of Mercy," unidentified editorial, January 21, 1985, 03.04, 2, 22; JJM news release, "Statement by JJM on Conviction of Sanctuary Workers," May 12, 1985, 03.04, 2, 23.

11. "Mass Congressmen Back Bombing," by Wayne Woodlief, *Boston Herald*, April 16, 1986, 07, 9, 237.

12. "Bomb Threats Plague Capitol," by Wayne Woodlief, *Boston Herald*, April 17, 1986, 07, 9, 237.

13. Jim McGovern, "El Salvador's Sadness," *Boston Herald*, September 20, 1986, 03.04, 2, 34.

14. "Moakley Asks Reagan Administration to Allow for Political Sanctuary in US," *Taunton Daily Gazette*, September 25, 1986, 07, 9, 237.

15. Leogrande, *Our Own Backyard*, 476–80.

16. "Law-maker to Press His Fight for Respite for Latin Refugees," *New Bedford Standard Times*, October 11, 1986, 07, 9, 237.

17. JJM, OH-01.

18. "Moakley Vows to Continue Fight to Stop Salvadoran Deportations," *New Bedford Standard Times*, October 15, 1986; "Moakley Seeks Deportation Solution," by Viveca Novak, *Taunton Daily Gazette*, October 17, 1986, 07, 9, 237.

19. "Thatcher Lobbies against GTE Pact," by Alyson Harris, *Taunton Daily Gazette*, September 5, 1985, 07, 9, 219.

20. John A. Farrell, *Tip O'Neill and the American Century* (Boston: Little, Brown, 2001), 610–11.

21. "Ocean Spray Breaks Ground for New Plant," *Enterprise*, June 25, 1987, 07, 10, 250.

22. Farrell, *Tip O'Neill and the American Century*, 673–75.

23. "Mass Delegation Ponders Life after Tip O'Neill," by David Armstrong, *Enterprise*, January 29, 1987, 07, 10, 250.

24. Theodore Draper, *A Very Thin Line: The Iran-Contra Affairs* (New York: Simon and Schuster, 1991).

25. "Moakley Says Contra Vote an 'Accounting' for Money," *Taunton Daily Gazette*, March 12, 1987, 07, 10, 250.

26. Leogrande, *Our Own Backyard*, 260–84.

27. JJM to Senator [Claude] Pepper, May 1, 1987, 03.04, 2, 6. (Pepper had previously been a senator.)

28. A rich literature on Nicaragua includes Leogrande, *Our Own Backyard*; Joan Kruckewitt, *The Life and Death of Ben Linder* (Seven Stories Press, 2001).

29. "Moakley against Reagan's Refugee Deportation Idea," by Thomas Grose, *Taunton Daily Gazette*, May 16, 1987, 07, 10, 250; "Opening Statement of John Joseph Moakley," 03.04, 2, 38.

30. "Moakley's Illegal Alien Plan Attacked," by Bob Mitchell, *Taunton Daily Gazette*, June 4, 1987, 07, 10, 250; "Testimony by Honorable Patrick Swindall," July 23, 1987, 03.04, 2, 37.

31. "Moakley's Illegal Alien Plan Attacked," by Bob Mitchell, *Taunton Daily Gazette*, June 4, 1987, 07, 10, 250.

32. Dr. Charles Clements, author interview.

33. "Day after Testifying to Congress, Evans Is Fired," by Paul Nyden, *Charleston Gazette*, May 16, 1987, 03.04, 2, 36; David Evans, author interview.

34. JJM letter to editor, *Charleston Gazette*, May 26, 1987, 03.04, 2, 36; David Evans, author interview.

35. Photograph in Teresa Whitfield, *Paying the Price: Ignacio Ellacuria and the Murdered Jesuits of El Salvador* (Philadelphia: Temple University Press, 1995); "Human Rights and Salvadoran Refugees in the United States," Dr. Segundo Montes, 03.04, 2, 37.

36. Leogrande, *Our Own Backyard*, 481–83, 492; "Meese Signs Order Giving Nicaraguans Haven in US," *Washington Post*, July 9, 1987, 03.04, 2, 34.

37. "Moakley Fights for Refugee Bill," by Tom Squitieri, *Boston Herald*, November 28, 1988, 07, 11, 276.

38. "Prospects Good for Passage of Deportation Bill—Moakley," by Bob Mitchell, *Taunton Daily Gazette*, July 29, 1987, 07, 10, 250.

39. Wade Henderson to Randolph Ryan, August 14, 1987, 03.04, 2, 34.

40. "Southie Gives Duke the Big Green Light," *Boston Herald*, March 16, 1987; "Moakley Praises Dukakis," *Taunton Daily Gazette*, n.d., 07, 10, 250.

41. "Party Pros Created System to Balance Activists' Influence," *Boston Globe*, May 11, 1988; "Dukakis Adopts Centrist Stance," by Don Oberdorfer, *Washington Post*, June 16, 1988, 07, 11, 270.

42. "State of the State in the Capitol: Has O'Neill's Absence Hurt?" by Michael Kranish, *Boston Globe*, February 7, 1988, 07, 10, 267.

43. "Moakley Serves His Constituents," by Thelma O'Brien, *Bridgewater Independent*, March 30, 1988, 07, 11, 268.

44. "Glenn, Nunn, Good Choices for Veep," by Bob Mitchell, *Taunton Daily*

Gazette, July 16, 1988; "Selection Seen as Aiding Democrats," *Boston Globe*, July 13, 1988, 07, 11, 271.

45. "Smashing Salvadoran Unions," *Los Angeles Herald Examiner*, May 20, 1988, 07, 11, 270.

46. "Nicaraguan Coffee Importers Fighting a Last Minute Embargo," by Ellen J. Bartlett, *Boston Globe*, May 10, 1988, 07, 11, 270.

47. Leogrande, *Our Own Backyard*, 526–49.

48. Adam Clymer, *Edward M. Kennedy: A Biography* (New York: Harper Perennial, 2009), 431–32; Photo, *Taunton Daily Gazette*, October 13, 1988, 07, 11, 274; "Immigration Bill Passes House, Goes to Senate," by Roy O'Hanlon, *Irish Echo*, 07, 11, 275.

49. "Jamaica Plain Residents, Congressman Moakley Discuss Paths to Peace in Central America," *Jamaica Plain Citizen*, September 22; "Moakley Fights Clock to Pass Anti-deportation Legislation," *Taunton Daily Gazette*, September 22, 07 11, 274.

50. "Moakley Rails at Senate," *Boston Globe*, October 5, 1988, 07, 11, 275.

51. "Moakley Fights for Refugee Bill," by Tom Squitieri, *Boston Herald*, November 28, 1988, 07, 11, 276.

52. "D.C. Delegate Slated to Be Chairman of N.E. Caucus," by Dinah Wisenberg, *Boston Globe*, November 30, 1988, 07, 11, 276; "Atkins Wins Fight for Panel Seat," *Boston Globe*, December 7, 1988; "Mass Delegation Fight Ushers in New Era," *New Bedford Standard Times*, n.d., 07, 11, 277.

10. THE JESUIT MURDERS

1. "Packing Some Clout," unidentified clipping; "101st Congress Fashions Its Priorities," *Boston Herald*, January 2, 1989; "Bay State Congressmen Have Numerous Priorities," *Enterprise*, January 9, 1989, Series 07, Box 10, Folder 277.

2. "Moakley Urges Refugee Action," *Boston Herald*, February 13, 1989, 07, 10, 277.

3. "Talking Points on HR 45," 03.04, 4, 50.

4. "Pressure on Atkins Just Part of Job," *Enterprise*, May 1, 1989, 07, 10, 277.

5. "Democrats Looking to Clear House," by Tom Squitieri, *Boston Herald*, May 29, 1989, 07, 11, 279; Anthony Champagne et al., *The Austin/Boston Connection: Five Decades of House Democratic Leadership, 1937–1989* (College Station: Texas A&M University Press, 2009), 254–56.

6. "Frank: I'll Name Gay Republicans," *Boston Herald*, June 7, 1989, 07, 11, 279.

7. "Moakley Likely to Head Rules Panel," by Michael Kranish, *Boston Globe*, May 31, 1989, 07, 10, 278; "Representative Claude Pepper Remembered as a Fighter till the End," *Enterprise*, May 31, 1989, 07, 11, 279.

8. "Wright's Actions 'Courageous; Foley 'Congenial' Says Moakley," by Bob Mitchell, *Taunton Daily Gazette*, June 3, 1989; "Mass Rep Now Rules Powerful House Panel," by Tom Squitieri, *Boston Herald*, June 8, 1989, 07, 11, 279.

9. William M. Leogrande, *The United States in Central America 1977–1992* (Chapel Hill: University of North Carolina Press, 1998), 553–66.

10. *Congressional Record*, October 25, 1989, in 03.04, 5, 63.

11. "Memory for Moakley," *Boston Herald*, November 27, 1989, 07, 11, 278.

12. Dean Baker, *The United States since 1980* (Cambridge: Cambridge University Press, 2007), 109–11.

13. Leogrande, *The United States in Central America*, 568–75.

14. Teresa Whitfield, *Paying the Price: Ignacio Ellacuria and the Murdered Jesuits of El Salvador* (Philadelphia: Temple University Press, 1995), 1–7.

15. Ibid., 71–78.

16. Jim McGovern, author interview.

17. Whitfield, *Paying the Price*, 75–76.

18. Leogrande, *The United States in Central America*, 458–59.

19. Whitfield, *Paying the Price*, 81; Esther Cassidy, "Enemies of War," documentary film.

20. Whitfield, *Paying the Price*, 80; Cassidy, "Enemies of War."

21. Whitfield, *Paying the Price*, 85–88.

22. Ibid., 83–84.

23. Michael Posner to James A. Baker, November 30, 1989, 03.04, 14, 246.

24. "Interim Report of the Speaker's Task Force on El Salvador," April 30, 1990.

25. Esther Cassidy, "Enemies of War."

26. Jim McGovern, author interview.

27. JJM to President Alfredo Cristiani, December 13, 1989; JJM to Ambassador Miguel Salaverria, December 21, 1989, 03.04, 14, 238.

28. "Testimony before the Special Committee," December 19, 1989, 03.04, 14, 242.

29. Jane Franklin, *The U.S. Invasion of Panama: The Truth behind Operation "Just Cause"* (Independent Commission of Inquiry, 1999); *The Panama Deception*, film; Herbert S. Parmet, *George Bush: The Life of a Lone Star Yankee* (New York: Scribner, 1997), 392–419.

30. Leonel Gomez, OH-21.

31. Ibid.; Jim McGovern, author interview.

32. Whitfield, *Paying the Price*, 96; "Are We Shielding the Killer's of Salvador's Priests?" James A. Goldston and Anne Manuel, *New York Times*, January 21, 1990, 03.04, 14, 246.

33. Cassidy, "Enemies of War."

34. "Aid Fight Is Likely as Salvador Links Army to Slayings," *New York Times*, January 9, 1990, 03.04, 8, 131.

35. Whitfield, *Paying the Price*, 93–97.

36. Typescript, January 10, 1990, "Briefing by Frank Smyth," 03.04, 14, 244.

37. Typescript, "Clover Club Speech," January 27, 1990, 03.04, 14, 244.

38. Patrick J. Burns, president, Society of Jesus, to JJM, December 20, 1989; Burns to President Bush, December 21, 1989 (cc to JJM) 03.04, 14, 241; Paul S. Tipton, S.J., to JJM, January 11, 1990, 03.04, 14, 242; Boston College president J. Donald Monan, author interview.

39. AP typescript, February 1, 1990, 03.04, 8, 131.

40. Cassidy, "Enemies of War."

41. Whitfield, *Paying the Price*, 166–67; Cassidy, "Enemies of War."

42. Beacon Society speech, April 4, 1992, 03.04, 10, 173.

43. Whitfield, *Paying the Price*, 167.

44. McGovern, in Cassidy, "Enemies of War."

45. Beacon Society speech.

46. JJM, OH-001.

47. "Confidential Telegram Subject: Cristiani Meeting with Codel, Moakley," 03.04, 14, 244.

48. "Statement by Congressman Joe Moakley on behalf of the U.S. Congressional Delegation," February 14, 1990, 03.04, 16, 272.

49. Typescript, "The Jesuit Case: Considerations for a Further Investigation," February 16, 1990, 03.04, 5, 69.

50. Leogrande, *The United States in Central America*, 559–64.

51. Typescript, "Moakley-Murtha Provisions," 03.04, 5, 66; "Memo from Jim to JJM," March 21, 1990, 03.04, 17, 278; Leogrande, *The United States in Central America*, 573–75.

52. "Interim Report of the Speaker's Task Force on El Salvador," April 30, 1990, 03.04, 17, 278.

53. Typescript, "Moakley-Murtha Provisions," in May 16, 1990, Gerry Studds to Zone 7 Members, 03.04, 6, 77.

54. Leogrande, *The United States in Central America*, 573–75.

55. "September 14 El Salvador Task Force Staff Report," 03.04, 14, 245.

56. Whitfield, *Paying the Price*, 183–84.

57. Ibid., quotation 184, 184–87.

58. "Fourth Criminal Court Communique," November 17, 1990, Box 14, Folder 247; typescript, "Confidential," JJM to Bernard Aronson, October 10, 1990; JJM to [FBI Director] William Sessions, October 16, 1990; news release, October 18, 1990, Box 15, Folder 258.

59. JJM, OH-01.

60. "A War Won for Refugees," *Boston Globe*, October 25, 1990, 07, 12, 293; Jim McGovern, author interview.

11. "WELLCOM SENADOR SMOKLIN"

1. Oscar Santamaria, author interview; William M. Leogrande, *Our Own Backyard: The United States in Central America, 1977–1992* (Chapel Hill: University of North Carolina Press: 1998), 575–76.

2. Herbert Parmet, *George Bush: The Life of a Lone Star Yankee* (New York: Scribner, 1997), 442–511; Teresa Whitfield, *Paying the Price: Ignacio Ellacuria and the Murdered Jesuits of El Salvador* (Philadelphia: Temple University Press, 1995), 267–71.

3. Jim McGovern, author interview.

4. Ibid.

5. Whitfield, *Paying the Price*, 267–68, 277–80.

6. Eduardo Sancho (aka Ferman Cienfuegos), Roberto Canas, author interviews; Charles Clements, *Witness to War* (New York: Bantam, 1985), 129–31.

7. "Tribute to Joe Moakley, Washington, D.C., April 4, 2001, Remarks by U.S. Rep. Jim McGovern," Moakley website.

8. Roberto Canas, author interview.

9. JJM et al. to President George Bush, June 5, 1991, 03.04, 8, 123.

10. Whitfield, *Paying the Price*, 285.

11. Jim McGovern, author interview. Whether Walker or Hercules acted on their own initiative or under orders remains unclear.

12. This description is based on the author's visit; "The Congressman and the Rebels," by Lee Hockstader, *Washington Post*, July 1, 1991, 03.04, 8, 125; Jim McGovern, author interview.

13. "The Congressman and the Rebels," by Lee Hockstader, *Washington Post*, July 1, 1991, 03.04, 8, 125.

14. Maria Ida Hernandez, Carlos Bonilla Aves, Enrique Otero, Geraldo Arturo Leyva, and Luis Rivas, author interviews.

15. McGovern, "Tribute to Joe Moakley," Moakley website; Jim McGovern, author interview.

16. Carlos Bonilla Aves, Enrique Otero, Geraldo Arturo Leyva, Luis Rivas, and Maria Ida Hernandez, author interviews.

17. McGovern, "Tribute to Joe Moakley."

18. Jose Maria Tojeira, author interview.

19. "Remarks of U.S. Rep. Joe Moakley," University of Central America—San Salvador, El Salvador, July 1, 1991.

20. Jose Maria Tojeira, author interview.

21. Whitfield, *Paying the Price*, 357–58. McGovern holds a more charitable view of Walker's role, insisting that the Task Force could not have done its work without his cooperation; author interview.

22. JJM, Beacon Society speech, April 4, 1992, 03.04, 10, 173.

23. Whitfield, *Paying the Price*, 359.

24. Parmet, *George Bush*, 495–96.

25. Leogrande, *Our Own Backyard*, 575–76.

26. Whitfield, *Paying the Price*, 356–65.

27. *Washington Post*, October 14, 1991, 03.04, 7, 108. The op-ed also appeared in the Minneapolis *Star Tribune*, October 23.

28. Whitfield, *Paying the Price*, n. 54, 478.

29. "Statement of Representative Joe Moakley, Chairman of the Speaker's Task Force on El Salvador," November 18, 1991.

30. "Officers Linked to Salvador Killings," by Pamela Constable, November 18, 1991, 1; "The Waning of War in El Salvador," *Boston Globe*, November 19, 1991, 19.

31. Memo, Jim to JJM, Box 8, Folder 133. "El Salvador Aid Options Memo, 1991," Folder 134; "JJM et al. to Secretary James A. Baker, February 4, 1992, 9, 170.

32. Whitfield, *Paying the Price*; Charlie Clements, author interview.

33. General Juan Rafael Bustillo to JJM, February 7, 1992, 03.04, 10, 166.

34. General Rene Emilio Ponce to JJM, April 21, 1992, 03.04, 10, 174.

35. JJM et al. to Secretary of State James A. Baker, May 28, 1992, 03.04, 10, 176; Oscar Santamaria, author interview.

36. Whitfield, *Paying the Price*, 385–89.

37. Ana Guadalupe Martinez, author interview; official deposition to Salvadoran Court, translated by Congressional Research Service.

38. FMLN communique, January 4, 1991; "US Suspects Rebels Killed Americans in El Salvador," by George Gedda, Associated Press typescript; both in 03.04, 9, 143.

39. "Execution in El Salvador," *Newsweek*, January 14, 1991; "Salvador Deaths Merit Probe," *Boston Herald*, n.d., 03.04, 9, 143.

40. "US Targets Salvador Rebel Chief for Prosecution," by Doyle McManus and Ronald Ostrow, *Los Angeles Times*, January 15, 1991; Mercedes del Carmen Letona to JJM, October 30, 1991 (author's translation) 03.04, 9, 144.

41. "Killing of 15 in El Salvador Laid to Army," by Tom Gibb, *Washington Post*, 03.04, 9, 147.

42. JJM et al. to Ferman Cienfuegos et al., November 5, 1991, 03.04, 9, 137.

43. "Wanted Salvadorans Turn Themselves In," by Christopher Marquis, Miami *Herald*, March 19, 1992, 03.04, 9, 143.

44. Memos to Joe from Jim, n.d., 03.04, 9, 143.

45. News release, December 12, 1991, 03.04, 9, 154.

46. Ana Guadalupe Martinez, author interview; Leonel Gomez, "Mi Amigo Joe," *Diario Latino*, October 24, 2008; Gomez, OH-021; "Wanted Salvadorans Turn Themselves In," Miami *Herald*, March 19, 1992, 03.04, 9, 143; "Letter Agreement Governing Terms of Surrender by Two Salvadoran Citizens," attached to memo by Greg Craig, March 6, 1992, 03.04, 9, 143.

47. "Wanted Salvadorans Turn Themselves In," Miami *Herald*, March 19, 1992, 03.04, 9, 143.

48. Nigel Hamilton, *Bill Clinton: An American Journey: Great Expectations* (New York: Random House, 2003), 577–688; Bill Clinton, *My Life* (New York: Knopf, 2004), 374–446.

12. DEATH AND RESURRECTION

1. Alex Wadden, *Clinton's Legacy? A New Democrat in Governance* (Houndmills: Palgrave, 2002), 1–21.

2. "Challenge Portends a Hard Sell," *Boston Globe*, February 4, 1993, 07, Box 14, Folder 336. Further news articles are from this series, unless otherwise noted.

3. "Clinton Will Offer High-stake Tax Hikes," by Joe Battenfeld and Andrew Miga, *Boston Herald*, February 14, 1993, 14, 336.

4. Bill Clinton, *My Life* (New York: Knopf, 2004), 461–62, 493, 496.

5. "Moakley's Budget Clout Raises the Bill, Critics Say," by John A. Farrell, *Boston Globe*, May 27, 1993, 14, 340.

6. "Pols Pull out All the Stops," by Joe Battenfeld, *Boston Herald*, May 28, 1993, Box 14, Folder 339.

7. "House Approves Deficit Package," by John A. Farrell, *Boston Globe*, August

6, 1993, 14, 342; Nigel Hamilton, *Bill Clinton: Mastering the Presidency* (New York: Public Affairs, 2007), 160–63.

8. "Harbor Saga a Parable over Cuts," by John A. Farrell, *Boston Globe*, n.d., 14, 336; quotation in "Moakley: Don't Expect Water, Sewer Rate Relief," *Patriot Ledger*, February 12, 1993, 14, 336.

9. "Meehan Runs Afoul of Colleagues," by Don Aucoin, *Boston Globe*, August 6, 1993, 14, 342.

10. Adam Clymer, *Edward M. Kennedy: A Biography* (New York: Harper Perennial, 2009), 537–38.

11. "Point, Counterpoint," *Boston Herald*, August 29, 1993, 14, 342; "Moakley Is Seen as Out of Step," by Joe Battenfeld, *Boston Herald*, September 23, 1993, 14, 343.

12. "Irish Post Has Bay State Pols in an Old-fashioned Donnybrook," by Joe Battenfeld, *Boston Herald*, February 6, 1993, 14, 336.

13. Barbara Sinclair, "The President as Legislative Leader," in *The Clinton Legacy*, Colin Campbell and Bert A. Rockman, eds. (New York: Chatham House, 2000), 74–77.

14. "NAFTA Boosted in Gillette Visit," by Michael E. Knell, *Boston Herald*, August 23, 1993, 14, 342.

15. "Looks Like a Close Shave for Clinton," by Meg Vaillancourt and Frederick Biddle, *Boston Globe*, October 29, 1993, 14, 344.

16. "Labor Leaders Miffed at Joe K's NAFTA Boosting," *Boston Herald*, October 24, 1993, 14, 344.

17. "Bill Bellies Up to the Bar," by Joseph Mallia, *Boston Herald*, October 30, 1993, 14, 344.

18. "Clinton Cites JFK to Push NAFTA," *Boston Globe*, October 30, 1993, 14, 344.

19. "VP Pushes Northeast on NAFTA," by John Diamond, *Lynn Daily Evening Item*, n.d., 14, 344.

20. *Taunton Daily Gazette*, November 18, 1993, 14, 345.

21. "House Passes NAFTA," *Boston Herald*, November 18, 1993, 14, 345.

22. "As Result Became Clearer, Moakley Felt Relief," *Boston Globe*, November 18, 1993, 14, 345.

23. "People Line Up in Snow to Pay Last Respects to Tip O'Neill," *New Bedford Standard Times*, January 9, 1994; "Friends Bid Tip Final Farewell," by Robert Trott, *Boston Herald*, January 11, 1994, 14, 334.

24. Wadden, *Clinton's Legacy?*, 88–111; quotation 92.

25. Ibid., 88–100; quotation 97.

26. Bill Clinton, *My Life*, 535.

27. "Moakley to Play Key Role in Debate," by John Diamond, *Daily Transcript*, November 12, 1993, 14, 345; Sean Ryan, author interview.

28. Wadden, *Clinton's Legacy?*, 101–10.

29. "Rep. Moakley Gives Insider's View of Health Reform," *Acuity*, n.d., 14, 344.

30. "Health Care Reform Debate Puts Moakley in the Spotlight," by Andrew Mollison, *Patriot Ledger*, July 9, 1994, 14, 347.

31. "Representative Moakley Opposes Invasion of Haiti," *Taunton Daily Gazette*, September 15, 1994, 14, 348.

32. Wadden, *Clinton's Legacy?*, 100–103; "Clash on Crime Bill Paints a House Sharply Divided," *Boston Globe*, August 13, 1994, 14, 347.

33. Hamilton, *Bill Clinton*, 333–48.

34. "Moakley Holds Debate Hostage to Murphy Pledge," by Peter J. Howe and Bruce Mohl, October 21, 1994; "In Ninth District, a Fine Candidate Who Is Going Nowhere," by Jeff Jacoby, *Boston Globe*, November 1, 14, 349.

35. Jim McGovern, author interview; Commonwealth of Massachusetts, Public Document 43, 1994.

36. Clymer, *Edward M. Kennedy*, 538–44; "Moakley, Bulger Back Kennedy," *Boston Globe*, November 4, 1994, 14, 349.

37. Sean Ryan, author interview.

38. JJM speech at McCormack Institute, February 13, 1995, in series 04, 16, 286.

39. "Moakley at Wife's Side as She Recovers from Surgery," by Joe Battenfeld, *Boston Herald*, July 21, 1993, 144, 341.

40. "Moakley and Wife Wage Toughest Battle of All," by Andrew Miga, *Boston Herald*, May 24, 1994, 17, 388.

41. Fred Clark, OH-20.

42. Jim McGovern, author interview.

43. News release, "Statement by Congressman Joe Moakley," March 27, 1995, Series 07.03, 6, 233.

44. "Face-off in Congress," *Patriot Ledger*, May 27, 1995, 17, 388.

45. "Moakley Awaiting Transplant," [*Brockton*] *Enterprise*, June 15, 1995, 17, Folder 388.

46. "Moakley Breathes on His Own," *Boston Globe*, July 13, 1995, 17, 390; "Moakley Condition Upgraded Following Liver Transplant," *Taunton Daily Gazette*, August 1, 1995, 17, 391; Jim McGovern, author interview.

47. *Globe* Photo, September 20, 1995, 16, 392.

48. "A Last-minute Change of Heart," *Brockton Enterprise*, September 14, 1995, 17, 392.

49. "Moakley, at 11th hour, Decides Not to Retire," by Bob Hohler, *Boston Globe*, September 14, 1995, 17, 392.

50. *Daily Transcript*, September 15, 1995, 17, 392.

51. "His Wife's Sacrifice Shaped the Decision," by Peter Gelzinis, *Boston Herald*, September 14, 1995, Box 17, 392.

52. "Gabby's Press Conference an Instant Hall-of-Famer," by Howie Carr, *Boston Herald*, September 15, 1995, 17, 392.

53. "A Clear Choice for Moakley," by Eileen McNamara, *Boston Globe*, September 16, 1995, 17, 392.

54. *Globe* interview, n.d., 17, 392.

55. Sean Ryan, author interview.

56. "Boston Baked Washington," by Mary McGrory, *Washington Post*, n.d.; also *Boston Globe*, April 28, 1993, 14, 338.

57. "Moakley Receives Honor from Salvadorans," unidentified clipping, 14, 334; Jim McGovern, author interview.

58. Jim McGovern, Ana Guadalupe Martinez, Roger Kineavy, author interviews; Mark Danner, *The Massacre at El Mozote* (New York: Vintage, 1994).

59. OH-01. Castro-brand convertible couches were widely advertised on television in the 1950s and 1960s.

60. JJM to President Clinton, April 12, 1995, 03.06, 8, 85; "Moakley Asks Clinton to End Cuba Embargo," by Bob Hohler, *Boston Globe*, April 13, 1995, Folder 386; "U.S. Should End Its Embargo against Cuba," by Elizabeth Shannon, *Boston Globe*, May 4, 1995, 03.06, 8, 85.

61. "Moakley Meets Castro, Talks Trade, Relations," by Colum Lynch, *Boston Globe*, October 25, 1995; "Moakley Accepts Offer to Visit Castro in Cuba," by Andrew Miga, *Boston Herald*, October 25, 1995.

62. JJM, "Talking with Castro," *Boston Globe*, October 26, 1995; "Moakley Plans Trade Visit to Cuba," by Colum Lynch, *Boston Globe*, October 26, 1995, 177, 394.

63. Secretary of State Warren Christopher to Speaker Newt Gingrich, September 20, 1995, 03.06, 8, 84.

64. Ileana Ros-Lehtinen to President Clinton, October 26, 1995, 03.06, 8, 85.

65. JJM, OH-01.

66. January 20, 1996, *Florida Sun Sentinel*, 03.06, 8, 84.

67. "Moakley Finds Ups and Downs in His Cuba Visit," by Steve Fainaru, *Boston Globe*, January 19, 1995, 03.06, 8, 84.

68. Ibid.

69. "Helms-Burton Legislation Becomes Law; Global Community Protests and Cuba Threatens Retaliation," *Cuba INFO*, vol. 8, no. 4, March 21, 1996, 03.06, 8, 84; Sebastian Balfour, *Castro*, 3rd. ed. (Harlow, England: Pearson Longman, 2009), 158–60; Bill Clinton to JJM, August 7, 1996, 03.06, 8, 86.

70. Fred Clark, Sean Ryan, author interviews.

71. News release, March 16, 1996, series 07.03, 7, 292; "Tribute to Evelyn Moakley," by Jim McGovern, 07.03, 7, 294; "Evelyn Moakley Eulogized as Witty, Gracious Woman," by Joe Heaney, March 21, *Boston Herald*, 07.01, 18, 415.

72. "Moakley Asks Effort for Inmate in Mexico," by Steve Fainaru, *Boston Globe*, April 10, 1996; "Islands Bill Gets Solid Backing," *Patriot Ledger*, April 18, 1996 18, 416.

73. "Gryska, Moakley Focus on Economics," *Medfield Suburban Press*, October 31, 1996 18, 410; "Stakes Are High in the Battle of the Brahmins," by Mary McGrory, *Boston Globe*, October 5, 1996, Box 18, Folder 409; "Bridge Honors Moakley's Late Wife," by Thomas G. Palmer, *Boston Globe*, October 5, 1996, 18, 405.

74. Jim McGovern, author interview; *Taunton Daily Gazette*, November 7, 1996, 18, 410, Commonwealth of Massachusetts, Public Document 43, 1994.

13. RETURN TO SANTA MARTA

1. Michael Patrick MacDonald, *All Souls: A Family Story from Southie* (New York: Ballantine, 1999), 1–15.

2. Dick Lehr and Gerard O'Neill, *Black Mass: The True Story of an Unholy Alliance between the FBI and the Irish Mob* (New York: Perennial, 2000).

3. Ibid., 205–16; Sean Ryan, author interview.

4. JJM to Mark Robinson, January 22, 1997; "The Stadium: The Facts," by seven South Boston residents' groups, 04, 14, 171.

5. Statement by Robert Kraft, February 22, 1997, 04, 14, 171; Fred Clark, author interview.

6. "Moakley's on the Case," by David Nyhan, *Boston Globe*, February 26, 1997, 07, 19, 432.

7. Jose Maria Tojeira to JJM, May 23, 1997; JJM and McGovern to Tojeira, August 4, 1997; 03.04, 11, 204.

8. Steve LaRose, author interview.

9. JJM and McGovern to "Dear Colleague," May 21, 1997; JJM et al. to Ambassador Ann Patterson, June 12, 1997; Barbara Larkin to JJM, September 5, 1997, 03.04, 11, 198.

10. Memo to JJM from Steve, n.d., 03.04, 11, 198.

11. JJM speech, November 15, 1997, typescript, 03.06, 11, 199.

12. Ibid., 03.04, 11, 204; Jose Maria Tojeira, Steve La Rose, author interviews.

13. "Proyecto intercambio policia Boston y agentes CAM," November 18, 1997, *El Mundo*; "EEUU y El Salvador: por tratado de extradicion," *Latino*, November 18, 1997; 03.04, 11, 208; briefing book, 03.04, 11, 207.

14. Briefing book, 03.04, 11, 207.

15. LaRose, OH-02.

16. Carlos Bonilla et al., author interviews.

17. Ana Maria Menjivar, author interview.

18. *Boston Globe*, November 22, 1997, 03.04, 11, 210.

19. *Worcester Telegram and Gazette*, November 22, 1997, 03.04, 11, 210.

20. Embassy post to El Salvador desk, December 5, 1997, 03.04, 12, 211.

21. JJM and McGovern to J. Brian Atwood and Franklin Raines, n.d., 03.04, 12, 211.

22. Sebastian Balfour, *Castro*, 3rd ed. (Harlow, England: Pearson Longman, 2009), 162–64.

23. "Clash of Titans," by Johanna McGeary, *Time*, January 26, 1998; "Pope May Illuminate Cuba's Darkness," by Peter Gelzinis, *Boston Herald*, January 20, 1998; 03.06, 9, 95.

24. "Arriving in Cuba, Law Says Change Will Occur Slowly," *Boston Globe*, January 24, 1998, 03.06, 9, 95.

25. "For Cubans Awaiting Renewal a Better Life Not Yet Possible," unidentified clipping; "Loyalty Holds amid Cuba's Decay," by Jo-Ann Moriarty, *Metro West Sunday Republican*, 03.06, 9, 95.

26. Steve La Rose, author interview.

27. "Bay Staters Chat with a Mellow Castro on Many Topics," *Lawrence Eagle Tribune*, January 25, 1998; "Castro Meets Massachusetts Congressmen," *Woburn Daily Times Chronicle*, January 26, 1998, 03.06, 9, 94.

28. William Delahunt, author interview.

29. JJM et al. to Sandy Berger, February 2, 1998, 03.06, 9, 101; Memo to membership of subcommittee on trade, May 4, 1998, 03.06, 9, 91; JJM et al. to Fidel Castro, July 16, 1998, 03.06, 9, 89; JJM news release, March 19, 1998, 07.03, 9, 471.

30. Bill Clinton, *My Life* (New York: Alfred A. Knopf, 2004), 774.

31. "Upbeat Hillary Promises to Fight Scandal," January 31, 1998, *Boston Herald*, 7.1, 20, 449.

32. "'Joe Mo' Knows Longevity, Devotion," *Taunton Daily Gazette*, January 31, 1998; *New England Newswatch*, January 30, 1998, 07.01, 20, 449.

33. *New England Newswatch*, January 30, 1998, 7.1, 20, 449.

34. "Democrats Say Speech Did the Job," *Patriot Ledger*, January 28, 1998, 7.1, 20, 450.

35. Roger H. Davidson et al., *Congress and Its Members*, 13th ed. (Washington, DC: CQ Press, 2012), 146–47.

36. "Democrats, Gingrich Spar over Ethics Plan," *Boston Globe*, June 19, 1997, 7.1, 20, 441.

37. "New Ethics Rules Are Approved, Including a Ban on Outsiders' Complaints," by Alison Mitchell, *New York Times*, September 19, 1997, 07.01, 20, 444.

38. "Moakley Laments a House Divided," by David Nyhan, *Boston Globe*, June 26, 1998, 7.1, 20, 455.

39. "With Pals like These, President Faces Fight," *Boston Herald*, August 27, 1998, 07.01, 20, 457.

40. "Clinton Cheered to Find a Friendly Venue," by Brian McGrory, *Boston Globe*, August 28, 1998, 07.01, 20, 457.

41. *Taunton Daily Gazette*, September 14, 1998, 07.01, 20, 458.

42. "Democrat Gains Blunt Impeachment Fervor," *Boston Herald*, November 4, 1998, 7.1, 20, 461.

43. Clinton, *My Life*, 824.

44. "Congressman Moakley Hits Republicans on Medicare, Housing, Education Cuts," *Randolph Mariner*, August 7, 1996, 7.1, 19, 420.

45. "Fast Track Must Be Fixed," JJM, *Boston Herald*, October 10, 1997, 7.1, 20, 446.

46. "Bitter Battle Splits House," *Metrowest Daily News*, December 19, 1998, 07.01, 21, 464.

47. "Members Make Their Arguments," *Boston Globe*, December 19, 1998, 7.1, 21, 465.

14. MAN OF THE CENTURY

1. Thomas H. O'Connor, *The Hub: Boston Past and Present* (Boston: Northeastern University Press, 2001), 271–74.

2. David S. Nelson to JJM, March 7, 1989; Robert O'Brien to Fred Clark, March 30, 1990; Peter L. Brown to JJM, May 10, 1990; Stephen Breyer to JJM, December 14, 1990; 04, 15, 173.

3. Sean Ryan, author interview.

4. "Federal Courthouse Area Master Plan, June 1994," 04, 15, 180; "Judge Breyer

and the Taj Mahal," by Jack Anderson and Michael Binstein, *Washington Post*, May 19, 1994; "Courthouse Cost Inquiry Linked to Breyer Hearing in Report," *Boston Globe*, June 22, 1994; "Critics Keep Heat on Fan Pier Courthouse Plan," *Boston Herald*, June 7, 1994, 04, 15, 184.

5. "A Courthouse that Acquits Itself Well," *Washington Post*, October 3, 1998; "Taped Remarks of Congressman JJM," September 25, 1998; 04, 15, 189.

6. Sean Ryan, author interview; "In a Cloud of Long-term MBTA Construction Plans, a Silver Line," *Boston Globe*, August 17, 1998, 7.1, 20, 457; Ryan Memo to JJM, February 16, 2000, 7.1, 22, 482.

7. Photo, March 30, 1999, *Boston Globe*, 7.1, 21, 467; "Airport a Natural Adjunct to Logan," 7.1, 21, 467; "Logan Runway Nixed till at Least 2002," by Laura Brown, *Boston Herald*; "Moakley and the Power of Positive Politics," by Joan Vennochi, *Boston Globe*, January 28, 2000; 7.1, 22, 480.

8. "Moakley Slams Gov over Massport Pick," *Boston Herald*, September 14, 1999; "Gov. Lt. Gov. Swift Rap 'Sexist' Comment by Moakley," *Boston Herald*, September 15, 1999, 7.1, 22, 473.

9. JJM and Jim McGovern to President Bill Clinton, November 13 and November 19, 1998; Clinton to JJM, December 4, 1998; Ambassador Anne Patterson to McGovern, n.d.; 03.04, 12, 215; www.iadb.org/regions.

10. Typescript, UCA speech, November 12, 1999; JJM to Sister Pauline McShain, December 27, 1999, 03.04, 12, 221.

11. Typescript, El Salvador Trip Itinerary, November 1999, 03.04, 12, 220.

12. Steve LaRose, author interview.

13. "Long List of Horrors at US Army School," JJM, *Boston Globe*, n.d., 03.06, 13, 146; JJM speech, typescript, March 30 1999, 03.06, 13, 150.

14. JJM to "Dear Colleague," March 15, 1999, 03.06, 13, 144; "House Kills Training Funds to School of the Americas," by John Lancaster, *Washington Post*, July 31, 1999, 03.06, Box 13, Folder 146; SOA Watch newsletter, January 24, 2000, 03.06, 13, 150.

15. "Mexico Returns Jailed Ex-Boston Man to US," *Boston Globe*, February 4, 1998, 03.06, 11, 122.

16. JJM to President Clinton, September 18, 1996; Clinton to JJM, October 10, 1996, March 9, 1998; 03.06, 11, 127.

17. JJM et al. to President Alvaro Arzu, June 15, 1998, September 14, 1999. Francisco Goldman, *The Art of Political Murder: Who Killed the Bishop?* (New York: Grove Press, 2008), tells this story in chilling detail.

18. JJM, Jim McGovern, Joseph Kennedy III to Secretary Madeline Albright, April 3, 1998; JJM and McGovern to President Bill Clinton, August 7, 1998; 03.04, 13, 233.

19. "Moakley Rips Gore Switch on Elian case," *Boston Herald*, April 1, 2000, 07.01, Box 22, Folder 484; Sebastian Balfour, *Castro*, 3rd ed. (Harlow, England: Pearson Longman, 2009), 177.

20. Steve La Rose, author interview.

21. "Moakley to Reaffirm Fidel-ity," by Peter Gelzinis, *Boston Herald*, March 26, 2000, 7.1, 22, 484.

22. *Boston Globe*, Jordana Hart, April 20, 2000; *New Bedford Standard Times*, Joanna Massey, April 25; 2000, 03.06, 9, 103.

23. "Mass. Group Sees New Kind of Civic Education in Cuba," by Jordana Hart, *Boston Globe*, April 18, 2000, 03.06, 9, 103.

24. Steve LaRose, author interview.

25. Fred Clark, e-mail to author, May 10, 2012, author interview; "Moakley Sends a Message," by Scott van Voorhis, *Boston Herald*, April 25, 2000, 7.1, 22, 484; "Pritzkers Compromise on Fan Pier," *Boston Globe*, n.d., 7.1, 23, 487.

26. "Hub Bridge on the Edge," *Boston Globe*, March 30, 1999, 7.1, 21, 452; "Menino's Rejection Leaves Old Bridge without Protection in New Boston," *Boston Globe*, December 5, 1999, 7.1, 22, 479; Clark to author, May 10, 2012.

27. "$65 Million Deal for South Boston," *Boston Globe*, May 24, 2000, 7.1, 23, 487.

28. "Moakley to Menino: Handle Southie Yourself"; "Angry Council Presses Kelly on Linkage," *Boston Herald*, n.d., 7.1, 23, 489; Clark e-mail to author, May 10, 2012.

29. Suffolk University news release, January 13, 2000; Dedication Program; Milton *Record Transcript*, January 21, 2000; 7.1, 22, 481.

30. "A Neighborhood Gathering," *Boston Herald*, September 24, 2000, 7.1, 23, 492; Fred Clark, author interview.

31. "Moakley, Frank Roll to Easy Re-elections," *Boston Globe*, November 8, 2000; "Last Rites for GOP in Bay State?" by Jeff Jacoby, *Boston Globe*, November 9, 2000.

32. Fred Clark, author interview.

33. "Minority Party Urges Bush to Listen and Compromise," by Susan Milligan, *Boston Globe*, December 15, 2000, 7.1, Box 23, 498. There could be a one-vote majority because one senator was independent.

34. Steve LaRose, author interview.

35. "Pontiff Awarded Congressional Honor," *Boston Herald*, January 9, 2001; "For Pope, a Medal, for 9th C.D., a Blessing," *Boston Globe*, January 9, 2001; JJM, Remarks, *Congressional Record*, January 20, 2001; 03.06, 11, 115.

36. LaRose, author interview; *Boston Globe*, ibid.

37. JJM news release, January 12, 2001; Memo, January 12, 2001, LaRose to Karin Walser and Kevin Ryan; 03.06, 11, 115.

38. "Salvador Murder Probe Gives Moakley a Certain Kind of Sheen," *Boston Globe*, January 21, 2001.

SELECTED BIBLIOGRAPHY

All archival work done at John Joseph Moakley Archive and Institute,
Suffolk University, Boston, Mass.

BOOKS

Arnson, Cynthia J. *Crossroads: Congress, the President and Central America 1976–1993.* 2nd ed. University City: Pennsylvania State University Press, 1993.

Balfour, Sebastian. *Castro.* 3rd ed. Harlow, England: Pearson Longman, 2009.

Beatty, Jack. *The Rascal King: The Life and Times of James Michael Curley 1874–1958.* Boston: Addison Wesley, 1992.

Bulger, William M. *While the Music Lasts: My Life in Politics.* Boston: Houghton Mifflin, 1996.

Champagne, Anthony, et al. *The Austin/Boston Connection: Five Decades of House Democratic Leadership, 1937–1989.* College Station: Texas A&M University Press, 2009.

Clements, Charles. *Witness to War.* New York: Bantam, 1985.

Clinton, Bill. *My Life.* New York: Knopf, 2004.

Clymer, Adam. *Edward M. Kennedy: A Biography.* New York: Harper Perennial, 2009.

Cowie, Jefferson. *Stayin' Alive: The 1970s and the Last Days of the Working Class.* New York: New Press, 2010.

Craig, Barbara Hinkson. *Chadha: The Story of an Epic Constitutional Struggle.* New York: Oxford, 1988.

Danner, Mark. *The Massacre at El Mozote.* New York: Vintage, 1993.

Davidson, Roger H. et al. *Congress and Its Members.* 13th ed. Washington, DC: CQ Press, 2012.

Farrell, John A. *Tip O'Neill and the Democratic Century.* Boston: Little, Brown and Co., 2001.

Formisano, Ronald P. *Boston against Busing: Race, Class and Ethnicity in the 1960s and 1970s.* Chapel Hill: University of North Carolina Press, 2004.

Hamilton, Nigel. *Bill Clinton: An American Journey: Great Expectations.* New York: Random House, 2003.

———. *Bill Clinton: Mastering the Presidency.* New York: Public Affairs, 2007.

———. *American Caesars: Lives of the Presidents from Franklin D. Roosevelt to George W. Bush.* New Haven: Yale, 2010.

Hillson, Jon. *The Battle of Boston: Busing and the Struggle for School Desegregation.* New York: Pathfinder Press, 1977.

Lehr, Dick, and Gerard O'Neill. *Black Mass: The True Story of an Unholy Alliance between the FBI and the Irish Mob.* New York: Perennial, 2000.

Leogrande, William M. *Our Own Backyard: The United States in Central America 1977–1992.* Chapel Hill: University of North Carolina Press, 1998.

MacDonald, Michael Patrick. *All Souls: A Family Story from Southie.* New York: Ballantine, 1999.

Parmet, Herbert S. *George Bush: The Life of a Lone Star Yankee.* New York: Scribner, 1997.

O'Connor, Thomas H. *South Boston My Home Town: The History of an Ethnic Neighborhood.* Boston: Northeastern University Press, 1994.

———. *The Boston Irish: A Political History.* Boston: Northeastern University Press, 1995.

———. *Boston Catholics: A History of the Church and Its People.* Boston: Northeastern University Press, 2001.

———. *The Hub: Boston Past and Present.* Boston: Northeastern University Press, 2001.

O' Neill, Thomas P., Jr. *Man of the House: The Life and Political Memoirs of Speaker Tip O'Neill.* New York: Little, Brown, and Co., 1987.

Wadden, Alex. *Clinton's Legacy? A New Democrat in Governance.* Houndmills, England: Palgrave, 2002.

Whitfield, Teresa. *Paying the Price: Ignacio Ellacuria and the Murdered Jesuits of El Salvador.* Philadelphia: Temple University Press, 1995.

U.S. INTERVIEWS

William Bulger	February 11, 2011
Fred Clark	November 23, 2010
Beryl Cohen	March 3, 2011
Charlie Clements	December 9, 2011
William Delahunt	March 8, 2012
David E. Evans	December 15, 2011 (telephone)
Charles Fiske	October 21, 2011
Ed del Tufo	April 3, 2011
Sue Kay	September 26, 2011
Roger Kineavy	July 22, 2011
Mel King	April 15, 2011
Stephen LaRose	May 15, 2012
Jack Moakley	August 2, 2010
Tom Moakley	October 23, 2010
Joe Moynihan	January 19, 2011
Patrick McCarthy	May 7, 2011
Jim McGovern	February 6, 2012
Padraig O'Malley	June 6, 2011
Carol Pryor, Ed Crotty, and Fran Price	October 1, 2011
Bill Shaevel	March 17, 2011
Sean Ryan	March 23, 2012
Robert Kevin Ryan	May 14, 2012 (telephone)
James Woodard	May 14, 2011

EL SALVADOR INTERVIEWS

Carlos Bonilla Aves, Maria Ida Hernandez,	January 6, 2012
Geraldo Arturo Leyva, Enrique Otero, Luis Rivas	
Roberto Canas	January 4, 2012
Hector Dada	January 3, 2012
Ana Guadalupe Martinez	January 4, 2012
Gerson Martinez	January 4, 2012
Eduardo Sancho (aka Ferman Cienfuegos)	January 4, 2012
Oscar Santamaria	January 3, 2012
Jose Maria Tojeira	January 3, 2012

INDEX

Abrams, Elliot, 145, 184
Alarcon, Ricardo, 234
Albert, Carl, 95
ARENA (Nationalist republican Alliance) Party, 183–84, 196
Armey, Dick, 210
Aronson, Bernard, 167, 180, 184, 186, 195
Arrigal, Herbie, 31
Arroyo, Felix, 125
Atkins, Chet, 158–59
Atlacatl Battalion, 175
Atwater, Lee, 161–62
Aviles, Carlos, 171–72, 175, 179

Baker, James A., 183, 185
Batson, Ruth, 46–48, 85
Battenfeld, Joe, 204
Benavides Morales, Guillermo Alfredo, 171, 174, 179, 193–95
Blute, Peter, 201, 205, 228
Boland, Edward, 159
Bolling, Royal, 52
Bonilla Aves, Carlos, 188, 231–32
Bonior, David, 202, 206
Boston: Big Dig and, 242; described in 1950s, 35–37; public schools and, 76–98
Boston African-Americans, 47, 54, 74
Boston Irish-Americans, 35, 49, 78
Brooke, Edward, 87, 93–94
Browder, Ann, 113
Buckland, Eric, 171, 175, 179–81
Buckley, Ernest, 32
Bulger, James "Whitey," 226
Bulger, William, 5, 14, 27, 41–42, 79, 99, 212, 217, 227, 250
Burke, James, 56
Burke, William, 38

Bush, George H. W., 120, 158, 160, 166, 170, 183, 194
Bush, George W., 3, 12, 254–55
Bustillo, General Juan Rafael, 172, 177, 179, 194–97
Byrd, Robert, 158

Canales, Maria Teresa, 146
Capuano, Michael, 239
Card, Andrew, 3
Carr, Howie, 216
Carr, William, 31–33
Carter, Jimmy, 100–104, 117–18
Carter, Martin, 29–30
Casper, Joe, 70–71
Cassidy, Esther, 168, 173, 254
Castro, Fidel, 10, 218–20, 234
Cellucci, Governor Argeo Paul, 239
Cerna, Lucia, 167, 169
Chadha case, 135–37
Chamorroro, Violetta, 177
Cheney, Barbara, 3, 11, 13
Cheney, Richard, 173, 175
Christopher, Warren, 220
Cienfuegos, Ferman (nom de guerre of Eduardo Sancho), 171, 185
Clark, Fred, 3, 7, 11–12, 15, 222, 253
Clements, Dr. Charles, 152, 185, 196
Clinton, Hillary Rodham, 209, 236
Clinton, William Jefferson: healthcare and, 209–10, 223; impeachment of, 235–40; New Democrats and, 202; North American Free Trade Act and, 207; 1992 election victory and, 200–201
Cochran, Deborah, 121–23
Cohen, Beryl, 39, 59, 68
Collins, John, 40, 52

143–48, 151–57, 160–61,163–64, 181–82; El Salvador reconstruction and, 217–18, 245–47; "Enemies of War" documentary and, 254; energy policy and, 103–4; Evelyn Duffy and, 3, 32–33, 37, 44, 111, 213–15, 222; funeral of, 11–15; Grenada invasion and, 139; GTE contract and, 148–49; health care issue and, 209–10; historical preservation and, 108; honors received, 4–11; House of Representatives and, 82–83; leadership, 100–101; impeachment of Bill Clinton and, 235–40; Israel-Egypt trip, 104–6; Jesuits and 216–17; John Paul II visit, 255; on Libya bombing, 146; liver transplant, 214–15; Logan Airport runway, 58, 244–45; Massachusetts House, campaigns and serves in, 31, 33–40; Massachusetts Senate, 41–42, 43–59; Naval service, 24–26; Newt Gingrich and, 212, 237–38; on North American Free Trade Act (NAFTA) 206–8; organ donation, 124; Picket-Dawson case, 197–200; "retirement" news conference, 215–16; retirement (2001) news conference, 1–3; Rules Committee and, 83–85; School of the Americas and, 247–48; South Boston development issues and, 227, 241–44, 251–52; South Boston "Person of the Century," 253–54; Soviet Jewry and, 105–6; Tip O'Neill and, 80–81, 120, 141–42, 149, 156; transit issues and 106–9, 244; visits Santa Marta, El Salvador, 185–88, 230–32; Watergate and, 82

Moakley, Joseph A. (father): early life, 18–20, 26, 43–44; death, 53

Moakley, Mary (née Scappini, mother), 16, 18–21, 43

Moakley, Robert and Tom (brothers), 4, 18–19, 37, 43

Moakley, Thomas (Mochler), 17
Monan, J. Donald, 193
Montes, Segundo, 153, 164
Morgan v. Hennigan, 86
Morrison, Bruce, 163
Moynihan, Joseph, 5–6
Murphy, Michael, 211
Murtha, John, 177–79

National Association for the Advancement of Colored People (NAACP), 46, 49
Neal, Richard, 9, 158, 233, 235
Nelson, Alan, 152
Nelson, David, 66–68
Nicaragua: "contras," 147, 150–51; mining of its harbors, 139; peace process and, 157, 162, 177
Nixon, Richard, 81–82
Noriega, Manuel, 169

Ochoa, Sigfrido, 175
O'Bryant, John, 101
O'Connor, Thomas, 18, 40
O'Leary, James, 90
Olver, John, 201
O'Malley, Padraig, 12, 73
O'Neill, Thomas ("Tip"): "Camscam" and, 140–41; Carter and, 100–101; as congressional leader, 80–81, 92–93; congressional race and, 33–34; El Salvador and, 130; funeral of, 208–9; Moakley and, 74, 84, 117–18, 120; retires, 149; Vietnam and, 61–63
Otero, Enrique, 188

Panama invasion, 169
Parks, Paul, 46–47
Patterson, Anne, 229, 232
Pepper, Claude, 162
Perez de Cuellar, Javier, 195–96
Pickett, David, 197–200
Ponce, Rene Emilio, 172, 174–77, 179, 185, 191, 194–97